THE
MCMAHON LINE

A Study in the Relations between India
China and Tibet, 1904 to 1914

Volume II: Hardinge, McMahon and
the Simla Conference

by
ALASTAIR LAMB

LONDON: Routledge & Kegan Paul
TORONTO: University of Toronto Press
1966

First published 1966
in Great Britain by
Routledge & Kegan Paul Ltd
and in Canada by
University of Toronto Press

Printed in Great Britain
by W. & J. Mackay & Co Ltd
Chatham

CONTENTS

PART THREE: THE SIMLA CONFERENCE AND THE McMAHON LINE 1913 TO 1914

APPENDICES

IN VOLUME II

MAPS

IN VOLUME II

PART ONE
The Assam Himalayan Crisis
1910–12

XVI

CHINESE MOVES IN 1910–11: TIBET
BURMA AND THE HIMALAYAN
STATES

CHINESE projects for the domination of Tibet, to a degree
which the Manchus had not enjoyed since the eighteenth
century, appeared to be on the point of success in February 1910.
The occupation of Lhasa by Chao Erh-feng's men made it
possible for the Chinese to accelerate their programme for the
reform of the administrative structure of Central Tibet. They
did not, as yet, propose to incorporate the Dalai Lama's territory
into a Chinese province along the lines they had followed in the
1880s with the newly reconquered Chinese Turkestan (Sinkiang)
and as Chao Erh-feng was then planning to do in the Marches:
there were still advantages in ruling Lhasa through a Tibetan
puppet government. With an army at his back, however, and
with the Dalai Lama well out of the way, Amban Lien Yü began
to show even less regard for the sentiments of Tibetan conserva-
tism than he had in the past. The resignation of Wen Tsung-yao,
the Assistant Amban, which followed the Dalai Lama's flight,
appears to have marked the conclusion of a policy debate in
Lhasa. Wen, Western educated and speaking fluent English,
while convinced that China should take Tibet under her wing,
yet argued that the process should be a gradual one. The
Tibetans, Wen told a British official in 1912, were a different
race from the Chinese and had their own peculiar customs and
habits. They should be won over to China, not bullied into submission. He was impressed by the way the British had handled
the Tibetans during the Younghusband Mission of 1904.

271

Tibetans were continually telling him, Wen remarked, that 'the British treated them like brothers, while the Chinese treated them like dogs'.[1] With Wen's departure the idea of treating the Tibetans like brothers went quite out of fashion in the Amban's Yamen. Lien Yü took pleasure in making high Tibetan officials kneel in his presence. Outrages perpetrated by Chinese troops upon Tibetans went unpunished.

For all his scorn of things Tibetan, however, Lien Yü managed to find sufficient Tibetan collaborators to serve his political needs. Tsarong Shape, who had come to the 1908 Trade Regulations negotiations in the company of Chang Yin-tang, was a Tibetan official of considerable seniority and prestige who allied himself to the Chinese.[2] The Panchen Lama, after he had considered and rejected the idea of following the Dalai Lama into exile in British India, soon used his great spiritual influence on behalf of the Amban's policy; and by 1911 he had moved his residence from Shigatse to Lhasa.[3] Some of the Lhasa monasteries discovered that there were financial advantages in supporting the Chinese, however objectionable this step might have been on religious or patriotic grounds. Lien Yü, there can be no doubt, had a party in Lhasa sufficient for his needs so long as he was backed by Chinese military strength and so long as the main line of communication between Central Tibet and Szechuan remained open.

With a puppet régime to run the day-to-day administration, the Chinese were able to execute a number of projects for modernisation of Central Tibet and for the consolidation of their influence there. Before 1910 a Chinese school had already been established in Lhasa. In 1910 Lien Yü began to open similar schools, designed to teach Chinese to the Tibetans, in the provincial towns: such a school was opened at Gyantse on 22 July 1910. In Lhasa impressive new barracks, the Trap-chi barracks, were completed in September 1910. With an outer

[1] FO 371/1327, no. 29539, Jordan to Grey, 28 June 1912. See also: FO 371/1610, no. 14001, Jordan to Grey, 27 March 1913; and FO 371/855, no. 34635, Max Müller to Grey, 9 September 1910.

Wen, it is interesting to note, was one of the first senior Chinese officials to take his wife and family with him to Tibet.

[2] FO 371/855, no. 32604, IO to FO, 6 September 1910.

[3] FO 371/1078, no. 27291, Weir, Gyantse Annual Report 1910–11, 31 March 1911.

wall six feet thick and ten feet high, they could accommodate up to 1,200 men. A telephone system was installed to link the new barracks to Lien Yü's Yamen.[4] In late 1910 or early 1911 a Chinese of exceptional ability, Teng Wei-ping, whom the London *Times* described as 'an excellent organiser who speaks both French and English', arrived in Lhasa to take charge of the Chinese Post Office there. He began at once to plan a link between the Tibetan capital and both China and India by telegraph and wireless.[5] At about this time a body of some 200 Chinese Military Police arrived in Central Tibet to take over the maintenance of law and order at the trade marts. By this date, in the neighbourhood of the Trade Agencies at least, the Chinese were removing more and more of the work of dispensing justice from Tibetan hands.[6]

The final objective of Chinese policy in Central Tibet in the late Manchu period is not entirely clear. Would the Manchu Government, had it been given time enough, have attempted the elimination of all signs and symbols of Tibetan autonomy and the conversion of the entire Tibetan region into one or more Chinese provinces? We do not know. It seems more than probable, however, that the survival of the Tibetan puppet régime was guaranteed only until the day that the Chinese had put their finishing touches to the work of reshaping the administration of the Tibetan Marches; whereupon it would be Lhasa's turn to see its territory divided up into a host of Chinese *hsien* or magistrates' districts.

In the spring of 1911 Chao Erh-feng's brother, Chao Erh-hsün, was recalled to Peking; and Chao Erh-feng, no doubt convinced that his work of conquest and consolidation in the Marches was nearing completion, took over the Szechuan Viceroyalty. His old command was entrusted to one of his lieutenants, Fu Sung-mu. At this moment the Chinese power in Eastern Tibet appeared to all observers to be beyond challenge. It is true that Hsiang-ch'eng, which had caused Chao Erh-feng so much trouble in 1906, once more rebelled

[4] Ibid.

[5] *The Times*, 30 May 1911.

[6] FO 371/1078, no. 27291, Weir, Gyantse Annual Report 1910–11, 31 March 1911, and Macdonald, Yatung Annual Report 1910–11, 30 May 1911.

against him in late 1910, with the local Chinese garrison joining forces with the Tibetans; but Chao had no difficulty in restoring control, punishing the rebels with his accustomed ferocity. Only one Tibetan district east of the Mekong had not yet been brought under direct Chinese rule, Nyarong, a region which had been since the 1860s under the administration of Lhasa, whose rights here had been confirmed by the Manchus as a reward for aid in putting down a revolt. Chao Erh-feng, in 1908 and 1909, had been refused permission by Peking to take over Nyarong after attempts to purchase the district from the Dalai Lama had failed. In the summer of 1911, while on his way to Chengtu to take up his new appointment, Chao finally, and on his own responsibility, annexed Nyarong, driving out the Tibetan authorities and replacing them with Chinese magistrates. This action, which was particularly resented by the Dalai Lama and his Ministers in exile in India, meant that no vestige of Lhasa authority now remained between the upper Mekong and Tachienlu on the Szechuan border. Accordingly, in August 1911 Fu Sung-mu, Chao's successor in the Marches, memorialised the Throne to the effect that the whole of Eastern Tibet, which he defined as extending westwards to Giamda, a place a bare 100 miles east from Lhasa, should be formally declared to have now become a Chinese Province, Sikang (or Western Kham), consisting of thirty-three *hsien* (magistrates' districts). Some twenty-seven of these *hsien*, all to the east of the Salween, had already been established. The six *hsien* to the west of the Salween, however, were still projects only; and they had not yet come into full operation when the outbreak of the Chinese Revolution brought about a collapse of Chinese power in Central Tibet and a severe setback to the process of Chinese reorganisation in the Marches.[7]

Chinese consolidation of power in Tibet, as has already been noted, gave rise to a measure of Anglo-Chinese friction at the trade marts and along the border between Central Tibet and British India in the region of Nepal, Sikkim and Western Bhutan. It also produced tension along another stretch of the Indo-Tibetan border in a district which had up to now played a relatively small part in the evolution of British Himalayan policy. During 1910–11 Chinese troops from Lhasa undertook

[7] Teichman, *Eastern Tibet*, op. cit., pp. 32–35.

the subjugation of Pome, a Tibetan district in that region where the Tsangpo turns abruptly south to cut its way through the Assam Himalaya and become the Brahmaputra. Pome, it would seem, had hitherto enjoyed a very real degree of independence from the rule of the Dalai Lama's Government in Lhasa, and it now showed no signs of welcoming an increase in direct Chinese influence in its local administration. While the expedition to Pome was being planned, Chao Erh-feng decided to add to his domain in the Marches the district immediately to the east of Pome, Zayul, which was situated on the upper reaches of the Lohit Brahmaputra (Zayul Chu). Both Pome and Zayul touched to their south upon the tribal tracts of the Assam hills into which the British had not to date made any serious attempt to extend their direct administration. This tribal area of largely unexplored mountain and jungle immediately became the subject of Anglo-Chinese competition; and, at least from the British point of view, the result was the creation of a boundary problem far more serious than any which had arisen along the Indo-Tibetan border since the Tibetans were expelled from Sikkim in 1888. This problem of the Assam Himalaya will be discussed in some detail later on.

Zayul, and its neighbour Pome, were of interest to the Chinese because they commanded the shortest route between Lhasa and Yunnan Province, a desirable alternative to the main Szechuan-Lhasa road (Map no. 3). Both Zayul and Pome, moreover, contained tracts of land at, by Tibetan standards, very low altitudes. The Tsangpo Valley where it started to cut through the Assam Himalaya had a bottom below 5,000 feet above sea-level. In the Zayul valley rice cultivation was possible. Here, it seemed to Chao Erh-feng, Chinese colonists might fare much better than they had in the bleak neighbourhood of Batang. In August 1910 Chao decided to experiment in Chinese settlement in Zayul, which, so an advertisement posted at Chengtu and other large cities in Szechuan then announced, 'is a wide plain where the climate resembles that of Chengtu' and 'where they used to produce rice'. In Zayul, Chao's announcement continued, there were vast expanses of unpopulated fertile land available. Water was plentiful. The few natives who lived there were peaceful and friendly. Chinese settlers who volunteered to come to Zayul, Chao promised, would be protected from all attacks by the Tibetans, and would be provided with oxen, ploughs and seed, to be paid for on easy terms over a three-year period. In Central Szechuan, the advertisement pointed out, peasants were expected to pay one-half or more of their harvest as rent. With what remained, Chao Erh-feng asked, 'how can you support your parents, your wife and your children?' Why, moreover, struggle against such burdens and difficulties in Szechuan when the promised land awaited?

> Beyond the Barrier . . . [of the Tibetan border] . . . all that is needed is hard work and no slackness; when the land you open up will be just as though you had bought it, a possession for all time for your descendants, yet without repayment. How good a thing that would be!

As in the earlier Batang scheme, prospective settlers were to be given their travelling expenses. Those with a bit of capital were told that they could take over as much land as their resources could manage. No land tax would be charged for the first three years of the scheme. 'Come forward early,' Chao Erh-feng cried, 'to occupy the good lands, so that others shall not be beforehand in occupying them.'[8]

Zayul, by this time (August 1910), was firmly under Chinese control. Those Tibetan officials opposed to China had been removed from office and duly chastened. A Chinese garrison of some 300 men was established at Chikong to the north of Rima, the administrative centre of Zayul.[9] There seemed no reason, in British eyes, why Chao Erh-feng's colonisation scheme might not achieve some success, and it was possible that a Chinese agricultural colony would grow like some insidious fungus on the borders of Eastern Assam and Northern Burma.

By the middle of 1910, as we have already seen, Chinese administration was also being extended into Pome (sometimes referred to as Bomi, Pomed, Poyul and a number of other variant names), a region which Chao Erh-feng considered another likely home for Chinese peasants. In Pome, however, Chinese rule was not so easily imposed as had been the case in

[8] FO 371/855, no. 37194, Max Müller to Grey, 27 September 1910.
[9] PEF 1910/13, no. 1450, Bailey to India, 8 August 1911; FO 371/1078, no. 22724, Wilkinson to Jordan, 1 May 1911.

Zayul. The Pome people, who by some accounts were of mixed Tibetan and Chinese blood—the latter deriving from Chinese troops who settled here in the late eighteenth century— possessed a tradition of political independence which they did not seem disposed to abandon without a struggle.[10] In late 1910 the Pome people killed a senior Chinese official. The Chinese replied with a punitive expedition which provoked open rebellion. In early 1911 Chung Ying, who had been in command of the flying column which entered Lhasa in February 1910, was sent to Pome with some 300 men in the hope that he could pacify the district. He met with scant success, and was soon recalled and replaced by Lo Ch'ing-ch'i, the Amban Lien Yü's private secretary, who had recently returned from an abortive mission to Darjeeling to persuade the Dalai Lama to come home to Tibet. Lo Ch'ing-ch'i had with him perhaps 1,000 of the best troops in the Lhasa garrison, and he was soon reinforced by a contingent of Chao Erh-feng's men from the Marches, and by most of the garrison in Zayul. This force achieved some initial successes, but it was quite unable to subdue the Pome tribesmen, who took to guerrilla campaigning in the hills. The Chinese supply and medical services were not up to the strain imposed upon them. Lo Ch'ing-ch'i's army diminished rapidly in size and its morale deteriorated drastically. When Amban Lien Yü recalled the survivors back to Lhasa in late 1911 they were already on the verge of mutiny. As soon as they learned of the Revolution which had just broken out in China they refused any longer to obey their officers and they put their commander to death.[11]

The Chinese were in control of Pome and Zayul for a very short time. By late 1911 the Pome venture had ended in disaster; and the Tibetans massacred the remaining Chinese in Zayul in the early summer of 1912. The Chinese, however, were in contact with the tribal areas of the Assam Himalaya

[10] For an account of Pome, see F. M. Bailey, *Report on an Exploration on the North-East Frontier, 1913*, Simla, 1914, p. 1; see also, P. Carrasco, *Land and Polity in Tibet*, Seattle, 1959, p. 137. The story of descent from Chinese soldiers is to be found in FO 371/855, no. 31883, J. R. Muir, Report on E. Tibet, 14 June 1910.

[11] This version of the Pome campaign is mainly based on the information which Major Liu, who took part, provided the Indian Government in 1912. See FO 371/1329, no. 43284, Gould to Bell, 10 September 1912.

adjacent to Pome and Zayul long enough to have appreciated the need to acquire some kind of influence over the non-Buddhist tribesmen who lived along this newly established Chinese frontier. South of Pome, in the valley of the Brahmaputra-Tsangpo (here called the Dihang or Siang), was the home of Abor tribes of considerable ferocity with a long history of clashes with their neighbours both to the north and the south. Below Zayul on the Lohit Brahmaputra lived Mishmi tribesmen whose good behaviour was of obvious importance if the banks of the Zayul Chu were to be settled by Chinese colonists. The nature of the tribal problem in the Assam Himalaya will be discussed in detail later on in this book. Suffice it to note here that the Chinese, once in districts like Pome and Zayul, could no more avoid some relations with the Assam hill tribes than could the British from their territory in the Brahmaputra valley in Assam. Some control of the tribes was essential to a peaceful frontier. When in 1910 Chao Erh-feng began to take steps to extend Chinese influence into the tribal areas, especially those adjacent to Zayul which were occupied by Mishmis, he was only doing what any sensible administrator would have done in the same circumstances, attempting to secure his flank from disturbance as cheaply and as simply as possible. We will have occasion to return to this question farther on. The British, however, did not see Chinese policy in this light. Accustomed as they were to applying a conspiracy-type theory of history to Russian moves towards the Indian borders, it was easy for them to make a similar analysis of Chinese policy. Chinese contacts with the Assam hill tribes were seen in Simla as further evidence of a general Chinese offensive directed against the north-eastern borders of the British Empire in India and Burma, and launched along a front extending from Nepal to the Burma-Yunnan border. Chinese claims to suzerainty in Nepal and Bhutan, Chinese interest in the Assam Himalaya, Chinese refusal to accept the British alignment of the Burmese border, all these in British minds tended to become combined as but different aspects of the same plot. As Sir Henry McMahon wrote of these events of 1910 and 1911 in his *Final Memorandum on the Simla Conference*, dated 8 July 1914:

No sooner had the Chinese forces arrived in Lhasa than it became evident that China was scarcely in search of those peaceful and neighbourly relations between India and China, which had been contemplated by His Majesty's Government when concluding the Agreement of 1906. . . . The peace of our North-East Frontier was seriously menaced by a series of Chinese aggressions along the border line from Bhutan to Upper Burma; whilst it became evident that a Chinese Tibet would involve incessant intrigues with the States of Nepal, Sikkim and Bhutan. Through the hostile attitude of the Chinese a situation had arisen indeed which threatened to cancel all the advantages of our previous arrangements in regard to Tibet, and to involve grave political responsibilities and heavy military expenditure on the North-East Frontier of India.[12]

Did the Chinese, in fact, see things in quite this light? Were they, as McMahon and his colleagues obviously thought, throwing down the gauntlet before the British Empire and challenging the Indian Government to hold its frontiers if it could? Were, in Chinese minds, Nepal, Bhutan, the Assam Himalaya and North-Eastern Burma as closely related to each other as some British officials believed? The answer to all these questions should, most probably, be negative. There was not, in these years 1910 to 1912, a single and concerted aggressive Chinese threat to the integrity of India's northern borders. There was not, indeed, at this period anything like a single and concerted Chinese policy in Central Asia. The Manchu Dynasty, in the last years of its life, was moving in a general direction. It intended to establish Chinese rule in Central Asia beyond challenge. How this was accomplished, however, was left to a number of bodies whose relations with each other were frequently far from harmonious. Chinese policy in Tibet, for example, was determined in part by special Peking Boards concerned with Tibet and Mongolia, in part by the Wai-wu-pu or Chinese Foreign Office, in part by the Amban's Yamen in Lhasa, in part by the Chinese leaders in the Marches, in part by the Amban at Sining in Kansu Province, in part by the Szechuan Provincial Government and in part by the Yunnan Provincial Government. Co-ordination between these various organisations can only be described as primitive. Occasions were rare indeed when the Provinces of Kansu, Szechuan and

[12] FO 371/1931, no. 43390, IO to FO, 26 August 1914.

Yunnan were able to act in concert. Szechuanese and Yunnanese mutual jealousy and suspicion were proverbially acute;
and in the early Republican period the two Provinces were
sometimes at war with each other. It was unlikely, therefore,
that Yunnanese pressure on the Burmese border was carefully
correlated, for instance, with the actions of the Chinese Amban
at Lhasa.

The British Legation in Peking, not surprisingly, had a clearer
and more realistic picture of the nature of Chinese policy in
Central Asia than did the Government of India. When the
Wai-wu-pu in the course of 1910 declared that Nepal was a
Chinese vassal state, India expressed an alarm which was not
entirely shared by Max Müller and Jordan in Peking. In Simla
it seemed as if the Chinese were now about to embark upon a
scheme to detach the Gurkhas from their loyalties to the
British. In fact, it is likely that they were doing no more than
restate their conviction since the end of the eighteenth century
that Nepal was a Chinese tributary state. Chinese declarations
to this effect in 1910 and 1911 were perhaps really no more
significant than the Chinese reception of a Nepalese tribute
mission to Peking in 1908. Jordan was probably correct when
in April 1911 he summed up the Chinese attitude to Nepal in
these words:

> Nepal is now the only country which sends tribute to the Court
> of Peking, and China will cling with tenacity to this last vestige
> of the cherished traditions of the extensive overlordship which
> she at one time exercised in Eastern Asia.[13]

Late Manchu claim to suzerainty over Nepal, in other words,
was to a very great extent symbolical. Chinese officials in Tibet
may have from time to time seen in Nepalese intrigues a
method for annoying the British; but in Peking the main
practical objective of a policy towards Nepal, it is probable, was
to diminish Nepalese prestige in Tibet and was not directed
specifically against the British. The Gurkhas maintained a
Resident in Lhasa. They were able, partly because of the
memory of their victory over Tibet in 1854–6, to exert a great
deal of influence over the course of Tibetan politics; and it
was without doubt useful for the Chinese to be able to publish

[13] FO 535/14, no. 33, Jordan to Grey, 1 April 1911.

for internal Tibetan consumption the fact that Nepal was a Chinese tributary state. This was, it seems likely, the main Chinese interest in Nepal in 1910-11. In 1912, however, as we shall see, the new Chinese Republic under President Yuan Shih-k'ai did give some thought to the prospect of persuading Nepal to help the Chinese retain their hold on Tibet in the face of local rebellion; but this was a policy of desperation, and defensive rather than offensive in nature. The Gurkhas in 1912, as in 1910-11, denied that they had ever been under Chinese suzerainty and declared that the quinquennial tribute missions were no more than demonstrations of 'friendly and complimentary relations'. In early 1911 they showed nothing but pleasure when Jordan formally told the Wai-wu-pu that China had no rights whatsoever in Nepal.[14]

The problem (to the British) of Nepal in relation to the presence of Chinese power in Tibet, indeed, lay less in the prospect of a Sino-Nepalese alliance than in the danger that the Gurkhas would decide to attack the Chinese. Frontier disturbances were certainly possible of a kind which it was British policy to avoid. With a powerful China in Tibet, moreover, the Indian Government found the Nepalese Durbar harder to handle. Its Prime Minister was faced with the temptation to take a leaf out of the book of the Amir of Afghanistan and play one of his neighbours off against the other. All this, however, could hardly be described as the result of deliberate Chinese planning. Chandra Shamsher Jang on the whole resisted, perhaps wisely, Chinese temptations. Despite many alarmist memoranda by Indian officials, Nepal gave the Indian Government surprisingly little trouble during the successive Tibetan crises of 1910-13. If the Chinese had indeed plotted to threaten India from this direction, then they can only be said to have failed miserably.

Bhutan, in theory at least, was more seriously threatened by Chinese claims than ever was Nepal. The Gurkhas had an army that could match any force the Chinese were likely to send against them. Bhutan was virtually without organised defences. If the Chinese chose to enforce their claims to suzerainty over Bhutan, claims which the Wai-wu-pu affirmed on several occasions during 1910-11 in the face of British protests, it was

[14] FO 535/15, no. 54, Manners Smith to India, 7 March 1912.

likely that they could succeed. During 1910 Bell, who had immediate control over British relations with this Himalayan State, reported that there were signs of increasing Chinese pressure on Bhutan. For instance, the Chinese had recently insisted, Bell was told, on the circulation of Chinese rupees in Sir Ugyen Wangchuk's territory. In the middle of 1910 the Chinese were said to be assembling troops at Tsöna, an administrative centre very close to the extreme north-eastern tip of Bhutan, which might perhaps be the prelude to an invasion: in fact, however, these troops were part of the Pome operation. There is no evidence that anything beyond the assertion of symbolic claims was planned for Bhutan which, during 1910–11, received less Chinese attention than it had when Chang Yin-tang was in Tibet. We may conclude that, in all probability, Chinese claims to Bhutanese overlordship were likewise intended mainly at that time to impress the Tibetans and to maintain 'face'.[15]

Chinese policy towards Bhutan and Nepal, if it was not directed specifically against the British, was at least part of the Chinese attempt to consolidate their power on the Tibetan plateau. Chinese policy towards the Burmese border (Maps no. 2 and no. 4), however, was certainly unrelated, except in the widest sense as an expression of the same general outlook, to the Tibetan question. It developed from the British annexation of Upper Burma in 1886, which resulted in the creation of a new Sino-British border stretching from the north-westerly limit of French Indochina, on the Mekong, to the Himalayan sources of the Irrawaddy. The Chinese, who had long been accustomed to look on Burma as a member of the community of Ch'ing tributary states, much resented Lord Dufferin's suppression of the Mandalay kingdom. The Tsungli Yamen (the Chinese Foreign Office of that period) were persuaded to accept this *fait accompli* only after the British had agreed, in return, to abandon the Colman Macaulay Mission to Lhasa which was then preparing in Darjeeling. The Tsungli Yamen, however, did not agree to any definition of the term 'Burma'; and the alignment of the Sino-Burmese border remained the subject of some future Anglo-Chinese negotiation. It was a question,

[15] Correspondence relating to Bhutan for this period, and also to Nepal, is to be found in PEF 1912, Vols. 25, 26 and 27.

moreover, which the Chinese, with their habitual approach to frontier matters, were unlikely to raise on their own accord.[16]

During the negotiation of the Anglo-Chinese Convention of 1894 and its modification in 1897 the British secured Chinese acceptance of a boundary alignment of sorts from the Mekong northwards to lat. 25° 35' N., a point roughly half-way between Myitkyina in Burma and Tengyueh in Yunnan. Sections of this alignment were demarcated on the ground in 1898-9, and thenceforward remained undisputed. One section, along the middle reaches of this alignment, was laid down *ex parte* by Sir George Scott in 1898-9 and to this section by 1914 the Chinese had still not recorded their assent; but neither had they offered a serious challenge to it as the *de facto* boundary. North of lat. 25° 35' N., however, the Chinese had maintained their claim to a boundary which was quite unacceptable to the British. Ever since the British annexation of Upper Burma they had insisted that the Yunnan western boundary touched upon the east bank of the Nmaihka branch of the upper Irrawaddy. In September 1892, during negotiations between the Chinese Legation in London and the British Foreign Office on Burmese frontier issues, the Chinese Minister, Sieh *Tajen*, declared formally to Lord Rosebery that Chinese territory extended to the Irrawaddy, and that the British should recognise this fact, if only as compensation to China for the altered status of Burma. The tribes in this region, Sieh argued, had long acknowledged Chinese supremacy, and Chinese traders and settlers had been active here, in a district which was in many ways much sinified. Where Chinese civilisation flourished, so Sieh stated, there was Chinese territory. The British rejected the Chinese claim to an Irrawaddy boundary for a number of weighty reasons. Its acceptance would, it was felt, give China a vantage-point whence she could infiltrate deep into British Burma. Chinese possession of this tract would provide a handy

[16] The only available detailed published account of the history of the border between British Burma and Yunnan is Dorothy Woodman, *The Making of Burma*, London, 1962.

In the brief account of the Sino-Burmese frontier given here, I have relied mainly on two India Office, Secret and Political Department Confidential Memoranda; B.174, *Burma-China Frontier: N'Maikha Section*, and B.185, *Burma-China Frontier: N'Maihka Section, Pt. II*. These give an admirable summary of correspondence up to early 1911.

refuge for rebels and malcontents from British territory. A smuggling trade would inevitably flourish along the waterway of the Irrawaddy. The result of all these developments would be an increase in British military expenditure to guard and keep the peace on this difficult frontier. From the British point of view but one boundary alignment on the eastern side of Kachin State was acceptable: this followed the watershed between the Nmaihka and the Salween.

In 1892 the Chinese rejected the Nmaihka-Salween watershed alignment. In early 1898 they despatched from Yunnan a Chinese official with an escort of, so it was reported in Rangoon, some 200 men to demonstrate that China was in effective control of the Nmaihka valley. British protests to Peking having produced no result, Lord Curzon's Indian Government resolved to defend this disputed tract. In February 1900 H. F. Hertz, suitably escorted, encountered Chinese troops at Hpare, at the southern end of the British-claimed watershed alignment, and drove them back into Yunnan with the loss of some seventy Chinese lives. In 1902 it was again reported that Chinese forces had crossed the Nmaihka-Salween watershed. Satow protested to the Wai-wu-pu, which agreed to refer the matter to Yunnan. In early 1903 the Yunnan Provincial authorities despatched officials to investigate on the spot, who reported that the watershed line was more than 100 *li* within Chinese territory. Prince Ch'ing of the Wai-wu-pu, on receipt of this news, suggested to Satow that a joint Anglo-Chinese boundary commission might now attempt to demarcate the frontier on the basis of the Yunnan Government's information, a proposal which was anathema to the Government of Burma. Satow, however, was authorised to propose that a joint Anglo-Chinese *inspection* of the disputed border might be made as a basis for further discussion. The Chinese agreed. The task of inspection was thereupon entrusted to G. L. J. Litton, the British Consul at Tengyueh, who had already in the last few years explored much of the country along the Nmaihka-Salween watershed, and to Shih, the Tengyueh *Taotai*. Litton was to be assisted by Leverson, the Deputy Commissioner for Bhamo. The joint inspection took place from March to May 1905. Shih seemed to be in a reasonable frame of mind, and, had he not been abruptly transferred before the proceedings were complete,

Litton thought that some useful result might have been achieved. Shih's removal was interpreted by the British as an act of deliberate obstruction on the Chinese part.

As a result of the 1905 inspection Litton concluded that:

1. We find that, as a matter of fact, there is not now, and is not in the least likely to be in the future, any sort of effective control or administration by the Chinese beyond the watershed. . . . We therefore recommend, in the first place, that no other line but the watershed should be accepted.

2. We find that, from the geographical and ethnographical points of view, the line proposed is not only a convenient, but may be called an ideal frontier as far north as the confines of Tibet. It is a conspicuous and unmistakable range of mountains only passable at wide intervals, and both sides of the crest of the range are entirely uninhabitable for an average distance of six to eight miles from the crests. . . . This range divides all the Kachins (on the Burma side) from all the Chinese (on the Yunnan side). Further, all the Lisa, with the exception of a few scattered hamlets, and all the Lu Tzu, would be on the Chinese side.

3. We find that the adoption of any other frontier would be highly detrimental to the interests of Burma, and in the long run scarcely less injurious to the interests of China. Chinese territorial claims on the N'Maikha side could not be recognised without forming an enclave where all the discontented, restless or criminal spirits could find a safe refuge beyond the reach of the British Government. This would greatly increase the expense and difficulty of even a partial administration.[17]

Litton added that, since the Chinese did, in fact, receive tribute from a few villages to the west of the proposed watershed line, they might well be compensated for such small loss of revenue; but that this was the only concession which he would advise. In 1906, immediately after the Anglo-Chinese Convention on the Chinese adhesion to the Lhasa Convention had been signed, Satow informed the Wai-wu-pu of Litton's conclusions, which he said now represented British policy. If the Chinese did not accept the watershed line, he declared, the British would proceed to extend their direct administration, which at that time

[17] India Office, Secret and Political Department Confidential Memoranda, B.174, quoting Litton's report which was sent to London under cover of India Foreign Letter of 17 August 1905.

could not be said to run much to the north of Myitkyina, right up to the crest of the Nmaihka-Salween divide. The Chinese refused to abandon their claims to the Nmaihka valley, and requested that further inspections on the ground take place. The British then considered a number of further concessions, such as a modification of the boundary alignment in the region of the Wa States, to induce the Chinese to accept the watershed line: but it became clear by 1908 that these would be fruitless. The Indian Government, in any case, was vehemently opposed to the idea of any concessions at all.

In January 1908 the Burmese Government discovered that, in the previous autumn, a Chinese official and fifty Chinese soldiers had crossed the watershed and erected a boundary pillar at Hpala on a small tributary of the Nmaihka. The Lieutenant-Governor proposed, therefore, that British forces should once more begin active patrolling in this disputed tract which had been left undisturbed since H. F. Hertz's clash with the Chinese at Hpare in 1900. Morley disliked the plan, and was worried lest it should result in the permanent establishment of police posts in remote districts where their security and supply would be extremely expensive. Finally, in November 1908, he reluctantly agreed to permit W. F. Hertz, the Deputy Commissioner of Myitkyina, and brother of H. F. Hertz, to make a limited tour with an escort of no more than 100 men, on the clear understanding that it would not lead to anything like a permanent occupation of these hitherto unadministered regions. Armed conflict with the Chinese was at all costs to be avoided. In January 1909, the Chinese having in the meanwhile taken no further action, Hertz's tour was cancelled.

In February–March 1910 a fresh crisis developed. A large party from the Chinese side, apparently composed of followers of the Chinese-subject Chief of Tengkeng, occupied the village of Pienma (or Hpimaw) on the western side of the watershed. The cause of this act appeared to be the refusal of the Pienma people to pay to the Tengkeng Chief an increased tax on the coffin-wood which they were accustomed to export to Yunnan. Archibald Rose, British Consul at Tengyueh, on investigating the incident concluded that it involved more than a petty dispute over traditional dues, and that it was likely that the Yunnan authorities intended to support the Tengkeng Chief and

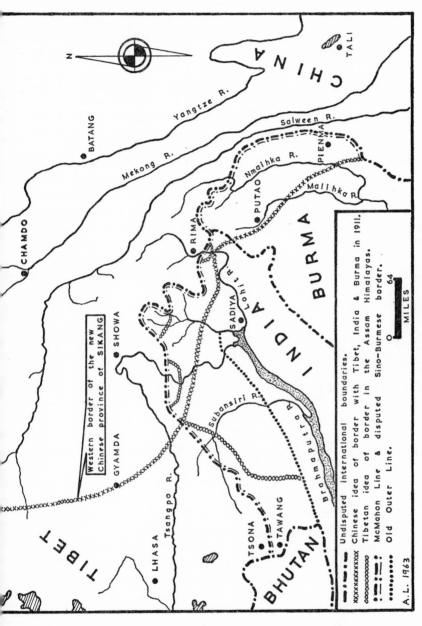

4 *Chinese and Tibetan ideas of the alignment of the Indian North-East Frontier, 1910–12*

take Pienma under permanent Chinese occupation as, Rose thought, the prelude to a campaign to bring all the disputed territory under Chinese administration. A new-drilled army, Rose noted, was at that moment being trained in Yunnan. In July 1910 a further Chinese transgression of the watershed line was reported in the shape of the visit of a Chinese official with escort to the district of Hkamtilong at the headwaters of the Malihka or western tributary of the Irrawaddy. At about this time, moreover, the nature of Chinese interest in Pienma was becoming clearer. The Chinese had, it seemed, established at least three schools in this district, indicating a cultural spearhead, as it were, for the advance of Chinese government. All this caused the Burmese Government to revive the proposal for Hertz's tour, which the Indian Government now approved. Hertz, with an escort of some 500 men, was to go up to the disputed neighbourhood of Pienma, levy a nominal tribute, promise British protection to the local chiefs, and knock down any Chinese boundary pillars he might come across. An expedition to Hkamtilong was authorised as well. Under the command of J. T. O. Barnard, it was to visit this remote corner of northern Burma where Chinese penetration had been reported, and to make it clear to the Kachins and other tribes there that they were British subjects.

In January 1911 Hertz and his escort entered Pienma unopposed. Chinese administration there, it was discovered, consisted of one elderly Chinese schoolmaster, whom Hertz had no difficulty in persuading to return to Yunnan. Hertz's orders precluded any permanent British occupation of Pienma; so no sooner had the old schoolmaster gone than he himself withdrew. The Chinese then began to protest against this invasion, as they described it, of their territory. In Yunnan a boycott of British goods was hastily organised, and it was rumoured that new-drilled troops would soon set out for the disputed territory. In February 1911 the Chinese were said to have reoccupied Pienma in force (the report was soon found to be untrue), and the Burmese Government proposed to send Hertz out once again. Both the India Office and the Indian Government, however, opposed this plan on the grounds that no further action should be taken until Jordan had been given a chance to reopen negotiations in Peking on the Burmese boundary question. Hertz, indeed, had reported that the Chinese claim to Pienma was not entirely without foundation, since the Tengkeng Chief had long possessed rights over the district; but, he argued, these pertained to the Tengkeng Chief as an individual rather than as a Chinese subject.

The reports in 1910 of the Chinese occupation of Pienma presented the Indian Government with a problem very similar to that which arose from Chinese penetration into the Assam Himalaya. Both in Northern Burma and in the Assam Hills the British did not at that time carry out direct administration; and their claim to the territory in question was theoretical rather than practical. In both areas the British could easily enough send expeditions to expel uninvited intruders; but then arose the problem of what to do next. Writing privately to Morley on the proposed expedition under Hertz to Pienma, Minto noted that:

> What it seems to me we should be quite clear about is our line of action *after* the expedition. . . . It is out of the question that we should sit down under further Chinese encroachment and the expedition could easily assert our authority.[18]

In other words, it was no use sending an expedition of this kind unless it resulted in some form of permanent British occupation. Morley, however, still obsessed with the idea of non-interference on the Indian frontiers, did not see things quite in the same light, as his reply to Minto, dated 18 July 1910, makes clear. Morley wrote that:

> I quite understand your interest in the movements of China, and the stir of the old Adam in you, that makes you dwell on the propriety of 'showing our teeth'. But there are questions that cannot be decided in India, nor from the Indian point by itself. H.M.G. have to survey the whole theatre of Chinese operations, which are manifold just now; and if the effect of showing our teeth too ferociously about the N'Maikha-Salween watershed were to provoke a Chinese boycott of British goods, it would be very awkward, and public opinion here in such a case would be very apt to ask whether the game was worth the candle. I had a long talk with Grey and Hardinge at the F.O. yesterday afternoon . . . [17 July 1910] . . . and we discussed the Chinese situation as a whole, with no notion of

[18] Morley Papers (D.573/24), Minto to Morley, 30 June 1910.

knocking under to the Pigtails, yet with a lively appreciation of the trouble that they have it in their power to give us, if they think that even virtuous England is going to treat China to what they call the policy of 'the carved melon', and to take a bit here and a slice there. When, again, you speak of the necessity of H.M.G. being 'aware of the impossibility of our withdrawing' after the Burma expedition has asserted our claim, I am not by any means so certain. That will depend. Who knows—such are the chances and changes of human things—but that you and Curzon may combine, breathing fire and slaughter against me for scuttle on the Salween!! Curzon, however, burnt his finger in his charge about scuttling out of Somaliland, and he may be more careful in the future, though he is not a willing learner. Anyhow sufficient for the day is the evil thereof, and the 500 policemen . . . [of W. F. Hertz's escort] . . . will doubtless march up to the boundary ridge when the rains permit. After what we said in 1906, we cannot do less than that. Of course, if China were a decent place, we should settle the boundary by arbitration, joint commission and other resources of civilisation; only these devices are not well suited to people who speak disdainfully of latitude and longitude, and work their oracle by forged maps.[19]

The Indian Government agreed with Morley about China not being 'a decent place'; but they were by no means convinced that he did not indeed intend to scuttle on the Salween and in the Assam Himalaya as well. With such an anxiety in their minds, they were inclined to believe that the Chinese had made an alarmingly accurate estimate of the likely reaction in England to aggression along the remoter tracts of the British Indian frontier. At this period, when Morley adhered so tenaciously to his concept of non-interference, many British officials in India could not bring themselves to believe that it was a coincidence that the Chinese had embarked upon a forward policy. The Chinese, they felt, must have sensed British weakness and indecision, and have decided to exploit it as best they could.

Such an Indocentric outlook, indeed, was to play a decisive part in the Government of India's devising of counter measures designed both to frustrate the Chinese and circumvent John Morley and his Cabinet colleagues. It did not, however, represent a particularly accurate appreciation of the nature

[19] Morley Papers (D.573/5), Morley to Minto, 18 July 1910.

of Chinese policy at this period. Max Müller, writing in April 1910 to Sir Edward Grey, interpreted the general Chinese forward policy, which he detected to be in progress in Turkestan, Mongolia, Tibet and on the Burmese frontier, as an essentially opportunist one of asserting traditional Chinese rights, however tenuous they might be, when circumstances favoured their assertion.[20] There was no master plan and there were no specific local objectives outlined in advance. There was certainly no plot for aggression against the British Indian Empire. This view seems, on the basis of the available evidence, more reasonable than that implied by Sir Henry McMahon in the passage quoted above. It was absurd, at any rate, to attempt to relate too closely Chinese moves in Tibet with Chinese moves on the Burma-Yunnan border. In both regions Chinese actions in 1910 had a long history behind them. The problem of the Nmaihka-Salween watershed went back to at least 1892: the problem of the nature of China's position in Tibet and her relationship with the Himalayan States could be traced to the Burma-Tibet Convention of 1886 and the Sikkim-Tibet Convention of 1890. Given the general direction of Chinese Central Asian policy in the first decade of the twentieth century, it was inevitable that these two problems should become more acute.

[20] FO 371/854, no. 16007, Max Müller to Grey, 22 April 1910.

XVII

BACKGROUND TO THE ASSAM
HIMALAYAN BOUNDARY PROBLEM[1]

I. THE PROBLEM

THEIR operations in Pome and Zayul during the course of 1910 and 1911 brought the Chinese into contact with some of the hill tribes living to the south of the main crests of the Assam Himalayan range, thus causing the British to begin to take a very active notice of a region which, ever since they first came into territorial contact with it in 1826, they had as a matter of policy generally left alone. From 1826, when by the Treaty of Yandaboo the British acquired Assam from the Burmese,[2] until 1910 the hill country along this section of the Indo-Tibetan marches, from Bhutan to Burma, was looked upon by the Indian Government as a convenient buffer between British and Tibetan territory. In 1910, however, as a result of Chinese activity, these mountains and jungles were seen to be a zone of serious weakness in the land defences of the Indian Empire.

The Assam Himalaya can be divided for our present purpose into two distinct regions. Firstly, adjacent to the eastern border of the Himalayan kingdom of Bhutan lies what may conveniently be called the Tawang Tract (Map no. 6)—between 1913 and 1919 this was officially described as part of the Western Section of the North-East Frontier, in 1919 it became

---

[1] Much of the information in Chapter XVII has already been published in Lamb, *China-India Border*, op. cit., pp. 115–30.

[2] At first the British attempted to administer Assam through a native dynasty; but they abandoned this experiment in 1838 when Assam became a Non-Regulation Province of British India.

known as the Balipara Frontier Tract, and more recently it has become the Kameng Division of the North-East Frontier Agency (NEFA). The Tawang Tract is a strip of territory some eighty miles wide which extends from the crests of the main Himalayan range right down to the Brahmaputra valley of Assam. Secondly, from the Tawang Tract eastwards to the Burmese border is that belt of mountain, over 100 miles deep

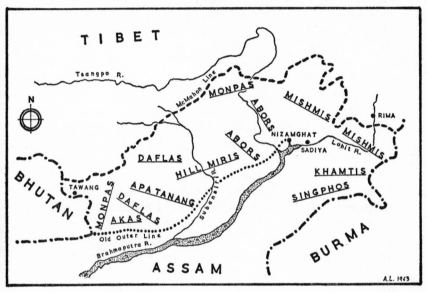

5   *Tribes of the Assam Himalayas*

in places, where live the 'aboriginal' tribes of the Assam Himalaya along the valleys of the Subansiri, Dihang (or Siang), Dibang, and Lohit river systems (Map no. 5). At present both Tawang and the hills to the east of it are administered as part of NEFA;[3] but the two regions, Tawang and the land of the 'aboriginal' tribes, are different from each other in a number of significant ways which have not always been appreciated in

[3] NEFA, of course, also embraces some hill tracts to the south of the main east-west axis of the valley of the Brahmaputra and its Lohit tributary, tracts which do not touch upon the Indo-Tibetan border. Since this work is concerned with British relations with Chinese and Tibetan territory, these portions of NEFA are ignored; and I have tended to use NEFA as a convenient term for the Assam Himalaya between the McMahon Line boundary of 1914 and the northern edge of the Assam plains.

recent accounts of the present problems of the Himalayan borders of India. As we shall see, Tibetan relations with Tawang were by no means the same as Tibetan relations with the hill country farther east.

2. THE TAWANG TRACT

The Tawang Tract (Map no. 6) can be subdivided into three main zones. In the extreme north, wedged in as it were into a triangular space bounded by the Bhutanese border, by the alignment which in 1914 became known as the McMahon Line, and by a mountain range crossed by the 13,940-foot-high Se La (Pass), is to be found what might be termed Tawang proper, the neighbourhood of the great Tibetan monastery of Tawang, a daughter house of Drebung monastery near Lhasa and sheltering between 500 and 700 monks.[4] South-east of the Se La is the second zone, the valley of the Bichom tributary of the Kameng River in which lies the administrative centre of Dirangdzong. Farther south, and separated from the Bichom by the Bomdi La, 9,640 feet, is the third zone, the valley of the Tenga tributary of the Kameng with the important villages of Rupa and Shergaon, the latter, as the crow flies, just over twenty-five miles north of Udalguri in the Assam plains. The southern boundary of the Tawang Tract, indeed, was generally said (before 1914) to run east-west just eleven miles north of Udalguri and thirty miles north of the Brahmaputra River.

All three zones of the Tawang Tract, a district which is known to the Tibetans as Mönyul, share with much of Bhutan a common geographical feature to which the explorer Kingdon Ward once drew attention.[5] In much of the Himalayan range

[4] Tawang monastery was founded in the seventeenth century by Lama Mera, a close friend of the fifth Dalai Lama. The sixth Dalai Lama was born near Tawang, his footprint is still displayed there to the faithful, and the monastery preserves relics of his mother. See V. Elwin, 'The Dalai Lama comes to India', *Geographical Magazine*, August 1959.

[5] F. Kingdon Ward, 'The Assam Himalaya: travels in Balipara', Pt. 1, *Journal of the Royal Central Asian Society*, XXV, 1938, pp. 610–11. See also F. Kingdon Ward, *Assam Adventure*, London, 1941.

The term Mönyul, which usually refers to the Tsöna district and the Tawang Tract, is sometimes used by Tibetans to describe a number of other remote districts along the Himalayan range. I am indebted to H. E. Richardson for this information.

there exist fairly wide river basins opening up the hills to the monsoon and resulting in the extension of the zone of high rainfall towards the crests: the result, on the whole, is a climate which is abhorrent to Tibetans. Between the Tista valley in Sikkim, however, and the valley of the Subansiri system to the east of the Tawang Tract, the forward ranges, relatively unbreached by major rivers, are a far more effective barrier against the rains than they are elsewhere. Here there are interior valleys as low as 5,000 feet above sea-level which are still cool enough and dry enough to make them attractive to settlers of the Tibetan or Bhutanese hillman type.

Thus the Tawang Tract, almost to the very edge of the Assam plains, is inhabited by tribes which, on any realistic scheme of classification, must be more closely related to Tibet than to the Indian lowlands. These are the Mönpas, Buddhist, greatly Tibetanised in language and culture, similar to the inhabitants of Eastern Bhutan and, more remotely, to such Himalayan groups as the Lepchas of Sikkim. The Mönpas, as one might expect, are most influenced by Tibet in Tawang proper, right on the edge of the Tibetan plateau. The Mönpas of the Dirangdzong region, the Sherchokpa as they are called, have many clearly non-Tibetan features; and so, to an even greater extent, do the Mönpas of Rupa and Shergaon, the Sherdukpen. But all the Mönpas, even those most removed from the Tibetan centres of the Tsangpo Valley, belong, culturally, to the north rather than to the south.[6] A recent (1963) account gives the total Mönpa population in the Kameng Division of NEFA (as the Tawang Tract is now called) as 36,600 including 2,600 Sherdukpen.[7] Until 1914 in theory, and until considerably later in practice (as we shall see), the Mönpas were under some measure of Tibetan political control, albeit exerted through complex and, in districts like Rupa and Shergaon, rather remote channels. 'Mönyul', so Kingdon Ward remarked of the Tawang

[6] For an account of the Mönpas of Tawang, see Aitchison, *Treaties*, op. cit., XII (1931), pp. 100–1; Verier Elwin, *A Philosophy for NEFA*, Shillong, 1960, pp. 10–13; R. R. P. Sharma, *The Sherdukpens*, Shillong, 1961; R. S. Kennedy, *Ethnological Report on Akas, Khoas, Mijis and the Monbas of Tawang*, Shillong, 1914.

[7] S. N. Sarma, 'Assam's relations with NEFA', *United Asia*, Vol. 15, no. 5, May 1963, pp. 358–9.

Tract in 1938, 'is in fact an outlying district of Tibet like the Chumbi Valley',[8] a conclusion which in recent times, especially since the Chinese Communists began to contest the validity of the McMahon Line border, it has been fashionable in some quarters to deny or obscure. There can be no doubt, however, from a study of British relations with the Tawang Tract since 1826, that at least until 1914 the Indian Government considered this district to be just what Kingdon Ward said it was, 'an outlying district of Tibet', and that there were good reasons for this view.

The British first came into direct territorial contact with the Tawang Tract as a result of the Treaty of Yandaboo of 24 February 1826, when they acquired Assam from the Burmese; but they were aware of the region's existence before this date. An important trade route from Tibet to Assam passed through Tawang by which an annual Tibetan trading venture visited the plains, bringing quantities of silver (worth at least a lakh of rupees) and loads of rock salt, which were bartered to Assamese merchants for, so Hamilton tells us, '*Tussa* cloth, a kind of coarse silk cloth manufactured by the native women of Assam from the Queen downwards; iron and lac found in Assam, and other skins, buffalo horns; pearls; and corals, first imported from Bengal', as well as for much rice.[9] The total value of this trade in 1809 was estimated to amount to about 2,00,000 rupees, and apart from salt and silver the Tibetans sent down woollen cloth, gold dust, musk, ponies, yak tails and Chinese silks. Burmese raids in the second and third decades of the nineteenth century disrupted the trade through Tawang;[10] but in 1833 the British made a fairly successful attempt to revive it when Lieutenant Rutherford established an annual fair at

[8] Kingdon Ward, 'Balipara', loc. cit., p. 613.

[9] Quoted by Alexander Mackenzie, *History of the Relations of the Government with the Hill Tribes of the North-East Frontier of Bengal*, Calcutta, 1884, p. 15.

Hamilton compiled, mainly from official sources, two accounts of British India and its neighbours which were both published in the second decade of the nineteenth century. See W. Hamilton, *A Geographical, Statistical and Historical Description of Hindostan*, 2 vols., London, 1820; W. Hamilton, *East India Gazetteer*, London, 1815.

[10] R. B. Pemberton, *Report on the Eastern Frontier of British India*, Calcutta, 1835, p. 81.

Udalguri, which Alexander Mackenzie, the historian of the Assam frontier, writing in 1884 on the basis of his own experiences in the 1870s, described in these words:

> A very interesting spectacle may be seen there . . . [Udalguri] . . . annually. Traders from all parts of Thibet, from Lassa and places east, west, and even north of it are present in crowds, some of them clad in Chinese dresses, using Chinese implements, and looking to all intents Chinese. Many have their families with them, and carry their goods on sturdy ponies, of which some hundreds are brought down to the fair yearly. In 1852 Government sanctioned a proposal to move the site to Mungledye . . . [Mangaldai near the north bank of the Brahmaputra] . . . which was expected to be more convenient for the Bengal and Assam traders. It was found, however, that such a change would not be popular. The hill caravans would not venture so far into the plains, and existing arrangements were left undisturbed.[11]

The British acquisition of Assam inevitably brought the Indian Government into some sort of political contact with the authorities in the Tawang Tract. The Mönpas nearest the plains had acquired in the course of time certain territorial rights to the south of the foothills which marked the limit of their normal occupation. What these rights were is by no means clear; but it is certain that some of the non-Mönpa inhabitants of the Kariapara Duar were in pre-British times in the habit of paying dues of one kind or another to their Mönpa neighbours, dues which were, or could be, interpreted as implying a measure of political subordination. R. B. Pemberton, who in the 1830s had made a special study of the northern frontier of Assam and Bengal, reported that the Kariapara Duar was shared between Tawang and Assam, the Tawang authorities, whom he described as direct subordinates of Lhasa, occupying the Duar during the cold season and abandoning it during the hot weather,[12] a practice which was the result, no doubt, of the seasonal migration of some of the Sherdukpen Mönpas which, so Elwin tells us, still goes on.[13] In the early nineteenth century,

---

[11] Mackenzie, *North-East Frontier*, op. cit., p. 16.
[12] R. B. Pemberton, *Report on Bootan*, Calcutta, 1839, p. 50.
[13] Elwin, *NEFA*, op. cit., p. 12.

however, it would seem that the British considered that sovereignty over the Duar was held rather by Tawang than by the authorities in Assam: as Robinson wrote in 1841 in his *Account of Assam*, based on much official information; 'this Duwar is held by the Towung Raja, a chieftain immediately dependent

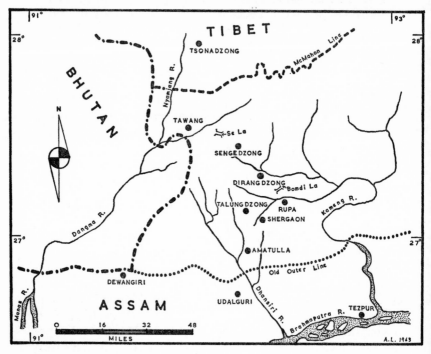

6 *The Tawang Tract*

upon Lassa'.[14] The British finally acquired sovereignty over Kariapara in 1844, when Major Francis Jenkins, the Governor-General's Agent for the North-East Frontier, persuaded six Mönpa chiefs to surrender all claims in the Duar in exchange for the annual payment of Rs. 5,000, a sum which, it was calculated, represented one-third of the revenue of the district in question.[15]

The chiefs from the Tawang Tract who signed the 1844 agreement appear to have been members of the Sherchokpa

[14] W. Robinson, *A Descriptive Account of Assam*, London, 1841.
[15] For the text of this agreement, see Appendix VIII.

and Sherdukpen Mönpas from Dirangdzong, Rupa and Sher-gaon, groups whose political status was at that time not fully understood by the British. Jenkins certainly regarded them as representatives of 'the Tawang Raja', a personage about whom he could say little except that he was 'not under the Government of Bootan, but is a feudatory of the Raja or Governor of Lassa'. He thought that British friendship with the Tawang authorities could be of some commercial advantage, since the trade route through Tawang was not only the shortest between British India and Lhasa but also

> there are by this route no intermediate independent authorities, the territories of the two great Governments of Britain and China . . . [as Tibetan suzerain] . . . are here coterminous, and this is the nearest route by which the produce of the North Western Provinces of China, and the Eastern Provinces of Tibet and Tartary could be brought into the British domi-nions.[16]

In 1873 the Tawang trade route still seemed attractive, even though it had not developed significantly since Jenkins's day. In that year Alexander Mackenzie, then Junior Secretary to the Bengal Government, recommended Tawang to Lord North-brook's attention because 'the Tawang country is held by Bhuteas who are entirely independent of Bhutan proper, and directly under Thibet. On all occasions Thibetan officials take part in whatever is done there. . . . Here, then . . . we are in actual contact with Tibet.' On the Tawang route, it was hoped, there would be no opportunity for meddlesome local chiefs like those in Bhutan or Sikkim to interfere with and obstruct the transit trade between British territory and that of the Lhasa Government. The Tawang route, at all events, Mackenzie argued, was potentially at least as valuable as that through Darjeeling.[17]

Mackenzie's implied conclusion that on the British-Tawang border relations were likely to be smoother than they were

---

[16] Enclosures to Secret Letters from India, Vol. 114, no. 36, Jenkins to India, 19 August 1847.

[17] *Accounts and Papers*, 1874, xlix, f. 567, 'Report on Trade Routes and Fairs on the Northern Frontiers of India', enclosing Mackenzie to India, 23 June 1873.

elsewhere along the Himalayas was not, in fact, supported by a great deal of evidence. During 1852–3, indeed, a crisis developed on this particular frontier which nearly resulted in an armed clash between the British and the Tawang authorities. Trouble arose over the Rs. 5,000 which the British had agreed to pay to the Tawang people in 1844. This sum had been handed over each year to one of the chiefs of, it would seem, the Sherdukpen or Sherchokpa Mönpas, who came down to the Udalguri fair for this purpose. These chiefs, who, the British thought, enjoyed wider powers than was actually the case, were known as the *Satraja*, the Seven Rajas, and the most important of their number was known to the Indian Government as the Gelong (or Gelling) Raja: it was he who collected the money. In 1852 the Gelong Raja, having received the Rs. 5,000, tried to hold on to it; and as a result was obliged to seek asylum in British territory. His Raja colleagues reported his defection to their superiors, who appear to have been, though the British did not know it at the time, the monks of Tawang monastery north of the Se La. The Tawang monks, probably with help from the authorities at Tsöna, the Tibetan administrative centre just north of what later became the McMahon Line, despatched an armed force to the British border to lend weight to their request for the Gelong Raja's extradition. The British refused, and immediately sent a force of their own to the border, 400 infantry and two six-pounder guns. The Tibetans thereupon proposed a compromise. If the British would sign a paper declaring that the Gelong Raja had died, then the Tibetans would withdraw in peace and, apparently, without the Rs. 5,000. The British declined to help the Tibetans save face. Long discussions followed, as a result of which the British eventually agreed to continue paying the Rs. 5,000 if the Tibetans would pardon the Gelong Raja, who would continue to reside in British territory (Appendix IX). In 1861 the Gelong Raja seems to have made peace with his masters and returned to Tawang; but soon he was again forced to take refuge south of the border. In 1864 a party of hillmen, on the orders of the Tawang authorities, crossed the British border and murdered the Gelong Raja, an act which much annoyed the Indian Government. For a while reprisals were seriously considered; but eventually it was decided to overlook the incident on the understanding that if there was further trouble the payment of Rs. 5,000 should be stopped for a while.[18]

In the cold season of 1872–3, presumably to reduce the risk of future frontier violations, Major Graham, Deputy Commissioner for Darrang, undertook to lay down the Tawang-British border as part of a general demarcation of the Bhutan-British border then in progress. Graham discussed the proposed alignment with a number of Mönpa chiefs (the *Satrajas*), who made it clear that they could make no binding agreements without the consent of their superiors in Tibet. During these talks four Tibetan officials appeared on the scene. 'I found they looked like priests', Graham reported, 'and appeared to be men of distinction and position. They were treated with great respect by, and took precedence of, the Rajas, and lastly the Rajas said the strangers had come from Lhasa on a tour of inspection.' Who exactly these four officials were is not certain. They may have been representatives of the great Tawang monastery; but it seems more likely that they were sent either by Lhasa (perhaps from Drebung monastery, Tawang's mother house) or by the authorities in Tsöna. Their presence, at all events, made the demarcation possible, since they persuaded the Mönpas to agree upon a boundary alignment, running east-west roughly eleven miles north of Udalguri.[19] This, it is interesting to note, seems to have been the only stretch of what the British considered to be the Indo-Tibetan border ever to have been laid down with Tibetan participation; but it was a line which the Indian Government abandoned when, in 1914, it decided upon the McMahon Line which at this point ran some sixty miles farther north.

In 1875, with the return to India of the explorer (Pundit) Nain Singh, who had travelled from Ladakh to Assam by way of Tibet and Tawang on behalf of the Great Trigonometrical Survey of India, the British acquired their first reasonably accurate picture of the country, people and politics of the

[18] Mackenzie, *North-East Frontier*, op. cit., pp. 16–17; L. W. Shakespear, *History of Upper Assam, Upper Burmah and North-Eastern Frontier*, London, 1914, p. 101; Aitchison, *Treaties*, op. cit., XII (1931), p. 78; B. C. Allen, *Assam District Gazetteers V: Darrang*, Allahabad, 1905, pp. 54–55.

[19] Secret Letters from India, Vol. 15, 1873, f. 523; Mackenzie, *North-East Frontier*, op. cit., p. 18; Mackenzie to India, 23 June 1873, loc. cit.

Tawang Tract, a picture somewhat amplified by Bailey and Morshead in 1913 and by Nevill in 1914.[20] It became clear that the Tawang Tract, Mönyul, while all of it was under some measure of Tibetan rule, yet that rule was neither uniformly nor, in some parts of the Tract, directly applied. Tawang proper, to the north of the Se La in the valleys of the Tawang and Nyamjang rivers, which was the seat of the great Tawang monastery, was an integral part of the Tibetan administrative district of Tsöna. The two Dzongpön (or District Governors) of Tsöna were accustomed to spend the cold weather in Tawang, which they considered, as it were, their winter capital. Of course, the Tawang monastery, a daughter house of the important Drebung monastery near Lhasa, was extremely influential in the region, and monastic representatives dominated the *Trukdri*, or local council, which regulated the day-to-day conduct of affairs in Tawang proper. South of the Se La, in the districts of Dirangdzong and Rupa and Shergaon, the Tsöna Dzongpön do not appear to have exercised direct authority except in the small village of Sengedzong, situated right at the southern foot of the Se La, which was more a private estate belonging *ex officio* to the Tsöna Dzongpön than a part of Tsöna district. South of the Se La, with this one exception, was the domain of Tawang monastery extending right down to the British border. Tawang monks maintained district officers at Dirangdzong in the valley of the Bichom tributary of the Kameng, and at Talungdzong at the very head of the valley of one of the branches of the Tenga tributary of the Kameng. Every year in the cold weather, when the fairs in Assam were in operation, the Talungdzong officials moved farther south to

---

[20] For Nain Singh's narrative, see Capt. H. Trotter, 'Account of the Pundit's journey in Great Tibet from Leh in Ladakh to Lhasa, and of his return to India via Assam', *Journal of the Royal Geographical Society*, Vol. 47, 1877.

For accounts of the journey of Bailey and Morshead through Tawang in 1913, see F. M. Bailey, *No Passport for Tibet*, London, 1957; Bailey, *Report*, op. cit.; F. M. Bailey, 'Exploration on the Tsangpo or Upper Brahmaputra', *Geographical Journal*, Vol. XLIV, 1914, pp. 341–64.

For accounts of Nevill's visit to Tawang in early 1914, see Sir Robert Reid, *History of the Frontier Areas Bordering on Assam from 1883–1941*, Shillong, 1942, pp. 286–8; PEF 1913/28, Nevill to Assam, 21 June 1914, enclosing diary of a visit to Tawang.

Amatulla, right on the British border, where they could watch the traffic to and from Udalguri. The Dirangdzong and Talungdzong officials collected taxes and were responsible for defence against the Bhutanese on the west and the non-Buddhist tribes on the east. The degree of their direct involvement in administration at the village level, however, seems to have varied from place to place. The Sherdukpen Mönpas, apparently, enjoyed a considerable measure of local autonomy, and the control of the Tawang monks in their valleys was at times little more than nominal. Tawang administration south of the Se La was not thought by British observers like Bailey and Nevill to have very much to recommend it. The Mönpas were oppressed by heavy taxes in return for which they received far less protection against raids from the neighbouring tribal areas than they had a right to expect.[21]

In recent years it has often been argued that the Tawang Tract never, strictly speaking, formed part of Tibet. The Mönpas there, it has been said, were subordinate to Tawang monastery in a religious sense only, and the taxes which they paid were religious dues.[22] This line of argument, of course, cannot possibly apply to Tawang north of the Se La, which was within the Tsöna district and was as Tibetan as Phari at the head of the Chumbi Valley, a town which in function it in many ways resembled. The status of the Tawang monastic estates south of the Se La is not so easy to define, and evidence of sorts can indeed be produced to support the contention that their relationship to Tibet was spiritual only. The evidence, however, on examination is not particularly convincing. The Tawang monks, like many other such bodies in Tibet, undoubtedly carried out temporal administration. The monastic Dzongpöns at Dirangdzong and Talungdzong did not confine themselves to Buddhist matters only, if it is at all possible to make a distinction between spiritual and temporal questions

[21] For a brief account of the administration of Tawang, apart from the works relating to Nain Singh, Bailey and Nevill to which reference has already been made, see General Staff, India, *Military Report on the Bhareli River Area and Tawang, 1920*, Calcutta, 1921.

[22] See, for example, Government of India, Ministry of External Affairs, *Report of the Officials of the Governments of India and the People's Republic of China on the Boundary Question*, New Delhi, 1961, p. 124.

within the theocratic framework of the Tibetan State. The revenue which they collected was taxation, not voluntary religious tithing. In administering south of the Se La, moreover, the Tawang monks were not acting on their own behalf, but rather they were agents of their mother monastery, Drebung at Lhasa, which had a very definite role in Tibetan government both lay and religious. The seal of Drebung, for example, was attached to the Lhasa Convention of 1904.

It has further been argued of late, in an attempt to lend support to the validity in international law of the McMahon Line boundary, that the Tawang Tract not only was not Tibetan, in a temporal sense, but also that it had, in effect, come under a measure of British protection long before 1914.[23] The sum of Rs. 5,000 which the British had been paying to chiefs in the Tract ever since 1844, so proponents of this view declare, was a subsidy which implied admission by its recipients of political dependence upon the British Indian Government. In fact, however, a glance at the 1844 agreement, of which the text is printed here as Appendix VIII, shows that the Mönpa signatories accepted the sum of Rs. 5,000 per annum in exchange for their relinquishment of rights in the Kariapara Duar of Assam. They were, in a way, leasing this Duar to the British. It could, indeed, be argued that in a sense the British, at least in respect to Kariapara Duar, were dependent upon the authorities in the Tawang Tract. Arguments about the political implications of the agreements of 1844 and 1853 relating to this Rs. 5,000, it would seem, are unlikely to be particularly fruitful. The Mönpas, after collecting the Rs. 5,000 from the British at Udalguri, handed it over to the Tawang monastery, which, in turn, sent all but Rs. 500 of it on to Drebung near Lhasa: thus, as A. W. Botham, the Chief Secretary to the Assam Government,

[23] E.g., ibid., pp. 203–4.

In 1876 Sherdukpen chiefs from Rupa and Shergaon were invited to attend a Durbar at Tezpur to hear Queen Victoria proclaimed Empress of India. This action rather suggests that the British, in practice, had come to look on the Mönpas immediately adjacent to their territory as to have come to some extent under their influence: but this influence could not possibly be construed to have extended north of the Bomdi La. It is interesting that the Indian side in the Sino-Indian border discussions of 1960 does not appear to have made any use of this episode. See V. Elwin, *India's North-East Frontier in the Nineteenth Century*, Bombay, 1959, p. 353 n.

remarked in 1922, in a not entirely successful attempt at humour, 'Tawang being a dependency of Lhasa, and Tibet being a dependency of China, we are in a way paying tribute to China for part of the Darrang District' of Assam in which the Kariapara Duar lay.[24]

In 1910 the Chinese sent a small body of troops to Tsöna.[25] Had the Chinese Revolution not broken out in late 1911 to spell the doom of the Chinese projects in Pome and Zayul, there can be little doubt that sooner or later Chinese officials would have entered the Tawang Tract and made their way down to the British border eleven miles to the north of Udalguri. As a result, Chinese rule would have penetrated right through the Himalayan barrier to the very edge of the Assam plains. This, to the British, most undesirable outcome of Chinese policy in Tibet was avoided through circumstances over which the Indian Government had no control. The Tawang-British border did not become critical during 1910–12. The dangers which its very existence implied, however, did not escape the notice of British strategists. As the Indian General Staff noted in June 1912:

> The demarcation of the frontier line about Tawang requires careful consideration. The present boundary (demarcated) is south of Tawang, running westwards along the foothills from near Udalguri to the southern Bhutan border, and thus a dangerous wedge of territory is thrust between the Miri . . . [non-Buddhist tribal] . . . country and Bhutan. A comparatively easy and much used trade route traverses this wedge from north to south, by which the Chinese would be able to exert influence or pressure on Bhutan, while we have no approach to this salient from a flank, as we have in the case of the Chumbi salient. A rectification of the boundary here is therefore imperative.[26]

It should cause no surprise, therefore, that this 'wedge' was incorporated within British territory by the McMahon Line of 1914; but the account of how this was done is best left to a later chapter.

[24] Reid, *Assam Frontier*, op. cit., p. 303.

[25] Bailey, *Report*, op. cit., p. 25.

[26] PEF 1910/14, General Staff Note on the North-East Frontier, 1 June 1912.

3. THE NON-BUDDHIST HILL TRIBES

The Assam Himalayan range to the east of the Tawang Tract is deeply penetrated or cut right through by several extensive river systems. The basins of the Subansiri, the Siang or Dihang, the Dibang, and the Lohit open up vast areas of jungle and mountain to the monsoon. The result is a climatic zone, in places extending almost to the crest of the range, unsuited to that Tibetan type of settlement which we find in Bhutàn and Tawang. In this belt of mountains and foothills, in places over 100 miles deep and stretching for some 300 miles to the Burmese border, live the non-Buddhist hill tribes who may be described as 'aboriginal' in the sense that they have managed to preserve cultures relatively uninfluenced by the civilisations of either the Indian plains or the Tibetan plateau. There are, by a recent estimate, about 186,000 of these tribesmen,[27] belonging to numerous small groups which have been classified into seven or eight major categories (Map no. 5). They have no writing of their own. Their history is little understood. Their languages have generally been assigned to the Tibeto-Burman group. Physically, most of them seem to be of Mongoloid type, and some anthropologists have detected a general relationship between them and such groups as the Shans of Burma. Some of the tribes have not progressed much beyond the food-gathering stage; but others, like the Apa Tanangs, have developed a most sophisticated economy based on wet-rice cultivation. It is not easy to make any particularly useful generalisation about the culture and economy of these peoples; and, fortunately, for the purposes of this book it is not necessary to do so.[28]

[27] Sarma, loc. cit., pp. 358–9. Elwin, *NEFA*, op. cit., p. 6, suggests a somewhat larger figure.

[28] For some descriptive accounts of the non-Buddhist tribes of NEFA, see Elwin, *NEFA*, op. cit.; E. T. Dalton, *Descriptive Ethnology of Bengal*, Calcutta, 1872; G. Dunbar (Duff-Sutherland-Dunbar), *Other Men's Lives*, London, 1938; V. Elwin, *India's North-East Frontier in the Nineteenth Century*, Bombay, 1959; T. K. M. Baruah, *The Idu Mishmis*, Shillong, 1960; U. Graham Bower, 'The Daflas of the Subansiri Area', *Journal of the Royal Central Asian Society*, 1949; U. Graham Bower, *The Hidden Land*, London, 1953; C. von Fürer-Haimendorf, *Ethnographic Notes on the Tribes of the Subansiri Region*, Shillong, 1947; C. von Fürer-Haimendorf, 'The Tribes of the Subansiri Region',

The non-Buddhist hill tribes of the Assam Himalaya are not Tibetans in any sense of the word, though a few groups living along the eastern edge of the Tawang Tract have to some degree been affected by the Tibetanised cultures of their Mönpa neighbours. In a few places along the north of the tribal hills, for example in the upper Siang and Siyom valleys, Tibetans or Mönpas have settled in small numbers and have mixed to some degree with the 'aboriginals'; but such instances are very much the exception. However, if the tribes are on the whole not Tibetan, it is equally true that, as Sir Robert Reid, Governor of Assam from 1937 to 1942, once told the Royal Central Asian Society, 'they are not Indian in any sense of the word, neither in origin, nor in appearance, nor in habits, nor in outlook'.[29] The same, indeed, could be said for other groups within the subcontinent who have escaped by virtue of the isolation of their habitat the impact of Indo-Aryan culture; and the significance of the non-Indian aspect of the Assam frontier peoples should not be exaggerated. The main point, of course, is that these people live on a frontier. They are not, as elsewhere, islands in an Indo-Aryan sea: they are a buffer between two quite distinct cultural worlds, those of the Indian plains and of Tibet. Their existence has prevented the evolution of a reasonably clear-cut cultural boundary line of the kind which, as has already been noted, separated Assam from Tibet along the Tawang Tract.

For reasons as much administrative as scientific, during the course of the nineteenth century these tribes were classified into six main groups, the Akas, Daflas, Apa Tanangs, Miris, Abors and Mishmis, to which more recently further categories have been added. This classification is of some value in that it provides a convenient nomenclature for major tribal regions of the

[29] Sir R. Reid, 'India's North-East Frontier', *Journal of the Royal Central Asian Society*, Vol. 31, 1944, p. 174.

Journal of the Royal Central Asian Society, 1948; C. von Fürer-Haimendorf, *Himalayan Barbary*, London, 1955; C. von Fürer-Haimendorf, *The Apa Tanis and their Neighbours*, London, 1963; G. A. Grierson, *Linguistic Survey of India*, III, Calcutta, 1909; J. P. Mills, 'Mishmis of the Lohit Valley, Assam', *Journal of the Royal Anthropological Institute*, 1952; S. Roy, *Aspects of Padam-Minyong Culture*, Shillong, 1960; B. K. Shukla, *The Daflas*, Shillong, 1959.

Assam Himalayas. The Akas and some of the Daflas live between the Tawang Tract and the Subansiri basin. More Daflas, as well as the Apa Tanangs and Miris are to be found along the Subansiri and its tributaries. The river system of the Siang or Dihang is Abor country. In the basin of the Dibang and along the Lohit are to be found Mishmis. To the professional anthropologist, of course, this tribal classification is far less useful. The Abors (or Adis as they now prefer to be called), for example, are by no means a homogeneous category: Verrier Elwin subdivides them into the Minyongs, Padams, Pasis, Panggis, Shimongs, Boris, Ashings, Tangams, Gallongs, Ramos, Bokars and Pailibos, each with its distinctive characteristics. Many of the names for the major tribal groupings, moreover, are of Assamese rather than tribal origin. Abor, for instance, means in Assamese 'unruly' or 'disobedient': the term Adi, meaning simply 'hillmen', has now been substituted for it.

From a political point of view the names of the tribes are of minor importance. The essential fact is that there were a large number of small tribal groups, with governmental organisations which had rarely evolved beyond the village level; and that it is meaningless to talk of anything like an Abor or Mishmi or Dafla *state*. Lieutenant-Colonel G. L. S. Ward, who took part in military operations in the Mishmi hills in 1899–1900, described clearly the position in one region at least when he noted that 'there is absolutely no settled government among the Mishmis—each village, and even each house being quite independent, managing its own affairs. Every man is his own master.'[30] British treaties with the hill tribes, of which a number were concluded during the nineteenth century, were made not with any major tribal category as such, but with groups of village headmen each able to bind no more than his own particular community. Maps of what is now NEFA which show the distribution of the major tribal categories tend to be rather misleading, suggesting that these categories controlled clearly defined territories extending from the foothills to the crest of the range, rather as did the authorities in Nepal and Bhutan.

During the course of the nineteenth century it became clear that not only were the tribes divided into cultural groups, to which segments of the hills could be assigned, but that also

[30] G. L. S. Ward, *Military Report on the Mishmi Country*, Simla, 1901.

within such segments there were horizontal divisions, as it were, which prevented the evolution of anything approaching a pan-tribal organisation. Students of these tribes, like E. T. Dalton, whose *Descriptive Ethnology of Bengal*, though published in 1872, is still a work of the greatest interest, failed to find, except in the Mishmi country along the Lohit, any evidence of much north-south mobility on the part of the inhabitants of the Assam Himalaya. Among the tribesmen along the foothills adjacent to British territory there was abundant evidence of indirect contact with the Tibetan world in the shape of such objects as brass vessels, small bronze bells, glass beads and iron knives and swords; but it was almost impossible to find anyone who had actually visited the land beyond the high peaks whence these things originated. The Padam Abors, for example, Dalton found 'for some reason throw a veil of mystery over their inter-course, and always repudiating direct trade with Tibetans, tell you of the existence of barbarous tribes on the high snow ranges behind them: and you meet with no one of the clan who will acknowledge to have passed this barrier of savages'.[31] So also, he found, the hill Miris and the Daflas always spoke of the wild peoples who lived to the north between them and Tibet. The explanation for this phenomenon of horizontal stratification was, basically, an economic one. The tribal groups immediately adjacent to the markets of Assam and Tibet supplied the interior peoples with such goods as they required, and their geographical position conferred on them a monopoly of this trade which they guarded jealously. The interior peoples could not avoid all contact with the outside world, since they had to obtain salt, a substance rare in the Assam Himalayas. This could be acquired either from Assam or from Tibet; and there existed a divide, the 'salt divide' so Mills and Fürer-Haimendorf have termed it, separating those who looked south from those who looked north for this essential commodity.[32] Only along the Lohit Valley between Assam and Tibetan Zayul was there anything remotely comparable to the through Indo-Tibetan trade route of the Tawang Tract; and

[31] Dalton, op. cit., p. 28.
[32] Fürer-Haimendorf, *Himalayan Barbary*, op. cit., p. 234; Fürer-Haimendorf, *Tribes of the Subansiri*, op. cit., p. 43; J. P. Mills, 'Problems of the Assam-Tibet Frontier', *Journal of the Royal Central Asian Society*, 1950.

commerce up and down the Lohit had failed to bring about any significant political unification of the Mishmi tribes.

The lowest tribal groups in this scheme of horizontal stratification, those living along the edge of the Assam plains, had a very long history of contact with the rulers to their south. Tribal raids in search of plunder or slaves into the plains were common. The Daflas and Abors seem to have been especially feared in this respect. The Ahoms, who had ruled Assam for centuries before the coming of the British, evolved a system which minimised the effects of tribal raiding. Annual sums were paid to the tribes nearest to the border, either in exchange for the surrender of territorial rights which the tribes considered they had acquired along the edge of the plains (*posa*), or more or less as bribes to the tribesmen to persuade them to keep the peace ('blackmail'). *Posa*, according to Mackenzie, was 'really a well-ascertained revenue payment' which in some cases was collected by the tribes themselves from the cultivators of the frontier tracts involved;[33] and it probably originated from the process of Assamese colonisation of land into which the neighbouring hillmen had been accustomed to migrate during the cold season just as did the Sherdukpen Mönpas into the Kariapara Duar. The British, when they acquired control of Assam in 1826, took over this system; but they tried to stop the tribes from collecting direct from the peasants: instead, they endeavoured to turn *posa* into a direct payment by Government to the tribes, a change which the tribes did not always accept with good grace.

The system of payments to the hill tribes which the British took over from Ahom practice, and which they endeavoured to rationalise through a series of written agreements with tribal headmen, was a complicated one. In general, however, it was not intended to imply, any more than it had in Ahom times, that the Assam Government had assumed sovereignty over the tribal hills (at least, in so far as the tracts along the Tibetan border was concerned—some tribes like the Khamtis and the Singphos definitely acknowledged that they had come under British protection). Many of the British treaties with these tribes are very careful to state the existence of a frontier between the tribes and British territory. An engagement with some Aka

[33] Mackenzie, *North-East Frontier*, op. cit., p. 21.

chiefs of 1844, for example, bound the tribesmen to obey British law while they were in British territory, which meant, the text implied, the plains not the hills. This distinction is made clear beyond doubt in a group of engagements with Abor chiefs in the 1860s. Article 2 of the treaty with some Minyong Abor headmen, or *gams*, of November 1862, states that

> the limit of British territory which extends to the foot of the hills is recognized by the Meyong Abors, who hereby engage to respect it.[34]

Throughout the text of this treaty it is emphasised that the British are only claiming sovereignty up 'to the foot of the hills', and they only wish to control the tribesmen in respect to actions which take place south of this line. In another treaty of 1862 the tribes concerned were to be given annually 100 iron hoes, 40 mounds of salt, 100 bottles of rum, and 2 mounds of tobacco 'to enable the Abors of the clans or communities mentioned in the preamble to keep a Police' to prevent transgressions of the British frontier;[35] this could be regarded as aid, like American help to Vietnam to keep out the Communists, rather than the payment of a subsidy with the implication of assumed sovereignty.

The British, in the nineteenth and early twentieth centuries, did not consider that the non-Buddhist tribal areas of the Assam Himalayas formed part of their Indian Empire. On the other hand, unlike the Tawang Tract, which they admitted was part of Tibet, they did not consider these regions to form part of the dominions of any other Power. There could be no question that the non-Buddhist tribes immediately adjacent to the British border—those in the interior were another matter—were under Tibetan rule. If tribal groups violated the British frontier, as they occasionally did, the Indian Government felt itself free to order a suspension of *posa* and other such payments, to impose an economic blockade on the tribes in question and prevent them from visiting the markets of Assam, and, in the last resort, to send punitive expeditions into tribal territory. Some of these operations, like the Bebejiya Mishmi Expedition of 1899–1900, were planned on an elaborate scale: in 1899 it was intended to

[34] See Appendix X.
[35] Aitchison, *Treaties*, XII (1931), pp. 160–2.

send a force of some 1,200 men into Mishmi country, though in the end only about 100 set out.[36] The Indian Government did not regard these campaigns of tribal pacification as being of international interest; and it never considered for one moment informing the Chinese, whom it acknowledged had a legitimate concern in Tibetan affairs, that a British force was about to be despatched into the Assam Himalayas. While the tribal hills were not inside the limits of British territory, yet it was felt that they fell within the sphere of British influence, and that the Indian Government was fully entitled to take what action it saw fit there to protect its interests. There seemed no need, however, before 1910 to have this situation confirmed by any international agreement.

In the second half of the nineteenth century the problem of keeping the peace along this mountain border was somewhat complicated by economic developments in Assam. The tea industry began to take an interest in the Himalayan foothills. Timber companies looked with envy at the forest wealth along the edge of the tribal hills. It became obvious that, uncontrolled, the expansion of commercial enterprises of this kind into tribal territory was bound to result in disturbances which might oblige Government to undertake expensive punitive expeditions. Some regulation of the frontier regions was essential. Accordingly, the Bengal Eastern Frontier Regulation of 1873 was introduced, creating the so-called 'Inner Line' which has been such a thorn in the flesh of subsequent generations of would-be explorers. Mackenzie has defined this Regulation as one which

> gives power to the Lieutenant Governor [of Bengal and with responsibility for Assam] to prescribe a line, to be called 'the inner line' in each and any of the districts affected, beyond which no British subjects of certain classes or foreign residents can pass without a license. The pass or license, when given, may be subject to such conditions as may appear necessary. And rules are laid down regarding trade, the possession of land beyond the line, and other matters, which give the executive Government an effective control. The regulation also provides for the preservation of elephants, and authorizes Government to lay down rules for their capture.[37]

[36] Reid, *Assam Frontier*, op. cit., pp. 204–9.
[37] Mackenzie, *North-East Frontier*, op. cit., p. 55.

The problem of elephant catching was an acute one, since the trappers of this beast were continually wandering into tribal territory and finding themselves enslaved by the hillmen. The Inner Line was not the international boundary of the Indian Empire;[38] it was a device to create a buffer zone, as it were, between the international boundary and regularly administered territory, a tract which marked the transition between the tribal hills and the Assamese plains. By limiting access from the south to this area it was hoped to minimise the risk of trouble with the tribes. At the same time, tribesmen who crossed the international boundary from the north, but remained beyond the Inner Line, still passed under British jurisdiction should the authorities choose to exercise it. It has been said that the Inner Line disrupted trade between the tribes and the plains.[39] This does not, in fact, seem to have been the case. While making it more difficult for plainsmen to penetrate into the tribal areas, it does not seem to have limited in any significant way the attendance of hillmen at such markets as that held annually at the administrative centre of Sadiya.[40]

The Inner Line, while not the international boundary, yet served many of the functions of that boundary; and British writers tended to treat it as the effective limit of Indian territory, thus adding further complexity to Sino-Indian boundary disputes in recent years. The definition of the Inner Line in the Darrang and Lakhimpur Districts of Assam adjacent to the Himalayan range, which took place in 1875–6, rather tended to obscure the definition of the international boundary, or Outer Line, which was made here at the same time. In recent years it has been possible for apologists of the Indian side in the Sino-Indian dispute to deny that there was ever an Outer Line at all other than that which was defined by the McMahon

[38] Sir E. Gait, *A History of Assam*, Calcutta, 1926, pp. 334–5.

[39] S. N. Sarma, loc. cit., p. 363.

[40] In 1876, for example, no less than 3,600 tribesmen attended the Udalguri fair and 3,000 the fair at Sadiya. Elwin, *NEFA*, op. cit., p. 3.

For an account of the Sadiya fair, see *Accounts and Papers* 1874, XLIX, f. 567, Report on the Trade Routes and Fairs on the Northern Frontier of India, enclosing Report on the Sudya Fair by Major W. S. Clarke, 21 February 1873.

Line in 1914.[41] Of the existence of the Outer Line, however, there can be no real doubt. It had been implied in such instruments as the British agreement with some Abor *gams* which has been referred to above. It followed the line of 'the foot of the hills' a few miles to the north of what became the course of the Inner Line. It was laid down on the ground for part of its length, from the south-east corner of the Tawang Tract to the Baroi River at lat. 27°, long. 93° 20', in 1875, following the foothills alignment. From the Baroi River to Nizamghat on the Dibang the Outer Line was not demarcated; but by definition it followed 'a readily recognisable line along the foot of the hills'. Eastward of Nizamghat there was no Outer Line at all, it would seem, the Inner Line alone marking the limits of British jurisdiction.[42] The situation of the Outer Line along the Assam Himalayas is shown with some precision in the map *The Province of Eastern Bengal and Assam*, thirty-two miles to the inch, which was specially prepared by the Foreign Department, Government of India, in 1908 to illustrate the second volume of the 1909 edition of Aitchison's *Collection of Treaties*. The demarcated border, indicated by alternating dots and dashes, is shown here continuing from the southern border of Bhutan to the Baroi River, where it is replaced by alternating dashes and crosses, indicating delimited but not demarcated: at Nizamghat dashes and crosses give way to a dotted line following the Inner Line alignment eastwards. This particular map marks the tribal hills of the Assam Himalayas, but not the Tawang Tract, with a light yellow wash indicating that while

[41] For example, Sir Olaf Caroe, 'The Sino-Indian Frontier Dispute', *Asian Review*, April 1963, p. 72. Sir Olaf Caroe takes the London *Times* severely to task for publishing, on 21 November 1962, a map showing the Indo-Tibetan border before 1914 on the foothills alignment. This 'much ado about maps', as *The Times* once said of an official Indian protest on this point, has arisen because of a certain confusion. The *Tibetan* frontier may well not have followed the foothills alignment in the Assam Himalayas before 1914 (though we have seen that in the Tawang Tract this is just what the Tibetan frontier did); but the foothills marked the line of the *British Indian* frontier. It did not follow of necessity that the British frontier was also the Tibetan frontier: along much of the tribal foothills to the east of the Tawang Tract it clearly was not.

[42] India Office, Political and Secret Department Confidential Memoranda, B.180, *North-Eastern Frontier of India: Tribal Territory North of Assam*, 3 December 1910.

outside the international boundary yet this area is in some unspecified way within the general British sphere of influence. The Outer Line, it should be noted, was not based on any ethnic demarcation between Assamese and tribal territory. Many hill tribes had established permanent or seasonal settlements south of the Outer Line. The Outer Line followed the convenient geographical alignment of the foot of the hills which, it has been said, rise 'like a wall from the valley'.

During the nineteenth century British officials penetrated from time to time into the tribal hills beyond the foothill line; but, with the exception of the Lohit Valley, they only travelled short distances north of British territory. As early as 1826, for example, Captain Bedford had made a short expedition into Abor country; and by the end of the century Europeans had come into contact with the southern fringes of most of the main tribal groups. The interior tribes, however, remained but little known: the Apa Tanangs, for instance, were first seen by a European in their home country in 1890 when the tea planter H. M. Crowe made the adventurous journey up the lower Subansiri valley.[43] By 1910, it is certain, no British official had made his way up into the Assam Himalaya to anywhere near the beginning of Tibetan territory, except along the Lohit. It seems very unlikely, moreover, that agents of the Ahom rulers of Assam before 1826 had bettered the British in this respect. In some parts of the Assam Himalayas, along the Subansiri for example, British officers had still not travelled all the way up from the plains to Tibet by the time of the Transfer of Power in 1947. The claim, raised in recent years as a result of the Sino-Indian boundary dispute, that in NEFA the British, and the Ahoms before them, had exercised effective administration all along the Assam Himalayas right up to what became in 1914 the McMahon Line, is not supported by very impressive evidence.[44]

Only on the Lohit, in the country of the Mishmis, had British and other European travellers, official and unofficial, managed to make their way to territory under undoubted Tibetan control. The Lohit, which linked Sadiya in Assam to

[43] Elwin, *NEFA*, op. cit., p. 13.
[44] See, for example, Government of India, Ministry of External Affairs, *Report of the Officials*, op. cit., p. 201.

Tibetan Zayul, was seen from the earliest days of British rule in Assam as a potential trade route leading to the inner provinces of the Chinese Empire. Lieutenant Wilcox, who made his way for more than sixty miles up the Lohit from Sadiya in 1826, noted that many of the Mishmis near the British frontier were in possession of such articles as Chinese pipes, Chinese and Tibetan swords, coats of Tibetan wool, and beads of glass and carnelian of Chinese or Tibetan workmanship.[45] J. M'Cosh, writing in 1837, pointed to the Lohit and neighbouring routes by which, 'in the event of it ever becoming necessary to take vengeance on the Chinese, an armed force embarking on the Brahmaputra could march across the mountains and enter Yunnan, one of the richest provinces of the Empire'.[46] The Lohit Valley, accordingly, was attacked by explorers with an enthusiasm which was not seen on the Dihang or the Subansiri. The journeys of Lieutenant Wilcox and Captain Bedford in 1826 were followed by that of Dr. Griffith in 1836, who reached the half-way point between Sadiya and Tibetan territory.[47] In 1844–5 Lieutenant Rowlatt tried unsuccessfully to reach Tibet by this route.[48] In 1851 the French missionary Father Krick travelled all the way to Walong, which he considered to be the Tibetan border and where he was obliged to turn back. In 1854, accompanied by Father Boury, Krick made another attempt to enter Tibet by the Lohit route; but the two priests were murdered by Mishmi tribesmen, leading, in the following year, to a small British punitive expedition up the valley under the command of Lieutenant Eden.[49] In December 1867 the Indian Government, in an attempt to establish communications with the French Catholic missionaries in Eastern Tibet, sent messengers from Sadiya up the Lohit, who, after travelling for

[45] R. Wilcox, 'Memoir of a Survey of Assam and the Neighbouring Countries executed in 1825–6–7–8', *Asiatic Researches*, XVII, Calcutta, 1832, p. 373.

[46] J. M'Cosh, *Topography of Assam*, Calcutta, 1837, p. 12.

[47] W. Hunter, *A Statistical Account of Assam*, 2 vols., London 1879, Vol. 1, p. 322. See also Bengal Secretariat Press, *Selection of Papers regarding the Hill Tracts between Assam and Burmah and on the Upper Brahmaputra*, Calcutta, 1873, p. 119.

[48] B. C. Allen, *Assam District Gazetteers, Vol. VIII: Lakhimpur*, Calcutta, 1905, p. 82.

[49] Dalton, *Ethnology*, op. cit., p. 14.

fifteen days, were turned back by a party of Tibetans engaged, it would seem, in collecting revenue from the Mishmis.[50] In 1869–70 the enterprising T. T. Cooper, self-styled 'pioneer of commerce' in quest of a channel by which Indian tea could reach Central Asian markets, tried to go up the Lohit. The Mishmis made him turn back long before the Tibetan border was reached.[51] In 1879 the Khamti chief Chowsam, evidently acting on behalf of the British, tried to get to Tibet by this route, but was not allowed to cross the Mishmi-Tibet border.[52] In January 1886 J. F. Needham, the Assistant Political Officer, Sadiya, with responsibility for British relations with the eastern Assam hill tribes, and Captain E. H. Molesworth, commanding the Lakhimpur Frontier Police, made their way to within one mile of Rima, the Tibetan administrative centre of Zayul, a feat which was only possible because Chowsam, who preceded them, had managed to prevent the Mishmi tribes from giving the Tibetans advance warning of their progress. Needham was convinced that the Lohit route, though in 1886 of little commercial importance, might well be developed into a major trade route 'for supplying Eastern Tibet with English goods'; and he proposed to Government that a road be built along it to the Tibetan border.[53] Lord Dufferin's administration, with its hands full in Burma and with one Tibetan venture, the Colman Macaulay Mission, already projected, was not enthusiastic. Roads of this kind were not to be attempted 'unless on clear evidence of their necessity and utility', which could not be detected in Needham's report.[54] The Lohit road was later to

[50] BCCA, p. 120; Collections to Despatches, Vol. 99, 1868, no. 160.

[51] T. T. Cooper, *The Mishmee Hills*, London, 1873.

[52] J. F. Needham, 'Journey along the Lohit Brahmaputra between Sadiya in Upper Assam and Rima in South-Eastern Tibet', *Royal Geographical Society Supplementary Papers*, Vol. II, 1889.

The Khamtis are a Buddhist tribe, related to the Burmese Shans, who migrated into Assam from Hkamtilong in the early nineteenth century. They live on the southern bank of the Lohit in the neighbourhood of Sadiya. To their south are the Singphos, related to the Burmese Kachins and, like the Khamtis, recent arrivals in Assam. Both the Khamtis and the Singphos, unlike the non-Buddhist tribes of the Assam Himalayas, had during the course of the nineteenth century accepted the status of British subjects.

[53] Needham, 'Journey', loc. cit.

[54] Letters from India, Vol. 48, 1886, India to Assam, 14 September 1886.

be championed with great verve by Sir Thomas Holdich, who persuaded the Indian Government at the time of the Young-husband Mission to think about opening a trade mart in Zayul; but, on closer examination, the prospects of the Lohit seemed no more promising in 1904 than they had in 1886.[55]

These journeys up the Lohit, while they brought British officials right through to Tibetan territory, could hardly be interpreted to imply British administration. In the Lohit valley, as elsewhere along the tribal areas of the Assam Himalayas, British policy was one which Morley was later to describe as 'non-interference'. This dated back, in fact, to the pre-British period of Ahom rule, and it was sanctified by the Inner and Outer Lines of the 1870s. Mackenzie, referring specifically to the Abor country, summed up British policy thus:

> It is not open to us on the Abor frontier to have recourse to the policy of permanent occupation and direct management which we shall find successfully carried out in the Naga, Garrow, Cossyah, Jynteeah, and Chittagong Hill Tracts. To annex the Abor Hills would only bring us into contact with tribes still wilder and less known, nor should we find a resting place for the foot of annexation till we had planted it on the plateau of High Asia; perhaps not even then.[56]

The Indian Government certainly had no intention of pushing 'the foot of annexation' up the Lohit Valley, however attractive it might be as a potential trade route, until the Tibetan border was reached. It was not certain, indeed, where the Tibetan border was. Father Krick thought the first Tibetan village was Walong, a few miles south of the McMahon Line boundary of 1914,[57] and Needham seems to have agreed. There was evidence, however, that while Tibetans did not live below Walong, yet Tibetan influence had been established over Mishmi tribesmen living farther down the Lohit. Griffith, who reached in 1836 the point where the Lohit is joined by its tributary the Delei, some distance below Walong, was turned back by the Mishmis, so he thought, because they feared Tibetan reprisal if they were to

[55] Sir T. Holdich, *Tibet the Mysterious*, London, 1908, pp. 333–6.

[56] Mackenzie, *North-East Frontier*, op. cit., p. 55.

[57] Dalton, *Ethnology*, op. cit., p. 14.

allow strangers through their territory.[58] On the lower reaches of the Du, a tributary of the Lohit just to the east of the Delei, Lieutenant Rowlatt in 1844–5 met Tibetan Lamas who persuaded him to turn back.[59] In 1869–70 Cooper was told by members of one Mishmi group, the Miju, 'that they were subjects of the Tibetan Government, by whose order they had prevented me from reaching Tibet'.[60] Ward, on the basis of his experiences in the Mishmi country in 1899–1900, supported Cooper. 'There is no doubt', he observed, 'that there was 'intercourse to some extent between the Mishmis and the Tibetans. The Meju Mishmis are regarded as the watchdogs of the Tibetans, as they give them early information of the approach of strangers to the Tibetan frontier.'[61] J. F. Needham, in 1886, while inclined to agree with Krick that Walong was the Mishmi-Tibet frontier, doubted that there could be found here anything like an international boundary in the European sense. 'In the absence of any strongly marked geographical division,' he reported, 'it seems probable that Tibetan authority in the south-western extremity of the Zayul valley depends rather on the casual exertion of force than upon any recognised distinction between the natives of Zayul and their Mishmi neighbours.' In 1836, for example, a small Tibetan force had gone down the Lohit well below Walong to take part in a conflict between two Mishmi groups.[62] There did not seem to be any particularly sharply defined resting-place for 'the foot of annexation'.

There was, we have seen, some evidence that in the nineteenth century the Tibetans had established some influence over at least the Mishmis living nearest to Zayul. Had they also established a measure of influence over the other hill tribes to their south along the upper valleys of the Assam Himalayas? The Indian Government in 1910 still had no reliable information on this point; but it certainly shared John Morley's

---

[58] Bengal Secretariat Press, *Papers*, op. cit., p. 119. See also W. Griffith, 'Visit to the Mishmee Hills', *Journal of the Asiatic Society of Bengal*, Vol. VI, 1837; W. Griffith, *Journal of Travels in Assam, Burma, Bootan, etc.*, Calcutta, 1847.

[59] Dalton, *Ethnology*, op. cit., p. 14.

[60] Cooper, *Mishmee Hills*, op. cit., p. 245.

[61] Ward, *Report*, op. cit.

[62] Needham, 'Journey', loc. cit.

suspicion that 'at the back of the Abor hills lies foreign territory, Tibet, and between the Abors and Tibet proper there may be tribes which are more or less under Tibetan influence'.[63] On the basis of travellers' reports and other sources which have become available since 1910, it is now possible to say that Morley was correct, and that in several places Tibetan influence had penetrated south of the main crests of the Assam Himalayas. The Tibetans, no more than the British, were able to avoid all contact with the hill tribes along their frontier, peoples whom they called *Lopas*. Moreover, in a few regions there had been taking place over the years a measure of actual Tibetan or Tibetan-type (Bhutanese or Mönpa) colonisation into tribal territory.[64]

Early in the twentieth century Tibetans from a number of districts in Eastern Tibet migrated into the Assam Himalayas by the headwaters of the Dibang. They were seeking *Pemakö*, a Buddhist holy land about which old prophecies existed;[65] and they thought that they had found it in the country of the Chulikatta Mishmis. Several thousand settlers arrived, but by 1909 most of them had either died or, disillusioned, had set out for their home districts. In 1913 a mere handful remained, who were fighting a rearguard battle against hostile Mishmis.[66] A few years later the Tibetans had completely abandoned the Dibang basin, unable to withstand the attacks of the tribesmen.[67] On the Tsangpo-Siang, however, settlers advancing from the north were more successful. These were mainly Bhutanese and

[63] PEF 1910/13, Morley to Minto, 4 September 1908.

[64] The main source of information on this subject in a European language remains Bailey, *Report*, op. cit., a work much used in such later compilations as Carrasco, op. cit.

Bailey was no trained anthropologist or political scientist; but in 1913 as during his other journeys he showed remarkable powers of observation and clear thought. His *Report*, while certainly no literary masterpiece, must rank among the most accurate and informative accounts of Central Asian exploration yet written. Bailey later revised and partly rewrote it for publication under the title *No Passport for Tibet*: but it is to be regretted that in the process he omitted much useful information contained in the *Report*. I am much indebted to Colonel Bailey for letting me have his last remaining spare copy of the *Report*.

[65] J. Bacot, *Le Tibet Révolté*, Paris, 1912, p. 10.

[66] Bailey, *Report*, op. cit., p. 3; Bailey, *No Passport*, op. cit., pp. 35–38.

[67] So Colonel Bailey tells me.

Mönpas from Tawang, and many of them established themselves along the upper reaches of the Siyom (the Pachakshiri country). The Bhutanese migration appears to have begun in the early nineteenth century; and in 1913 some of the colonists still regarded themselves as subjects of the Tongsa Penlop, though they also recognised to some extent the authority of Kongpo and Pome to their north. Under their influence some of the neighbouring tribes, presumably of the Abor group, had become Tibetanised and had embraced Buddhism. Other tribes remained hostile to the settlers—these settlers, whether from Bhutan or elsewhere, are generally referred to as Mönpas. In 1905, after a particularly violent attack by Abors, the Mönpas built a fort at Jido on the Siang, a point more than ten miles as the crow flies below the alignment which the McMahon Line was to follow in 1914. The Mönpas, in 1913, were claiming the right to raise revenue as far down the Siang as Simong (forty miles as the crow flies below the McMahon Line). The available information, which is not entirely satisfactory, suggests that there was a slow but steady process of southward Mönpa advance down the Siang during the nineteenth and early twentieth centuries (Map no. 8). The Tibetans regarded these Mönpas as their subjects, and many of them, particularly those on the upper Siyom, had apparently become dependants of the *lHa-klu* (*Lhalu*), one of the great feudal families of Tibet (Map no. 7).[68]

All along the frontier between Tibetan and tribal (*Lopa*) territory from Tawang eastwards the Tibetans were in some kind of contact with the nearest tribal groups.[69] In some places certain *Lopas* had acquired trading rights in Tibetan territory. In others the Tibetans were accustomed to pay subsidies in cash or kind to the *Lopas* in an attempt to dissuade them from raiding into Tibet. This kind of 'protection money' was particularly heavy along the eastern border of the Tawang Tract. On the upper Subansiri, where that river becomes the Tsari

[68] Bailey, *Report*, op. cit., pp. 2–3; Carrasco, op. cit., pp. 101, 104.

For an account of the mixed population in the region where the Dihang-Siang becomes the Tsangpo, see F. Kingdon Ward, *The Riddle of the Tsangpo Gorges*, London, 1926, p. 110; F. Kingdon Ward, 'Through the Gorges of the Tsangpo', *Journal of the Central Asian Society*, XIII, 1926, p. 142.

[69] Bailey, *Report*, op. cit., pp. 17–21.

Chu of Tibet, the Tibetans had a special interest in *Lopa* territory to their south (Map no. 7). Here, in what the Tibetans know as Tsari, the 1914 McMahon Line defined the boundary as just south of the Tibetan village of Migyitun. As a division

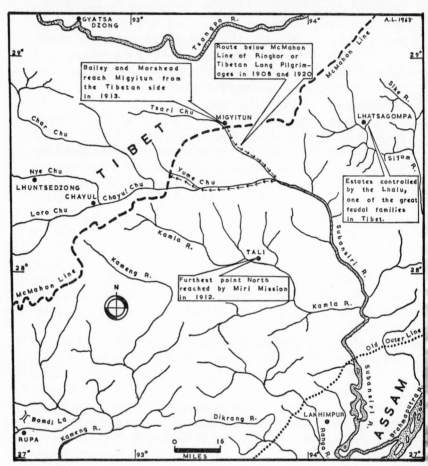

7   *The Subansiri Valley*

between Tibetan and *Lopa* country this was reasonable, but, as we shall see in a later chapter, it ignored, deliberately, the fact that the entire region was regarded by the Tibetans as being sacred, and that every twelve years a pilgrimage, the *Ringkor* or 'Long Pilgrimage', was made by hundreds of thousands of

Tibetans down the Subansiri-Tsari to its junction with the Chayul Chu, a point some twenty miles or so south of the McMahon Line. The pilgrims returned to Tibet along the Chayul Chu. This periodic excursion into *Lopa* territory was only possible if the tribes were first heavily bribed to leave the devout travellers unmolested.[70]

In 1910 the Indian Government, it has been noted already, knew very little indeed about the nature of the Tibetan relations with the non-Buddhist tribes of the Assam Himalayas; but it had little doubt that relationships must have existed which would provide the basis for a Tibetan claim to sovereignty over some at least of the territory on the Assamese side of the range. With the Chinese in Pome and Zayul, so close to the tribal hills, this was an alarming thought. The Chinese, as the Indian Government well knew from its experiences with Bhutan and Nepal, were adept at extracting the utmost political advantage from traditional relationships. When it was discovered during the course of 1910 that the Chinese were indeed endeavouring to establish their influence over some of the hill tribes, the security of the entire Himalayan frontier of Assam, where hitherto the British had on the whole adhered to their policy of non-interference, seemed to be threatened. The fact that the British did not know quite how extensive the relationships were which the Chinese might exploit only served to make the situation appear more critical than it actually was.

[70] Apart from the *Ringkor* or 'Long Pilgrimage' there was also the Kingkor or 'Short Pilgrimage', an annual event which was confined to Tsari north of what was to be the McMahon Line. For an account of the *Ringkor* and *Kingkor*, see Bailey, *Report*, op. cit., pp. 10–12; F. Ludlow, 'The Sources of the Subansiri and Siyom', *Himalayan Journal*, X, 1938, pp. 9–10; Anon, 'Sources of the Subansiri and Siyom', *Himalayan Journal*, IX, 1937, pp. 145–6.

XVIII

THE ASSAM BORDER CRISIS: 1910 TO 1912[1]

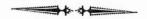

I. NOEL WILLIAMSON AND THE POLICY OF NON-INTERFERENCE, 1905 TO 1910

THE policy of non-interference in the Assam Himalayas meant that British officials only crossed the Inner Line at infrequent intervals. The Outer Line they tended to avoid unless it was necessary to send an expedition over it to punish the tribesmen for some outrage against British subjects or some violation of the British frontier. For much of the early history of the Inner Line Regulation the British officer most directly concerned with the frontier non-Buddhist tribes was J. F. Needham, Assistant Political Officer, Sadiya, and a man of considerable energy and enterprise, as his venture up the Lohit in the winter of 1885–6 has shown; but, except in the Lohit Valley, Needham's penetration into tribal territory was very superficial. In 1884, two years after his appointment to Sadiya, he visited the village of Membo (or Mebu), one of the Abor settlements closest to Sadiya and, it would seem, just on the British side of the Outer Line (which was here defined but not demarcated). Needham reported that the last British visit to Membo had been in 1854, thirty years earlier.[2] Needham never revisited Membo (Map no. 8). In 1905, when he retired, the presence of a British official in the strip between the Inner and Outer Lines was still a very rare event indeed.

[1] Some of the information in Chapter XVIII has already appeared in Lamb, *China-India Border*, op. cit., pp. 130–42.

[2] J. F. Needham, *Report on the Abor villages beyond the British Frontier*, 1884 (in Royal Geographical Society Library, cat. no. Z.48.3).

With the opening of the twentieth century the wisdom of the prevailing policy towards the Inner Line began to be challenged by those Assam officials, Needham included, who were directly concerned with its administration. The actual Line was no longer well marked: since its demarcation in the 1870s many of the pillars indicating its alignment had been removed, or had been eaten by insects, or had become buried beneath jungle growths. It was not always easy, therefore, to specify the exact point beyond which British subjects could not go without passes, especially as the original recording of the Line was not everywhere of the highest quality. There were forces at work, moreover, that indicated either that the Inner Line, wherever precisely it might run, should be modified or that the regulations concerning its crossing should be revised. In the late 1890s, for example, tribesmen from several Abor groups had started migrating south of the Inner Line with the intention of settling more or less permanently in British territory, a process which could hardly fail to affect the nature of British relations with the tribes concerned. At about the same time several timber companies in Assam began to take an active interest in the *Simul* trees (cotton trees or *Bombax malabaricum*) which grew in the forests between the two Lines. Two such companies, the Sissi Saw Mills and Trading Co. Ltd. and the Meckla Nuddee Saw Mills, petitioned Government in November 1906 for a revision of the Inner Line Regulations.[3]

For several years these two companies, and others like them, had been faced with a dwindling supply of suitable timber on the British side of the Inner Line. They had endeavoured to obtain passes from the appropriate authorities, in this case the office of the District Commissioner, Lakhimpur, to enable them to work to the north of the Line; but they had met with difficulties, since the District Commissioner was not sure that he had the power to authorise large-scale commercial operations outside fully administered British territory. The timber companies, therefore, had resorted to unofficial methods, employing Assamese contractors who in turn engaged tribesmen, mainly

[3] PEF 1910/13, Memorial from the Sissi Saw Mills and Trading Co. Ltd. and the Meckla Nuddee Saw Mills to the Honourable L. Hare, C.S.I., C.I.E., November 1906.

Miris, to cut down trees in the forbidden zone. The contractors, without bothering about passes, then sent elephants across the line to extract the felled timber. These operations presented the hill tribes with an excellent opportunity to demand what amounted to 'protection money', an opportunity which they exploited to the full. Since the timber companies, albeit indirectly, were working forests which lay within the Outer Line, the international boundary of British India, they naturally resented paying blackmail to the tribesmen who were, technically speaking, foreigners. Moreover, as the scale of the exploitation of the inter-Line jungle increased, so did the size of the blackmail: the managers of the two petitioning companies claimed that costs were now reaching a point where the end-product of their timber, Indian tea chests, could not compete with those manufactured in Norway and Japan. The petitioners requested that, firstly, the Inner Line be advanced so that it merged with the Outer Line along the foot of the hills; and, secondly, that Government provide protection against tribal exactions on loggers working in the inter-Line tracts.

The timber companies seem to have first raised the question of the Inner Line in 1902, when the Assam Government heard them out with little sympathy. When they petitioned in 1906, however, the administration of Assam had just undergone a major revolution following Curzon's partition of Bengal. It had been combined with East Bengal to form a Lieutenant-Governor's Province—Assam had previously been under a Chief Commissioner—and its newly appointed head, Lancelot Hare, was disposed to consider a change in the Inner Line Regulation which the last Chief Commissioner, Sir Bampfylde Fuller, had rejected in 1904. By this date, moreover, Needham had given up the task of conducting British relations with the tribes of the eastern half of the Assam Himalaya. His place was taken by Noel Williamson, a young men whose ambition it was to explore as deep into tribal hill country as he could and who was by conviction as well as by inclination opposed to the restrictions of the policy of non-interference.

Sir Lancelot Hare, writing to Lord Minto in September 1907, agreed with the timber companies that the tribes should not be allowed to extort what were politely called 'royalties' from the loggers in the inter-Line tracts, which were, after all, as British as anywhere else within the Indian Empire.[4] The tribes should be told to stop this annoying practice, and, if necessary, be obliged by force to give it up. Williamson should be permitted to tour extensively between the Lines, explaining to the villages there, and to tribesmen from villages to the north, the new policy of Government. Hare anticipated no trouble, but felt it would be as well for Williamson to have with him an impressive escort, perhaps 150 police. He did not see that any particular advantage would derive from pushing back the Inner Line. The main need, he felt, was to establish British relations with the tribes on a new basis. The old system of *posa*, in theory a cash commutation for the revenue which the tribes used to levy on the plains villages, but in practice by now nothing more than a subsidy, should be ended. Instead, the Assistant Political Officer, Sadiya (Williamson), should be given an equivalent sum which he could use to buy presents for friendly and well-behaved tribal *gams*, those who helped Williamson during the course of, so Hare hoped, frequent tours along the inter-Line tract. Thus tribal co-operation would be visibly rewarded. Such a flexible and positive policy, directed towards the winning of the friendship of tribesmen both between the Lines and along the northern border of the Outer Line, was particularly desirable now that hillmen were settling in significant numbers below the Inner Line. Hare saw no great danger in this southward migration, provided that it was properly supervised and provided that the new settlers in British territory were not stirred up by their fellow tribesmen beyond the border. The Abor, for example, was 'not the intractable savage he was once thought to be. He is,' Hare said, 'less bloodthirsty than the Naga, has more aptitude for concerted action, and is probably no less amenable to civilising influences.' Abors, and tribesmen like them, were welcome. The Christian missionaries, Hare imagined, once enough tribesmen had come down, would open schools for them as they had for the Khasis and other such groups south of the Brahmaputra.

This was a policy with far-reaching implications. If the fringes of the tribal areas became 'civilised' to any degree, and if British officers toured actively right up to the Outer Line, then very shortly the Outer Line, rather than the Inner Line,

[4] PEF 1910/13, East Bengal and Assam to India, 9 September 1907.

would become the real limit of British administration. The troubles of the timber companies would then be to all intents and purposes solved without the necessity of a formal advance of the Inner Line. However, it must also have been clear to officers like Williamson, and probably to Hare as well, that the extension of active British administration up to the Outer Line would inevitably involve a measure of direct British contact with the tribal territory beyond: and the outcome, even if disguised, would be the northward placing of the 'foot of annexation'. The implications of Hare's proposals did not, of course, escape the notice of Lord Minto's advisers. The Indian Government, while in general sympathetic to the timber companies and appreciating that something should be done to bring the tribesmen in the inter-Line zone under a greater measure of British control, was very anxious that in the process the British should not embark on anything which might result in an actual advance of their territorial frontiers. They were particularly worried about the consequences of too-frequent tours by British officers into unadministered tracts. Sooner or later, they must have foreseen, there would be an 'incident' with incalculable consequences. Such tours, indeed, Williamson was already making. In 1905 he had travelled along the edge of the Abor country where the Dihang, Sisseri and Dibang rivers emerged from the hills. In the winter of 1907–8, shortly after the East Bengal and Assam Government had made its suggestions on future policy towards the Inner Line, he travelled up the Lohit to Sati, a village a few miles downstream from Walong (Map no. 9). Williamson thought that Walong was the first inhabited point in Tibet. He could easily, he reported, have followed Needham's footsteps all the way to Rima; but he refrained from crossing the Tibetan border in accordance with Government standing orders.[5]

In June 1908 Lord Minto approved a new policy for the Assam frontier.[6] It was, for reasons which have already been suggested, milder than Hare might have wished: but, for all that, it implied a radical change in the British attitude to these

[5] N. Williamson, 'The Lohit-Brahmaputra between Assam and South-Eastern Tibet, November 1907 to January 1908', *Geographical Journal*, Vol. 34, no. 4, 1909.
[6] PEF 1910/13, Minto to Morley, 11 June 1908.

hill districts. The tribes were to be prohibited, forcibly if need be, from extorting blackmail in the inter-Line zone. Tribesmen who had settled between the Lines should be obliged to pay Government a poll tax: if they refused, they should be expelled. Tribesmen who lived north of the Outer Line, yet cultivated land to the south of it, should pay taxes to the British for that land. The old system of *posa* payments, where possible, should be replaced by a flexible scheme of distributing gifts at the discretion of Williamson. Tribesmen should be encouraged to settle south of the Inner Line and to visit fairs at such places as Sadiya: it was the wish of the Indian Government that the hill people should become aware of the benefits of modern civilisation. Tribes occupying territory between the Lines should be required to receive British officials who might choose to visit them on duty. Measures should be taken to prevent excessive exploitation of the reserves of *Simul* timber beyond the Inner Line. Finally, Williamson was to make a tour through the villages just to the north of the Outer Line to explain the new policy: but, it was emphasised, such tours would not be repeated in the future except in very special circumstances. There was to be no regular British patrolling beyond the international boundary. If Williamson's tour in the Abor country, which the Indian Government had most in mind, was a success, then it might perhaps be followed up by a similar venture into the Mishmi districts of the Lohit Valley.

Morley was not entirely pleased with these proposals.[7] 'The policy of non-interference', he told Minto in September 1908, 'is in my opinion essentially sound.' He wondered what would happen if the tribes, even those living between the Inner and Outer Lines, refused to obey Williamson's orders or declined to pay the taxes which the new policy would impose. Would this mean a series of punitive expeditions, leading to occupation? And where would that occupation stop if it once started? On the other hand, Morley agreed that the complaints of the timber companies concerning tribal blackmail of loggers in the inter-Line zone had much substance, and that something should be done to end this evil. Perhaps a tour by Williamson through the districts in question would do no harm. He could negotiate with the tribes some compensation for the loss of their blackmail,

[7] PEF 1910/13, Morley to Minto, 4 September 1908.

which, Morley noted, they 'undoubtedly consider a legitimate source of revenue'. As to the proposal that Williamson should then go on to visit tribal villages along the northern edge of the Outer Line, Morley was clearly unhappy: he did not approve it, but neither did he forbid it in so many words.

With Morley's opinion to hand, the Indian Government decided to authorise Williamson to tour between the Lines in the 1908–9 cold season, but to defer the crossing of the Outer Line until the end of 1909.[8] Williamson's main objectives were to contact the tribes in the inter-Line zone, find out all he could about them, explain to them the new ideas of Government about such matters as blackmail, and endeavour to establish some fresh system whereby they could derive some benefit from the exploitation of the natural resources beyond the Inner Line. The problem was to give the tribes something without at the same time seeming to acknowledge their rights to royalties or blackmail; and its solution was left very much to Williamson's discretion.

Williamson, and probably some of his superiors in the Eastern Bengal and Assam Government as well, had by this time—the end of 1908—decided that a more active British policy along the Assam Himalayan frontier was a matter of some urgency, and that more was at stake than the profits of the timber companies. The nature of Chinese ambitions in Tibet was becoming clearer. Williamson, there can be no doubt, was convinced that it was not only in Bhutan that the Chinese hoped to assert their influence south of the main Himalayan range. His journey up the Lohit had shown him that this route was extremely vulnerable to Chinese penetration; and, no doubt, the same could be said for the upper Siang Valley, a part of the world about which the British at that time knew virtually nothing. It would be foolish, in the face of the gathering Chinese storm, to pay too great a respect to the sanctity of the Outer Line. He decided to ignore his instructions which specified that he should not tour beyond the international boundary until the end of 1909, if then; and he resolved to make his way as far up the Dihang-Siang Valley as he could at the first opportunity. In late 1908 he met by chance one of the *gams*, or headmen, of the Abor village of Kebang who had come down to the plains.

[8] PEF 1910/13, East Bengal and Assam to Williamson, 31 October 1908.

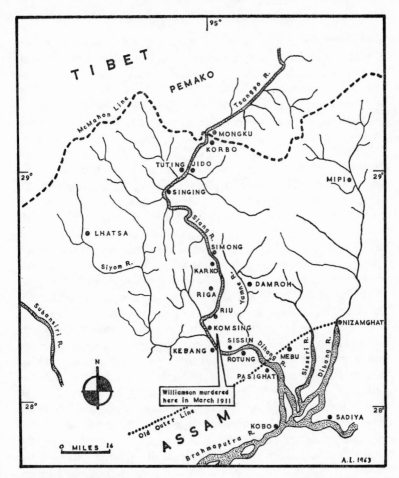

8　*The Dihang-Siang Valley*

The *gam*, so Williamson later reported, invited him to visit his village, on the west bank of the Dihang more than twenty miles upstream of the Outer Line; and Williamson accepted, not as a Government officer but as a private person. Accompanied by Colonel D. M. Lumsden and Rev. W. L. B. Jackman (an American missionary with an excellent command of the Abor language), he set out up the Dihang in January 1909 (Map no. 8). At Kebang, the home of the friendly *gam*, the party was politely turned back. The Abors were by no means hostile, and one of the *gams* of Riu, a village on the east bank of the Dihang

331

about twenty miles north of Kebang, even suggested that Williamson would be welcome there in the following year. This year, it was said, the idea of foreign visitors was still too novel, and the tribesmen should be given time to get used to it. On his way back from Kebang Williamson became seriously ill, so that his authorised tour between the two Lines had to be postponed for a while.[9]

The fiction of the private visit to Kebang was accepted by Government, which, presented with a *fait accompli*, could hardly do otherwise. Moreover, Williamson's report on the friendly treatment he received from the Abors weakened the argument that tours by British officers beyond the Outer Line would only lead to 'incidents'. Accordingly, both the Indian Government and the India Office, the latter with some reluctance, found themselves obliged to agree that when Williamson at last did make his tour between the Lines, for which instructions had been issued in October 1908, he should combine it with visits to a number of Abor settlements to the north of the Outer Line. No date, however, was set.[10] In the cold season of 1909–10, instead of visiting Abor country, Williamson made a second journey up the Lohit to beyond the Tibetan border, during the course of which he was able to meet an important Tibetan official from Rima:[11] and in January and February 1911 he once more travelled up the Lohit.[12] It was not, in fact, until March 1911 that Williamson embarked on the long-delayed Abor tour, which was to end in tragedy and to provide the immediate occasion for the termination, albeit tacitly, of the policy of non-interference. By this date, of course, the Chinese threat to the Assam border, which Williamson had foreseen as early as 1908, had assumed a gravity which even the most dedicated followers of Morley could not overlook.

[9] PEF 1910/13, East Bengal and Assam to India, 29 June 1909; Colonel D. M. Lumsden's Diary of his recent attempt to reach the Sangpoo Falls.

This was the first visit to Kebang by Europeans; but not the first by employees of the Indian Government. In 1901 two Gurkha surveyors in the service of the Great Trigonometrical Survey of India made their way up the Dihang to Kebang, which point then marked the northern limit of any survey at all in this region. See G. Dunbar, *Frontiers*, London, 1932, p. 81.

[10] PEF 1910/13, Morley to Minto, 1 September 1909.

[11] PEF 1910/13, East Bengal and Assam to India, 26 May 1910.

[12] PEF 1910/13, Williamson's Diary, January to February 1911.

2. CHINESE INFILTRATION INTO THE ASSAM
HIMALAYAS, 1910

In May 1910 a chief of the Miju Mishmis of Pangam on the Lohit, Tungno by name, came down to Sadiya with an alarming story. Two Tibetans, he reported to Williamson, had recently visited his village with the news that 1,000 Chinese troops had just arrived at Rima and demanded taxes from the Tibetan Governor, who, on refusing to pay, was promptly imprisoned. The Chinese, moreover, who had now taken over the administration of Zayul, had sent Tibetan messengers into the Mishmi country to instruct the chiefs, that of Pangam included, 'to cut a track from Tibet to Assam broad enough for two horsemen to ride abreast'. Tungno, the Pangam chief, refused to obey this order on the grounds, or so at least he told the British, that he was a British subject under the jurisdiction of the Assistant Political Officer, Sadiya.[13] Two months later, in July, another Miju Mishmi, called Halam, told Williamson that a party of Chinese from Rima had recently come down the Lohit to just below Walong and planted boundary markers at the Yepak River, a stream which flowed into the Lohit from the west (Map no. 9).[14] In October, Mishmis visiting Sadiya said that the Chinese had now forbidden all trade between the Mishmis and Tibet in an attempt, it would seem, to establish a *cordon sanitaire* between the tribes and Tibetan Zayul, a region which, as we have already noted, Chao Erh-feng had selected for Chinese colonisation.[15]

Some of this news was rather encouraging from the British point of view, suggesting that the Chinese intended on the Lohit to establish a boundary a good distance away from Sadiya. Walong, near which place the Chinese boundary flags were erected, had, after all, been accepted by British officers like Needham and Williamson as the effective Tibetan border; and it was pleasant to find the Chinese of like mind. On the other hand, the Chinese orders to Tungno of Pangam, whose village was many miles downstream from Walong, were

[13] PEF 1910/13, East Bengal and Assam to India, 26 May 1910.
[14] PEF 1910/13, East Bengal and Assam to India, 4 July 1910.
[15] India Office, Political and Secret Department Confidential Memoranda, B.189, Chinese Activity on the Mishmi Border.

definitely not reassuring. It looked as if the Chinese, while intending to establish their actual limit of administration at Walong, their equivalent, in other words, of the Inner Line, yet proposed to build up a sphere of influence below that place which might well extend all the way to the British Inner Line. On the Lohit, unlike tracts farther to the west, there was no recognised British Outer Line: here the Inner Line did, in effect, double duty, being the *de facto* limit of British sovereignty as well as of British administration. The Pangam chief, Tungno, could claim that he was a British subject, but, so the East Bengal and Assam Government declared, they 'cannot admit that he is in any way entitled to put forward such a claim. The Mishmis receive no *posa*, they pay no taxes to Government, no attempt has ever been made to interfere in their internal and domestic affairs, and so long as they abstained from molesting British subjects they were left completely undisturbed.' But, the East Bengal and Assam Government continued, 'the Mishmis, however, were not subjects of Tibet, and they must certainly have had more respect for the British Government than for any other foreign power with which they were brought in contact'.[16]

The East Bengal and Assam Government saw three possible answers to the Mishmi problem. First: the Mishmis could be left as they were, 'savage and independent tribes between British territory and Tibet'. Ideally, this was the best policy, following the well-established principle of doing nothing when in doubt. However, it was extremely unlikely that the Chinese in Rima would leave the Mishmis alone, even if the British did. Second: the Mishmis could be taken under British protection, a course which would present a number of difficult administrative problems. The Tibetan border was nearly 150 miles upstream on the Lohit from Sadiya. As the East Bengal and Assam Government pointed out:

It is clear that if we extend our territory up to the Tibetan frontier we must advance our posts many miles beyond our present situation and locate them in a sparsely inhabited and mountainous country. Further, though we know something of the route to Rima, it is difficult to see how we could define our boundary to the north or south of Rima, or protect our marches when defined. On the other hand, Rima must be far

16 PEF 1910/13, East Bengal and Assam to India, 26 May 1910.

from the Chinese base, and it is doubtful whether the Chinese would venture to disregard a definite pronouncement that we would not tolerate any advance beyond the western boundary of Tibet.[17]

Third: the British might decide that 'the Chinese should be allowed to absorb the Mishmis if they wish to do so'. But, so the Eastern Bengal and Assam Government noted in a remarkable understatement, 'to allow the Chinese to extend their influence right down to the foot of the hills bordering on the valley of the Brahmaputra might be productive of serious administrative inconvenience'. The only sensible course, on this analysis, was to declare that all the Mishmis were British subjects and to announce that British territory extended up the Lohit to Walong.[18]

The Chinese penetration into Mishmi country, even if on a very small scale, had serious implications for the whole Assam border, not merely the Lohit Valley. As Charles Bell pointed out, Assam was to all intents and purposes undefended.[19] As Bell quoted from the *Military Report on Assam* of the Indian General Staff,

> that Assam would ever stand the slightest chance of being invaded by a civilized military Power has never been contemplated, and consequently no strategic plan, no defences, no organization whatsoever exists to repel a serious invasion. . . . Assam's one and only protection against a serious invasion is the chain of hills surrounding her frontier.

Now, it seemed, the Chinese were well placed to penetrate unopposed this mountain barrier. Unless something was done, Chinese troops might suddenly turn up within a few miles of Sadiya; and the Lohit was not the only danger area. All along the Assam Himalayas there were routes which an enterprising commander could negotiate. Mountains, as Hannibal and Napoleon had demonstrated, were rarely the perfect defence they might seem to arm-chair strategists. Bell, accordingly, proposed that the British at this moment, before it was too late, should extend their influence deep into all the hill areas between them and the Chinese, perhaps by concluding treaties with as many tribal groups as possible; the model for these treaties, of

[17] Ibid.   [18] Ibid.   [19] PEF 1910/13, Bell to India, 20 August 1910.

course, Bell suggested, should be that which he had just made with Bhutan. Once the tribes were placed under British protection the Indian Government would at least have a legal right to protest against Chinese infiltration into tribal territory, a right which the British did not at present possess. Even with treaties, however, the safety of the tribal tracts depended on British vigilance. Bell recommended that the tribal hills be divided into at least two frontier districts, each watched over by a British officer specially appointed for that purpose and directly subordinate to the Central Government.

As Bell certainly appreciated, any policy towards the threatened North-East Frontier which was both effective and likely to win the approval of the Home Government would probably have to satisfy two criteria which to some extent conflicted with each other. An adequate defence of the tribal hills against Chinese infiltration inevitably involved the establishment there of some measure of British influence. Yet it was clear that the Cabinet would not be happy to see the Indian Government take steps which might be interpreted in England, not to mention Russia and elsewhere, as indicating an extension of British territorial limits in the direction of Tibet. But, as we have just seen, during the course of 1910 the East Bengal and Assam Government concluded that it would be indeed rash to leave any longer the international status of the Assam Himalayas in its present nebulous state. Sir Lancelot Hare was in no doubt that India should assume sovereignty over the Lohit valley, even if this involved an addition to the burden of British administration. Lord Minto, during the last weeks of his term of office, was likewise prepared to consider a northward advance of the British border. In October 1910 he advised the India Office that the best solution to the Assam problem was to 'gain a buffer' by 'extending the outer line' towards Tibet. The new Outer Line, he thought, should run

> from the east of the wedge shaped portion of Tibetan territory of the Towang district, which runs down to the British frontier north of Odalguri, in a north-easterly direction to lat. 29°, long. 94°, thence in a south-easterly direction to the Zayul Chu as far east and as near Rima as possible, thence across the Zayul Cu to the Zayul-Irrawaddy divide, and then along that divide until it joins the Irrawaddy-Salween divide. Tribes in

this area are believed to be mostly independent, and some of them are already under our influence.[20]

This was the first of a series of proposed boundary alignments which were to lead, in 1914, to the McMahon Line. It is interesting that at this stage the Indian Government were still excluding the entire Tawang Tract from British territory.

The India Office, where the Marquess of Crewe was taking over from Lord Morley, was definitely uneasy at the implications of this plan. It could not see how, in fact, the Outer Line could be advanced without also advancing the area of British administration with all that suggested in terms of manpower and money. As Minto would shortly be leaving India, it seemed wisest, however, to make no definite answer until Minto's successor, Hardinge, had been given an opportunity to investigate and form his own conclusions.[21] Lord Hardinge of Penshurst, lately Sir Charles Hardinge of the Foreign Office, had been one of the chief architects of the policy which produced the Anglo-Russian Convention of 1907. No doubt the India Office thought that he would be less enthusiastic about territorial advances into Central Asia than Lord Minto, who, Morley had sometimes suspected over the past five years, had a secret leaning towards solutions of a definitely Curzonian flavour in matters relating to the Indian frontiers.

Hardinge, who arrived in India in November 1910, lost no time in acquainting himself with the Assam border problem. On 22 November he had a long discussion at Calcutta with Sir Lancelot Hare, of whom he seems to have formed a most unfavourable impression.[22] He was not convinced by Hare's anxiety about the intentions of the Chinese and told him that

any forward move of the administrative frontier was strongly to be deprecated. Chinese aggression would, in Lord Hardinge's view, be met, not in the tribal territory bordering Assam, but

[20] PEF 1910/13, Minto to Morley, 23 October 1910.
[21] PEF 1910/13, Morley to Minto, 25 October 1910.
[22] Morley Papers (D.573/26), Hardinge to Morley, 4 May 1911. Hardinge wrote that 'Hare has turned out to be a complete failure in Eastern Bengal, which I believe to be the worst-administered province in the whole of India'.
For the meeting between Hare and Hardinge, see Reid, *Assam Frontier*, op. cit., p. 221.

by attack on the coast of China. He was, therefore, opposed to running risks or spending money on endeavours to create a strategic frontier in advance of the administrative border, and he was unable to agree to any promise of support being held out to the Mishmis or other tribes beyond our frontier who might appeal for help against Chinese aggression. Frontier officers should, Lord Hardinge thought, confine themselves to cultivating friendly relations with the border tribes and punishing them for acts of hostility within our limits.[23]

In other words, Hardinge was prepared to approve such ventures as the Dafla Expedition of November 1910, in which Dafla attacks on British subjects engaged in trapping wild elephants between the Lines had been punished by a small punitive force of 100 military police under Williamson and Sir G. Duff-Sutherland-Dunbar;[24] but he saw no need at present for any changes in the alignment of the British border. He summed up his policy in these words:

> We recognise that the action of the Chinese may ultimately compel us to fix a line beyond which no further advance can be permitted; but we see no necessity at present for incurring the risks and responsibilities entailed by a forward movement into the tribal territory now beyond our control.[25]

Frontier officers, for the time being, should confine themselves to 'cultivating friendly relations' with the tribesmen beyond the Outer Line and to carrying on the established policy of punishing outrages committed on British territory or against British subjects. However,

> should it be possible to obtain further information about the country beyond the 'outer line' without risk of complications, we should be prepared to authorise explorations for the purpose, but we would not permit any general increase in activity in this direction, nor can we recommend that any sort of promise should be given to the tribes that may rely on our support or protection in the event of Tibetan or Chinese aggression.[26]

[23] PEF 1910/13, Hardinge to Crewe, 22 December 1910.
[24] For an account of the Dafla Expedition of November 1910, see PEF 1910/16, File no. 1918/6.
[25] PEF 1910/13, Hardinge to Crewe, 22 December 1910.
[26] Ibid.

Hardinge's remark about meeting a Chinese invasion of Assam with an 'attack on the coast of China' may at first sight seem rather strange. What Hardinge meant, of course, speaking as an old Foreign Office man, was that the Indian Government should not look on the Assam border problem in purely Indian terms. A Chinese attack on the territory of British India was a Chinese attack on Great Britain, to be countered where it seemed fittest in the light of global British strategy. An Anglo-Chinese war would, in all probability, not be decided by any battle on the Sino-Indian border, but by British pressure on the Chinese heartland. All this was sensible enough, but it did not answer the question raised by the East Bengal and Assam Government, which was what exactly should it now do on the Assam border. Hardinge, at this stage, did not quite see what the Assam border problem was. He failed, just as we have seen from the Morley-Minto correspondence how Morley sometimes failed, to appreciate the subtleties of prestige to which the Indian Government traditionally attached such importance. The idea that a border tribe like the Mishmis could be allowed to come under Chinese influence, which Hardinge appeared to accept with equanimity, was to an old Indian official like Sir Hugh Barnes, now a member of the Council of India, 'inconceivable'.[27] Sir Arthur Hirtzl, Secretary to the Political and Secret Department at the India Office, was very surprised by Hardinge's attitude. In a private letter to Sir Richmond Ritchie, the Permanent Undersecretary of State for India, he summed up his views both on the Assam danger and on Hardinge's attitude to it, which, since they touch on the root of the matter, are worth quoting at length. Wrote Hirtzl:

> The levity with which Hardinge talks about attacking the coast of China amazes me. But quite apart from that, it is a bad matter, for no attempt is made to argue the case or explain the grounds for their conclusions; and though of course the *onus probandi* lies on the other side, still the Secretary of State is surely entitled to know why the other side is overruled.
>
> If anything goes wrong in Assam, there will be very voiceful public opinion against us. There are no European industries along the North West frontier, and one fat Hindu banya more

[27] PEF 1910/13, no. 4300/1910, Minute by Sir H. Barnes, 15 December 1910.

or less doesn't matter—yet! But in Lakhimpur District there are over 70,000 acres of tea gardens turning out 30,000,000 pounds of tea annually, and employing over 200 Europeans and 100,000 Indians. The European capital risk in tea must be enormous, and there are other industries as well (e.g. coal, over ¼ million tons a year). These gardens lie at the foot of the hills inhabited by savages; their defence rests with 1 battalion of native infantry and one battalion of military police (850 men). Think of the howl the planters would let out, and the rise in the price of tea! The Government of India, of course, know all this, but in a document of this kind . . . [Hardinge's despatch of 22 December 1910 to the Marquess of Crewe] . . . they ought to show that they know it; and if they don't, I think the Secretary of State should call them down from the high atmosphere of 'attacks on the coast of China' to the more prosaic level of border protection and administration.[28]

The Chinese threat to Assam, in fact, however remote it might seem to be, could not be ignored, because of the enormous economic importance of the Assam tea industry. British capital was involved, and British capital had its voices in Parliament. The India Office, however dedicated its head might be to Morley's ideal of non-interference—and the evidence suggests that Lord Crewe did not differ much in this respect from his predecessor—could not afford to have the Assam border treated to a display of the techniques of masterly inactivity. It is certain that Hardinge would have sooner or later, if he did not so decide of his own accord, have been instructed to be more active at the 'prosaic level of border protection and administration' in Assam, had not the course of events made this unavoidable in any case.

3. WILLIAMSON'S DEATH

Hardinge's rejection of the East Bengal and Assam Government's proposals gave rise to depression but not to despair. Williamson, who, in the words of one of his friends, 'was absolutely fearless, and entirely bent on his own way of doing things',[29] decided, presumably with the tacit approval of Sir Lancelot Hare, to take matters into his own hands. In early January 1911, without seeking any formal permission, he set out

[28] PEF 1910/13, Hirtzl to Ritchie, 12 January 1911.
[29] G. Dunbar, *Frontiers*, London, 1932, p. 92.

up the Lohit 'to find out as accurately as possible what the Chinese are doing round Rima'.[30] On 4 February he reached a place called Menilkrai, just south of the Yepak River and on the west bank of the Lohit, where Krick in 1851 had seen a large boulder which he stated was the recognised boundary between Tibet and the Mishmi country. Beside this same boulder Williamson found the boundary markers which the Chinese had erected in 1910 (Map no. 9). They consisted of two flags, one now reduced to tatters, the other with the Chinese dragon still visible. On the following day Williamson crossed the Yepak and visited the hamlet of Walong, where he found the inhabitants were at this time all Mishmis. The Walong people told him that the Menilkrai boulder had been twice visited by the Chinese in 1910, once by a party under the command of a junior officer, and once by three Chinese of obviously elevated rank. They said that there were only about forty Chinese soldiers at Rima; but at least 500 Chinese troops were stationed at Chikong, about three days' journey farther north. Later that day Williamson met a Tibetan trader coming down from Rima who told him that 'the Chinese are treating the Tibetans with some consideration and the occupation of this portion of Tibet does not weigh heavy on the inhabitants'. Williamson made no attempt to remove the Chinese boundary markers, even though he was convinced that the Chinese had no claim to the south bank of the Yepak: Walong was the farthest south that they could argue their territory ran in this quarter. Since erecting the boundary flags, so Williamson discovered from his Mishmi informants, the Chinese had made no attempt to interfere with the tribes on the Lohit south of their border, and the reported Chinese ban on Mishmi trade with Tibet was now lifted, if, indeed, it had ever been imposed. All, in fact, seemed fairly quiet on the Lohit front.

The Lohit, however, was not the only route by which the Chinese could possibly menace Assam. If the Tsangpo and the Brahmaputra were the same river, as was generally suspected, though still not proved, then the Dihang or Siang Valley, which connected the Tibetan to the Assamese sections, might well turn out to be a road through the Himalayan range as negotiable as that from Rima to Sadiya. The investigation of this route

[30] PEF 1910/13, Williamson's Diary, January and February 1911.

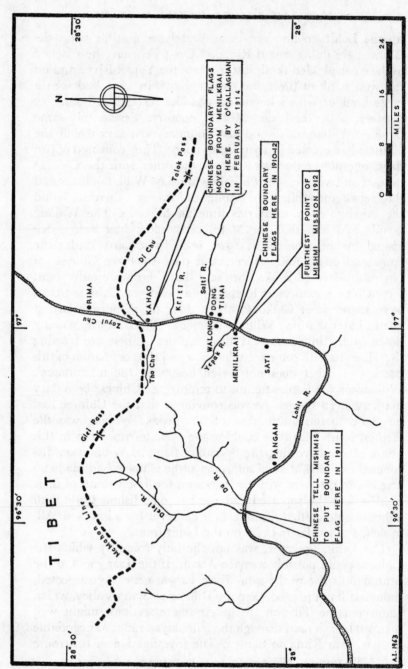

The following labels appear on the map:

- CHINESE BOUNDARY FLAGS MOVED FROM MENILKRAI TO HERE BY O'CALLAGHAN IN FEBRUARY 1914
- CHINESE BOUNDARY FLAGS HERE IN 1910-12
- FURTHEST POINT OF MISHMI MISSION 1912
- CHINESE TELL MISHMIS TO PUT BOUNDARY FLAG HERE IN 1911

Place names: RIMA, KAHAO, WALONG, DONG, TINAI, MENILKRAI, SATI, PANGAM

Rivers: Di Chu, Kriti R., Salti R., Zayul Chu, Tho Chu, Yepak R., Lohit R., Du R., Delei R.

Passes: Talok Pass, Glei Pass

TIBET

McMahon Line

A.I. 1963

9   The upper Lohit Valley

had certainly been one of Williamson's objectives during his visit to Abor country in January and February 1909; but on that occasion he had, as we have seen, failed to get anywhere near the Tibetan border. He now resolved to revisit the Dihang Valley with the intention of going much farther north than he had in 1909, 'in order to enquire into the extent of Tibetan influence on that side'.[31] This was an important question if the Dihang-Brahmaputra turned out, as Williamson was sure it would, to be the same river as the Tsangpo; for the Chinese were at that moment showing an active interest in Pome, a district on the Tsangpo at the very point where that stream should begin to cut its way through the Assam Himalayas. The Amban Lien Yü, so Bell learnt from the Dalai Lama in November 1910, had just demanded that the Pobas, the people of Pome, should submit to the Chinese, and clearly intended to back this request with force. Who were the Pobas? Bell thought 'it is quite possible that the phrase "Pobas" includes some of the tribes, Abors, Daflas, Akas etc., who live on the northern border of Assam'.[32] Thus it seemed probable that as soon as the Chinese began serious military campaigning in Pome they would also find themselves trying to bring some of those hill tribes of the upper Dihang or Siang Valley under their influence. Williamson thought that the Chinese, at all costs, should be forestalled. Something like Bell's scheme for creating a cordon of tribal treaties along the hills might have achieved this end; but it had been ruled out by Government. Williamson, therefore, realised that if anything was to be done he would have to do it himself on his own authority.

The exact details of Williamson's plan will now probably never be known. He enlisted as an ally one Dr. Gregorson, a tea-estate doctor with exploring interests. The two men proposed to travel, unofficially and at their own risk, as far up the Dihang-Siang as they could, perhaps as far as the much-discussed falls on the Tsangpo in Tibetan territory. Gregorson's interest was mainly geographical: the honour of being the discoverer of this fabulous waterfall, perhaps greater than Niagara or Victoria, was an irresistible temptation. Williamson, however, certainly

[31] PEF 1910/13, Hardinge to Crewe, 13 April 1911.
[32] FO 371/855, no. 45042, Dalai Lama to Bell, 6 November 1910; FO 371/1078, no. 283, Bell to India, 28 November 1910.

had a number of political objectives in mind. Apart from finding out the limits of Tibetan rule and determining whether the Chinese had made any progress in this quarter, he hoped, we may be sure, that his presence would be taken by the tribes as a symbol of the power of the British Empire: and it may well be that he intended to take the tribes under British protection, presenting his superiors, on his return, with a *fait accompli* which they would find it very difficult to repudiate. This, however, is speculation. Williamson and Gregorson never returned from their journey.

The two travellers left Sadiya on 14 March 1911, accompanied by a military police orderly, a coolie sirdar named Lal Bahadur, Dr. Gregorson's Tibetan servant, thirty-five Nepalese porters and four Miris. They made their way up the west bank of the Dihang to the Abor village of Rotung, just beyond which, on 22 March, they crossed over to the east bank against the advice of Williamson's old friend the *gam* of Kebang (Map no. 8). Across the Dihang, at the Abor settlement of Sissin, some of the porters fell sick. It was decided to send the three worst cases back to Pasighat on the British-administered frontier, while Dr. Gregorson remained at Sissin with the other invalids and Williamson continued on upstream to Komsing. The three sick Nepalese porters were accompanied by a Miri, to whom Williamson entrusted letters to be delivered to the British authorities at Pasighat. These letters were impressive objects, in white envelopes with black borders (in mourning for Edward VII) and sealed with red sealing wax. When, on 29 March, the Miri reached Rotung on the west bank of the Dihang, he could not resist showing the letters to the local Abors; and when asked what they meant, explained that the white stood for the two white men, the black for their escort and porters, and the red seals meant that Williamson was very angry with the Abors. The Rotung men convinced by this explanation, decided that the letters must not be delivered. As soon as the Miri and the three sick Nepalese had left Rotung they were ambushed and killed. When news of this reached Kebang the tribesmen there decided to set out to dispose of Williamson, Gregorson and the rest, so that no report of the affair would ever reach the plains. The arguments for restraint of Williamson's friendly *gam* were of no avail. A war party set out, crossed the Dihang and killed

Gregorson and all but one of his companions. They then went on to Komsing and slaughtered Williamson, who had put up a gallant defence until his ammunition was exhausted. Only five members of his party managed to evade the Abors and, eventually, to make their way back to British territory.[33]

The first reaction in London to news of Williamson's death was to ask what Williamson was doing across the Outer Line in the first place. Who had authorised him to make this journey? Did the East Bengal and Assam Government not realise that policy had laid it down that the Outer Line was not to be crossed by British officials without express permission from the Supreme Government?[34] The East Bengal and Assam authorities managed to put up a defence of sorts. A tour by Williamson in Abor country, including the crossing of the Outer Line, had, in fact, been authorised in 1909; and Williamson, it was now argued, was merely acting rather belatedly on that authority.[35] This was not very convincing, particularly as it transpired that the East Bengal and Assam Government had, in fact, refused Williamson permission to make an official tour, while allowing him to go as a private person and at his own risk.[36] But even if Williamson had not been on duty when he was killed, and even if the Home Government felt that what he had done to bring about his death deserved reprimand rather than sympathy, the fact remained that in a period when the Chinese were active all along the north of the Assam Himalayas it would hardly do to admit publicly that the Indian Government had not the power to punish outrages of this sort by tribes living so close to the British border. There were many people in Assam who thought that the Chinese had something to do with Williamson's murder, a view that was not seriously held in official circles.[37] However, there could be no escaping the fact that this incident

[33] See A. Hamilton, *In Abor Jungles*, London, 1912; also Bailey, *No Passport*, op. cit., pp. 28–30. The Abor Blue Book, which was published towards the end of 1911, contains the official accounts of the circumstances of Williamson's death. See Cd. 5961, *East India (North-East Frontier)*, *Operations Against the Abors*, 1911.

[34] PEF 1910/13, India to East Bengal and Assam, 8 May 1911.

[35] PEF 1910/13, East Bengal to India, 22 April 1911.

[36] PEF 1910/13, no. 900/1911, Minute by Hirtzl.

[37] PEF 1910/13, no. 866/1911, Major-General Bower to Lieutenant-General Sir B. Duff.

had received a great deal of publicity and had focused attention on the weakness of the British position along the Assam border. As Sir Richmond Ritchie put it to Lord Morley, 'the massacre of Mr. Williamson's party by the Abors revives the question of our policy towards the tribes on the Assam frontier in connection with the aggressive action of the Chinese in South East Tibet'.[38]

Williamson's murder made it impossible for Lord Hardinge, had he so wished, to deny that a more active policy was called for along at least the Abor section of the Assam Himalayan border. During the summer of 1911 fresh information about Chinese intentions came to light to suggest that the implementation of such a policy was indeed a matter of some urgency. In June, D. H. Felce, manager of the Imperial Tea Company's estate at Tarajuli, heard from one of his employees of the arrival of four mysterious persons in the Aka country north of Tezpur. These men, so the Aka chief of the village of Tagi Raja was reported to have said, were very pale in complexion, they had pigtails and wore loose trousers, and they were unarmed save for small knives. They carried packs on their backs. A. R. Giles, Superintendent of Police, Darrang, was convinced that they were Chinese, perhaps surveyors or explorers who had come down by way of the Tawang Tract.[39] At about this time the Chinese operations in Pome were reaching a climax. Colonel Willoughby, the British Military Attaché in Peking, reported that the Pome situation would inevitably lead the Chinese into Abor country, and he pointed out that there were now (July 1911) Chinese outposts only 130 miles away from Komsing, where Williamson had met his death.[40]

The Chinese were also reported to be active on the Mishmi border in the Lohit Valley during the summer of 1911. This had from the first seemed in India to be the most threatened section of the frontier, because it contained a known through route from Chinese-held Tibet to India along which the forces of Chao Erh-feng, rather than those, far weaker, of the Amban Lien Yü, could advance. It was, moreover, close to the Hkamtilong region of Upper Burma where, since early 1910, Chinese infiltra-

[38] PEF 1910/13, Ritchie to Morley, 8 April 1911.

[39] FO 371/1065, no. 33488, Felce to Giles, 20 June 1911; PEF 1910/13, Hardinge to Secretary of State, 7 July 1911.

[40] PEF 1910/13, Jordan to Grey, 22 July 1911.

tion deep into British territory had been reported. Thus the account of F. M. Bailey's passage down the Lohit in July 1911, the final stage of his adventurous overland journey from Peking to India, was closely studied by the Indian Government. On 15 July, at Tinai on the east bank of the Lohit opposite Walong, Bailey met two Mishmi chiefs on their way to the Chinese headquarters at Chikong. They told him that the year before the Chinese had summoned them to make their submission to the Chikong authorities, but that they had disobeyed this command. Recently fresh orders had reached them to the effect that if they did not come to Chikong at once Chinese troops would be sent to fetch them by force. Bailey advised them, before going to the Chinese, to see what the Assistant Political Officer, Sadiya (W. C. M. Dundas), thought about it. The Mishmis agreed, and for a while they kept Bailey company as he made his way downstream; but they eventually got bored and wandered off to some unknown destination in the jungle. Shortly after this Bailey came across two more Mishmi chiefs *en route* for Chikong, whom he also dissuaded from going on. On 20 July, at the Mishmi village of Minzong, Bailey came across two Tibetans, officials, they said, sent by the Chinese to round up the Mishmis and told that they would be decapitated if they did not perform their task satisfactorily. These Tibetans had just learnt that the garrison at Chikong, some 350 men, had been called away to Pome, where things were not going well for the Chinese, news which seemed to please them greatly: they were overdue and unwilling to face the wrath of their employers which they now hoped they might escape. Bailey believed that the departure of the Chinese from Chikong meant that their meeting with the Mishmi chiefs would be postponed for a while; but that the Chinese would not abandon their plans in this direction.[41] Indeed, in October, a few months after Bailey's return to India, the Mishmi chief of Pangam, Tungno, told Dundas at Sadiya that two Tibetans had been in his territory issuing fresh summonses. Tungno also reported that earlier in the year a party of Chinese officials had come down the Delei tributary of the Lohit; but of this venture the British

[41] PEF 1910/13, Bailey to India, 8 August 1911. See also Bailey, *China-Tibet-Assam*, op. cit., pp. 141–7.

discovered a great deal more later on, and its account here is accordingly postponed.[42]

These indications that the Chinese were unlikely, as long as they remained in Tibet, to leave the Assam hill tribes alone, combined with the need to do something about avenging Williamson's murder by the Abors, obliged Lord Hardinge to formulate a policy more to the point than that of launching an attack on the Chinese coast. By the end of June the outlines had been sketched in; and on 21 September Hardinge presented Lord Crewe with a detailed account of what he had in mind. This marked the end, for the time being, of Morley's ideal of non-interference, and the beginning of a chain of events which were to make possible the definition of the McMahon Line in 1914. The new policy was designed both to punish the Abors and to frustrate the Chinese, the latter being by far the most important objective. It was based mainly on proposals which Lord Minto had made just before his departure from India in late 1910, and which the East Bengal and Assam Government had been making ever since.

4. THE ABOR EXPEDITION

The first point was to punish the Abors. A punitive expedition against them had been recommended by the East Bengal and Assam Government in May 1911, approved by Hardinge in June and authorised by Lord Crewe in July. Even though Williamson's fatal journey had been 'made without the cognisance or sanction of the Local Government' and was 'contrary to the well known standing orders prohibiting the crossing of the "Outer Line" without permission', yet the hill tribes could not be permitted to go about slaughtering British officers with impunity. The proposed Abor expedition should set out in October 1911, capture Williamson's murderers and bring them to trial, and teach the tribes a lesson in this quarter which they would not forget for many years to come. The expedition, however, should do more than this. It should be used to 'secure as soon as possible a sound strategical boundary between China *cum* Tibet and the tribal territory from Bhutan up to and including the Mishmi country, and this should . . . now be the

[42] Political and Secret Department Confidential Memo. B.189.

main object of our policy'. Thus the Abor expedition should give birth, as it were, to daughter expeditions into the Mishmi country along the Dibang and Lohit rivers and the Miri country along the Subansiri, districts in no way involved in the Williamson affair. These ventures, the Mishmi Mission and the Miri Mission as they came to be called, were, as was the Abor expedition itself, to find out the exact limits of Tibetan territory as the first step in defining a new international boundary 'as far as possible removed from our present administered areas and preventing Chinese intriguing within our limits'. Where the limits of Tibetan territory were clear, as just below Walong on the Lohit, for example, boundary cairns were to be erected.[43]

When Hardinge first outlined this plan, on 29 June, he emphasised that he did not have it in mind to extend British administration up to the proposed new boundary.[44] Indeed, he did not even intend to place the tribes living between the new boundary and the old Outer Line under British protection. The boundary cairns were really intended to stake out a British claim and strengthen British hands in the event of some future negotiations with the Chinese. The new boundary was to indicate not so much the northern limits of British sovereignty as the southern limits of Chinese and Tibetan sovereignty. There would be created, in fact, what Hirtzl at the India Office called 'a multiplicity of lines'.[45] The old Inner Line would still mark the British administrative border. The old Outer Line would continue to indicate the effective limits of touring by British political officers. The new northern boundary, finally, would define a kind of no-man's-land into which the Chinese must not be allowed to set foot.

The idea of adding a third line to the existing arrangement of the Inner and Outer Lines was not without its subtlety: if the Chinese could be induced to respect the new line, then the scheme would satisfy the two criteria which Bell had remarked on in the summer of 1910, namely the defence against China without a corresponding advance in British administrative responsibilities. In fact, of course, the plan could never work out quite like this. Men at the India Office like Sir Arthur

[43] PEF 1910/13, Hardinge to Crewe, 21 September 1911.
[44] PEF 1910/13, Hardinge to Secretary of State, 29 June 1911.
[45] PEF 1910/13, no. 1081/1911, Hirtzl's minute.

Hirtzl and Sir Hugh Barnes, wise in the realities of Indian government, appreciated that any advance of the border, whatever that border might be called, would mean an advance of the area in which the inhabitants could look to British protection. In the Mishmi country, for example, the new border would be designed to keep the Chinese from penetrating far south of Walong. If the Chinese did move into Mishmi tribal country below this point, and the tribes appealed for British help, the Indian Government could not decline to protect the Mishmis against the Chinese. Grey at the Foreign Office, likewise, was not too happy about Hardinge's proposed creation of 'something in the nature of a triple frontier', which, he thought, 'would surely lead to much confusion'. Grey did not believe that there was any point in trying to annex territory without controlling it. As he put it, in a letter to the India Office on 21 July 1911:

> A policy of sending expeditions into unadministered territory with a view to claiming a frontier, and of subsequently withdrawing, is open to objection as leading to difficulties similar to those encountered in the case of the recent expedition to the Pienma district,[46] and that it would consequently be preferable, whenever possible, to decide upon a suitable and defensible frontier by local exploration and then not only to lay claim to it but to take steps to administer the country enclosed.[47]

The idea of three lines of boundary, if Hardinge had ever held it, had certainly been abandoned by September 1911. The new boundary, Hardinge said, was to be created by advancing the Outer Line. The inter-Line zone, hitherto only a few miles wide, would now be expanded to embrace the greater part of the southern slopes of the Assam Himalayas. Here a policy would be applied not unlike that which Williamson and Sir Lancelot Hare had been urging during Lord Minto's administration, a policy which Hardinge described as 'loose political control'. In normal circumstances the tribes between the two Lines, now widely separated, would be left as much as possible to their own devices. If, however, the Chinese moved

[46] See p. 288 above. Here at Pienma, no sooner had Hertz withdrawn than the Chinese were reported to have returned.
[47] PEF 1910/13, FO to IO, 21 July 1911.

into tribal territory, or if the tribes violated either the Inner Line or the new Outer Line, or, even, if the tribes appeared to be acquiring 'an undue sense of independence', the Indian Government would act. This did not mean that during periods of peace and calm the British should ignore the inter-Line areas entirely. In some places they would have to establish permanent outposts, as, for example, on the upper Lohit; in others they could perhaps rely on nothing more concrete than tribal treaties.[48] Grey and the Foreign Office were still not convinced of the wisdom of a policy which, even in this revised form, implied 'claiming territory which we are not prepared to hold and administer'; but they would accept the opinion of the Indian Government, and would argue the point no more.[49]

Once a rough alignment of the new boundary had been decided upon, Hardinge proposed, 'a formal intimation should be made to China of the limits of the country under our control'. Such a declaration, indeed, was vital to the whole scheme as Hardinge saw it. The Chinese, he felt, were unlikely to cross a line when to do so would be to invite British retribution: he had evidently decided to ignore the example of the Sino-Burmese border where the Chinese were continually crossing lines of just this kind. It is likely, moreover, that Hardinge saw the need for some diplomatic shield behind which the Abor Expedition and its associated missions could take place. The Tibetan Government in exile had already indicated that it considered it had jurisdiction over some Assam Himalayan districts; and in August 1911 the Indian Government had informed its officers on the Tibetan frontier that 'it is not desirable that matters regarding the Abors, Mishmis and other tribes on the North-East Frontier should be discussed with the Dalai Lama and his Ministers'.[50] There would certainly be some diplomatic complications if, the moment the Abor expedition set out into the hills, the Chinese were to declare that the British were embarking upon military operations in Chinese territory. It seemed wisest to strike first with a general statement of the area of British influence, and then proceed to occupy it.

[48] PEF 1910/13, Hardinge to Crewe, 21 September 1911.
[49] PEF 1910/13, FO to IO, 6 November 1911.
[50] FO 371/1065, no. 35166, Bell to India, 5 August 1911, and India to Weir, 15 August 1911.

Grey, however, thought otherwise. A declaration such as Hardinge had in mind would only give the Chinese advance warning of British intentions, and, far from deterring them, would actually encourage them to penetrate as far as they could into tribal territory while they were still in a position to do so.[51] Grey, therefore, insisted that 'no formal intimation of the extent of the territory claimed by His Majesty's Government shall be made to China until a definite decision has been made as to the frontier to be held, based on the results of the present expeditions'.[52]

The new Outer Line alignment which Lord Hardinge had in mind was precisely that which Minto had proposed in October 1910. It would start at the foot of the hills at the extreme south-east corner of the Tawang Tract and then run north-east to the crest of the Assam Himalayas somewhere in the region of lat. 29°, long. 94°, whence it would follow roughly lat. 29° until long. 96°, then turn south-east to the Lohit Valley below Rima and end at the Burmese border on the Lohit-Irrawaddy watershed.[53] This alignment, which, except in the Mishmi country on the Lohit, passed through terrain to all intents and purposes at that time unknown to the British, marked out the general sphere of British influence in the tribal areas which, while in practice of little significance, had yet been indicated on a number of maps. The map appended to Vol. II of the 1909 edition of Aitchison's *Collection of Treaties*, to which reference has already been made, indicated this region as an area of lightly coloured wash beyond the Outer Line. The proposed new alignment was the basis for the McMahon Line of 1914; but, unlike the McMahon Line, it left within Tibet the entire Tawang Tract right down to the foothills above Udalguri, an unsatisfactory state of affairs, as the Indian General Staff were quick to point out.[54]

[51] PEF 1910/13, FO to IO, 26 October 1911.

[52] PEF 1910/13, FO to IO, 6 November 1911.

[53] PEF 1910/13, Hardinge to Crewe, 21 September 1911. The bulk of the important document is printed in Reid, *Assam Frontier*, op. cit., pp. 226–8.

[54] In the Indian General Staff 'Note on the North-East Frontier' of June 1912, the text of which is to be found in PEF 1910/14, it was remarked that Tawang was 'a dangerous wedge of territory' between Bhutan and the tribal hills. The General Staff proposed that the whole of Tawang, including

In late September and early October 1911 orders were issued for the Abor Expedition and the Miri and Mishmi Missions. The Abor Expedition was entrusted to the command of Major-General Hamilton Bower, with A. Bentinck as Political Officer. Its objectives were; firstly, to avenge the deaths of Williamson and Gregorson and apprehend the Abors responsible; secondly, to visit as many Abor villages as possible on both sides of the Dihang-Siang Valley so that the tribesmen could be informed that they were now under British control 'of a loose political nature'; thirdly, to prove that the Tsangpo and the Brahmaputra were one and the same river, linked by the Dihang-Siang; fourthly, to persuade or compel any Chinese who might be on the southern side of 'recognised Tibetan-Chinese limits' to withdraw northwards; and finally, to acquire information upon which proposals for the alignment of the new boundary where it crossed the Dihang-Siang could be based.[55] The Mishmi Mission, which was to be headed by W. C. M. Dundas, Assistant Political Officer, Sadiya, was to be subdivided into two separate but related operations.[56] One column was to go up the Lohit to the Chinese boundary flags at the Yepak River; a second column, in which F. M. Bailey was included, would explore the basins of the Dibang and Sisseri rivers lying between the Lohit and the Dihang-Siang. The Dibang and Sisseri part of the scheme, taking place in almost completely unknown country, could not be planned in detail: its main function was to study the extent and nature of Tibetan and Chinese influence, if any, and to ascertain a good boundary alignment. The Lohit part, however, was to be in a region which the British, by Assam Himalayan standards, knew very well; and for it detailed instructions were provided. Firstly, it was to

[55] PEF 1910/13, India to Major-General H. Bower, 25 September 1911.
[56] PEF 1910/13, India to W. C. M. Dundas, 5 October 1911.

Tsöna, should be included within British India, which involved an even more advanced frontier than that of the McMahon Line of 1914. From the middle of 1912 there ceased to be any doubt that the Tawang Tract, at least as far north as the Se La, should be included in British territory. The evolution of the border alignment in this quarter will be discussed later on in connection with the negotiating of the McMahon Line.

The General Staff Note of 1 June 1912 is printed in Reid, *Assam Frontier*, op. cit., p. 280.

visit the Yepak River, and to erect a cairn beside the Chinese boundary flags[57] 'so as to mark in an unmistakable manner the boundary between India and Tibet'; secondly, it should endeavour to explore to the west of the Lohit Valley so as to determine the border alignment leading towards the headwaters of the Dibang and linking up with the other column of the Mishmi Mission; thirdly, it was to start work on the construction of a cart road up the Lohit to the Yepak; finally, it should expel, albeit politely, Chinese and Tibetan officials from what would now be British territory. The Miri Mission, the venture up the Subansiri and its tributaries which was to be in the charge of G. C. Kerwood, received similar instructions; 'the main object of the Mission', the Indian Government told Kerwood, 'will be to establish friendly relations with the tribes and to survey and explore the country in order to obtain information which will enable a satisfactory frontier to be demarcated between India and Tibetan-Chinese territory'.[58]

Major-General Hamilton Bower's main Abor expeditionary force set out into the hills in late October 1911. With over 1,000 troops and several thousand Naga porters it had no trouble overwhelming the Abors and bringing Williamson's murderers to justice. Total British casualties came to five killed and six wounded. By January 1912 the military side of the operation was over, though survey work went on for a little longer. British officers travelled up the Dihang-Siang to lat. 28° 55', near the settlement of Singing, a point far farther north than had been reached before, but still some thirty miles short of what was to become the McMahon Line (Map no. 8). Parts of some of the tributaries of the Dihang-Siang, like the Siyom and the Yamne, were also explored. The conclusion, as far as the Chinese threat was concerned, seems to have been that no immediate danger existed on this front, but that, since on the upper reaches of the Dihang-Siang Abor villages tended to give way to settlements of Mönpas and other Buddhist groups who had migrated down from Tibet, it would be as well to push the British boundary as far north as possible. It was as yet, however, impossible to specify a precise boundary alignment. Bentinck, who was in charge of the political side of the work in Abor country, noted

[57] In the event, no boundary cairns were erected.
[58] PEF 1910/13, India to G. C. Kerwood, 5 October 1911.

a feature of tribal life in the Abor hills which later was to be discussed by Mills and Fürer-Haimendorf, namely the tendency for villages to attempt to impose restrictions on trade passing through them to the tribes deeper in the hills. Bentinck referred to those Abor settlements nearest British territory which, 'so far from forming the door opening on those beyond, have acted as the curtain shutting us off from them and them from us': and thus, tribes which would logically have traded with the Indian plains found themselves obliged to trade with Tibet across the snowy ranges. North of Simong, a village roughly half-way between the old Outer Line and the McMahon Line of 1914, trade, especially in salt, was entirely with Tibet. Some means, Bentinck argued, would have to be found to free internal communications in the tribal hills before British influence could be expected to be felt on a continuing basis much beyond the villages along the old Outer Line, no matter where the new international boundary might be drawn on the map.[59]

The Miri Mission to the Subansiri basin, like the surveying parties attached to the Abor Expedition, failed in the season 1911–12 to reach the limits of Tibetan territory, though at the village of Tali on the Kamla tributary of the Subansiri it came across signs of an active trade with Tibet in which Tibetan salt was bartered for hides and rice, the last commodity produced mainly by the Apa Tanang people (Map no. 7). The Mission was not able to get beyond Tali, because of the hostile attitude of the local population, and Tali was more than forty miles as the crow flies from the nearest point on the 1914 McMahon alignment; but here, at any rate, the Mission was able to establish a total absence of direct Tibetan political influence. Tibetan goods, beads, brass bells, swords and the like, abounded in the Tali region, but, so Kerwood, the Mission leader, was informed, Tibetans never came this far south. It seemed very unlikely that a significant threat of Chinese infiltration could exist here.[60]

The area of greatest danger remained, as it had appeared to be ever since 1910, the Lohit Valley (Map no. 9). The

[59] PEF 1910/14, A. Bentinck, Political Report on the Abor Expedition, 23 April 1912.

[60] PEF 1910/14, G. C. Kerwood, Miri Mission Report 1911–12, 24 May 1912.

departure of the Mishmi Mission was hastened because of reports that the Chinese were again summoning Mishmi chiefs to Chikong and were considering the advance of their boundary flags up to seven marches below Walong.[61] When Dundas and his party reached the Yepak River, on 3 January 1912, they found that the Chinese, the day before, had put up fresh boundary markers beside the old ones of 1910. The new markers consisted of a red flag bearing a four-clawed dragon and a red placard bearing in Chinese and Tibetan the following inscription: 'Zayul, southern limit, boundary of Manchu Empire.' The Mishmi Mission stayed in the neighbourhood of Walong until 31 January, during which time they were in communication with the Chinese authorities in Zayul, who, far from protesting at the presence of a British force so close to the border, actually sent it welcome gifts of chickens, eggs and other produce.[62] There was no evidence to suggest that in January 1912 the Chinese were busy advancing down the Lohit towards the Assam plains; but then, at this moment the Chinese force in Zayul had been reduced to a mere token, the bulk of the garrison having been diverted to the unsuccessful Pome campaign. When Bailey came through Rima in July 1911 there had been a Chinese garrison of more than forty soldiers; by January 1912 this had shrunk to two men. It seemed likely, however, that the Chinese would shortly return in force to revive the forward policy in the Mishmi country which the Pome operations had interrupted. The full significance of the outbreak of the Chinese Revolution was not yet apparent. The mutinies of Chinese forces in Central Tibet, it then seemed, would most probably result in the despatch of strong reinforcements from Szechuan Province. In these circumstances the discovery which the Mishmi Mission made concerning recent Chinese activity along the Delei tributary of the Lohit had serious implications.

The Delei flows south from the Glei Pass to the Lohit, which it joins some ninety miles from Sadiya. In December 1911 Dundas sent a small party under Captain Hardcastle to explore this tributary and contact the isolated Mishmi communities who lived along its upper reaches. Hardcastle learnt from one of the Mishmi chiefs here, a certain Mazanon, the following

[61] PEF 1910/13, Hardinge to Secretary of State, 10 October 1911.
[62] FO 371/1335, No. 13372, Mishmi Mission Diary.

story. In about May 1911 a Chinese official calling himself 'Ta Loh', with an escort of some fifty Chinese soldiers and 100 Tibetans, crossed the Glei Pass and spent a week in the Delei Valley. He summoned the Mishmi headmen to his camp and ordered them to clear a path down the Delei to its junction with the Lohit. The Mishmis, or so Mazanon reported, explained that the route was a very difficult one and that 'Ta Loh' would be better advised, if he wished to get into the main Lohit Valley, to do so by way of Rima and Walong. The Chinese official seemed willing to accept this advice. He then gave the Mishmis a document which he said they should show any Chinese or British officials who might come their way. He also gave them a flag, with orders to erect it at the Delei-Lohit junction. The Mishmis, if Mazanon's story is to be believed, refused both the document and the flag. The Chinese then presented them with nine loads of salt, which they accepted unconditionally. The Tibetans accompanying 'Ta Loh' described him as a 'big man', whom it would be rash to offend, and advised the Mishmis to give him presents, which, Mazanon said, they did not do. The Chinese party then recrossed the Glei Pass, going eastward in the direction of the Pome country. Mazanon's story indicated that the Mishmis had, except for the nine bags of salt, in no way committed themselves to the Chinese. From another source, three Tibetans visiting the upper Delei Valley, Hardcastle derived a different version of these events which suggested that the Mishmis had been more submissive to the Chinese than Mazanon would care to admit to a British officer. According to the Tibetans, the Chinese official 'Ta Loh', whom they called 'Chang Ta Lao-yeh', had explained to the assembled Mishmi chiefs that from now on they must obey Chinese orders and regard themselves as Chinese subjects, and had given to each of them a kind of passport or warrant of protection, written in Tibetan and Chinese, and issued in the name of Chao Erh-feng. Captain Hardcastle managed to collect fifteen of these documents, which one of the members of the Mishmi Mission, Captain Jeffery, translated from the Chinese text, thus confirming the Tibetans' version.[63]

Captain Hardcastle's information added one more detail to

[63] PEF 1910/14, Hardinge to Secretary of State, 28 January 1912. See also Political and Secret Department Confidential Memoranda, B.189.

the picture that was forming in British minds of the boundary between China and the British Indian Empire as the Chinese saw it (Map no. 4). When the experience gained since 1910 in the Assam Himalayas was married to discoveries which Hertz, Barnard and Clerk had made between 1910 and 1912 as to the nature of Chinese claims over Hkamtilong and the upper Nmaihka Valley in Burma, it became clear that the Chinese had evolved a border alignment most unacceptable in British eyes. Starting, on the Yunnan side, at the Salween-Irrawaddy watershed in the neighbourhood of Pienma, this line ran north-west across the upper reaches of the Nmaihka and Malihka tributaries of the Irrawaddy to the well-established Mishmi-Tibet boundary point on the Lohit just below Walong. From here it ran slightly south-west to meet the Lohit again at its junction with the Delei tributary: this was one of the implications of the story that Mazanon told Captain Hardcastle. What was the Chinese idea of the alignment west of the Lohit-Delei junction was unknown; but it seemed likely that their line would follow a gently north-westerly course across the upper tributaries of the basins of the Dibang and Sisseri to meet the Dihang-Siang not far north of the farthest point reached by the surveying parties attached to the Abor Expedition, perhaps somewhere between Singing and Jido.[64] This line, along both its Burmese and Assamese stretches, included within the Chinese sphere much territory which the Indian Government, as its knowledge of the districts involved improved, was becoming increasingly convinced ought to be British.

5. LOOSE POLITICAL CONTROL

By the spring of 1912 the Indian Government had discovered a great deal about those districts along its North-East Frontier from which it hoped to exclude the Chinese. The Abor Expedition and its associated missions in the Assam Himalayas,

[64] The Dibang column of the Mishmi Mission learnt that the Chinese had been attempting to make contact with the Mishmis living on the upper reaches of the Dri or upper Dibang. By 1912, however, Chinese officials had not actually set foot in the Dibang basin, using Tibetan traders as the link between them and the tribes. See PEF 1910/14, F. M. Bailey, Report on the work of the Dibang Column—Mishmi Mission 1911–12.

together with the operations in the extreme north of Burma under Hertz, Barnard and Clerk, had yielded information which, if not sufficient for the definition of a boundary alignment as precise as the McMahon Line was to be in 1914, was enough to enable Lord Hardinge to specify in general the kind of course his proposed new Outer Line should follow.[65] Further exploration would be needed to add details here and there; and British parties were to be active in Assam and Burma up to late 1913. The main points, however, had been established, and the problem in 1912 was how to make the new boundary an effective one. What could be done to prevent the Chinese, once they had recovered from the crisis of their Revolution—as some observers in India in 1912 thought they soon would—from continuing to infiltrate down towards the Assam plains? Should the Chinese Government be told about the new British Outer Line, as yet neither delimited nor demarcated? Should the British extend their administration right up to the new Line, or should they, as they had in the days before the Chinese threat, preserve an attitude of non-interference towards the hill tribes? Lord Hardinge's policy of 'loose political control' was designed to answer this kind of question.

'Loose political control' was also to be applied to the extreme north of British Burma, where, as in the Assam Himalayas, the Chinese had been extending their influence towards the edges of directly administered British territory. There were many similarities between the Burmese and Assamese situations, and an effective British policy had to relate to both regions. In one respect, however, the Assam Himalayan boundary involved a problem which was not present to a significant degree in Burma. In Northern Burma, as in Assam, it was clear that the effective exclusion of the Chinese would involve an intensification of British administration and its extension into regions which, in

[65] Unlike the expeditions into the Assam Himalayas, the British ventures into the extreme north of Burma resulted, in 1913, in a number of armed clashes between small Chinese parties in the Ahkyang Valley (a tributary of the Nmaihka) and the British expedition led by J. T. O. Barnard. In April 1913, during one such encounter, Barnard was wounded. There can be no doubt that had the Chinese attempted to penetrate into the Assam Himalayas with the same determination that they showed on the Yunnan-Burma border, the problem of defining what was to be known as the McMahon Line would have been very much more difficult.

the past, had been left very much to their own devices. Permanent posts would probably have to be established: this was soon to be done at Putao (Fort Hertz) near the head of the Malihka Valley and at Pienma (Hpimaw) near the Salween-Irrawaddy divide. Roads would have to be pushed into remote hill tracts. The cost of British government in Burma would rise. In theory, however, there would be in Burma no increase in the extent of British sovereignty. The British, so it was maintained, had acquired title to the upper valleys of the Irrawaddy basin when they took over the Mandalay kingdom in 1886. Here they were defending what they already possessed, and were not taking over new territory. It was not so easy to say this in relation to the Assam Himalayas. Even if it could be argued that the non-Buddhist hill tribes had long been considered by the Indian Government to fall within the general sphere of British influence, yet there existed no treaty or formal declaration to this effect. It could equally well be argued that the tribal areas constituted foreign territory, and that by advancing the Outer Line Lord Hardinge was increasing the size of the British Empire. This was an interpretation of the events in Assam which both the India Office and the Foreign Office hoped to avoid, if possible. Imperial expansion had no place on the electoral platform of Mr. Asquith's Liberal Government. Moreover, if the tribal areas beyond the old Outer Line were, in fact, foreign territory, who could demonstrate with absolute certainty that they were not part of Tibet? The British had promised the Russians in 1907 that they would not annex Tibetan territory. The advance of the Outer Line, if it were once publicly admitted to imply the advance of British sovereignty, could well involve British explanations in St. Petersburg, as it indeed did in 1914.

The Abor Expedition involved the despatch of a British armed force beyond the Outer Line. It had been approved, of course, by the Secretary of State for India, Lord Crewe; but formal consent for it from Parliament had not been sought, an omission which may well have involved a breach of the Government of India Act, 1858. Section 55 of this Act reads thus:

> Except for preventing or repelling actual invasion of His Majesty's Indian possessions, or under other sudden and urgent necessity, the revenues of India shall not, without the consent

of both Houses of Parliament, be applicable to defray the expenses of any military operation carried on *beyond the external frontiers* of such possessions by His Majesty's forces charged upon such revenues.[66]

Did the old Outer Line in fact constitute an external frontier? Both the Indian Government and the India Office rather thought that it did. They appreciated, however, that any public statement to this effect, such as would be involved in the quest for parliamentary approval for the Abor Expedition, might prove an irresistible invitation to the Chinese to start raising formal claims in the Assam Himalayas which, so far, they had not done. It was decided, therefore, to ignore the implications of the Outer Line in relation to Section 55 of the 1858 Act. In an attempt to avoid awkward questions, moreover, the India Office took great care to edit certain documents which it could not escape including in the Abor Blue Book, 'with a view to eliminating as far as possible the *international* aspect of the case'.[67] The press were kept as far away from the Abor Expedition as could be arranged, and an attempt was made to keep the Miri and Mishmi Missions secret.[68]

It was not possible, of course, to prevent shrewd Parliamentary critics from exploiting the Government of India Act of 1858; the best that could be done was to see that such persons were no better informed than was absolutely necessary. Sir William Byles, a Yorkshire member with no love for punitive campaigns, was the first to raise publicly the issue of Section 55 of the 1858 Act; and it was to a great extent to silence his awkward queries that the Abor Blue Book was presented. On 31 October and 7 November he asked whether the Abor Expedition, and the Mishmi Mission as well, did not involve considerations arising from the 1858 Act. He was told that neither the

[66] My italics. See PEF 1910/15, File no. 1918/4, for text of the 1858 Act and its implications for the Abor Expedition.

[67] FO 371/1066, no. 47933, Shuckburgh to Max Müller, 4 November 1911.

[68] FO 371/1066, no. 48949, India to East Bengal and Assam, 26 October 1911.

Press correspondents were not allowed to accompany the Abor Expedition or the missions; they had to rely for news on the Official Reporter, Major Poole, whose discretion earned him the nickname 'The Stagnant Poole'. See Bailey, *No Passport*, op. cit., p. 29.

Mishmis nor the Abors were beyond the British external frontiers. Byles was unconvinced. On 14 November he pointed to a number of maps, including that in the *Imperial Gazetteer of India*, showing the Mishmis and Abors outside British territory. He was informed that 'the maps in the *Imperial Gazetteer* do not purport to show with scientific exactitude the frontier between India and Tibet, which has never been demarcated'; and that, as far as the 1858 Act was concerned, the tribes in question could be considered to live within British territory. On 28 November, still dissatisfied, Byles asked whether one purpose of the Abor Expedition was to lay down a Sino-Indian border; and, if so, if China had been consulted. He was referred to item no. 19 in the Abor Blue Book, which had just been issued. This heavily edited version of Hardinge's despatch of 21 September 1911 can hardly have made him much wiser; but he could not avoid accepting the assurance of E. S. Montagu, the Parliamentary Under-Secretary of State for India, that 'it is not intended as a result of the [Abor] expedition to increase the area administered by the Government of India'.[69]

Parliamentary questions by Byles and some of his colleagues helped Lord Crewe decide that the new British policy of 'loose political control' in the Assam Himalayas should be as like the old policy of non-interference as it was possible to make it. The new policy, in any case, as Hirtzl noted, 'had nothing to do with the punitive expedition against the Abors, though that expedition was the means of beginning to give effect to it. It was necessitated solely by the advance of the Chinese.'[70] In the spring of 1912, with Chinese power all but swept away from Tibet by the tide of rebellion, it seemed in some quarters in London as if the quest for a permanent solution to the Assam border problem could well be postponed for a while. The purely local problem of conducting relations between Assam and the Abor tribes had not, in the past, involved the British occupation of positions beyond the old Outer Line. With the Chinese threat declining, there could be no urgent need for such outposts now.

Lord Hardinge, however, had by now become a convert to the view which the East Bengal and Assam Government had

[69] For Parliamentary Questions on the Abor Expedition, see PEF 1910/15, File no. 1918/4.

[70] PEF 1910/14, Hirtzl to Ritchie, 26 April 1912.

been urging since 1906, that, if only for reasons of local Assamese administration, British relations with the hill tribes should not be allowed to revert to that system which had operated in the days of non-interference. As the Lieutenant-Governor of East Bengal and Assam, Sir C. S. Bayley, put it in February 1912:

> The Abors have always been the most troublesome tribe on this frontier, and past experience has proved the impossibility of exercising effective control over them from a post in the plains. This experience is not unique, for the Nagas and Lushais were only brought under control when their country was permanently occupied. The policy hitherto adopted of sending expeditions into the Abor country, inflicting punishment, and withdrawing the force, has invariably been misunderstood by the tribes concerned. The temporary occupation has soon been forgotten and fresh trouble has ensued. It should now be definitely abandoned both on the ground of its want of success and because the presence of an aggressive and intriguing neighbour, whom it is absolutely necessary to debar from obtaining influence over the hill tribes on our border, necessitates a reconsideration of the whole position not only in regard to the Abor tract alone, but in respect of the whole frontier, from Bhutan to the Hkamti country and the unadministered regions north of Burma.[71]

In other words, just as the tribal problem had created the justification for measures designed to frustrate the Chinese, so now those measures might also be made to result in some permanent solution to the tribal problem. The two issues were so closely related that they could not be separated. If the tribes were not brought under some more effective British control, the frontier could not be guarded; and if the frontier was not better guarded than it had been in the past, it would be difficult to control the tribes. Both objectives, so Lord Hardinge, in support of the opinion of the East Bengal and Assam Government, advised, could best be achieved by a policy of establishing a few permanent posts in the tribal country beyond the hitherto accepted limits of British administration. There should be one such post in the Abor country, where Rotung on the west bank of the Dihang-Siang seemed a good site. There should be

[71] Reid, *Assam Frontier*, op. cit., p. 241, quoting Bayley to India, 22 February 1912.

another post at Menilkrai, just below Walong on the Lohit.[72] Such were the implications of 'loose political control'.

The Home Government had not seen 'loose political control' in quite this light. As E. S. Montagu put it:

> I take it that loose political control implies objection to any sort of kind of interference by foreign powers, and I believe that this could best be achieved as a general rule by patrols or expeditions from well-maintained bases in our own territory, and need not involve posts in tribal territory at all.[73]

Lord Crewe agreed. As far as the Rotung post was concerned, he was, 'on grounds of general policy' very 'unwilling to sanction the establishment of permanent police posts in the Abor country'. The Indian Government could have posts at Pasighat and Kobo, both places which could be described as potential 'well-maintained bases in our own territory'. They could not have any permanent base in the hills beyond the old Outer Line.[74] This decision was vehemently opposed by Hardinge; and there were several senior officials at the India Office, Sir Arthur Hirtzl included, who doubted its wisdom.[75] In late 1912, after six months of argument, Lord Crewe was persuaded to modify his decision somewhat. There would be, as he had always said, no permanent *police* or *military* post at Rotung. He would allow, however, the Indian Government to establish a *trading* post there, open for part of each year. He emphasised that 'this is in no sense an administrative or political step'. However, the new trading post was not significantly different from the old police post: it would be permitted an escort of some 100 rifles. It would be closed down during the rains; but then it is likely that the proposed police post would likewise have operated only in the cold season.[76]

From the point of view of preventing future Chinese infiltration, the proposed post at Menilkrai was clearly of far greater importance than that at Rotung. There could be no doubt that the Chinese, between 1910 and 1912, had been trying to

[72] FO 535/15, no. 49, Hardinge to Secretary of State, 21 March 1912.
[73] PEF 1910/14, no. 1493/1912, Minute by Montagu, 1 May 1912.
[74] FO 535/15, no. 49, Secretary of State to Hardinge, 6 April 1912.
[75] PEF 1910/14, Hirtzl to Ritchie, 26 April 1912.
[76] PEF 1910/14, Secretary of State to Hardinge, 3 October 1912.

establish some influence over the Mishmi tribes adjacent to their border in Zayul, and that, if their fortunes in Tibet improved, they would do so again. Moreover, the Lohit Valley could well turn out to be the back door into that Hkamtilong country which the Chinese had since 1910 been approaching from the Yunnanese side. To abandon the Lohit would be to leave this door ajar. There were arguments for the maintenance of a British presence here which Lord Crewe made no attempt to refute. If the Lohit were not policed by the Indian Government, the Chinese might conclude that the British had given up their claims here, and might rush in to fill the vacuum. This was no academic point. While, during the course of 1912, it became increasingly obvious to British observers that, as a result of the Chinese Revolution, the Chinese had suffered a disastrous setback in their plans for Central Tibet, yet it then seemed that they still maintained a tenuous grasp on Zayul. In April 1912, so the Chengtu Chinese press reported, the Szechuan Government had despatched a special investigating officer, Chiang Feng-ch'i, to the Zayul border to talk things over with the Mishmi Mission (which, of course, had already returned home). Three Chinese surveyors were also sent to this sector of the border where English troops 'were furtively sneaking in'.[77] On 9 June 1912, it was later to transpire, Chiang Feng-ch'i reached the Yepak River and put up a fresh boundary marker there to proclaim it a point on the southern frontier of the Chinese Republic.[78] In November 1912 it was formally announced in Peking that Zayul had been turned into a Chinese *hsien* or magistrate's district.[79]

It was easy enough to authorise the establishment of a permanent British post up the Lohit; but it was not so easy in practice to place such a post on an operational basis. The track up the Lohit Valley from Sadiya to the Tibetan border passed through some of the most unpleasant country in the world. Few of the early travellers in this region can be said to have enjoyed their experience. Major Bliss, who commanded the escort for the Mishmi Mission in 1911–12, reported that 'the communications in the Mishmi country are by far the worst that in a

[77] Political and Secret Department Confidential Memoranda, B.189.
[78] PEF 1913/28, O'Callaghan's Tour Diary, 7 March 1914.
[79] FO 535/15, no. 283, Secretary of State to Hardinge, 5 November 1912.

considerable experience I have met with'.[80] The route to the site of the proposed post, at Menilkrai near Walong, passed through jungle infested with leeches of incredible ferocity, ran along knife-edge ridges and beside sheer precipices, crossed raging torrents and mountain slopes subject to frequent land-slides. The difficulty of the way made it essential that a British force should remain at Menilkrai, since it was clearly impossible to dash through this kind of country to cope with emergencies as they arose: it also made it extremely hard to keep such a force supplied and reinforced. Hence, the Menilkrai post depended on the construction of a good road up the Lohit Valley. The Lohit road was started in 1912, in the hope that it would be completed by the end of the year. It proved to be a task so arduous and expensive that by 1914, when it had only reached a point a few miles beyond Sadiya, it was quietly abandoned, and with it the Menilkrai post.[81] The project was not revived until the 1940s, and not completed during the period of British rule in India.

If the policy of 'loose political control' did not give rise to dramatic feats of engineering, it still produced some significant changes in the machinery for the conduct of British relations with the Assam hill tribes along the Tibetan border. Some of the Abor and Mishmi groups were brought, albeit tacitly, under British protection. The orders issued to Abor villagers during the course of the Abor Expedition, and the relations established between the Mishmi Mission and the tribes along the Lohit, implied a far greater degree of British involvement in tribal affairs than would have been tolerable in the days of the policy of non-interference.[82] The continued presence up to late 1913 of British exploring parties in the hill tracts, moreover, must have convinced the tribesmen that more than a punitive expedition of the traditional pattern was now afoot. The work of such bodies as the Mishmi Exploration Survey Detachment and the Abor Exploration Survey Detachment during 1912–13 was justified as necessary to secure the final geographical details for the definition of the new Outer Line; but, in fact, it had also

[80] Reid, *Assam Frontier*, op. cit., p. 239, quoting Major G. Bliss, *Brief Narrative of the Mishmi Mission, 1911–12*.

[81] PEF 1913/39, no. 1310/1914, Minute of 4 April 1914, for example.

[82] See Aitchison, *Treaties*, op. cit., XII (1931), pp. 165–6.

a clear political objective in bringing to the local populations the knowledge of the existence of the British Empire.[83] Had the First World War not intervened, it is likely that such official 'exploration' would have become a regular feature of the administration of the Assam Himalayas, which would, with its own momentum, have created *de facto* British posts in many remote mountain districts.

The permanence of the British presence in the frontier hills was symbolised by the appointment of Political Officers with special responsibility for relations with the hill tribes. The North-East Frontier along the Assam Himalayas was divided in 1912 into three sections, the Western, Central and Eastern Sections. The Western Section, concerned with the Tawang Tract and the western hill tribes like the Akas and Daflas, was in 1913 entrusted to Captain G. A. Nevill. In 1919, still under Nevill, it became the Balipara Frontier Tract. The Central and Eastern Sections, dealing with the Abor and Mishmi hills, were in 1912 combined under the command of W. C. M. Dundas, whose headquarters were at Sadiya. There was an Assistant Political Officer at Pasighat. In 1919 these sections became the Sadiya Frontier Tract.[84] Even though restrictions were placed from the outset upon the movements of the Political Officers on the Assam frontier—only along the Lohit were they permitted to make tours right up to the Tibetan border without special permission—yet their very existence guaranteed that a far closer watch on events in the Assam Himalayas would now be kept than in the days of Needham and Williamson.[85]

The North-East Frontier administration set up in 1912 and 1913 was to remain a part of the Indian governmental system, and to evolve into NEFA of the modern Indian Republic. Its creation, as Percival Landon shrewdly commented in the *Fortnightly Review* of October 1912, added greatly to the territorial extent of Assam and had more or less created 'a North Eastern

---

[83] See Colonel S. G. Burrard, *Records of the Survey of India IV: Explorations on the North-East Frontier during 1911-12-13*, Calcutta, 1914. This collection includes Major C. P. Gunter, *Report of the Mishmi Exploration Survey Detachment, 1912-13*, and Captain O. H. B. Trenchard, *Report of the Abor Exploration Survey Detachment, 1912-13*.

[84] Reid, *Assam Frontier*, op. cit., pp. 265, 303.

[85] See, for example, FO 535/16, no. 229, Assam to India, 5 April 1913.

Frontier Province'.[86] Landon thought that this was done 'almost surreptitiously' so that 'not one in a million' knew what was happening: and he was not far from the truth, for the implications of Section 55 of the Government of India Act of 1858 had indeed made it necessary to proceed with great caution in what amounted to a northward advance of the British frontier. It could never be frankly admitted that the frontier had, in fact, been advanced. The India Office, as we have seen, was already in November 1911 implying that the new Outer Line was really the same as the old Outer Line. The Indian Republic is still saying this today.

[86] Quoted in T. Das, *British Expansion in Tibet*, Calcutta, 1927, pp. 105–6.

PART TWO
British Policy and the Chinese Revolution
in Tibet, 1912 to 1913

XIX

THE CHINESE LOSE CONTROL OF
CENTRAL TIBET: NOVEMBER 1911
TO APRIL 1913

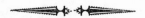

BRITISH anxieties as to the immediate danger on the Assam Himalayan frontier were much relieved by the outbreak of the Chinese Revolution which, by November 1911, had begun to undermine the Chinese position in Central Tibet. In the last ten days of that month the British Trade Agents at Yatung and Gyantse reported that Chinese garrisons were refusing to obey the orders of the commanders and that senior Chinese officials with their families were seeking asylum within the compounds of the two Trade Agencies.[1] By December the Chinese troops in Lhasa had declared the Amban Lien Yü, a Manchu, deposed and had appointed General Chung Ying in his place. Chung, who had commanded the flying column which occupied Lhasa in early 1910, was reported to be sympathetic to the Revolution and popular with the soldiers. It looked for a while as if he might succeed in stabilising the position and in maintaining Chinese control of Lhasa and the other towns of Central Tibet. The situation, however, soon got completely out of hand.[2]

[1] FO 535/14, no. 98, Viceroy to Secretary of State, 25 November 1911; FO 371/1326, Yatung and Gyantse Diary for Novemver 1911.

[2] The precise details of the crisis in Lhasa are by no means clear. I have reconstructed this story from a large number of reports, sometimes contradictory, reaching the Gyantse and Yatung Trade Agencies. One of the better, but not entirely accurate, accounts of the first stages of the anti-Chinese rising in Lhasa is to be found in FO 371/1327, no. 26168, Gould to India, 13 May 1912.

Chung might have done something with the Lhasa garrison, but he was quite unable to cope with the soldiers who started to trickle back to the Tibetan capital in the last days of 1911 from the disastrous operations in Pome. The Pome survivors, on their retreat, had sacked and looted a number of Tibetan towns, including the administrative centre of Tsetang. They had put to death their commander, Lo Ch'ing-ch'i, and by the time they approached the gates of Lhasa they were no more than a mutinous rabble. The privations of the Pome fighting, where more than a third of their number had died, had completely destroyed their morale, and they now but wished sufficient money and transport to enable them to go home to China. Money, however, General Chung Ying did not have. He had, it is true, immediately after his election to command extorted a fairly large sum, perhaps as much as Rs. 2,50,000, from the Tibetan authorities by threatening to sack the Potala Palace; but this had all been distributed to the Chinese garrison in Lhasa in an attempt to purchase its continued loyalty. He had nothing to offer the survivors of the Pome expedition, who numbered somewhere between 500 and 800 men; and they promptly began to loot in Lhasa as they had been looting on the way there. Fighting, inevitably, broke out between the Chinese and Tibetans in the capital, which by March 1912 had spread to Shigatse and Gyantse.[3]

The Gyantse and Shigatse garrisons were small, not more than 300 men in all, and they showed no taste for a gallant fight to the death. With the help of David Macdonald, the British Trade Agent at Yatung, and Lal Bahadur, the Nepalese representative in Lhasa, they were soon persuaded to hand over their arms and ammunition to the Tibetans in return for a safe conduct and travelling money, and to set out for Chumbi on the Indian border, the first stage of their journey back to China. In Lhasa, Chung Ying by early March had likewise decided that his position was untenable. He approached the Tibetan authorities to discuss a cease-fire and safe conduct for his men. Negotiations took place on 20 and 21 March, which then broke down. The Chinese had no confidence in Tibetan promises. The

[3] FO 371/1326, no. 10602, Yatung and Gyantse Diaries for January 1912; no. 20611, Gyantse Diary for March 1912; no. 19889, Bell to India, 9 April 1912.

Tibetans, while willing to let the Chinese withdraw towards India, would not agree to Chung Ying's proposal that he and his men should be permitted to march to the Chinese advanced positions in Eastern Tibet. It is possible that Chung Ying felt that, even though the Dalai Lama had expressed himself in favour of a safe conduct for the Chinese, his wishes in this respect might well be disregarded by the fanatically anti-Chinese monks of Sera and Gaden monasteries. No sooner had negotiations broken down than Chung Ying's men attempted without success to capture Sera, an event which was the signal for renewed fighting between the Chinese and Tibetans. By the beginning of April Chung Ying was besieged in the new Lhasa barracks (Trapchi) and in one small monastery (Teng-yeling) which had remained pro-Chinese. His force numbered almost 1,000 men, nearly all new-drilled troops, equipped with modern weapons, including some light Krupp artillery; and he was, in theory, more than a match for the monk army opposing him. However, he was desperately short of funds, and his ammunition was inadequate for a long siege. Nor could he feel particularly sure of the loyalty of all his men, the majority of whom were Pome survivors. Only his own bodyguard, not more than 130 men in all, could be described as being thoroughly reliable. Also besieged in Lhasa at this time, but quite out of touch with the forces who acknowledged Chung Ying's command, was the Amban Lien Yü and a bodyguard of some sixty or so old-style Chinese soldiers who were holding out in the Amban's Yamen.[4]

Chung Ying must have appreciated that he could not hold out indefinitely. He thought, however, that if he could maintain a Chinese foothold in Lhasa long enough he would be relieved by an expeditionary force from the Chinese bases in the Tibetan Marches. In early 1912 the Chinese situation in Eastern Tibet was extremely unsettled. In December 1911 revolutionaries had put Chao Erh-feng to death and replaced him by Yin Ch'ang-heng, an ambitious and unscrupulous intriguer, barely 25 years old, who possessed none of the great prestige of the man whom he had overthrown. Chao Erh-feng's death gave the signal for a series of anti-Chinese risings in the Marches, the most serious perhaps being the attack on the Chinese garrison

[4] FO 371/1327, no. 26168, Gould to India, 13 May 1912.

at Chamdo by local tribesmen acting in concert with the 3,000 or so monks of Chamdo monastery. The Chinese, however, in most places had managed to ride out this initial storm. In Chamdo, for example, the Chinese garrison, commanded by P'eng Jih-sheng, defended itself with considerable resolution, in the process destroying Chamdo monastery, an act which much distressed the Dalai Lama and which his troops were to avenge in 1918. Yin Ch'ang-heng made it clear that he had no intention of departing from the Tibetan policy of Chao Erh-feng. 'Tibet', he announced, 'is a buttress on a national frontier —the hand, as it were, which protects the face—and its prosperity or otherwise is of most vital importance to China.' He proposed that preparations should begin at once for the despatch of a relief column of Lhasa; and he was supported in this plan by the recently formed Central Government of President Yuan Shih-k'ai.[5] Chung Ying, therefore, had good grounds for thinking that he had only to hang on for a few months and Yin Ch'ang-heng would come to his aid. We will return again later on to the story of Chinese relief expeditions in the Marches. Amban Lien Yü, we may be sure, was, like Chung Ying, waiting for the coming of Chinese salvation from the east. His position in Lhasa was doubly precarious. On the one hand, he was under attack from the Tibetans. On the other, he had been declared deposed by Chung Ying's supporters. No doubt he felt that if he managed to keep the Chinese flag flying over his Yamen he might win such favour with the Republic as to make possible his continued employment in Government service; and he might even be able to bring about the political downfall of Chung Ying, for whom he had no love whatsoever.

While waiting on developments in Eastern Tibet, the various Chinese factions in Lhasa do not seem entirely to have closed their minds to the possibility of coming to terms with the Tibetans. By the end of May, at all events, news reached the British that the Chinese were once more exploring the possibility of securing a cease-fire and were prepared, provided that they could do so with safety and honour, to withdraw to the Indian border. Tibetan pressure had been mounting. Tengyeling monastery was now under fire from artillery which the Tibetans

[5] FO 535/15, no. 67, Jordan to Grey, 27 April 1912.

had captured from the Chinese. Troops from all over Tibet were marching or preparing to march on Lhasa to join in the siege. Tsöna and Tawang, for example, sent a delegation to the Dalai Lama's Government in exile to report their intention to send fighting men to the capital.[6] Chung Ying had virtually lost tactical control over all but his own bodyguard; and the Chinese forces in Tengyeling and in the Trapchi barracks were more or less fighting a war of their own.

By May, moreover, the Tibetan side was also becoming convinced that a negotiated settlement which would bring the Lhasa fighting to an end would be desirable. The Tibetans in Lhasa were far from being a united body. While Sera and Gaden monasteries were leading the attacks against the Chinese, Drebung was following a far more moderate policy: the result was an increasing tension between two monastic factions which threatened to lead to civil war. The Dalai Lama, who had been at Kalimpong since February, was growing increasingly anxious to return to Tibet; but he was reluctant to leave his place of Indian exile until the situation in his capital became more settled. By May he had decided that it would be as well to come to terms with the Chinese. The Panchen Lama, who had during the period of Chinese supremacy involved himself more with Amban Lien Yü than it now seemed wise, was also anxious for a negotiated peace in which he could recover some of his lost prestige—and, perhaps, protect himself against the Dalai Lama's wrath—by playing the part of mediator. The Nepalese, too, were urging peace talks. Their merchants in Tibet had suffered considerable financial loss as a result both of the disturbed conditions and of damage to their property in Lhasa during the fighting. Katmandu had more than once indicated that it would be willing to send its army into Tibet to restore order, a plan which caused much British anxiety: hence British advice, as expressed to the Nepalese Prime Minister through Lieutenant-Colonel Showers, the British Resident in Nepal, was that the Durbar should attempt, through its representative in Tibet, to mediate between the Tibetans and Chinese. The British, moreover, had another interest in securing a cease-fire as soon as possible in that a number of British subjects resident in Lhasa, Ladakhi Moslems, numbering more than 150 men,

[6] FO 371/1326, no. 21900, Viceroy to Secretary of State, 21 May 1912.

women and children, had been complaining to the British Trade Agents of the losses they had suffered in the recent fighting and seeking British protection. Their shops had been looted. One Ladakhi had been killed and another wounded. The leader of the Ladakhi community, Gulam Mohammed, with twelve companions, was at present virtually besieged by the Chinese in the Lodakhis' mosque, which was unfortunately located in that eastern quarter of Lhasa where the Chinese were making their main stand.[7]

In the first week of May a cease-fire of brief duration was actually agreed upon by the Tibetans and Chinese; but it produced no settlement. The Tibetan authorities, acting presumably on the orders of the Dalai Lama, were willing to allow the Chinese to withdraw if they first surrendered their arms, which the Chinese, not surprisingly, refused to do. The monks of Gaden and Sera were violently opposed to any terms at all for their enemies; and it is likely that they would have ignored any safe conduct which the Chinese might have been given. No doubt Chung Ying was well aware of this fact. After three days of uneasy truce, fighting broke out again in Lhasa on 6 May.[8]

By the end of May the Indian Government had resolved upon a scheme by which it could act as a mediator in the crisis, having concluded that the main obstacle to the Chinese and Tibetans coming to terms was a mutual distrust. The result was its instructions to one of the few trusted native agents it then had at its disposal who had any prospect of free movement in Tibet, Laden La, Superintendant of Darjeeling Police. Laden La, a Sikkimese whose uncle was Lama Ugyen Gyatso (once much relied upon by the Bengal Government as a source of intelligence on Tibetan affairs), had been connected with all the phases of British Tibetan policy from the day of the Younghusband Mission. He had been attached to the Panchen Lama's suite during that Incarnation's visit to India in 1905–6. Since 1910 he had been employed as a liaison officer between the Indian Government and the Dalai Lama, whose confidence he appeared to enjoy. Laden La was now told to make his way to Lhasa and persuade the Chinese to surrender, under his super-

[7] FO 371/1326, no. 25090, contains a collection of papers relating to these events.

[8] Loc. cit., Gould to India, 13 May 1913.

vision, and to see that they were not molested during their retreat to the Indian frontier. Lord Hardinge justified Laden La's deputation by pointing out to his masters in London the steadily increasing urgency of the Tibetan situation. The Nepalese, he said, were becoming more and more bellicose; and they were now declaring that, whatever the outcome of the struggle between the Chinese and the Tibetans, they would demand compensation for the losses suffered by their subjects, and that, if need be, they would use their army to exact payment. The longer the fighting in Lhasa continued, the harder it would be to restrain the Nepalese. At the same time, the Dalai Lama had at last made up his mind to cross from British territory back into Tibet; he finally left Kalimpong for Chumbi on 24 June.[9] Hardinge observed that it would be most undesirable for the Lama, who had, in Tibetan eyes at least, been living for the last two years under British protection, to get himself involved in the Lhasa hostilities. What if he should come under Chinese attack? Could the British avoid taking steps then to ensure his safety? And what would the Russians say if they did? Moreover, if in such a situation the British did nothing, could they restrain the Gurkhas from active intervention? These were the arguments for the Laden La mission, and powerful ones at that; but there can be little doubt, as we shall see later on, that Hardinge saw in the Sikkimese policeman something more than a mediator in the immediate Tibetan crisis: he could well turn out to be the beginning of that Lhasa Residency which Younghusband had sought to secure through the Separate Article of the Lhasa Convention of 1904. Hardinge was to be frustrated by London. Laden La, before he reached the Tibetan capital, was halted on the urgent instructions of Lord Crewe and Sir Edward Grey. We will return to this story in another chapter.[10]

In early July, while the Lhasa situation was still much disturbed, the Dalai Lama reached Phari at the head of the Chumbi Valley. His departure from British India was in one way a great relief to Lord Hardinge's Government. During the last few months, while he was preparing to leave, he had caused the British considerable embarrassment and had made the Indian Government walk out on to the very thin ice of issues

[9] FO 535/15, no. 125, Viceroy to Secretary of State, 24 July 1912.
[10] See Ch. XXI.

related to the Anglo-Russian Convention of 1907. On the other hand, once in Tibet the Dalai Lama was free to pursue again an independent foreign policy. This fact was made clear enough when it transpired that waiting to meet him at Phari was none other than Dorjiev, who had come for this purpose from Mongolia and who had recently been in St. Petersburg. Was the old story of secret Russo-Tibetan intrigue going to start all over again? In the event, Dorjiev did not remain long in Tibet, leaving for an unknown destination. The Dalai Lama, meanwhile, had an interview with the Panchen Lama at Ralung, a point on the Lhasa road about thirty miles from Gyantse, during which the two Incarnations apparently resolved, if only for the time being, their major differences. The Dalai Lama then settled down at Samding Monastery, on Lake Palti (Yamdok Tso), to wait until Lhasa had become safe enough for his return to the Potala Palace.[11] He did not set foot in Lhasa, which he had fled in such haste in February 1910, until 23 January 1913.[12]

In early August 1912, with the help of the Nepalese Representative at Lhasa, Lieutenant Lal Bahadur, the Chinese and Tibetans reopened truce discussions which had been broken off in May. The Chinese proposed the following terms: the Chinese troops would deposit their arms and ammunition in a locked

[11] FO 535/15, no. 145, Viceroy to Secretary of State, 9 July 1912; no. 163, IO to FO, 26 July 1912; FO 371/1327, no. 32864, Viceroy to Secretary of State, 2 August 1912; David Macdonald, *Twenty Years in Tibet*, London, 1932, pp. 97–99. Macdonald, who was the British Trade Agent at Yatung, had lunch with Dorjiev on this occasion at the Phari dak bungalow. Dorjiev, who Macdonald thought was still high in the Dalai Lama's favour, asked if it would be possible for him to return to Russia by way of India. Macdonald said there was nothing to stop him making a formal application to the Indian Government, but Dorjiev never did.

The meeting between the two Lamas appears to have taken place on 16 July 1912. A day or so earlier both the Dalai and Panchen Lamas were at Gyantse at the same time; but the Dalai Lama then confined himself to talking to the Tashilhumpo Incarnation over the Gyantse Trade Agency telephone, during the course of which conversation he instructed the Panchen Lama to meet him at Ralung. This must have been the first time in recorded history that the two chief Incarnations of the Yellow Church communicated with each other by this means; and it may possibly have been the last. See FO 371/1327, no. 30553, Viceroy to Secretary of State, 16 July 1912; no. 32224, Viceroy to Secretary of State, 22 July 1912.

[12] See Aitchison, *Treaties*, 1929 ed., Vol. XIV, p. 20.

warehouse, over which they would mount guard until orders for the final disposal of this material had been received from Peking: the Tibetans would provide funds to defray the cost of Chinese withdrawal to India: the safety of the Chinese during their withdrawal should be guaranteed by the mediator (Nepal), whose representative would also sign the truce agreement: both the Chinese and the Tibetans, the moment a cease-fire was agreed to, would vacate the monasteries which they then occupied, the Tibetan forces leaving Sera and Gaden and the Chinese giving up Tengyeling. After some discussion, agreement along these lines was reached on 12 August. The Chinese were to store their arms in a warehouse under joint Chinese, Tibetan and Nepalese care. The Chinese troops were to be allowed to make their way unmolested to the Indian frontier. Chinese subjects remaining in Lhasa, such as Chinese traders, would be guaranteed the protection of the Tibetan authorities so long as they obeyed Tibetan laws.[13]

This was welcome news to the Indian Government, which had already made some arrangements for the evacuation through India to China of the Lhasa garrison and other Chinese forces in Tibet. In June, President Yuan Shih-k'ai had requested through Jordan that the Indian Government should help in such an evacuation should it ever become possible; and Jordan had offered the services of his Military Attaché, Lieutenant-Colonel Willoughby, as a liaison officer between the Chinese forces and the Indian authorities, an offer which Yuan gladly accepted. Willoughby had acquired much experience of the Chinese army and its ways, as well as some knowledge of the Chinese language. A few days after the signing of the truce of 12 August he arrived in India; and in early September his Chinese Repatriation Mission began its work on the Sikkim-Tibet border. By the end of November 1912 more than 1,000 Chinese officers and men, as well as some 180 women and children, had passed through his Mission headquarters on their way back to China by way of India. Willoughby, however, did not find that, once the truce was signed, all was plain sailing. Indeed, when in March 1913 he finally left the Sikkim frontier

[13] FO 535/15, no. 168, Viceroy to Secretary of State, 5 August 1912; FO 371/1328, no. 34386, Viceroy to Secretary of State, 12 August 1912; no. 37369, Viceroy to Secretary of State, 3 September 1912.

there were still a few Chinese troops hanging on in Chumbi, where General Chung Ying was exploiting every device he could think of to postpone his own departure.[14]

The Lhasa truce of 12 August, it seemed to British observers on the Tibetan border, involved three distinct bodies of Chinese troops. There were Amban Lien Yü and his escort, General Chung Ying and his bodyguard, and the defenders of Trapchi and Tengyeling, who had by this time long ceased to pay much attention to Chung Ying's orders. The men in Trapchi and Tengyeling, the survivors for the most part of the Pome expedition, were very eager indeed to get out of Tibet if they could do so with reasonable safety; but they were not too happy at the prospect of leaving their weapons in Lhasa, even though the Nepalese representative, Lal Bahadur, pledged that the Tibetans would not be allowed to make use of them: in the end, while leaving their rifles and ammunition, they retained the bolts to their arms, thus making the weapons quite useless. This caused the Tibetans considerable annoyance; and there can be no doubt that some of the more extreme monastic factions in

[14] FO 371/1610, no. 16114, Lieutenant-Colonel M. E. Willoughby, *Report on the work of the Mission engaged in the Repatriation of the Chinese Garrison of Lhasa which surrendered to the Tibetans in August 1912*, Simla, 1912.

Between his arrival on the Sikkim-Tibet border in September 1912 and his departure in late March 1913, nearly 2,000 Chinese men, women and children passed through his camp at Gnatong. A number of pro-Chinese Tibetans and Tibetan camp followers also sought a Chinese exile at this time. By the time Willoughby reached the border a number of Chinese troops had already come down through Sikkim to Calcutta. These were from the Shigatse and Gyantse garrisons.

General Chung Ying, when he finally left Lhasa, brought with him over 600 people, including a number of Tibetan women who had contracted local marriages with Chinese soldiers and who now wished to remain with their husbands.

Willoughby was, on the whole, very impressed by the good behaviour of the Chinese soldiers with whom he had to deal. Though in poor health and with their clothes in tatters, the Chinese troops from Lhasa were by no means an undisciplined rabble; and they gave Willoughby very little trouble while in the Gnatong transit camp.

Some of the Chinese troops from Tibet, particularly from the Shigatse and Gyantse garrisons, showed no desire to return to China and wished to settle in the Darjeeling district. A few Chinese appear to have been given permission to remain in British India. One wonders what the present fate of their descendants may be, given the prevailing state of Sino-Indian relations.

the capital had hoped to be able to wipe out the Chinese invaders with their own surrendered weapons. There was also much argument about the size of the sum of money which the Tibetan authorities would provide to meet the travelling expenses of the Chinese troops between Lhasa and the Indian border. By the middle of September, however, the Trapchi and Tengyeling men were on their way to Chumbi; and by the middle of October most of them had crossed over into India and set out on the final stages of their journey home. The problem of the withdrawal of Amban Lien Yü's party and of General Chung Ying and his bodyguard was not so easily solved.

In early September Chung Ying received orders from Peking appointing him Amban (or its Republican equivalent) at Lhasa in place of Lien Yü. Chung Ying was instructed to remain in the Tibetan capital, while Lien Yü was told to return to China. Chung Ying, accordingly, informed the Tibetans that he, and his personal escort, would stay where they were. He argued that this was no breach of the truce of 12 August, which only concerned those Chinese troops who had come to Lhasa since the beginning of 1910. There had always been an Amban and escort in the Tibetan capital. In staying on he was but complying with a well-established practice.[15] The Tibetans, who had hoped to see the last of the Chinese, were not prepared to accept this interpretation; and they lost no time in declaring that the 12 August truce had been violated. Amban Lien Yü, also, was disturbed by Chung Ying's decision. He was not convinced that the orders which had put Chung Ying in his place were, in fact, valid; and he resolved to remain in Tibet until the position had been clarified. He did, however, withdraw from Lhasa to a safer place, a few miles north of Gyantse, whence, if the need arose, he could run for shelter within the limits of the British Trade Agency. Both Lien Yü and Chung Ying were at this moment virtually out of contact with their superiors in Szechuan and Peking, since the British, in August, had decided to close the Indo-Tibetan frontier to nearly all Chinese communications as part of their policy of trying to force Yuan Shih-k'ai to open formal negotiations over the whole question of the future status of Tibet.[16]

[15] FO 535/15, no. 255, Viceroy to Secretary of State, 17 October 1912.
[16] See pp. 432, 435, below.

With Chung Ying's decision to remain in Lhasa, fighting again broke out in the Tibetan capital. Lien Yü, under considerable moral pressure from young Basil Gould, who was then acting as Gyantse Trade Agent, had by the beginning of November made his way by slow stages to Chumbi, still hoping to hear something definite from Peking.[17] Chung Ying by the end of November began to show signs of a weakening resolve, it becoming less and less likely that any relief force from the east would be able to reach him in the foreseeable future; but he declared that he would not agree to a truce with the Tibetans unless it were arranged under British supervision.[18] The Dalai Lama then proposed that Gould should go up to Lhasa from Gyantse for this purpose; which plan was perforce rejected by Lord Hardinge on the grounds that a British official visit to the Tibetan capital involved a breach of the Anglo-Russian Convention of 1907.[19]

On 11 December Amban Lien Yü finally crossed over into Sikkim from Chumbi, thus abandoning all hope that a change in the Chinese fortunes of war might restore him to office.[20] Chung Ying was now thinking very seriously of withdrawing from Lhasa. In the last week of November his position had improved somewhat. He had managed, it seems, to capture the warehouse where all the surrendered Chinese arms were stored, a *coup* which put him in a very strong bargaining posture *vis-à-vis* the Tibetan Government.[21] He agreed, therefore, to reopen negotiations with the Tibetans, again through the mediation of the Nepalese representative, Lal Bahadur; and on 14 December a fresh truce agreement was signed. The surrendered Chinese arms were to be placed under Nepalese guard, and not handed over to the Tibetans before Chung Ying and his party reached Chumbi. The Tibetans would provide transport and food for the Chinese during their withdrawal.

[17] FO 371/1329, no. 49528, Gould to India, 26 October 1912.

[18] FO 535/15, no. 284, IO to FO, 11 November 1912.

During the latter part of 1912 Chung Ying was in more or less constant touch with the British at the Gyantse Trade Agency. For some reason Chung Ying always addressed the Trade Agent in French.

[19] FO 371/1329, no. 51046, Viceroy to Secretary of State, 29 November 1912.

[20] FO 535/15, no. 304, Viceroy to Secretary of State, 12 December 1912.

[21] FO 535/15, no. 305, Viceroy to Secretary of State, 13 December 1912.

The Dalai Lama's Government promised to take no reprisals against either the Chinese traders who might choose to stay behind in Tibet or the monks of Tengyeling monastery who had fought so well on the Chinese side. The Amban's Yamen and other official Chinese buildings in Lhasa would be handed over to the Tibetans, who would then seal their doors pending a decision on the disposal of their contents. Chung Ying's party were guaranteed an unmolested passage to the Indian frontier.[22] On 16 December Chung Ying surrendered his arms according to this agreement, and on 19 December he and his party, which included many Chinese civilians, traders and their families, were escorted out of Lhasa by a Nepalese officer and sixteen Gurkha soldiers of the Nepalese Residency guard.[23]

A few days later Chung Ying reached Gyantse, where he called on Gould, the acting British Trade Agent. 'He was', Gould later wrote, 'a mountain of a man, several inches over six feet, and broad and thick in proportion.' Gould asked him to a Christmas dinner of 'turkey and the usual trimmings' at which Chung Ying ate four double helpings of everything and then returned to his camp to have what he described as 'a proper meal'.[24] From Gyantse, Chung Ying made his way to Chumbi, where he received his first clear orders from Peking for many months. He was told to remain in Tibet for as long as he possibly could, and he accordingly settled down for a protracted stay in the Chumbi Valley. In the middle of February he was reported to have married a Chumbi Tibetan girl.[25]

The continued presence of Chung Ying in Tibet was intensely irritating to the British. There were Indian suggestions that he might perhaps be forced out if he did not leave of his own accord, suggestions which Lord Crewe had no difficulty in rejecting.[26] Both the Tibetans and the British requested President Yuan Shih-k'ai to order Chung Ying to leave, but with no result.[27] Chung Ying, once settled in Chumbi, began to busy himself

---

[22] FO 535/16, no. 181, Gould to Bell, 14 February 1913.

[23] FO 535/15, no. 321, Viceroy to Secretary of State, 28 December 1912.

[24] B. J. Gould, *The Jewel in the Lotus, recollections of an Indian Political*, London, 1957, p. 25.

[25] FO 535/16, no. 104, Viceroy to Secretary of State, 23 February 1913.

[26] PEF 1913/16, no. 672/13, Viceroy to Secretary of State, 22 and 23 February 1913; FO 535/16, no. 114, IO to FO, 26 February 1913.

[27] FO 535/16, no. 116, Viceroy to Secretary of State, 28 February 1913.

with intrigues with the Nepalese, who did not appear unwilling to allow the uncertain situation in Tibet to continue: it gave them opportunities for direct intervention in Tibetan politics to the great increase in their prestige.[28] Chung Ying also was in clandestine correspondence with the Panchen Lama. His schemes were much encouraged by the main Chinese secret agent in India at that time, one Lu Hsing-chi, who ran a trading firm in Calcutta, the Thinyik Co. Through Lu Hsing-chi, Chung Ying was kept informed of the progress of Chinese plans in Eastern Tibet for the launching of an offensive for the recapture of Lhasa; and no doubt a revived hope for relief from the east strengthened his determination to hold on.[29]

By the beginning of March 1913, however, Chung Ying's position in Chumbi was becoming increasingly precarious. He had established his headquarters in the premises of the Chinese customs at Yatung, very close to the British border, where he evidently hoped that the British would protect him.[30] However, Tibetan troops were concentrating in Chumbi. By the middle of March over 250 armed Tibetans had cut him off from all contact with the north.[31] At the same time, he found that he was coming under attack in Peking, to which, in early February, Lien Yü had returned to intrigue against the man who had displaced him in Tibet.[32] Lien Yü blamed the whole Tibetan crisis on Chung Ying, whose brutality, he declared, had caused the Tibetans to rise against the Chinese. Lien Yü seems to have intrigued with skill. When Chung Ying eventually did return to China he was arrested, put on trial and executed by Yuan Shih-k'ai's Government for his Tibetan crimes.[33]

Faced with increasing Tibetan pressure in Chumbi and with

[28] FO 535/16, no. 198, Lieutenant-Colonel Showers to India, 11 March 1913.

[29] See pp. 402–411.

[30] FO 535/16, no. 148, Jordan to Grey, 23 March 1913.

[31] FO 535/16, no. 141, Viceroy to Secretary of State, 18 March 1913.

[32] FO 535/16, no. 163, Jordan to Grey, 5 March 1913.

[33] Teichman, *Eastern Tibet*, op. cit., p. 40. Chung Ying was executed in 1915. His chief crime was alleged to have been the murder of Lo Ch'ing-ch'i, the commander of the Pome expedition. There can be little doubt that Chung Ying was in this particular instance quite innocent. The Presidential Mandate of 22 March 1915, which outlines the case against Chung Ying, is based almost entirely on evidence provided by Lien Yü.

Lien Yü's intrigues in Peking, Chung Ying at last decided that he had no alternative but to cross over into Sikkim. Many of his followers had been doing this already during January and February. On 14 April, with about thirty companions, Chung Ying left Tibet for India, reaching Kalimpong a week later. He was a very worried man. He had, it is true, received permission from Peking via Lu Hsing-chi and the Thinyik Co. to leave, but he had also been told privately that if he did so his family in China would suffer and he himself would be decapitated.[34] As it turned out, this information was quite correct. Chung Ying's departure from Chumbi marked the end of that Chinese military domination of the Dalai Lama's dominions which had begun in February 1910 with the arrival of Chao Erh-feng's flying column under Chung Ying's command. The Chinese did not return to Central Tibet until forty-nine years later, but at no point between Chung Ying's final departure from Chumbi and the 'peaceful liberation' of Tibet in 1951 did they abandon their efforts to do so.

[34] FO 371/1611, no. 28928, Bell to India, 13 May 1913.

XX

THE CHINESE REACTION

I. THE NATURE OF REPUBLICAN CHINESE
CENTRAL ASIAN POLICY

THE Chinese Revolution which broke out in late 1911 had the profoundest effects upon the structure of Chinese society and politics. It did not, however, bring about any fundamental change in the nature of Chinese policy towards the Central Asian territories, though it may have resulted in some modifications in the language in which that policy was traditionally expressed. The Chinese Republic, from the day of its birth, showed every intention of holding on to Sinkiang, Tibet and Mongolia. When Tibet and Mongolia did slip from its grasp the Republic emphasised that this was but a temporary state of affairs which would not be accepted for long in Peking.

As far as Tibet was concerned, the Republic followed two distinct, though closely related, lines of action. On the one hand, it did its utmost to persuade the Tibetan people and authorities that their best interests lay in a continuation of the traditional relationship with China. The Republic being influenced by the concepts of European and American political thought, an element of self-determination was injected into Chinese Central Asian policy which had been notably absent in the Manchu period. It was argued that the Tibetans and Mongols, not to mention the Moslems of Turkestan, were all members of the family of the Chinese nation; and care was taken that representatives of the Central Asian peoples should attend Republican assemblies. Just as China, by the Revolution, had entered into an age of reform which would convert the country into a modern state capable of fending off the aggressions of the Powers, so should the Tibetans, Mongols and Moslems join in this great adventure. In Central Asia this kind of doctrine had its social implications. The concept of the Chinese Republic as a partnership of the five races, Chinese, Manchu, Mongol, Moslem and Tibetan, contained within it a threat to those feudal classes of Central Asia, lay and spiritual, upon whom the Manchus had until very recently based their policy. Many Chinese supporters of the Republic were indeed strongly anti-feudal in their outlook; but the advisers whom President Yuan Shih-k'ai gathered round him appreciated that it might well be necessary to come to terms with the Tibetan lama hierarchy and the tribal chieftains of Mongolia and Sinkiang. In Tibet, at least, the Chinese endeavoured to minimise the suggestion that the Republic was out to destroy the power of princes and lamas by proposing the return of something superficially very like the old Manchu apparatus for the application of Chinese power. President Yuan went to great lengths in an attempt to win over the Dalai Lama to his side, a policy which was followed with considerable assiduity in Nationalist days. He tried, when the Dalai Lama showed himself unwilling to be wooed, to turn to the Panchen Lama. Here he was rather more successful, though the scheme did not bear fruit in Yuan Shih-k'ai's lifetime. In 1923 the sixth Panchen Lama was to flee from Tibet and take refuge in China. His successor, the seventh (and present) Incarnation, was to be from the moment of his selection a Chinese puppet.

The policy of winning over the Tibetans, either by popular appeal or by intrigue with the authorities, was accompanied by a very real Chinese threat, the mailed fist in the velvet glove. The Chinese, from 1912 onwards, never for one moment gave up their plans for the repetition of Chao Erh-feng's feat, the occupation of Central Tibet by forces advancing from Chinese positions in the Marches. There were times, as in the years following the truce of Rongbatsa in 1918, when the Marches quietened down and the Sino-Tibetan border appeared to have been stabilised. But these were no more than enforced pauses while the Chinese devoted their main attention else-where, against the Japanese and then against the Communists. The Tibetans were intended to realise, and there can be no doubt that many Tibetan politicians did so realise, that it was

wiser to come to voluntary terms with the Chinese when they
were weak than to be forced to accept Chinese dictation from
a position of strength. This moral President Yuan Shih-k'ai did
his utmost to point to; and Chiang Kai-shek and Mao Tse-tung,
whatever their ideological differences in other respects, would be
in agreement with Yuan on this point.

To analyse the Chinese reaction to the events in Tibet which
followed the outbreak of the Chinese Revolution, we must consider both these lines of policy. Though related, they are not
always executed in strict phase with each other. There is a
history of Chinese attempts to persuade the Tibetans, people
and lamas, to join the Chinese Republican family. There is a
history of projects for Tibetan conquest by military commanders
in Szechuan and Yunnan Provinces. Sometimes these histories
are the product of the same master plan. More often they are
not. The Chinese authorities in the Marches, from the outset of
the Republican era, were under but the loosest rein from Peking;
and at times they were virtually independent. Both Yunnan
and Szechuan had their quota of civil wars, and there were
occasions when the two Provinces fought against each other.
Thus, during the period covered by the remaining pages of this
book, it is not always easy to extract from the complex story of
Sino-Tibetan relations anything like an effective unified policy,
beyond a general feeling on the part of all Chinese leaders that
Tibet had always belonged in some way to China and should
not be allowed to pass from China's grasp. There is, however, a
danger that the lack of control of Peking over the Szechuan and
Yunnan Provinces, especially the former, which had the main
interest in the affairs of Eastern Tibet, can be exaggerated.
When, for example, the British protested to the Peking Government against some fresh reported proposal by Szechuan for
Tibetan conquest, it was very convenient for the Chinese
Foreign Office, the Wai-chiao-pu,[1] to be able to express regret

[1] The Wai-chiao-pu was the Chinese Republican Foreign Office. Until
1861 the Chinese did not possess a Foreign Office as such, relations with
tributary and other states being conducted through a wide range of central
and provincial bodies. In 1861, under pressure from the Powers, the Tsungli
Yamen was instituted by Imperial Decree as a central organ for the conduct
of Chinese foreign relations. The Tsungli Yamen was given its final form in
1864, when it was subdivided into five bureaux, four concerned with various
groups of Powers and one dealing with naval matters. The Tsungli Yamen

but also to observe that at present it could do nothing with those Szechuanese rebels. It is certainly possible that the power of the Central Government over the Provinces in early Republican days has been somewhat underestimated by Western historians.

Whatever the true nature of the relationship between Peking and Yunnan and Szechuan might be, however, there can be no doubt that from the point of view of ease of presentation there is much to be said for keeping the history of the fortunes of Chinese arms in the Tibetan Marches separate from the story of Chinese negotiations and intrigues with the authorities in Central Tibet. This expedient, at all events, will be adopted here. One section will deal with Chinese policy towards Lhasa and the Dalai and Panchen Lamas and their direct subjects; another will treat with matters relating to Eastern Tibet and the Tibetan hopes and failures of the Szechuanese and Yunnanese Governments.[2]

2. WOOING THE TIBETANS: YUAN SHIH-K'AI'S APPLICATION OF THE POLICY OF THE UNION OF THE FIVE RACES

From the outset the Chinese Republic resolved to include within its representative assemblies delegates from Tibet, Mongolia

---

[2] For a most stimulating study of Chinese external policy in modern times, indeed, at all time, I most strongly urge the reader to consult C. P. Fitzgerald, *The Chinese View of their Place in the World*, Chatham House Essays No. 1, London 1964.

---

survived until the Boxer troubles. In 1901, as part of the Chinese settlement with the Powers, the Tsungli Yamen became a full Ministry of the Manchu Imperial Government—it had hitherto been no more than a Government Board—with precedence over other Ministries. As such, it became known as the Wai-wu-pu. The Wai-wu-pu, like the Tsungli Yamen, was divided into bureaux, some of which dealt with such matters as mining, railway and telegraph concession, with customs, and with frontier affairs. Diplomatic relations with the Powers were carried on through the Bureau of Harmonious Intercourse. With the Republic the Wai-wu-pu was reorganised along more Western lines and became the Wai-chiao-pu. As such, with further changes in internal organisation, it survived to the end of the Kuomintang era.

See L. Tung, *China and Some Phases of International Law*, London, 1940, pp. 105–10; Y. C. Chang, 'The Organization of the Waichiaopu', *Chinese Social and Political Science Review*, Vol. 1, 1916.

and Sinkiang, thus indicating that the Central Asian peoples had as much to gain from the Revolution as the inhabitants of the eighteen provinces of China proper.[3] In early 1912 Yuan Shih-k'ai, well aware of the value of the spiritual support of the Dalai Lama, made overtures through the Yellow Temple in Peking to the leaders of the Tibetan Buddhist Church in the hope that it might be persuaded to rally to the side of the new Republic. In March 1912, in an attempt to persuade the Central Asian peoples that a new deal awaited them in Peking and that Chinese officials no longer intended to treat them as inferior beings, Yuan issued a most significant Decree. This document, dated 25 March, was to cause the British considerable anxiety; and they were to protest against its implications. It read as follows:

> Our people of Mongolia and Tibet, followers of the old religion, used to be a buttress on our North West Frontier, contented and loyal. But of late years the frontier officials have ill-performed their duties and have subjugated these pon-tiffs . . . [the Dalai and Panchen Lamas and the Urga Incarnation] . . . to grievous oppression . . . But now that the form of government has been changed to a Republic, and the five races . . . [Chinese, Tibetans, Mongols, Manchus, Moslems] . . . have been placed on a footing of equality, I, the President, do take a most solemn and unchangeable oath that all the oppression and irregular measures of the past will be abolished and done away with. Mongolia and Tibet should therefore all the more follow the wishes of the people as a whole, and should maintain peace and good order.[4]

In a Decree of 13 April President Yuan added that:

> The Five Races—Chinese, Manchu, Mongol, Mahommedan and Tibetan—are hereby exhorted each to intermarry freely with each other, firstly, in order to do away with the tradition of social distinction, and, secondly, in order to cultivate affection.[5]

Yuan Shih-k'ai, therefore, announced that all barriers against such a mingling of the races were now declared unlawful by the

[3] FO 535/15, no. 9, FO to IO, 13 January 1912.
[4] FO 371/1326, no. 16605, Jordan to Grey, 31 March 1912.
[5] FO 371/1326, no. 20650, Jordan to Grey, 27 April 1912.

Republic. Returning to this theme in a Decree (or Presidential Order) of 21 April 1912, Yuan added some remarks of great interest on the Republican concept of the political status of Tibet, which in many ways disagreed with the idea of Tibetan status which the Indian Government was hoping would now prevail. He declared that:

> Now that the Five Races are joined in democratic union, the lands comprised within the confines of Mongolia, Tibet and Turkestan all become a part of the territory of the Republic of China, and the races inhabiting these lands are all equally citizens of the Republic of China. The term *dependencies*, as used under the Monarchy, must therefore cease to be used, and henceforth as regards Mongolia, Turkestan and Tibet a complete scheme must be devised to arrive at a unified system of administration, and so promote unity in general among all races of the Republic. The reason why the Republican Government did not create a special Ministry to deal with dependencies was that Mongolia, Turkestan and Tibet are regarded on an equal footing with the provinces of China proper. For the future all administrative matters in connection with these territories will come within the sphere of internal administration. Now that the establishment of a single united Government is an accomplished fact, let all matters formerly dealt with by the Ministry of Dependencies be forthwith transferred to the control of the Ministry of the Interior, and all matters which belong to the province of other Ministries be handed over to the Ministries respectively concerned. Until the local politics have all been brought into harmony, all matters in Mongolia, Turkestan and Tibet should be dealt with in accordance with existing procedure. [6]

Part of the process of bringing the local politics of Tibet 'into harmony' involved the restoration of Chinese military power in Central Tibet by means of an expedition sent out from Szechuan: this we will consider later on. [7] A measure of harmony, however, and an increasingly important one as successive Szechuan projects aborted, could be achieved through negotiation and persuasion without the application of armed force, a fact which Yuan Shih-k'ai kept in mind throughout the period of the siege

[6] FO 371/1326, no. 20650, Jordan to Grey, 27 April 1912; FO 535/15, no. 67.

[7] See pp. 402–11.

of the Lhasa garrisons and which he did not ignore even after Chung Ying had finally left Tibetan soil for Sikkim.

Much recent writing on Tibet by European or American authors, and especially the works of Sir Charles Bell and Hugh Richardson, has presented an image of a Tibetan people united in their opposition to and dislike of all things Chinese. This, there can be little doubt, is a rather distorted picture. It is possible that few Tibetans were particularly taken with the idea of Chinese rule as such; and an opinion poll on the Tibetan Plateau in 1912 would certainly have produced an overwhelming 'No' to the question 'Would you like to see the Chinese back where they were in 1910?' On the other hand, the Chinese and Tibetans had been dealing with each other for a long time. China was the centre of sophisticated civilisation to which Tibetans looked. The Tibetan Buddhist Church was in a very real sense a part of the Chinese official establishment. The bulk of Tibetan trade in the early twentieth century was still with China; and upon this trade many influential Tibetan families depended for their fortunes. Tea, that essential substance in the Tibetan cuisine, was obtained from China; and even in the height of the 1912 crisis the Dalai Lama's Government gave no signs that it would welcome the replacement of Chinese tea by the Indian product, that dream of many mid-Victorian British 'pioneers of commerce'. In the years following the withdrawal of the Younghusband Mission the Chinese never seemed to experience serious difficulty in finding Tibetans to collaborate with them. After the Tibetans had turned on the Chinese in Central Tibet in early 1912, some of the leading collaborators had met with unpleasant fates. Tsarong Shape, the Tibetan representative who had signed the Trade Regulations of 1908, was put to death in the spring of 1912, along with his wife and two of his sons.[8] But many officials of the era of Chang Yin-tang and Lien Yü certainly survived, who did not dismiss entirely from their minds the possibility of coming to some compromise settlement with China. Some of the great Lhasa monasteries, always a powerful force in Tibetan politics, were fanatically opposed to the Chinese. Sera and Gaden played a prominent part in the attacks on the Lhasa garrisons. Yet it seems certain that Drebung was definitely lukewarm in its hostility to China; and one smaller monastery, Tengyeling,

[8] FO 371/1327, no. 29195, Yatung Trade Agency Diary, May 1912.

actively sided with the Chinese forces (which, in 1913, was to result in the total destruction of its buildings on the orders of the vengeful Dalai Lama). There were good reasons, therefore, why Yuan Shih-k'ai should continue to hope, despite the setbacks to Chinese arms, that some retention in Lhasa of the symbols of Chinese power could be secured through negotiation.

The Chinese possessed in their hand two cards of considerable value. The Panchen Lama, in the days since his visit to India, had on the whole tended to side with the Chinese, though he had done the best he could to hedge his bets and win the goodwill of the Dalai Lama's faction as well. The Chinese could reasonably assume that, with the collapse of their power in Lhasa, the Panchen Lama had become a very worried Incarnation indeed; and they could further anticipate that, however cordial the initial meeting between the Panchen and Dalai Lamas might be on the latter's return from Indian exile, yet sooner or later tensions would arise between the two theocrats which the Chinese might possibly exploit. The Dalai Lama, who in 1912 was certainly not in a strong enough position to dispose once and for all of his rival in Tashilhumpo, might well be shown that the best way to keep his competitor in his place was through relations with China.

A second weapon in the Chinese diplomatic armoury was Nepal. Previous chapters of this book have demonstrated that in every stage of the Tibetan crisis since Curzon, early in the twentieth century, decided that a threat of Russian intrigue in Lhasa existed, the Nepalese had been considered as a factor by the framers of British policy. Throughout 1912 the Nepalese had been diplomatically active in Tibet, and we have seen that their mediation greatly facilitated the eventual withdrawal of the Chinese forces from Lhasa. To some degree Nepalese interests in Tibet coincided with those of the Indian Government. In Katmandu there was no desire to see a strong power, be it Chinese or Russian, established to the north, where the Gurkha rulers had never quite abandoned their hopes for territorial conquest. Yet a Tibet quite free of Chinese influence, so astute Rana statesmen must surely have appreciated, would be a Tibet in danger of becoming a British protectorate in all but name. If so, then Nepal would be completely surrounded by districts controlled by the Indian Government; and this was not to Nepalese taste at all. The Nepalese, therefore, had good reason for hoping that out of the Tibetan crisis of 1912 would emerge, not an independent Tibet looking to British India, but rather a Tibet where the Chinese had recovered their powers such as they were in the days before the Younghusband Mission so disrupted the Tibetan political scene, strong enough to give the lie to claims of Tibetan independence yet not so strong as to overshadow the prestige of Katmandu. Thus the Nepalese did not look unfavourably on Chinese attempts to bring back to Lhasa something along the lines of an Amban and escort of ceremonial functions.

To the Tibetans, moreover, Nepal remained in 1912 what she had been since the late eighteenth century, a threat. The Gurkhas, in the 1780s, had invaded Tibet on two occasions. In the 1850s they had once more gone to war with the Lhasa Government and imposed upon it terms of peace which the Dalai Lama probably found somewhat humiliating. It seemed very likely that Tibet, once it was standing on its own feet, would again have to face Nepalese demands for territorial or economic concessions. Alone, the Tibetans were no match for the Gurkha army. They would, in such circumstances, have to turn either to China or to British India. The latter move, however much the Dalai Lama might personally favour it, would certainly be unpopular in many Tibetan circles: and, moreover, there was no guarantee that the British, in fact, would help. The Tibetans could hardly have failed to realise the importance which the Indian Government attached to the steady, uninterrupted flow of Gurkha recruits into the Indian Army. The Chinese, therefore, could argue with considerable force that they alone could protect Tibet from its aggressive Nepalese neighbour.

Chung Ying was certainly aware of the importance of Nepal, and so, it seems, was Yuan Shih-k'ai. In February 1913, when Chung Ying had given up his positions in Lhasa and was making his last struggles to keep a foothold in Tibet at all, in Chumbi, he proposed to the Peking Government that he should be authorised to approach Nepal with a suggestion that she enter formally 'the community of the five races'. Quite what this meant was not clear. Probably Chung Ying had in mind some Nepalese declaration of identity of interest with the Chinese. Peking was much taken with Chung Ying's idea; and on 13

February 1913 Chung wrote to the Nepalese Prime Minister to propose that Nepal be united with the five races and that, in witness of this fact, it should send a mission to Peking at once to congratulate the Republic on its birth. Here was an attempt to revive the old Nepalese tribute missions in a Republican form; and had the Nepalese agreed, there can be no doubt that the Tibetan authorities would have been much impressed. The Nepalese turned Chung Ying down, but quite politely: 'As Nepal is an ancient Hindu kingdom', the Prime Minister wrote, 'desirous of preserving her independence and her separate existence, she cannot entertain the idea of a union with the five affiliated races said to constitute the Republic of China.' Thus, at this stage the Chinese failed to win Nepalese acknowledgment of the Republic; but, even so, they were able to demonstrate the existence of some sort of relations between Peking and Katmandu and, by implication, that they could be of service to the Tibetans in persuading the Nepalese to act towards their northern neighbour with restraint.[9]

Chinese arguments were intended to convince the authorities in Central Tibet that it would be wise to come to some terms with the Republic and to agree to keep on in Lhasa a Republican successor to the Manchu post of Amban. It was implied that a distinction should be drawn between the Chinese forces who occupied Lhasa in early 1910, and who may well have been acting in breach of old arrangements, on the one hand, and the Amban and his traditional escort on the other. The Republic, so this presentation of the case ran, was not responsible for the excesses of Chao Erh-feng; and it was prepared to bring a fresh spirit to the conduct of Sino-Tibetan relations. Thus, in the early summer of 1912, Lien Yü told the Tibetans that he would be willing to agree to the surrender of all the Chinese forces then in Lhasa if the Tibetans, in return, would accept the continued presence in Lhasa of a Chinese representative with a suitable escort, which, according to Lien Yü, meant about 500 men.[10] It was only after Lien Yü came to realise that, whatever the outcome of the Tibetan crisis, it was very unlikely that Yuan Shih-k'ai would allow him to continue as Amban, that he

[9] FO 535/16, no. 83, Viceroy to Secretary of State, 8 February 1913; no. 198, Lieutenant-Colonel Showers to India, 11 March 1913.

[10] FO 371/1327, no. 25314, Viceroy to Secretary of State, 13 June 1912.

decided to give up his defence of the Amban's Yamen in Lhasa. Chung Ying's stand, likewise, was partly inspired by the hope that eventually the Tibetans would come to understand the value of having a Chinese representative in their capital, and would acknowledge that he had, in fact, taken over from Lien Yü as Amban.

Until August 1912 the Chinese had relied mainly upon Lien Yü and Chung Ying to put their case to the Tibetans. As the Tibetan crisis developed, however, and the position of the Chinese forces in Lhasa deteriorated, Yuan Shih-k'ai decided to explore other diplomatic approaches. One obvious measure was to send to Tibet a delegation of pro-Chinese Lamas who might argue the case for the continued Tibetan acceptance of Chinese suzerainty. Such a party, composed mainly of Mongols under the leadership of a Chinese official, Yang Feng by name, arrived in Darjeeling in early September 1912 with the intention of making its way to the Dalai Lama's place of residence in Tibet. Yang Feng was disguised as a monk, and the Chinese evidently hoped that he and his party would be able to cross the Tibetan border without attracting the attention of the British authorities. Indian intelligence, however, had improved considerably since the days of Curzon's administration when Dorjiev could pass unnoticed through British territory on his way to Russia. The true nature of Yang Feng's mission was discovered. It came to light, moreover, that his brother, Yang Fong, who was also a member of the party, had already been to Darjeeling in early 1910 when he had tried to persuade the Dalai Lama to return to Tibet and make his peace with the Chinese. The Indian Government, following a policy it had recently decided upon (which we will discuss later on), refused permission for this mission—the Lama Mission it came to be called—to cross the Indian border.[11] Yang Feng was obliged to reconcile himself to a long wait in Sikkim; and he was still to be seen in Kalimpong and Darjeeling by May 1913.[12]

[11] FO 535/15, no. 198, Viceroy to Secretary of State, 4 September 1912; no. 200, Grey to Jordan, 7 September 1912; no. 206, FO to IO, 11 September 1912.

[12] FO 371/1611, no. 23143, IO to FO, 19 May 1913; no. 25572, IO to FO, 2 June 1913. At the very end of May 1913 Yang Feng gave up and went to Calcutta, where he disappears from the records.

During this time he busied himself in minor intrigues, and managed to complicate slightly, so Lieutenant-Colonel Willoughby thought, the process of the repatriation of the Chinese garrisons in Tibet.[13]

While prevented from entering Tibet, Yang Feng was allowed to communicate with the Dalai Lama by way of the telegraph to Gyantse, his Tibetan messages, of course, as well as his telegraphic instructions from Peking, being carefully monitored by the Indian Government. Thus the British soon learned the nature of the proposals which Yuan Shih-k'ai had authorised Yang Feng to make on his behalf. A general discussion of the whole Tibetan question was to be opened between Yang Feng and the Dalai Lama. The Dalai Lama, it was hoped, would accept the retention of a Chinese representative in Lhasa, who would be Chung Ying. The Chinese were to point out that all the crises in Sino-Tibetan relations were due to the ineptitude of the Manchus, for which the Republic should not be blamed. If the Dalai Lama accepted the Republic, then Yuan Shih-k'ai would forgive him for his past actions against the Chinese and would restore to him all his titles. The Chinese, Yang Feng was told to promise, would offer some form of compensation for the damage done by the Lhasa garrisons during the troubles. Yuan Shih-k'ai, he was to conclude, hoped to send soon to Tibet a senior official who would investigate and who would be empowered to redress wrongs. If the Tibetans did not accept these overtures, Yang Feng was to hint, they might have to face the consequences of military reconquest by a force from Szechuan. These points were all put to the Dalai Lama on 27–29 November 1912. It was also then announced publicly that the Lama's titles had been restored and that Chung Ying had been formally appointed the new Amban.[14]

What the Dalai Lama made of Yang Feng's proposals is not known. Possibly he was more inclined to listen to Chinese offers than he had indicated to his British friends like Sir Charles Bell. At all events, Yuan Shih-k'ai appears to have concluded that a

[13] FO 371/1610, no. 16114, Willoughby's *Report*. Willoughby described Yang Feng as a patriotic Republican, about 27 years old, a native of Jehol, who spoke a very little English.

[14] FO 371/1329, no. 55846, intercepted Chinese telegrams dated 27 and 29 November 1912.

high Chinese official, bent on a mission of investigation and reconciliation, would, in fact, be received by the Tibetans.[15] On 15 November 1912 it was announced in Peking that one Fu Shih-yen, a graduate of the Academy of Frontier Affairs and a member of the Department of Mongolia and Tibet, had been appointed to a mission to Tibet to bring its leaders and people back into harmony with the other four races of the Chinese family. Fu Shih-yen, it was reported, was so enthusiastic about the task which had been entrusted to him that he actually offered to meet, out of his own pocket, all his expenses on the journey to and from Tibet.[16] Fu's mission does not seem to have progressed beyond the planning stage; but it represents a policy which the Republic did not easily abandon. Other officials were to be appointed to investigate the Tibetan situation; and the Simla Conference can in a sense be interpreted as an incidental consequence of one such appointment.

At the very beginning of 1913 the Indian Government learnt that yet another Chinese had been deputed to go to Tibet to try to put the case to the Dalai Lama and his supporters. This was a certain Lu Hsing-chi, whom the British were soon to consider the 'head of the Chinese Secret Service in India', and to think very seriously about deporting under Section 3 of the Foreigners Act III of 1864.[17] Lu Hsing-chi was connected with a Calcutta trading firm, the Thinyik Co., which had played an important part in arranging for the repatriation of the Chinese garrisons in Tibet through India. Whether this company had been established purely for political purposes, or whether its management, out of patriotism, had taken up political work in addition to the normal commercial operations, is not clear. Nor do we know the precise nature of Lu Hsing-chi's relationship with the

[15] It is not easy to interpret Tibetan attitudes towards their international status at this period. On the one hand they were certainly prepared to maintain some contact with the Chinese: on the other, as in the case of the letter which the *Tsongdu*, the Tibetan National Assembly, addressed to Lord Hardinge on 1 October 1912, they declared that they had broken off all connections with China, which was tantamount to a declaration of Tibetan political independence.

[16] FO 371/1329, no. 49006, Jordan to Grey, 30 October 1912; no. 55585, Jordan to Grey, 14 December 1912.

[17] PEF 1913/19, no. 1021/14, IO minutes on Viceroy to Secretary of State, 14 March 1914.

firm. Since October 1912, at all events, Lu had been one of the main channels of communication between President Yuan Shih-k'ai in Peking and the Chinese officials on the Tibetan border: and during the course of 1913 he was to emerge as one of the chief architects, and a very able one at that, of Chinese Tibetan policy. With Chung Ying's final withdrawal from Chumbi Lu Hsing-chi became the spearhead, as it were, of the Chinese diplomatic offensive against Central Tibet; and he eventually became, in place of Chung Ying, President Yuan's candidate for the office of Amban.

Lu Hsing-chi's mission was to keep some Chinese contact with the Tibetan and neighbouring authorities whatever the vicissitudes of Chinese military fortunes in Central Asia. It was Lu, it seems, who advised Chung Ying to attempt to open discussions with the Gurkhas on the question of Nepalese union with the family of the five races. It was Lu who encouraged Chung Ying to hold out in Chumbi even after he had been obliged to abandon Lhasa. After Chung Ying disappeared finally from the Tibetan scene, Lu intensified his intrigues with the Tibetans of all factions. His policy was outlined in a series of telegrams to Peking, all of which were intercepted, translated and carefully filed away for future reference by the Indian Government. Lu proposed, in the first place, that the Chinese continue, through conciliatory gestures, to try to win the Tibetans' love as well as their respect; and he advocated that the Tibetans be treated much along the lines proposed in the last days of the Manchu period by the Assistant Amban Wen Tsung-yao. At the same time, the Republican Government should endeavour to penetrate every level of Tibetan society with its own undercover agents: Lu urged a great expansion of the Chinese secret service in Tibet which was then operating under, it would seem, the local tactical command of one Tashi Wangdi. By persuasion or by pressure, Lu advised, the Tibetans should be made to recognise the Republic and to agree to the election of Tibetan representatives to the Chinese Parliament. The Dalai Lama should make his peace with the Chinese in a formal manner, sending a senior officer to Peking for this purpose and agreeing to the opening of Sino-Tibetan talks somewhere on his borders: Lu personally favoured Chamdo, where negotiations would not run the risk of British interference. While accepting the Dalai Lama as the logical head of the Tibetan Government, Lu never overlooked the possibility that it might be necessary to attempt to replace the Dalai Lama in this capacity by the Panchen Lama; he communicated frequently with the Tashilhumpo Incarnation, and his spies were well established in Shigatse.[18]

With Chung Ying's departure Lu Hsing-chi was appointed by Yuan Shih-k'ai to the post of 'Administrator of Tibet', by which we may probably understand the equivalent, in Republican terminology, of the old office of Lhasa Amban. As such, Lu not surprisingly wished to obtain permission to cross over from India to Tibet, permission which the Indian Government resolutely refused to give. In May, President Yuan Shih-k'ai secretly ordered the Dalai Lama to send an escort to the Sikkim border to convey Lu in state to Lhasa; but the Lama took no notice.[19] Lu, as his masters in Peking were beginning to realise more and more clearly, was suffering under considerable diplomatic disadvantage arising from the British resolve, expressed formally to the Peking Government in August 1912, to keep the Indo-Tibetan border firmly closed to all Chinese officials. The Chinese were sometimes allowed to use the telegraph which connected British India to Gyantse; but even the more technically naïve Chinese bureaucrats must have realised that messages sent along this line, by British operators, and in British telegraphic code, would almost certainly be read by Indian intelligence. Only if Lu were established in Tibet could he be free to exert his full diplomatic skill against the Tibetans. Thus throughout the summer of 1913 Lu Hsing-chi continued to look for methods to evade the British prohibition. It was most important, he told Yuan Shih-k'ai on more than one occasion, that he get to Lhasa soon, because:

> Fortunately the Dalai Lama has not hitherto categorically disclaimed allegiance to the Central Government; the British also continue to regard Tibet as a dependency of China; we must cling to these threads of opportunity.[20]

In his correspondence with the Dalai Lama and other leading

[18] FO 535/16, Viceroy to Secretary of State, 30 April 1913; FO 371/1610, no. 17522, IO to FO, 15 April 1913.
[19] PEF 1913/17, no. 2131/13, Viceroy to Secretary of State, 29 May 1913.
[20] FO 535/16, no. 304, Lu to Yuan, 28 May 1913.

Tibetans, Lu was conciliatory in tone, though he occasionally made veiled references to the military expeditions which the Chinese were preparing in Szechuan and Yunnan.[21] This mildness, however, should not delude one into thinking that Lu was advocating a Tibetan policy which diverged in any significant way from that of the majority of Chinese statesmen in Manchu, Republican, Nationalist and Communist times. Referring to Tibet, Lu urged Yuan Shih-k'ai to remember that 'territory formerly subject to the Manchus is now subject to the Republic, and no alteration can be made to its status'.[22] Thus, while advising conciliation towards the Central Tibetan authorities, Lu was also strongly in favour of plans for Tibetan reconquest from Szechuan; and he suggested that as soon as possible Chinese troops renew the Pome campaign which had been so disastrously interrupted by the outbreak of the Revolution.[23]

Lu Hsing-chi during the spring and summer of 1913 repeatedly informed the Dalai Lama that he was empowered to open full discussions on all aspects of the Tibetan problem in Lhasa or some other Tibetan centre. The Dalai Lama maintained that Lu would not be permitted to enter Tibet; but, he said, he would be very pleased to send a high official to talk with Lu at Darjeeling or some other such place on the British side of the Indian border. This proposal, it seems, was first made by the Dalai Lama, who told Bell about it, in late January or early February 1913. The high official the Dalai Lama had in mind for these discussions was the Lönchen Shatra, who, since Tsarong's fall, was the *doyen* of Tibetan politicians, and who, after a period of flirting with the idea of a closer Russo-Tibetan relationship, had now become convinced that only the British could help the thirteenth Dalai Lama maintain himself free from Chinese control. To each overture from Lu Hsing-chi, the Dalai Lama replied with a repeated offer for the opening of talks at Darjeeling; and, as we shall see, this offer eventually became one of the foundations upon which the Simla Conference, which opened in October 1913, was built.[24] With the

[21] FO 535/16, no. 160, Viceroy to Secretary of State, 28 March 1913.

[22] FO 535/16, no. 304, Lu to Yuan, 7 June 1913.

[23] FO 371/1611, no. 27086, IO to FO, 13 June 1913.

[24] FO 371/1609, no. 6124, Viceroy to Secretary of State, 4 February 1913; FO 371/1611, no. 28024, IO to FO, 18 June 1913.

Simla Conference Lu must have realised that his hopes had, for the time being, been frustrated. In late 1913 he left the Tibetan border for Calcutta to attend to his own commercial affairs; but, throughout the Simla Conference of October 1913 to July 1914 he remained a link between the Chinese delegation and Peking, and close attention was paid to his advice. Lu claimed that he was the Chinese Consul in India. The Indian Government refused to recognise him as such; but this did not deter Lu from performing many consular and diplomatic tasks.

The Chinese, though they had failed to persuade the Tibetans to acknowledge of their own free will their dependence to the Republic, never abandoned hope of doing so eventually. The opening of the Simla Conference, which the British regarded as a demonstration of the *de facto* independence of Tibet, was not seen in this light in Peking. On 13 November 1913, for example, when the Conference had been in progress for a month, Yuan Shih-k'ai dissolved the Republican Chinese Parliament and replaced it with an Administrative Council. In this new body he was careful to make provision for four representatives from Mongolia and four from Tibet, thus preparing for the day when Tibet was once more a full member of the Chinese family.[25] In recent times it has been stated that Chinese participation in the Simla Conference implied Chinese recognition of some very real measure of Tibetan independence. As we will see, China meant nothing of the sort. At no point since the outbreak of the Chinese Revolution did Yuan Shih-k'ai or any of his senior officials ever agree that Tibet was anything but part of China. In the official eyes of Peking the Five Races were still united.

3. EASTERN TIBET: PROJECTS FOR FOLLOWING IN THE FOOTSTEPS OF CHAO ERH-FENG

The Chinese Revolution brought about the downfall of Chao Erh-feng and many of his subordinates. Chao himself was executed on the orders of—some said by the very hands of—Yin Ch'ang-heng; and Chao's former second in command, Fu Sung-mu, was put in prison in Chengtu, though his life was

[25] FO 371/1613, no. 52286, Minute by Sir A. Nicolson, 14 November 1913.

spared and he was permitted eventually to retire to private life to write a history of the creation of Sikang Province.[26] The loss of Chao Erh-feng and of so many of the men whom he had trained was a severe blow to Chinese power in Eastern Tibet. It was not, however, of necessity a fatal blow. The Chinese forces in the Marches were undoubtedly still better trained and equipped than any troops at the disposal of the Tibetans. Yin Ch'ang-heng, while a man of lesser calibre than Chao and lacking that prestige which Chao's victories had built up, was a young and energetic commander who, it must have seemed in the early months of 1912, would soon put his house in order and send off an expedition to the relief of the Chinese garrisons besieged in Lhasa. Yin made it clear that the recovery of the Chinese position in Central Tibet was a task to which he gave a high priority.[27]

The Chinese, however, were not ready to march at once from the Marches towards Lhasa. News of the Revolution had brought with it a crop of anti-Chinese risings in Eastern Tibet. Hsiang-ch'eng, which Chao had reduced with such difficulty only a few years before, once more broke away from Chinese control. At Chamdo the Chinese garrison, under the command of P'eng Jih-sheng, found itself under furious attack from the monks, over 3,000 in number, of the great Tibetan monastery in that town. Throughout the Marches, from the Chinese advanced positions on the Mekong River back to the Szechuan border near Tachienlu, lines of communications were exposed to raids by armed nomads. Until order had once again been restored along the main roads, the relief expedition from Szechuan, the despatch of which there is no doubt President Yuan Shih-k'ai had approved, would have to be postponed.

In June, Yin Ch'ang-heng, with the support of the Acting Military Governor of Szechuan Province, Hu Ching-i, at last felt himself ready to launch the expedition which was going to save the Chinese forces in Central Tibet. On 16 June the venture was formally initiated at Chengtu. Yin declared that

[26] Teichman, *Eastern Tibet*, op. cit., p. 33; FO 535/15, no. 41, Wilkinson to Jordan, 1 February 1912; FO 371/1610, no. 17750, Jordan to Grey, 2 April 1913, enclosing a translation of Fu Sung-mu, *History of the Creation of Hsi-kang Province*.

[27] FO 535/15, no. 67, Jordan to Grey, 27 April 1912.

he was invincible. 'I,' he shouted to the assembled crowd, 'exposed the head of Butcher Chao in the midst of the army.' If he had faced Chao Erh-feng, and won, what had he to fear from the Tibetan rabble? The object of the campaign, he stated, was to bring Tibet back into the family of the five races under the Republic. The Tibetans had deserted that family in its hour of trial, and they should be punished. Yin, at this point, was putting some 700 men into the field, the vanguard of an army which was to number at least 8,000, so the Szechuan Government planned.[28]

The opening of the campaign seemed auspicious for the Chinese. By late July, when Yin Ch'ang-heng himself actually reached Tachienlu with, Jordan reported, some 4,000 men, P'eng Jih-sheng had weathered the storm at Chamdo and suppressed the rising of the monks, in the process destroying the great Chamdo monastery.[29] It seemed as if all Yin had to do was to clear the road between Tachienlu and Chamdo, and everything would be set for another dash to Lhasa like that of the flying column which, under Chung Ying's command, had made the Dalai Lama run for India in early 1910. At Tachienlu, Yin divided his force into two columns. One, under General Liu (Liu Jui-heng), was to advance towards Chamdo along the northern road, which ran through Dawu, Kantze and De-ge. The other, under Yin himself, was to push through by the southern road, by way of Litang, Batang and Draya. These two columns, in a giant pincer movement, were to converge on Chamdo, where they would unite for the march to Lhasa. This was in theory a good plan, and one which had been followed by Chao Erh-feng during his pacification of the Marches. Yin Ch'ang-heng, however, did not have troops in sufficient numbers and of suitable quality for the task. Provincial jealousies made him discourage the offers of contingents from Yunnan, which might have joined up with his columns by way of Atuntze; and, for the same reason, he rejected a proposal of President Yuan Shih-k'ai to send 20,000 Hupei troops to his aid. In early September Yin announced that he had cleared the main roads east of Batang, and that the country west of that

[28] FO 535/15, no. 108, Jordan to Grey, 18 June 1912; FO 371/1328, no. 37348, Wilkinson to Jordan, 21 June 1912.
[29] Teichman, *Eastern Tibet*, op. cit., p. 38.

town would soon be in his grasp. Louis King, a British Consular officer then stationed at Chengtu, however, told Jordan that Yin was being very optimistic indeed, and that even in the neighbourhood of Tachienlu Chinese control was anything but unchallenged.[30]

By the end of 1912 it was clear to many observers, Louis King included, that Yin's campaign had bogged down in a series of encounters with elusive Tibetan bands in the wild country between the main Chinese garrisons. In Hsiang-ch'eng the Tibetans, despite repeated reports to the contrary, appeared still to be in control, well equipped with modern rifles captured from the Chinese. Hsiang-ch'eng, in 1912 just as much as in 1905-6, posed a threat to the vital southern road from Tachienlu to Chamdo by way of Litang and Batang; and until Yin restored order here he was unlikely to risk extending his lines of communications westward beyond Chamdo. The Tibetan successes in Hsiang-ch'eng, in fact, made an effective Chinese relief of Chung Ying in Lhasa extremely improbable for the time being. Indeed, there is much evidence to suggest that by September 1912 Yin Ch'ang-heng and Hu Ching-i had given to the reconquest of Central Tibet a secondary priority and had decided that the logical development following the restoration of Chinese control east of Chamdo was the continuation of the policy of Chao Erh-feng and Fu Sung-mu for the creation of the new Chinese Province of Sikang.[31]

Sikang was to be both the administrative nucleus for the total incorporation of Tibet within the provincial structure of the Chinese state and a buffer between China and British India. There can be little doubt that the Chinese authorities, both in Chengtu and in Peking, believed that the British had more imperialistic intentions towards Tibet than the protestations of Sir John Jordan would suggest. The Abor Expedition and the Mishmi Mission were discussed with much apprehension in the Chinese press. A Chengtu newspaper, the *Kuo-min Pao*, for example, noted on 27 March 1912 that British activity up the

---

[30] FO 535/16, no. 45, Major D. S. Robertson, Report on the Chinese Military Situation in the Tibetan Marches, 3 January 1913; FO 371/1329, no. 46282, Jordan to Grey, 17 October 1912; no. 54747, Jordan to Grey, 5 December 1912.

[31] FO 371/1329, no. 50430, Wilkinson to Jordan, 4 September 1912.

Lohit was clearly directed towards Zayul and 'the Wild Men's Country' (i.e. the Mishmi tribal tracts). If the British obtained control of Zayul, the paper declared, then they could easily advance farther to the north-east to include both Batang and Chamdo within the sphere of influence of the Indian Empire. British influence in Eastern Tibet would eventually lead to British domination of Szechuan Province.[32] Another Chengtu paper, the *Yen-chin Pao*, so the British Consul-General in Chengtu, W. H. Wilkinson, told Jordan in late March 1912, was equally certain about the nature of British policy in Tibet. It stated in an editorial that:

> We learn that British troops in Tibet are continually instigating the Lamas to independence, and are prepared to aid and abet them. Their true desire is to make use of this to promote their colonization policy in Tibet.[33]

To keep a watch on British designs in the Zayul region, which was seen to be the strategic key to the control of Eastern Tibet from an Indian base, the Szechuan authorities in early 1912 despatched two missions of inspection, one under Chiang Feng-chi and another under Fu Hsieh-ch'en, chief of the Szechuan Survey Department.[34] Their reports convinced the Szechuan Government that Zayul and Pome could not be ignored. Chiang Feng-ch'i was instructed to investigate as well the situation in the Abor country and to make his way as far down the Tsangpo (or Siang) as he could. He was to be accompanied by an English interpreter in case he should meet with British troops.[35]

In late August 1912 Hu Ching-i, the Acting Military Governor of Szechuan, formally proposed to President Yuan Shih-k'ai that the project for the creation of Sikang Province be revived. Not only would it be a counter to British designs, but also it would be the only sure means of both consolidating Chinese power in Eastern Tibet and extending that power westwards to Lhasa and Central Tibet. New Chinese magistrates'

[32] PEF 1910/14, no. 3521, Political and Secret Department Memo. No. B189.

[33] FO 371/1327, no. 26168, Wilkinson to Jordan, 30 March 1912.

[34] FO 371/1326, no. 24384, Jordan to Grey, 18 May 1912; PEF 1910/14, no. 3521, Memo. No. B189.

[35] FO 371/1326, no. 24384, Jordan to Grey, 18 May 1912.

districts (*hsien*) should be created. Chinese colonists should once more be encouraged to move into Tibet. In Sikang, Hu said,

> the country is really fertile, a paradise not yet exploited. If we establish county organisation and settle the land with colonists, in a few years' time the land and other taxes will suffice to pay all expenses of administration and military occupation.[36]

The new Province of Sikang, it was proposed, would be administered from Chamdo. The head of its administration would be known as the 'Resident Pacificator of the Marches and Tibet', and would rank with a Provincial Governor-General. Yin Ch'ang-heng would be the first to hold this office. His seal was already being cut. By October 1912 President Yuan Shih-k'ai appears to have given his formal consent to the plan; and by the end of the year British observers had derived a clear picture of the territorial extent of the new Province.[37]

In the last years of the Manchu Dynasty Chao Erh-feng and Fu Sung-mu had established direct Chinese administration from the Szechuan border to a point no farther west than Chamdo on the Mekong. About the exact status of Chamdo doubts existed; but it can be said with some degree of certainty that it marked the *de facto* western limit of the Tibetan Marches under Chao's wardenship, and that beyond it lay the dominions of the Dalai Lama.[38] The Sikang Province which Yuan Shih-k'ai now approved extended considerably farther to the west. It included Zayul and Pome, and its claimed frontier with Lhasa territory was at Giamda, a little over 100 miles east of the Dalai Lama's capital.[39] This implied the existence of a Sino-Indian (as opposed to Indo-Tibetan) boundary in the Assam Himalayas extending westwards almost to the banks of the Subansiri. Along this frontier the Chinese, it was clear, would not be inactive. The Republic would certainly continue that policy towards the non-Buddhist hill tribes of the Assam

[36] FO 371/1329, no. 50430, Wilkinson to Jordan, 4 September 1912.

[37] FO 371/1329, no. 46282, Jordan to Grey, 17 October 1912; no. 47178, Jordan to Grey, 23 October 1912; no. 54747, Jordan to Grey, 5 December 1912.

[38] FO 371/1329, no. 55589, Porter to Jordan, 26 November 1912, enc. Memo. on Limits of Chao Erh-feng's Effective Administration in Eastern Tibet.

[39] FO 371/1329, no. 47178, Jordan to Grey, 23 October 1912.

Himalayas which Chao Erh-feng had advocated and which was described clearly enough in Fu Sung-mu's book published in early 1913. Fu pointed out that it would be impossible for the Government of Sikang to ignore the presence of such frontier peoples as the Abors and Mishmis (though he did not, of course, use these names for them); and the only satisfactory solution to the tribal problem was one in which 'the savages have been converted into Chinese'.[40]

While the majority of the Chinese officials concerned with Tibetan affairs—Lu Hsing-chi provides an example—were in favour of a Sikang Province which extended far to the west of Chamdo and included Pome and Zayul, in fact by late 1912 such a Province lay beyond China's grasp. Yin Ch'ang-heng was unable to take back Hsiang-ch'eng, though he from time to time reported to Peking that its capture was imminent. It seemed that here he was confronted not only by Tibetan tribesmen and monks, but also by a significant number of Chinese troops, veterans of the days of Chao Erh-feng who had declined to throw in their lot with the Republic. The repeated failures at Hsiang-ch'eng eventually wore Yin Ch'ang-heng out; and in May 1913 he was reported to have left his forces in the Marches to their own devices and returned to Chengtu. Yin had hoped that a quick Tibetan victory would enable him to seize power in Szechuan and dispose of Hu Ching-i, once his close friend and now his rival. On his return to Chengtu with no glorious victories to his credit, Yin set out on an elaborate campaign of intrigue against Hu. Yuan Shih-k'ai attempted in June to make peace between the two, confirming Yin as Administrator of the Marches (the term Pacificator was now dropped, perhaps as a tactful gesture to Yin to imply that the work of pacification had indeed been accomplished) and Hu as Governor of Szechuan. Yin refused to be content with this. On 3 July 1913 he staged a *coup d'état* in Chengtu, forcing Hu to withdraw to a temple outside the city and to announce his impending retirement. This success obliged President Yuan to raise Yin to the rank of Governor (*Tutu*).[41]

Yin's new title did little to strengthen his military position. The Chengtu treasury was all but exhausted. He could not

[40] FO 535/16, no. 194, Jordan to Grey, 2 April 1913.
[41] FO 535/16, no. 333, Alston to Grey, 14 July 1913.

reinforce the units engaged in siege or garrison duties in the Marches, and which in late 1913 numbered perhaps 7,000 men in all. A month after Yin's *coup*, moreover, the Szechuan army was faced with a major internal crisis when the 5th Division, based on Chungking, rebelled against the Chengtu Government. The Chinese forces in the Marches, belonging to the 3rd Division, remained loyal to Chengtu. In September 1913 a peace was patched up between the two factions. While this conflict was in progress, the Szechuan Government also found itself on the verge of war with the Government of Yunnan, thus ruling out anything like a joint effort in the Tibetan Marches. The effect of these conflicts and tensions was to reduce very seriously the morale, efficiency and unity of command of the Chinese in Eastern Tibet. As Major D. S. Robertson, British Military Attaché in Peking, summed up the situation in November 1913:

> As a general conclusion from what has been disclosed by the late disturbances as to the state of the Ssuchuan forces, it is safe to say that the latter are not fit at present to undertake, with any prospect of success, military operations such as the reconquest of Tibet in the face of an effective armed resistance by the Tibetans.[42]

By March 1913 President Yuan Shih-k'ai concluded that Chinese military operations in the Marches were unlikely to produce any dramatic results at present. He was being subjected, moreover, to very heavy British diplomatic pressure to impose a limit on the operations, now and in future, of the Szechuan army, and to agree to a definition of the boundaries of Sikang Province far more moderate than that which he himself had proposed. Yuan resolved, therefore, to attempt to open negotiations with the Tibetans in the Marches just as he was then trying to initiate discussions with the Dalai Lama's Government in Central Tibet. In March 1913 he appointed two 'Conciliators in Tibet', Wang Chien-ch'ing and Kuo Chang-kuang, whose task it would be to persuade the Tibetan leaders in Eastern Tibet to come to a conference at Chamdo.[43]

The commander of the Tibetan forces in the east, the Kalon

[42] FO 371/1612, no. 52945, Major D. S. Robertson, Report on Military Operations in Ssuchuan, 3 November 1913.

[43] FO 371/1612, no. 43257, Alston to Grey, 8 September 1913.

Lama, appears to have been prepared to listen to what the Chinese had to offer. While at that moment holding his own, he must have realised that the Chinese, in potential, were far stronger than the Tibetans. Once they had put their own house in order, it was more than probable that they would sooner or later produce a commander able to repeat the exploits of Chao Erh-feng. In the summer of 1913, therefore, the Kalon Lama began talks with the Chinese at Chamdo, when he proposed, so reports reaching Chengtu would indicate, these terms:

(1) the Dalai Lama would be recognised by the Chinese as the head of the Buddhist Church;

(2) in Tibet proper, the dominion of the Dalai Lama, the Tibetans would collect taxes, recruit troops and in other ways act as the Government, though with Chinese help if need be;

(3) the Chinese would lend Tibet money to finance schemes for the economic development of the country, and would help the Tibetans create a modern educational system;

(4) except in the event of the outbreak of civil war, the Chinese would send no troops into Tibet proper;

(5) the Chinese would create no new administrative posts in Tibet, and their representation there would not exceed what it was before 1910;

(6) the Chinese would increase the size of their annual cash payments to certain monasteries in Tibet;

(7) Tibet would enjoy all those advantages in relations with the Powers which China might have secured for herself.[44]

The Lönchen Shatra, chief Tibetan delegate at the Simla Conference which had just opened when news of these terms first reached the ears of the Indian Government, denied that there were any negotiations in progress between the Kalon Lama and the Chinese.[45] In fact, however, the negotiations without doubt took place; but they were broken off, apparently by the Chinese, some time in the autumn of 1913, only to be renewed again from time to time right up to 1918, when the situation in the Marches was to some extent stabilised by the truce of Rongbatsa. Chinese policy from the middle of 1913 onwards tended to produce an alternation of periods of negotiation and periods of active campaigning.

[44] FO 371/1613, no. 50007, Viceroy to Secretary of State, 1 November 1913.
[45] Loc. cit.

In November 1913, having failed to achieve any dramatic victory in the Marches, Yin Ch'ang-heng was summoned to Peking by President Yuan Shih-k'ai. No sooner had he reached the capital than he was arrested, the result, it was said, of a long series of intrigues by Chao Erh-hsun, the brother of Yin's victim Chao Erh-feng. Some of Yin's rivals in Szechuan petitioned the Central Government for his execution; but his life was spared out of deference to the wishes of Hu Ching-i, who appears to have forgiven Yin for his *coup* of July.[46] Yin, however, ceased to be a dominant factor in the situation in the Marches; and his departure from that scene was not regretted by the British. Yin was a Chinese of a type of which the British at that time had had very little experience, though they were to become familiar with the likes of him in the great era of the war lords. He was of humble origins; his father was a casual labourer and his mother a washerwoman. He was born in a squalid hut in a small village not far from Chengtu. His rise was due to his energy and ruthlessness, qualities which brought him to the notice of Chao Erh-feng, who became his patron. He had virtually no education. Sir John Jordan, who met Yin in Peking in December 1913, told his friend Sir Walter Langley at the Foreign Office in London that Yin 'struck me as the worst specimen of the new China I have come across and the impression was confirmed by his boasting that he had shot Chao Erh-feng with his own hand'.[47] Yin was replaced by Chang Yi, a Japanese-trained officer who, some observers thought, would get the Chinese forces on the move again in the Marches.[48] By the end of 1914 Chang Yi had given proof of no qualities beyond a monumental timidity. By the middle of that year there could be little doubt that the Chinese were on the defensive in Eastern Tibet; and it seemed extremely unlikely that they would in the immediate future be able to establish themselves in Pome and Zayul, let alone advance from their base at Chamdo for the reoccupation of Lhasa.[49]

[46] FO 535/16, no. 461, King to Alston, 3 November 1913; FO 371/1930, no. 20995, Porter to Jordan, 21 and 25 February 1914.
[47] Foreign Office, Jordan Papers, Jordan to Langley, 29 December 1913.
[48] FO 371/1929, no. 14205, King to Jordan, 15 January 1914.
[49] Teichman, *Eastern Tibet*, op. cit., pp. 42–47.

XXI

THE BRITISH REACTION

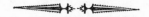

I. RELATIONS WITH THE DALAI LAMA

WITH the outbreak of the Chinese Revolution the Dalai Lama once more became an acute problem to the Indian Government. With Chinese power so rapidly on the wane in Central Tibet, the Lama would certainly make an attempt to return home. Once re-established in Lhasa, would he again turn to the Russians for support? How could he be prevented from doing so? The obvious answers, British aid to the Lama against the Chinese and the establishment of a British Resident in the Tibetan capital, appeared since 1907 to have been effectively removed from the repertoire of British policy by the Anglo-Russian Convention. Were there any methods by which the Indian Government could either circumvent the restrictions of this agreement which it had never welcomed or persuade the Home Government to initiate diplomatic overtures in St. Petersburg for its revision in respect to Tibet?

From the end of 1911 Lord Hardinge's administration can have been under no illusions that, after his exile in British India, the Dalai Lama had forgotten about the possible place of Russia in the Tibetan equation. We have seen how since his flight from Lhasa in 1904 he had maintained through Dorjiev some contact with the Imperial Government and how, even when in exile in Darjeeling, his Ministers had hinted that, failing British aid, he might feel obliged to throw himself on the mercy of the Tsar. As the Dalai Lama's return to Tibet became something more than a remote possibility, so did the Indian Government suspect that Russo-Tibetan relations might again develop into a threat to the security of the Himalayan border, unless countered by British activity in the border region.

In the early summer of 1911 the Dalai Lama wrote to the Tsar in quest of support against the Chinese, and he sent a copy of this letter to Isvolski, at that time Russian Ambassador in Paris: but the Russians, M. Neratov (the acting Russian Foreign Minister) told Buchanan (the British Ambassador in St. Petersburg), had no intention of replying to this appeal.[1] In December 1911, however, the Tsar received another letter from the Lama; and this time, Benckendorff informed Grey, the Tsar intended to make some reply, though in general and 'non-political' terms.[2] Since the Dalai Lama was still on British soil, the delivery of this document involved the co-operation of the Indian Government, which was secured rather reluctantly after some negotiation. At this time, in December 1911 and January 1912, King George V was visiting India.[3] The British were unwilling, while the King was there, to permit another monarch to make a direct approach, as it were, to a British guest: subtle questions of protocol were involved. Thus it was not until February 1912, when King George had been gone a month, that the Tsar's letter was allowed to be delivered, and even then only under conditions designed to minimise its impact: it was to be handed over by the Russian Consul-General in Calcutta, M. Reweliotty, to the Dalai Lama at Darjeeling in the presence of Charles Bell. The original letter was written in Russian, which Reweliotty translated into English and gave to Bell, who then provided the Tibetan version which was actually to be presented to the Lama. The ceremony of transmitting the Tsar's message took place on 10 February 1912. Bell presented to the Lama his version, whereupon, and, it would seem, rather to Bell's surprise, Reweliotty produced his own Tibetan text, which the Lama insisted on comparing with Bell's. After these formalities the Dalai Lama's Ministers tried to obtain a private interview with Reweliotty; an attempt which Bell foiled: as he reported to Hardinge, 'I judged that the courtesy due to a

[1] FO 371/1078, no. 19979, Buchanan to Grey, 24 May 1911.

[2] FO 371/1078, no. 50894, Benckendorff to Grey, 18 December 1911.

[3] King George V arrived at Bombay from London on 11 November 1911 and left Calcutta for England on 8 January 1912. See V. Smith, *Oxford History of India from the earliest times to 1911*, revised and continued to 1921 by S. M. Edwardes, Oxford, 1923, p. 779.

representative of the Russian Government required my presence at this interview also.' The Tibetan Ministers, in such constricting circumstances, made some vague enquiries as to the possibility of there being joint Anglo-Russian discussions over the future of Tibet, enquiries which Reweliotty had no choice but evade as best he could.[4]

The idea of some measure of joint Anglo-Russian intervention in Tibet appears to have fascinated the Dalai Lama. It had much to recommend it, from his point of view. The two Powers acting jointly would effectively prevent either one from acquiring a dominating influence over his Government. A united Anglo-Russian front, moreover, would severely limit the Chinese room for diplomatic manoeuvre. Accordingly, in a reply to the Tsar's letter which was not intended for British eyes, though its contents soon reached Bell by way of the Sikkimese policeman, Laden La, the Dalai Lama wrote:

> I beg that the Russian and British Governments will kindly discuss the Anglo-Russian Agreement [of 1907] deeply and carefully as soon as possible, so that all the Chinese officials and soldiers may be withdrawn from Tibet, and that the kingdom of Tibet may be restored to us.[5]

The Dalai Lama, however, was not convinced that Anglo-Russian mediation provided the only practicable answer to his problems. While it offered him the maximum of independence, yet it might not be nearly so rapid in its effects as active support to his cause from the Government of India, even if such support might carry with it some political strings. The Indian Government had refused him aid in 1910; but there was a possibility that, with the outbreak of the Chinese Revolution, it might have changed its mind. There could be no doubt that a British army could get the Dalai Lama back to Lhasa with greater despatch than any other means. Thus, while investigating the possibilities of joint Anglo-Russian mediation on his behalf, the Lama, who had learnt during his two exiles to be an opportunist politician of no mean skill, also explored the prospects of securing unilateral British aid. He must have appreciated, in

[4] FO 371/1326, no. 5618, Nicolson, 6 February 1912; no. 9614, Bell to India, 10 February 1912.

[5] FO 371/1326, no. 13403, Bell to India, 22 February 1912.

any case, that such aid would almost certainly bring the Russians back into the Tibetan question, though perhaps only after a British force had escorted him to his capital in triumph. It seems likely, therefore, that in the Lama's thinking British support and joint Anglo-Russian intervention were not mutually exclusive alternatives.

In February 1912, a few days after the Reweliotty interview, the Lama's Ministers first formally requested Bell for British military help in escorting the Lama home. One hundred British troops were asked for, a figure raised in early March to 500, with the added suggestion that the Tibetans might also buy some 200 British rifles. On 14 March the Lönchen Shatra, the chief Minister of the Tibetan Government-in-exile, accompanied by his son and by another Tibetan high official, dressed in ceremonial robes, called on Sir Henry McMahon, the Indian Foreign Secretary, at his office in Calcutta. They repeated the request for British help. They offered, in exchange, to place Tibet under British protection. 'Tibet', said the Lönchen Shatra, 'being a religious country, and its owner (the Dalai Lama) being a religious man, it could not exist without having some other power to help and support them.' McMahon treated all this with extreme caution. He permitted himself some vague phrases about Anglo-Tibetan friendship, but he offered no troops. The Lönchen Shatra, who was clearly disappointed, then dropped some veiled hints that, rejected by the British, the Dalai Lama might turn to the Russians. McMahon remained unimpressed, whereupon the Lönchen Shatra made one last request. If the British could not provide an armed escort for the Dalai Lama, they might at least depute a British official to accompany him on his journey home. McMahon made no comment beyond observing 'that the matter was a difficult one'. The interview then came to an end.[6]

The Tibetan requests were embarrassing to the Indian Government. McMahon, and probably Lord Hardinge, too, was certainly no longer opposed in principle to giving the Dalai Lama what help he could. The idea of a British companion had its attractions: it would get a British Resident to Lhasa by an indirect route; and the establishment of a Lhasa Residency was now being seriously considered in the Indian Foreign Office as

[6] FO 371/1326, no. 14007, Viceroy to Secretary of State, 14 March 1912.

an objective of British policy—in 1914 it was to be the subject of an article in the Simla Convention. However, any British involvement with the Dalai Lama at this juncture would involve a breach of the Anglo-Russian Convention of 1907, an agreement which was still held as sacrosanct in London. On the other hand, if the British made no gesture of goodwill at all to the Lama, he would most probably, as the Lönchen Shatra had hinted, be forced to revive that secret diplomacy with St. Petersburg which it had been the intention of the Younghusband Mission to frustrate and of the British negotiators of the 1907 agreement to prevent from ever again becoming an object of British concern.

Considerations such as these almost certainly lay behind the Indian Government's proposal, in late May 1912, to send a non-European official up to Lhasa to arrange a cease-fire between the Tibetans and Chinese and to smooth the way for the evacuation to India of the beleaguered Chinese garrison.[7] While justified on paper by the tense situation then prevailing in the Tibetan capital, there can be little doubt that here was a veiled attempt to comply with the Dalai Lama's request for the presence in Tibet of a British official during the period of his homecoming. Once in Tibet, moreover, there seemed no good reason why this official should not evolve into some kind of British Resident at Lhasa. The man selected was Laden La, to whom reference has already been made; and of whom Lord Hardinge telegraphed to Lord Crewe:

> Laden La is a British subject, a native of Sikkim; he is deputy superintendent in the Bengal police. He has been on special duty with the Dalai Lama since the latter arrived in India, and was attached to the Tashi [Panchen] Lama during his stay in this country [in 1905–6]. He had previously been employed on the Tibet Mission [of 1904]. Besides being a staunch Buddhist, which renders him acceptable to Tibetans, he is a man of great tact, ability and reliability, and has a thorough knowledge of English, Nepali and Tibetan languages.[8]

In other words, Laden La was as close an equivalent of Dorjiev as the British could hope to lay their hands on.

[7] See pp. 376, 377 above.
[8] FO 535/15, no. 95, Viceroy to Secretary of State, 8 June 1912.

The Laden La venture, there can be no doubt, took the Home Government by surprise. The proposal to send this Sikkimese policeman to Lhasa was first made by Hardinge to Lord Crewe, the Secretary of State, on 31 May.[9] On 5 June, when the Home Government had decided after discussion in Cabinet that 'Laden La's mission is viewed with some misapprehension by His Majesty's Government', it transpired that Laden La had already set out for Lhasa.[10] Both the India Office and the Foreign Office saw in this venture the source of a great deal of trouble. The Russians could well object that by sending an official, albeit a non-European, into Tibet the British had ignored the 1907 agreement. The Tibetans could, and probably would, interpret Laden La's deputation as a British promise, if only a tacit one, to support the Dalai Lama's party against the Chinese. Hence Hardinge was told to call Laden La back.[11] When the Viceroy replied, on 7 June, that Laden La was now probably beyond recall, the Foreign Office resolved to inform the Russians of the mission, and the Japanese as well, so as to minimise the diplomatic capital which could be made out of it.[12]

Despite 'clear the line' telegrams to the Gyantse Trade Agent, Laden La proved to be a hard man to stop. The orders for his recall finally caught up with him when he was $31\frac{1}{2}$ miles from Lhasa: and by this small distance did the Indian Government miss placing its representative in the Tibetan capital. Once there, Laden La would not have been removed with ease. Hardinge would probably have argued that to pull the British agent back would be the surest way to broadcast all over the Tibetan plateau that the British were not prepared to take any action in Tibet, news which could only dishearten the Dalai Lama's followers and encourage the Chinese garrisons to hold out. As it was, Hardinge was able to wring permission from his superiors for Laden La to remain a while in Tibet. From the Gyantse Trade Agency the Sikkimese policeman established communications with the various parties, both Tibetan and

[9] FO 535/15, no. 82, Viceroy to Secretary of State, 31 May 1912.
[10] FO 371/1326, no. 24187, Secretary of State to Viceroy, 5 June 1912; FO 535/15, no. 87, Viceroy to Secretary of State, 7 June 1912.
[11] FO 535/15, no. 93, Secretary of State to Viceroy, 6 June 1912.
[12] FO 371/1326, no. 24317, Minute by Grey.

Chinese, in Lhasa; and at Gyantse he behaved as if he was indeed, as the Tibetans were convinced he was, 'the officer deputed by the British Government to make peace between the Chinese and Tibetans'.[13] It need hardly be remarked that the Russians would have experienced no difficulty in interpreting such mediation as an interference in the internal affairs of Tibet contrary to the spirit of the first Article of the Tibetan section of the 1907 Convention.

Grey was afraid that the Laden La mission 'would end in the Tibetans claiming that we were under an obligation to assist them against the Chinese';[14] and Crewe thought that the Russians could probably use this episode to support their claims to increased influence in other parts of Chinese Central Asia, in Mongolia for example.[15] The best that the Home Government could do to avoid these dangers was to issue a declaration playing down the diplomatic implications of Laden La's presence in Tibet. On 25 June the Japanese and Russian Ambassadors in London were told by the Foreign Office that:

> Both the Chinese and Tibetan authorites at Lhasa have appealed to the Government of India to send an officer to Lhasa to arrange the surrender of the Chinese troops there and for their safe conduct to India. His Majesty's Government have not so far acceded to this request though a native policeman in the service of the Indian Government is in Tibet, but His Majesty's Government have not yet sanctioned his going to Lhasa.[16]

These were not very convincing words; but they were all that the Foreign Office could safely offer. Grey had no way of knowing what other Laden Las the Indian Government might have up its sleeve and who might at any moment turn up in Lhasa.

The Laden La project had its teeth removed through the prompt action of the Home Government. Lord Hardinge, however, did not then abandon all idea of making some gesture

[13] FO 535/15, no. 107, Viceroy to Secretary of State, 17 June 1912.
[14] FO 371/1327, no. 26186, Minute by Grey.
[15] Grey Papers (in Foreign Office Library), Vol. 59 General, Crewe to Grey, 25 June 1912.
[16] FO 371/1327, no. 25530, FO to Benckendorff, 25 June 1912, and no. 27011, Grey to Macdonald, 25 June 1912.

to the Dalai Lama beyond the conveyance of empty expressions of goodwill. When, in June 1912, the Dalai Lama, accompanied by some fifty officials and 150 retainers, really seemed about to set out for Tibet from Kalimpong, where he had been delaying since early in the year, Hardinge, no doubt advised by Bell, decided to send him a farewell message into which a considerable degree of political content could be read. This message would not only express the hope that the present cordial relations between the Indian and Tibetan Governments might continue—mere pious phrases—but also it would assure the Dalai Lama that the British would welcome letters from him after he had established himself once more in Tibet, and it would inform him that it was the British wish to see 'internal autonomy preserved in Tibet subject to the suzerainty of China, but without interference on the part of China'.[17]

The Home Government liked this proposal little better than it had the deputation of Laden La. In the opinion of the Foreign Office, any correspondence at all between the Indian Government and the Dalai Lama could be objected to by Russia invoking the 1907 agreement on Tibet. As Nicolson, who had negotiated that agreement, put it: 'I think we are sailing very close to the wind.' A case might be made for such correspondence while the Lama was still on British soil; but there must be no question of its continuation after the Lama's return. 'Direct correspondence between the Government of India and the Dalai Lama', Nicolson thought, would 'not be in accordance with the spirit of our convention with Russia.'[18] The Indian argument that the 1908 Trade Regulations had, in fact, authorised letters of this kind was not accepted by London. The Trade Regulations permitted direct Anglo-Tibetan communication on an extremely limited range of topics. As Grey minuted: 'The position seems to be that except on matters covered by Article 3 of the Trade Regulations we must only deal with Tibet through China.'[19]

[17] FO 535/15, no. 99, Viceroy to Secretary of State, 11 June 1912.
[18] FO 371/1327, no. 25530, Nicolson's minute on IO to FO, 14 June 1912.
[19] FO 371/1327, no. 27017, Grey's minute on IO to FO, 22 June 1912. The 1908 Trade Regulations only provided for Anglo-Tibetan communication on questions arising from the administration of the Tibet trade marts; other matters were reserved for Anglo-Chinese discussion.

The reference to the status of Tibet in the proposed message from the Viceroy was also objected to in London. It seemed, so the India Office thought, a bit 'unguarded'. In theory, however undesirable this might be in practice, the British still relied on the Chinese to keep the Tibetans up to their treaty obligations to the Indian Government. If the possibility of direct British pressure on the Tibetans, which might perhaps be called for at some future time, were ruled out because of Russia, then it might not be too wise to outlaw *all* Chinese interference in Tibetan affairs in all circumstances. To do so would be tantamount to declaring that the Tibetans could now behave as they wished without any control. The India Office, therefore, proposed this wording:

> The desire of the Government of India is to see the internal autonomy of Tibet under Chinese suzerainty maintained without Chinese interference so long as treaty obligations are duly performed and cordial relations preserved between Tibet and India.[20]

Subject to the making of the proposed changes in the text, however, Hardinge was grudgingly permitted to send his farewell message to the Dalai Lama.

The Indian Government had no choice but to accept the modifications and deletions suggested by London; but Lord Hardinge was unhappy about them. He refused, in any case, to feel himself unable, should future developments indicate the necessity for such a step, to send letters to and receive letters from the Dalai Lama whatever the Home Government might argue to the contrary.[21] The circumstances of the Dalai Lama's arrival at Phari at the head of the Chumbi Valley, on 9 July, supported the Viceroy's argument on this point. As has already been noted, the Lama was met at Phari by Dorjiev, who had recently been in St. Petersburg and who, in Hardinge's opinion, had certainly at one time in the past been a Russian agent and probably still was.[22] Hardinge, after all, had been

[20] FO 535/15, no. 104, IO to FO, 14 June 1912.
[21] FO 535/15, no. 163, IO to FO, 26 July 1912.
[22] See p. 378 above. Nicolson, it is interesting to note, did not share Hardinge's suspicions about Dorjiev on this occasion. 'I do not think', Nicolson minuted, 'we need be uneasy and I dare say Dorjieff wishes to

British Ambassador in St. Petersburg when the story of Dorjiev's mission to Russia of 1900 came to light. If Dorjiev could still continue to shuttle to and fro between St. Petersburg and Lhasa then the Indian Government must surely reserve to itself the right to send letters to the Dalai Lama: otherwise a situation like that which faced Lord Curzon on the eve of the Young-husband Mission might once more arise; and, Anglo-Russian Convention or no Anglo-Russian Convention, this no Government of India could ignore.

The situation in Central Tibet in 1912 certainly abounded in temptations for British intervention of a kind prohibited by the 1907 agreement. Apart from the continuing crisis of the siege of the Chinese garrison in Lhasa which, among other things, involved that perennial factor in Himalayan politics, the Nepalese, there was also the question of the Panchen Lama. Terrified lest the Dalai Lama would punish him for his collaboration with the Chinese, the Panchen Lama endeavoured on several occasions to place himself under British protection, offering in the process all sorts of concessions at Shigatse, a region which he tried to argue was not covered by the existing British treaties relating to Tibet.[23] Could the Indian Government afford to go on rejecting overtures from this quarter? Then there was the continued influence in Tibetan politics of Dorjiev, whose very presence in Tibet touched the Indian Government on its tender Russophobic nerve. Moreover, by 1912 the problem of external influences in Tibet was no longer confined to the three traditional powers, as it were, Britain, Russia and China. The Japanese were now also showing a growing interest in Tibetan affairs. No sooner, for example, had the Dalai Lama crossed over into Tibet and settled down at Samding Monastery to await the proper moment to re-enter Lhasa than he was joined by a certain Yasujiro Yajima, who assumed the role of military adviser to the Tibetan Government.[24] Hardinge had little doubt that Yajima was a Japanese

[23] See, for example, FO 371/1327, no. 27317, Gould to India, 28 May 1912.
[24] FO 535/15, no. 167, Viceroy to Secretary of State, 2 August 1912.

talk over matters concerning the Russian Buriats.' See FO 371/1327, no. 29267, Nicolson's minute on Viceroy to Secretary of State, 9 July 1912.

agent; and reports from the British Legation in Tokyo did nothing to make him change his mind.[25] Could the Indian Government, with both Russian and Japanese agents well entrenched at the seat of power in Tibet, afford not to have a British agent there as well?

Indian restraint was not encouraged by the Dalai Lama, who, so long as a Chinese threat to his position, either from the Lhasa garrison or from the Chinese forces in the Tibetan Marches, persisted, was clearly intending to do his best to involve the British with his cause. He had welcomed the Laden La mission, indeed, he had probably inspired it. Once in Tibet he went on corresponding with the British, hoping that Laden La or someone like him might yet go to Lhasa, and always in

[25] From various sources the Indian Government learnt quite a lot about Yasujiro Yajima. He had been an instructor to the Szechuan provincial army in 1908. He first turned up in Darjeeling in May 1911. In June 1912, without permission, he crossed the British frontier into Tibet. He was an armourer by profession. From MacDonald, British Minister in Tokyo, it transpired that Yajima had fought with the Japanese Army against Russia in 1904–5, and had then for a while been an instructor in the Toyama Military College. In 1907 he left the Imperial Army and joined a peculiar organisation called the Nippon Rikkokwa, which had been founded in 1897, so MacDonald said, 'with the object of educating and rearing poor students on Christian principles'. Since joining this body Yajima had been travelling about the world without any visible means of support 'for the purpose of fostering a hardy spirit and observing the manners and customs of different countries'. Between 1907 and 1912 he had followed this itinerary: Shanghai, Szechuan, Tibet, India, the United States, India, Japan, India and Tibet. His journeys, MacDonald thought, 'have no political significance whatever'; but MacDonald could hardly have expected to convince the Indian Government of this.

There could be no doubt, at all events, that in 1912 the Japanese were becoming very interested in political developments in Tibet. The Japanese press, for example, reported Tibetan affairs fully: the *Manshu Nichi Nichi Shimbun*, on 12 May 1912, went so far as to accuse the British of inspiring the Tibetan rising against the Chinese. Japanese diplomats showed great interest in British policy in Tibet and British plans in this direction *vis-a-vis* the Russians. From 1912 onwards the Foreign Office felt itself obliged to keep the Japanese at least as well informed as the Russians on the evolution of British Tibetan policy.

See FO 535/15, no. 167, Viceroy to Secretary of State, 2 August 1912; FO 371/1328, FO to IO, 22 August 1912; FO 371/1327, Viceroy to Secretary of State, 6 August 1912; FO 371/1329, no. 44227, MacDonald to Grey, 2 October 1912; FO 371/1327, no. 25704, MacDonald to Grey, 25 May 1912; FO 535/15, no. 246, Grey to MacDonald, 10 October 1912.

quest of signs and symbols of British support. In August 1912, for example, he proposed the deputation of an envoy to Lord Hardinge to convey formally his thanks for the British help and hospitality he had received since 1910; and on this occasion he made the following request, which perhaps reflects accurately enough the general nature of his political thinking at this time:

> Our hope is to learn the English language and to follow the custom of the British Government on which we depend and rely, and by doing this the prosperity of Tibet will be increased, and the great friendship between the British and Tibetans will remain unchanged forever. And for this reason, with the official deputed to India, we wish to send some energetic and clever sons of respectable families to London in charge of some officials to learn the language and customs.[26]

Thus began the strange story of the four Tibetan boys at Rugby, which is described in Appendix XI. In receiving this communication, let alone in giving it favourable consideration, the British were skating over the very thin ice indeed of the Anglo-Russian Convention, as, no doubt, the Dalai Lama hoped they would, perhaps breaking through in the process.

By the middle of 1912 Lord Hardinge was prepared to involve his Government to some extent in the cause of the Dalai Lama, though not, perhaps, to the extent of providing military support against the Chinese. He did not, of course, go as far as some of his subordinates, like Charles Bell, who would have been delighted to see the Lama escorted back to Lhasa by British troops. He appears to have concluded, however, that British interests would be well served by the presence of a British representative at the Tibetan capital, albeit a somewhat disguised one like Laden La; and he had lost much of his respect for the Anglo-Russian Agreement relating to Tibet for which he had to a great extent been responsible. Neither Grey nor Crewe in London were as yet willing to go as far as this. The Lhasa Residency still had for them implications which they could not accept. But in London as in Simla it had become obvious that the Tibetan policy of the post-Younghusband years could not continue much longer. An active, though essentially defensive, policy had already been accepted on the

[26] FO 371/1328, no. 40243, Bell to India, 10 August 1912.

Assam frontier which in many respects departed radically from the concept of non-interference. A new approach to the problem of British relations with the authorities in Central Tibet was called for now that the Chinese power there was so obviously disappearing. London did not deny that a very real Tibetan problem existed. It favoured, however, a rather different approach to its solution from that implied in the despatches from India.

The Indian Government since Curzon's day had seen in Tibet mainly a problem of frontier defence and administration. To Curzon, and, though to a rather less forcefully expressed degree, to Minto and Hardinge as well, it was almost unthinkable to accept the existence of a state in territorial juxtaposition with British India with which the British had no diplomatic contact at all. Just as the British insisted upon relations with Afghanistan and Nepal, so they had to have relations of some kind with Tibet. The first objective of these relations was the elimination of the influence of any other Power, and especially of any other European Power. Once this had been achieved, then border disputes and cognate local issues were reduced to manageable proportions. The key to the situation in Indian thinking, therefore, was the establishment of some degree of positive British influence at the heart of these border states as a measure both defensive and offensive, defensive in that it guaranteed the exclusion of rival influences in the future and offensive in that it eliminated any such influences already established. Thus it was inevitable, once it seemed likely that the Dalai Lama would be able to return to power in Central Tibet, that the Indian Government would try to ensure the continued existence of a favourable diplomatic relationship with him. Once, moreover, the Dalai Lama was free of the Chinese troops still holding out in Lhasa, the Indian Government could hardly escape thinking very seriously indeed about the creation of a permanent British political post in the Tibetan capital. India, therefore, had what might be called an essentially positive view of the future shape of Anglo-Tibetan relations. This view from 1912 until 1914, when a solution of sorts was arrived at, was not really very different from that held by Lord Curzon in 1903–4. One of the props of Curzon's Tibetan policy, for example, the Lhasa Residency, was once more being openly discussed in Indian official circles. One should not be surprised, therefore, to find Lord Hardinge observing, on 20 August 1912, that 'it has always appeared to us to be desirable to occupy the Chumbi Valley', though he added weighty reasons why 'we are unable . . . to recommend occupation at the present juncture'.[27] Viceregal talk about Chumbi, last heard at the time of the negotiating of the Tibet Trade Regulations in 1908, when the prolongation of British occupation was being considered, was an excellent indication of the point which thinking about Tibet in British India had reached.

For London this positive approach, at least in so far as Tibet was concerned, held fewer attractions. It clearly conflicted with the pattern of Anglo-Russian relations in Asia which had been formalised in 1907. The basic principle of the 1907 Convention was negative rather than positive. In certain areas of Asia, where hitherto the British and Russians had been actively competing with each other, the two parties to the Convention agreed *not* to take a number of specified actions. The Indian Government might say that if only it could get its man into such and such a regional centre, all would be well. The Liberal Government of Campbell-Bannerman and Asquith was inclined to argue that the same result could be achieved by getting the other side to agree to keep its man out. In the case of Tibet this difference between the basic attitudes of London and Simla produced an important variation in emphasis. India argued that now, with the Chinese collapse, there was the opportunity to do what was not done by the Younghusband Mission, to bring the Dalai Lama within the British diplomatic sphere. British support, if only moral, would suffice to keep the Chinese out of Central Tibet from now on, and British vigilance, perhaps exercised through a Lhasa Residency, would ensure that the Dalai Lama was not again allowed to be led astray by the wiles of Russia or of any other Power. London, on the other hand, was disposed to point out that, at this time, with the Chinese being forced out of Tibet and in a state of disorganisation at their centre owing to the Revolution, there was the opportunity to ensure the permanent exclusion of harmful Chinese power from Tibet by diplomatic means. The Chinese could perhaps be made to agree by treaty to a definition of Tibetan status which

[27] FO 535/15, no. 191, Viceroy to Secretary of State, 20 August 1912.

would meet British requirements. The 1907 Convention would probably still suffice to keep out the Russians in any significant way. Thus while in 1912 the Indian Government wrestled with the problem of positive British relations with the Tibetan Government, the India Office and the Foreign Office in London were exploring means to secure a diplomatic reduction of Chinese influence in Tibet to a degree no longer detrimental to British interests.

2. PRESSURE ON THE CHINESE

The British Legation in Peking had been delivering protests to the Chinese Government about the state of affairs in Tibet since at least 1886. In pre-Younghusband days these protests had been directed mainly against Tibetan actions with the expressed hope that the Chinese would make their Tibetan subjects behave themselves. In the years following the withdrawal of the British mission to Lhasa, Chinese rather than Tibetan actions had been the target. In both cases the Chinese had usually replied with soft answers and had then proceeded to let things go on just as before. It might well have been argued in 1912, therefore, that there was little point in continuing with this diplomatic charade. Just as in 1888 Lord Dufferin had been in the end obliged himself to expel the Tibetans from Sikkim, representations in Peking having produced no result at all, so it might now have seemed that only by the application of British physical pressure on the weak chinks in the Chinese armour could any worthwhile outcome be anticipated. Hardinge had seen this point, it is probable, when in 1910 he talked of solving the problem of the Assam Himalayan boundary on the coasts of China.[28] The Indian Government had always tended to advocate a tough policy towards the Chinese. Before 1912, however, it had generally been opposed by the British Foreign Office, which was reluctant to push Peking too forcefully. China, after all, had a role to play in the great game of rivalry in Asia between the Powers. Moreover, much value was attached in London to the China trade, which, it was thought, might suffer if the British pressed Peking too hard for Tibetan rights of little commercial importance. In 1912 the Foreign Office attitude in this respect underwent some change.

[28] See pp. 337, 338 above.

The outbreak of the Chinese Revolution in 1911 swept away the Manchu Dynasty. In its place emerged the Chinese Republic, weak, vulnerable and untried. This event took place at a time when four of the major Powers interested in Chinese spheres of influence, Britain, Russia, France and Japan, had joined together in an alliance which was directed primarily against the German Empire. Chinese goodwill was no longer a commodity in particular demand. China appeared to be on the verge of disintegration, with impending civil war in many of the eighteen Provinces and with the Powers doing their best to detach peripheral regions like Sinkiang, Outer Mongolia and Inner Mongolia. Japan had already swallowed Korea and was looking eagerly towards Manchuria. In these circumstances the new Chinese Republic needed foreign support far more than the Powers needed the help of Yuan Shih-k'ai's Government. Jordan could now back his protests to the Wai-chiao-pu with threats which he or Max Müller would never have made in 1910.

Jordan had no lack of grounds for protest during 1912. The Chinese statements of the union of the five races, Chinese plans for the reconquest of Central Tibet by expeditions from Szechuan and Yunnan, Chinese proposals for the creation of a new province out of Eastern Tibet, Sikang, Chinese delays in agreeing to the evacuation of the Lhasa garrison, Chinese intrigues with Nepal and the other Himalayan States, all these were the subject of notes from Jordan to President Yuan and his Ministry of Foreign Affairs. These notes, however, differed from those of an earlier age in two respects. Firstly, they contained within them a minatory element which was absent in so many previous British communications to China relating to Tibet. Secondly, they culminated, in August 1912, in what amounted to an ultimatum to the Chinese Government to make a clear statement of the nature of China's relation to Tibet which the British would find acceptable.

The most obvious weakness of the Chinese Republic in early 1912 was the fact that it was a new régime badly in need of international recognition.[29] It was clear that the Revolution had resulted in a change in the status of China proper. Did this mean that the status of China's former Manchu dependencies

[29] See also p. 477 below, note.

had changed as well? If so, would it not be reasonable to expect the Chinese, before they received recognition by the Powers as now being under the republican form of government, to declare what precisely the new status of these outlying regions, like Tibet, Mongolia and Sinkiang, was? So argued Lord Hardinge in March 1912, when he proposed that British recognition of the Republic should be conditional on a Chinese settlement of the Tibetan question. To Lord Hardinge at this stage such a solution clearly involved a Chinese acknowledgment of Tibetan political independence. How would the Chinese react to a demand of this kind? Would there be anti-British rioting in China, endangering British lives, property and trade? Hardinge, on the whole, thought not. He noted that

> so far as we know there has been no anti-Russian outbreak in connection with the support given by Russia to the Mongolian Government, and we have no reason to suppose that an anti-British outbreak will follow British opposition to the inclusion of Tibet in China.[30]

This parallel between the Mongolian and Tibetan situations, of which we will have more to say a bit later on, tended to dominate the thinking on Central Asia of British statesmen in 1912 and 1913. Hardinge argued that the Chinese should purchase British recognition in exchange for a number of specific agreements on frontier matters which had long disturbed the smooth path of Anglo-Chinese diplomacy. The invalidity of all Chinese claims over Nepal and Bhutan should be acknowledged. China should agree to the Salween-Irrawaddy watershed as the Yunnan-Burma border. China should promise to cease from 'encroaching on tribal territory on the north-east frontier [the Assam Himalayas] outside territory recognised locally as belonging to China, such tribal territory being under the control of Great Britain'.[31]

Lord Crewe was opposed in principle to the rather crude use of recognition to secure from China a satisfactory settlement of 'purely local disputes' along the Indian borders. He assumed, however, that

[30] FO 535/15, no. 44, Viceroy to Secretary of State, 23 March 1912.
[31] FO 535/15, no. 57, Viceroy to Secretary of State, 29 April 1912.

recognition must in any case be conditional on the new Government demonstrating its ability to control the outlying provinces of its empire. Without such control no guarantee as to the maintenance of foreign rights and interests would be of any practical value.[32]

In other words, while the Chinese could not, perhaps, be coerced into surrendering Tibet, or portions of it, altogether (if only because other Powers might use this as a precedent to the British disadvantage), there seemed no reason why recognition should not be made conditional upon the Chinese making their peace with the Dalai Lama. Since at present the Dalai Lama's party was apparently in the ascendant, such a Sino-Tibetan reconciliation would surely mean the Chinese recognition of a real measure of Tibetan autonomy, even if the fiction of Chinese 'suzerainty' might be invoked in the process. Sir Edward Grey agreed with this reasoning, noting that the Russians were already applying an analogous line of argument in relation to Mongolia.[33] Jordan in Peking, when consulted, also proved to be of like mind. He thought that the situation in Tibet with which the Chinese should be made to agree should not be Tibetan independence, but rather Tibetan autonomy under Chinese suzerainty.[34] This state of affairs Jordan described as the *status quo*, meaning the situation which the British imagined prevailed in Tibet on the eve of the Younghusband Mission of 1904. Jordan felt, unlike Max Müller in 1910, that the British could reasonably expect China to accept a Tibetan state where the Dalai Lama was very much the master in his own house and where the Chinese power was represented by no more than the Amban and a small ceremonial escort. It was with a Tibetan régime of this kind, though, of course, in the absence of the Dalai Lama, that the Lhasa Convention of 1904 had been concluded. Such a régime should be restored. The need now was to create a theoretical definition of a Tibet of this kind, its

[32] FO 535/15, no. 44, Viceroy to Secretary of State, 15 March 1912, IO covering letter of transmission to FO.

[33] PEF 1912/69, no. 1120/1912, FO to IO, 23 March 1912, and no. 1349/1912, FO to IO, 11 April 1912.

The Japanese, too, were endeavouring to obtain advantages in Chinese territory, in Manchuria and Inner Mongolia, in exchange for recognition.

[34] FO 535/15, no. 50, Jordan to Grey, 12 April 1912.

constitutional nature and its physical limits, which could be presented to the Chinese Government.

There was one serious disadvantage in the reliance upon recognition unsupported by other means of applying pressure on the Chinese. Recognition was an international matter. If other Powers decided to give the Chinese Republic their recognition, the British would more or less be forced to follow suit, Tibetan settlement or not.[35] Other methods would have to be explored. Jordan thought financial pressure might be applied. The new Republic would have to depend greatly upon foreign loans. The granting of financial aid by the British could well be made to appear to be conditional upon Chinese reasonableness over Tibet. Thus Jordan suggested to Grey in June 1912, when the Szechuan Provincial Government was reported to be on the point of launching a military expedition to relieve the Lhasa garrison, that

> should this project materialise, it might perhaps be advisable that I should be instructed to warn Yuan Shih-k'ai that we cannot be expected to give the Central Government financial assistance in order to set free provincial funds for the conduct of distant military enterprises.[36]

Jordan proceeded to make use of this gambit. For example, on 23 June 1912 he had an interview with Yuan Shih-k'ai in which the Chinese expedition from Szechuan to Tibet was discussed. In his memorandum on this occasion Jordan reported that:

> Sir John Jordan informed the President that the question of funds expended on this expedition was a very serious one. It practically amounted to this: that Szechuan Province, which should contribute nearly 1,000,000 taels annually towards the indemnity due to the Powers [the Boxer Indemnity], had defaulted in this payment, and was employing the funds to finance their Tibetan expedition. At the same time China was borrowing money from the Powers to make up this deficit in the Indemnity.
>
> Yuan ridiculed the idea of such a possibility, but Sir John Jordan insisted on its substantial accuracy, and warned the President that His Majesty's Government would not contribute

[35] See p. 477 below, note.
[36] FO 535/15, no. 90, Jordan to Grey, 8 June 1912.

towards any further advances to China if the expedition [from Szechuan into Tibet] went beyond Chinese territory. We could not be expected to release funds for distant ventures of this kind, or, in other words, to enable China to disturb the peace of Central Asia to the detriment of the interests of India.[37]

When Jordan tried to persuade, with minatory backing, President Yuan to abandon his Tibetan adventure, he did not only have British interests in mind. He believed that nothing would be more detrimental to the process of political re-organisation under the new Republic than a series of campaigns on the Central Asian fringes, which would divert money and resources badly needed at the centre. However, Jordan realised that Yuan Shih-k'ai probably possessed comparatively little control over provincial governments like those of Szechuan and Yunnan, whose leaders seemed bent on frontier wars whatever Peking might say. As Jordan told Grey:

> Strange as it may seem, the confusion which at present obtains in China proper only seems to stimulate the desire for aggressive action in outlying portions of the country, and a new and dangerous spirit of military enterprise is beginning to animate frontier provinces like Yunnan and Szechuan, which are practically independent of central control. It would greatly strengthen the hands of the Government here [in Peking] in dealing with Szechuan if arrangements could be made for the withdrawal of the beleaguered Chinese garrison at Lhasa, as all pretext for a military advance would then be removed.[38]

Jordan, perhaps, was more charitable than the facts warranted in his belief in Yuan Shih-k'ai's professions of distaste for Chinese forward moves in Tibet; but there can be little doubt that Peking, even had it wanted to, could not have stopped Chengtu from trying to follow in Chao Erh-feng's footsteps. It was pointless putting diplomatic pressure on Yuan and the Wai-chiao-pu to countermand military expeditions from the Marches so long as the temptation of the besieged Lhasa garrison continued in being. A Tibetan settlement demanded the Chinese evacuation of Central Tibet, which would be much expedited if the British took a hand. Once all the Chinese had been removed from the Dalai Lama's dominions, moreover, it

[37] FO 535/15, no. 150, Jordan's memo.
[38] FO 535/15, no. 150, Jordan to Grey, 26 June 1912.

would be much easier to maintain a diplomatic case for Chinese 'suzerainty' rather than 'sovereignty' over Lhasa territory. Hence the British offered to help in the Chinese evacuation by way of India; and hence the Chinese leaders still in Tibet resisted evacuation for as long as they could.

Supervising the withdrawal of the Lhasa garrisons to India was a step which the British could take mainly on their own soil and which carried relatively few seeds of future diplomatic complications. The Russians could hardly protest against such British aid to China provided the Indian Government could be restrained from sending its agents to Lhasa. But could the Chinese, in fact, be persuaded to surrender their Tibetan foothold without some measure of British pressure, in conflict with the terms of the 1907 Convention, on the Tibetan plateau? During 1912 the British explored a number of possible solutions to this problem. In June, for example, Lord Crewe wondered whether the Chinese garrison in Lhasa might be forced to surrender by the abrupt termination of rice imports into Tibet from India.[39] The Chinese, it appeared, were still able to get supplies of this cereal through the Tibetan siege lines. Lord Hardinge rejected the plan for administrative reasons—it would involve interference with the trade of Nepal, Sikkim and Bhutan as well as British India, and, in any case, the blockade could not be made effective without paying expensive compensation to the merchants customarily engaged in the Indo-Tibetan rice trade.[40] If any kind of blockade on the Indian border was to be resorted to, the Indian Government thought, it was best applied to people and information rather than goods. The Chinese in Tibet were now virtually cut off from direct communication with Yunnan and Szechuan. Orders, pay, news, reinforcements for them could only be despatched by way of British India. Why not declare the British border closed to all Chinese communications until a suitable Tibetan settlement had been arrived at? Such an embargo would certainly hurt the Chinese cause in several ways. It would weaken the moral and material strength of the Lhasa garrison. It would involve the Chinese in 'loss of face'. It was, accordingly, added to the British diplomatic armoury.

[39] FO 535/15, no. 117, Secretary of State to Viceroy, 19 June 1912.
[40] FO 535/15, no. 122, Viceroy to Secretary of State, 23 June 1912.

Perhaps the most effective British weapon at this time was one which was implicit in the entire Central Asian situation and which, for that reason, it was not necessary to describe to the Chinese in explicit terms. It was a weapon, moreover, which had been used before at earlier stages in the Tibetan question: it helped decide the Chinese, for example, to begin the negotiation of the Sikkim-Tibet Convention of 1890. If the Chinese did not come to some arrangement with the British about Tibet, thus at least still demonstrating that they were the legal suzerains, if not sovereigns, of that region, the Indian Government might find its patience exhausted and take some action on its own without consulting China at all. On the one hand, the British could perhaps let loose their Nepalese tributary on Tibet, using Gurkha troops to expel the remnants of Chinese power and guarantee future Chinese exclusion. On the other hand, the British might give some formal recognition to Tibet as a fully independent state able to make binding treaties on its own behalf without any Chinese participation whatsoever. Apart from the consequences of such a step for the Chinese position elsewhere in Central Asia, in Mongolia and Sinkiang, the result would be a severe blow to Chinese national pride. Rather than risk Nepalese intervention, or direct Anglo-Tibetan negotiations without the Chinese taking part, it seemed likely that President Yuan Shih-k'ai would conclude that 'suzerainty', even as the British understood that term, was better than nothing at all.

The various levers, potential and actual, which could be used to bring pressure to bear on the Government of Yuan Shih-k'ai, might perhaps result in the Chinese accepting a definition of Tibetan status which was to the British taste. What sort of Tibet would the British like the Chinese to agree to? This question was considered seriously in London and in India from the end of 1911, when the implications of the Chinese Revolution first began to be appreciated. Both the Foreign Office and the India Office soon concluded that, because of existing treaties, there could be no question at present of Tibet passing entirely out of the Chinese sphere. On the other hand, it was vital that the new Chinese Republic did not have the opportunity to do what it was suspected the Manchus had been trying to do, namely the total incorporation of Tibet within the

Chinese provincial structure, which would guarantee not only the intensification of the Assam boundary problem but also its extension westwards all along the Himalayan range. Hence Tibet, even if Chinese in name, must be a region where actual Chinese power was nominal. The definition of such a Tibet, so J. E. Shuckburg of the India Office reasoned in February 1912, should contain the following three points:[41]

1. The Chinese were suzerain in Tibet, not sovereign, which meant that while they could have their Amban at Lhasa they could not interfere in internal Tibetan administration.

2. Apart from the Amban's purely ceremonial, and small, escort, there could be no Chinese troops stationed in Tibet.

3. Again, apart from the Amban and his staff, there could be no Chinese civil officials stationed in Tibet.

In a way, a Tibet of this kind would be not unlike some of the self-governing members of the British Commonwealth, with the Amban as the Governor-General with purely ceremonial functions.

The Foreign Office agreed with the basic principles of Shuckburg's definition, though there was some argument about the precise shape in which it would be presented to the Chinese Government: the India Office would have liked a formal distinction drawn between sovereignty and suzerainty, while the Foreign Office were unwilling to see the word sovereignty, in any context, injected into the language of Anglo-Chinese diplomacy over Tibet; sovereignty, in the event, was omitted.[42] By July a memorandum along these lines had been drafted;[43] and in August, both the Foreign Office and the India Office feeling that the time was now ripe for presenting to China 'in formal and unambiguous language' British views on the status of Tibet, Jordan was instructed to deliver the final text of the memorandum to the Chinese Government.[44] He did so on 17 August 1912.[45]

[41] PEF 1912/29, no. 753/1912, Memo. by J. E. Shuckburg.

[42] FO 371/1328, no. 34809, IO to FO, 15 August 1912, with minute by Grey.

[43] FO 535/15, no. 152, IO to FO, 11 July 1912.

[44] FO 535/15, no. 178, IO to FO, 15 August 1912, and no. 183, IO to FO, 20 August 1912; FO 371/1328, no. 33657, FO to IO, 15 August 1912.

[45] FO 535/15, no. 193, Jordan to Grey, 17 August 1912, enc. text of memo.

The full text of Jordan's memorandum, one of the most important documents in the history of British dealings with Tibet, is printed as Appendix XII. After warning the Chinese of the risks they ran if they persisted in attempting to send an expedition from Szechuan to the relief of the Lhasa garrison, Jordan made the following five points:

1. The British Government, while recognising Chinese suzerainty in Tibet, denied that this status conferred on the Chinese Republic any right to intervene in Tibetan internal administration beyond the specifications of the 1st Article of the Anglo-Chinese Convention of 1906.

2. Chinese actions in Tibet since 1910, when they began to take over the internal administration of the country, and the declared policy of Yuan Shih-k'ai's Presidential Order of 21 April 1912, that Tibet was to be 'regarded as on an equal footing with the Provinces of China Proper', should be repudiated by the Chinese Government.

3. The Chinese could have an Amban at Lhasa, with 'a suitable escort', and with the right to advise the Tibetans on their foreign relations, but they could not have in Tibet an unlimited number of Chinese troops.

4. The British would require a written declaration along the lines of points 1–3 before they would be prepared to recognise the Chinese Republic.

5. Until the Chinese made such a declaration, the British would close the Sino-Indian border 'absolutely' to the Chinese; and the only Chinese who would be allowed to cross that border would be troops withdrawing to India from Lhasa.

The despatch of this memorandum to the Wai-chiao-pu committed the British, in effect, to a further round of Anglo-Chinese negotiations over Tibet. Yuan Shih-k'ai, Jordan must have known, was not likely to make, without some preliminary struggle, the declaration which the British requested. The first three points of the memorandum, moreover, did not in themselves provide anything like a complete answer to the Tibetan problem as the British saw it. In the first place, there was no reference to the physical limits of Tibet as that term was to be understood in the context of the memorandum. The Chinese were very weak indeed in Central Tibet. Their strength in Eastern Tibet, however, could not be ignored. There could be no question of the Chinese accepting 'suzerain' status in all the territory occupied by populations of Tibetan ethnic stock and culture. A boundary between Chinese 'suzerain' Tibet and Chinese 'sovereign' Tibet would have to be drawn; and here considerable room for manoeuvre existed for both China and the British. In the second place, Jordan's memorandum contained no provision for the exercise of British influence in Tibet under Chinese 'suzerainty'. Would the Indian Government now have the right, which, in fact, it was already exploiting, of direct communication with the Dalai Lama's Government over matters other than those arising from the conduct of the trade marts? It was clear that the Indian Government were going to fight hard for the recognition of this right which, in any case, they were determined to enjoy *de facto*. Thus implicit in Jordan's memorandum was the question of something like a British Residency at Lhasa, which in itself involved a further consideration. The British were limited in their relations with Tibet by treaty with Russia as well as with China. It was hardly likely that as drastic a definition of Tibetan status as that which Jordan was now seeking could be secured without arousing Russian interest; and the British could hardly expect to exploit such a definition without Russian consent. Hence, by sending this document to the Chinese Government the British were involving themselves in rather more than argument and discussion with President Yuan Shih-k'ai. They were treading on diplomatic ground which, in theory, had been sealed off once and for all by the Anglo-Russian Convention of 1907. Of this the British were well aware. The despatch of Jordan's memorandum was only authorised after the India Office and Foreign Office, in consultation with Lord Hardinge, had exhaustively discussed the wider implications of the Chinese Revolution in Central Asia within the general framework of Anglo-Russian relations in Asia.

3. RUSSIA, CENTRAL ASIA AND THE CHINESE REVOLUTION

The decision to present to the Chinese Jordan's memorandum of 17 August 1912 was only taken after the India Office and the Foreign Office had examined most carefully the political situa-

tion then prevailing not only in Tibet but also in Mongolia and
Sinkiang.[46] Both Mongolia and Sinkiang had been affected by
the Chinese Revolution, and their future status seemed as
uncertain as did the status of Tibet. In 1906–7, when the Anglo-
Russian Convention was being negotiated, the British had been
careful to prevent the widening of the agenda to include discussion of parts of Chinese Central Asia other than Tibet. They
had perceived that the Russians had a great interest in the
future of Mongolia and they had appreciated that the Russians
already possessed a position of great strength in Sinkiang; but
they were unwilling, not surprisingly, to afford gratuitous
recognition to Russian special rights in either region. The
absence of major political crises in Mongolia and Sinkiang at
that time made it practicable for Nicolson to confine his formal
discussions to Tibet. In 1912, with the whole of Chinese Central
Asia affected by the outbreak of the Chinese Revolution, it
proved no longer possible for British diplomats to isolate the
Tibetan question as they had in 1907. The Revolution had
seriously weakened, if not broken entirely, the bonds which held
Chinese Central Asia to Peking. It seemed as if Mongolia and
Sinkiang were falling into Russian hands. Could the British
accept this development without also securing for themselves a
new, and more powerful, position in Tibet? Moreover, as a
corollary, would it not be diplomatically sound to demand from
Russia acceptance of an alteration in the permitted nature of
British relations with Tibet in exchange for British acknowledgment of Russian gains in Mongolia and Sinkiang?

During the 1906–7 negotiations in St. Petersburg, Nicolson
had looked on Tibet as a region where he could make concessions in order to obtain Russian acceptance of the essential
British provisions relating to Afghanistan. He had not tried to
balance British gains in Tibet against Russian gains elsewhere:
he had given away points in Tibet in the hope that the Russians
would give away points elsewhere: in the process he had
created a number of diplomatic precedents which his British
successors were subsequently to find irksome. The British now
clearly required to strengthen their hand for the future in Tibet

[46] FO 535/15, no. 177, contains India Office views, transmitted to the
Foreign Office in IO to FO, 15 August 1912, and a selection of Foreign
Office minutes.

so as to obviate any recurrence of the unsettling events of 1910–12 when the Chinese dominated Lhasa. It was logical, therefore, for British diplomats to suggest that Russia might be prepared to exchange a modification of the Tibetan restrictions in the 1907 Convention for British acceptance of the new Russian position in Sinkiang and Mongolia, especially in the latter. But was there any reason why the Russians should, in fact, do this? Mongolia and Sinkiang already lay within their grasp, and the British had no treaty grounds for protest; yet the Russians could legitimately protest against any British intervention in internal Tibetan affairs. The Russians would be fools indeed if they did not ask for something more than that which they already had for the taking in return for their agreement to relax the Tibetan part of the 1907 agreement. By the end of 1912 it had become obvious to the British Foreign Office that a too drastic alteration of the status of Tibet and of the pattern of British relations with the Dalai Lama's Government would probably lead to a Russian demand for a modification in the Persian and Afghan sections of the 1907 Convention. A new British position *vis-à-vis* Tibet could well turn out to be expensive.

During the last years of the Manchu Dynasty the Chinese had been extremely active in Mongolia. Their policy, so Russian observers felt, marked 'the last act of a great drama performed before our eyes; the annihilation of a once powerful nation—the Mongols'; and the result would be that 'China with her more than four hundred million population would soon become the immediate neighbour of Russia'.[47] Chinese policy was being directed towards the destruction of the power of the Mongol feudal chiefs and the sinification of the Mongol population, the end result being the incorporation of Mongolia within China proper. This process, distasteful to the Russians, was also resented by the Mongol population at all social levels. In July 1911 the leading chiefs and lamas in Mongolia sent a delegation to seek Russian help against the Chinese. The Russians decided to exploit the opportunities thus presented to them, an initial step being the reinforcement of their Consular guards in Urga which was already under way when the Chinese Revolution erupted in October.

[47] Tang, *Russia in Manchuria and Mongolia*, op. cit., p. 295.

In December 1911 the Mongols, under the leadership of the Urga Hutukhtu (the chief Incarnation of the Tibetan Buddhist Church in Mongolia), formally declared that Mongolia was 'an independent state under a new government, endowed with authority to manage its affairs independently of others', and they stated that from this moment 'we Mongols shall obey neither Manchu nor Chinese officials, whose administrative authority is being completely abolished and who, as a consequence, should be sent home'.[48] The new Mongolian Government, however, appreciated that it could not expect to survive as such for long in the face of Chinese counter-attacks without foreign support, which Russia was alone in a position to provide. Russia had helped and encouraged the Mongolian independence movement, and she could now maintain it in being; but Russia would certainly demand a price. The Mongol payment for Russian help was to be embodied in the Russo-Mongol Agreement of 21 October/3 November 1912 and the annexed Protocol (see Appendix XIII).[49] These documents gave Russia very substantial commercial and political rights in Mongolia and what amounted to control over Mongol foreign relations. Russia thus achieved in Mongolia what some of the supporters of Curzon's Tibetan policy had hoped the British would obtain in Tibet through the Younghusband Mission. All this the Mongol leaders were probably prepared to concede gladly enough. They may well have been less satisfied with another consequence of Russian support in their hour of need. The Russians, while determined to see the destruction of Chinese power in Mongolia, were yet unwilling to see the new Mongolia acquire the full status of a sovereign state in international law.

There were sound reasons for this attitude. A fully independent Mongolia was hardly likely to be accepted by the Chinese Republic without some struggle. Too much 'face', as it were,

[48] Ibid., p. 300.

[49] Before taking this step the Russians had cleared the ground with the Japanese in July 1912 by recognising a Japanese sphere of interest in those parts of Mongolia, Inner Mongolia as they came to be called, which had not broken away from China, in return for which the Japanese accepted the special Russian interests in Outer Mongolia. Both Japanese and Russian diplomats denied that any such arrangement had been arrived at. See E. H. Zabriskie, *American-Russian Rivalry in the Far East: a study in diplomacy and power politics 1895–1914*, Philadelphia, 1946, p. 187.

was involved. To establish Mongolian independence, therefore, the Russians would probably have to intervene actively in a Sino-Mongol war, and in the process risk great expense as well as damage to their interests elsewhere in China. The Russian objectives in Mongolia, the protection of Russian commerce and the creation of a buffer between Russian and Chinese territory, could best be achieved by a Mongolia which was autonomous in its internal affairs yet which acknowledged Chinese suzerainty in the sense that the British had come to apply that term to Tibet. Russia would still get what she wanted and Chinese 'face' would be saved. This settlement of the Mongolian problem the Russians were to arrive at through the Russo-Chinese Declaration and exchange of notes regarding Outer Mongolia of 23 October/5 November 1913.[50] The Protocol attached to the Russo-Mongol Agreement of 21 October/3 November 1912 was acknowledged, but not the Agreement itself, with its implications of full Mongolian independence. Outer Mongolia, that is to say the portion of Mongol-inhabited territory which had broken away from China in 1911, was recognised as autonomous but 'under the suzerainty of China'. The Chinese agreed neither to send troops into Outer Mongolia nor to intervene in its internal affairs: however, they could maintain a representative, described in the Agreement as a 'Dignitary', in Urga with a suitable staff and escort. The Agreement, both in its wording and its implications, recalled very strongly the terms of the British memorandum on Tibet of 17 August 1912; and, indeed, the policies leading to these two documents were in many ways very similar.

The parallels between Russian interests in Mongolia and British interests in Tibet did not, of course, escape the notice of British observers. As *The Times* remarked on 3 December 1912:

> The analogy between the Tibetan and Mongolian cases is close. Over both territories Chinese claims were shadowy. Both territories were administratively independent until recent years, when China inaugurated the forward foreign policy that has resulted in two serious checks. Great Britain and Russia have both said practically the same thing in regard to Tibet and Mongolia respectively—no interference with their autonomy.

[50] Appendix XV.

Thus it was inevitable that the British, when formulating the policy behind the memorandum of 17 August 1912, should consider the possibility of coming to terms with the Russians. Perhaps, in exchange for a British recognition of the changed status of Outer Mongolia the Russians might be persuaded to overlook some disregard on the British part of the terms of the 1907 Anglo-Russian Agreement relating to Tibet. It was optimistic, however, to hope that such an exchange could be arranged without also considering other areas of Asia where Russia wished to increase her influence. Sinkiang, for instance, could not be ignored.

Sinkiang, Chinese Turkestan, had long been looked upon by the British as the essential buffer to Kashmir.[51] In the last decade of the nineteenth century the region had been the scene of competition between the British and the Russians, to a great extent carried on by the Russian Consulate in Kashgar and by the British agent in that city, whom the Chinese finally recognised as possessing Consular status in 1908. Sinkiang was in British strategic thinking a barrier between the Russian and British Empires. By the Pamirs Agreement of 1895, which defined the eastern end of the Russo-Afghan border, the British hoped that they had obtained some stability for Sinkiang in this role.[52] However, the western border of Sinkiang with Russia had never been defined. It was still possible for Russia to advance into Chinese-held territory from the Pamirs; and in 1901, with the establishment of a Russian armed post at Tashkurghan on the Chinese side of the Sarikol range, it looked as if a further Russian encroachment was about to begin. The result was a British attempt to obtain from China a defined boundary between Sinkiang and Kashmir so as to deprive the Russians, should they decide to annex Sinkiang, of the opportunity to exploit to their own political advantage disputes and uncertainties along the British frontier in the Karakoram. Between 1901 and 1912, in fact, the Russians did not come any closer to the British

51 See Lamb, *China-India Border*, op. cit., for a brief account of the history of the Sinkiang-Kashmir boundary and of British policy respecting its alignment.

52 The history of the Pamirs Agreement of 1895 is related in some considerable detail in G. J. Alder, *British India's Northern Frontier 1865–1895*, London, 1963.

border in Kashmir; but they continued to show an active interest in Sinkiang which suggested that it would be rash to overlook the possibility of another Russian forward move. With the outbreak of the Chinese Revolution many observers both in England and in India, including George Macartney (the British Consul at Kashgar), thought that Russia would now take over the whole province. There had been mutinies of Chinese troops, riots in Kashgar and other cities, and attacks against Russian subjects and Russian-protected persons. As, so St. Petersburg said, a measure of self-defence, in June 1912 the Russian Consular guard at Kashgar was reinforced by some 700 Cossacks with artillery support, and smaller bodies of troops were sent to other Russian Consular posts throughout Sinkiang. The Indian Government, watching closely these Russian moves as reported by George Macartney, concluded that unless something was done the present Russian augmentation of force would turn into a permanent military occupation, and Sinkiang would 'become, in fact if not in name, a Russian protectorate'.[53] But what could the British do; and should they, in fact, do anything?

While a Russian occupation of Sinkiang was certainly not welcomed, yet the India Office did not feel that the British had either the strength or the will to offer any physical opposition north of the Karakoram Range. If the Russians really wanted Sinkiang, it was theirs for the taking. In any case, the resultant British loss would not be disastrously great. A small diminution in prestige in an area where British prestige could hardly be said to be striking in the face of the active Russian Consulate at Kashgar, a small loss in trade in a region where the Russians, with their easier lines of communication, could compete advantageously in the market-place with goods coming from British India; neither of these results could possibly justify serious British alarm. The Russians, once in Sinkiang, would, of course, be very much nearer to the centres of population in British India; but they were likely to do little harm if British vigilance added strength to the natural obstacles presented by the mountains of Northern Kashmir. It would certainly be as well to make sure that the new Anglo-Russian border was kept as far north as possible. Any British diplomatic acceptance of

[53] FO 535/15, no. 177, Minute by R. T. Nugent, 26 August 1912.

Russian annexation or occupation of Sinkiang would be unthinkable without a satisfactory settlement of the resultant (if only *de facto*) Anglo-Russian border. On the whole, however, so Lord Crewe told the Foreign Office,

> there seems to be no plausible case for diplomatic action at present, and, indeed, it is for consideration whether it would not rather be advantageous to acquiesce in an eventual Russian occupation, provided that suitable compensation is given elsewhere. Such compensation . . . might be found in Tibet, where the terms of the Anglo-Russian Convention are making it increasingly difficult for His Majesty's Government to regulate their relations with the Dalai Lama and the Chinese in a manner consistent with their interests.[54]

Thus the new situation in Sinkiang, the result of the Chinese Revolution, suggested, as did the situation in Mongolia, the possibility of securing from Russia a relaxation, if only tacit, of the shackles which the Anglo-Russian Convention of 1907 imposed upon the British freedom of action in Tibet.

The idea of a revision of the 1907 Convention, which seemed so attractive to Lord Crewe, was received with a certain amount of scepticism by some officials in the Foreign Office, familiar as they were with the practical problems of Anglo-Russian diplomacy. Sir Eyre Crowe, than whom there can hardly have been at that time a more able diplomatist in the British service, noted that

> the difficulties of any revision of the agreement with Russia and of practically ousting the Chinese from Tibet after our having played into their hands during years of inactivity, if not encouragement, will undoubtedly be great. The policy of His Majesty's Government in first going to Lhasa and then retiring without making any arrangements for securing either a recognition of British or the stability of any native authority was much criticised at the time. It looks as if the India Office have now come to the conclusion that the policy of negation was a mistake. But, meanwhile, we have put serious obstacles in the way by tying our hands by the Russian agreement.[55]

Crowe thought, however, that it was certainly worth attempting

[54] FO 535/15, no. 177, IO to FO, 15 August 1912.
[55] FO 535/15, no. 177, Minute by Sir E. Crowe, 2 September 1912.

to remove some of these obstacles. Even the Indian Government, which could never be happy at the idea of British acceptance of a Russian advance to positions touching the Indian border, agreed that Sinkiang lay beyond the range of effective British resistance. If Sinkiang had to be surrendered to Russia, and provided a better Sinkiang-Kashmir border had been first secured, then the Russian granting of a free British hand in Tibet would, Lord Hardinge decided, be 'the ideal compensation'. The consensus of British official opinion, therefore, was that the revision of the Anglo-Russian Convention should at least be explored; and the opportunity lay conveniently to hand in Sazonov's proposed visit to England in September 1912.

Sazonov, the Russian Foreign Minister, hoped to talk over with members of the British Cabinet the unsatisfactory state of Anglo-Russian relations in and concerning Persia.[56] Since one part of the 1907 Convention would thus in effect be under discussion, it seemed to both Grey and Crewe that issues arising from another part might properly be raised simultaneously at this time. Sir George Buchanan, the British Ambassador in St. Petersburg, was therefore instructed to find out what Sazonov felt about adding Tibet and other Chinese Central Asian regions to the agenda of the forthcoming talks. Buchanan was, at first, hopeful that the Russians would be co-operative. The Russian press, he reported, had been most sympathetic to British problems in relation to Tibet. The *Novoe Vremya* of 10 September 1912, for example, drew the parallel between Britain in Tibet and Russia in Mongolia, urging the Russian

[56] A collection of papers relating to Sazonov's visit are to be found in G. P. Gooch and H. Temperley, ed., *British Documents on the Origins of the War 1898–1914*, Vol. IX, *The Balkan Wars*, Pt. I, *The Prelude; The Tripoli War*, London, 1933 (referred to hereafter as BD IX (1)), pp. 749–72.

1912 was a year of crisis in Persia following the Russian opposition to the American Financial Mission to Persia of 1911, led by W. Morgan Shuster. The Russians, attacked by Persian Nationalists, undertook the military occupation of Northern Persia which culminated, in March 1912, in their bombardment of the Shrine of *Imam* Reza at Meshed. The Russians, with their increased power in Persia, were seeking some modification of the partition into British and Russian spheres of influence of 1907. By this time the British were also dissatisfied with the 1907 partition and were prepared to discuss some modification of the so-called Neutral Zone.

See Sir P. Sykes, *A History of Persia*, 2 vols., London, 1951, Vol. II, Ch. LXXXIV.

Government to apply the same kind of pressure in relation to Mongolia as the British were then doing in relation to Tibet, this last remark being a reference to Jordan's memorandum of 17 August.[57] In a farewell conversation with the British Ambassador before leaving for London, Sazonov indicated that he was prepared to discuss Tibet and Mongolia as well as Persia, which Buchanan took to be encouraging.[58] This optimism, however, did not long survive the Russian Foreign Minister's arrival in England.

Sazonov made his position clear enough to Sir Edward Grey at Balmoral on 24 September. As Grey described this interview:

> I explained to M. Sazonof why a Chinese invasion of Tibet would disturb us by probably causing war between the Nepalese and Chinese. We had, I hoped, averted a Chinese invasion by diplomatic representations at Peking, and we hoped Tibetan autonomy under Chinese suzerainty would be preserved. If so, we desired nothing except the commercial treaty that we already had with Tibet. But unforeseen trouble might arise that might make it desirable for us to send some agent to Lhasa to keep us informed. I had no proposal to make at the moment, but a contingency might arise in which we should have to ask Russia for some relaxation on our side of the agreement about Tibet. M. Sazonof said that he would be ready to listen to this, but that he would require some *quid pro quo* for Russia. Mongolia was outside the Anglo-Russian agreement, and he could not regard that as *in pari materia* with Tibet. He assured me that Dorjief had no mission from Russia and was in Tibet on his own adventure.[59]

All this can be boiled down to the statement that Sazonov would not agree to a formal modification of the Tibet part of the 1907 Convention in exchange for a British acknowledgment of Russian freedom of action in Mongolia; he would require a compensating British concession within the framework of the 1907 Convention, which, of course, did not relate to Mongolia

[57] FO 535/15, no. 210, Buchanan to Grey, 11 September 1912.
[58] FO 535/15, no. 219, Buchanan to Grey, 18 September 1912.
[59] FO 535/15, no. 226, Note on Tibet by Sir E. Grey, 24 September 1912; BD IX (1), p. 758. For Sazonov's version of this interview, see J. J. Korostovetz, *Von Cinggis Khan zur Sowjetrepublik*, Berlin and Leipzig, 1926, p. 135, quoting from *Krasny Archiv III*.

at all. The kind of concession Sazonov had in mind emerged from his conversation with Lord Crewe, at Crewe Hall on 29 September. Crewe reported that:

> As to Tibet, about which Sir Edward Grey had already spoken, I said that we had no wish to enter it, but quite the contrary, and that in my view, the posting at Lhasa of a British officer as agent would not be worth the risk. But India must regard with concern any Chinese encroachment in Tibet, and we had told the Chinese Government so in terms undiplomatically frank. It might therefore be necessary to know what was going on in Tibet from a source on which we could rely. M. Sazonof said that if any definite change were made in the convention which would appear to our sole advantage, he would be seriously attacked at home. He hoped we should be willing, therefore, to obtain our information privately. I asked whether, if Chinese aggression caused us to take action apparently contrary to the convention, public opinion in Russia would not be more excited than if it were modified in cold blood to a slight extent. M. Sazonof emphatically disputed this, and said that, for example, our recent warning to China was now well known in Russia, and if as a sequel to a Chinese advance we were to occupy the Chumbi Valley, he did not believe that a word would be said. When I mentioned some rectification of the Nepal frontier, he said that this would be on a different footing, because it affected the subject-matter about which the convention was framed. On the whole, however, he thought it better to deal with any matter affecting Tibet as it naturally arose, and not to attempt a formal revision of any points. At the same time, if we were able to give material assistance in smoothing things with Afghanistan, he would be able to face opinion in Russia more easily in connection with other questions.[60]

All this was a rather long-winded way of saying that the Russians would not be prepared to accept any formal revision of the 1907 Convention without receiving compensation in the direction of Afghanistan, though they might (or they might not) acquiesce in informal breaches of the 1907 Convention without making such demands: this remained the Russian

[60] FO 535/15, no. 229, Note on a conversation between Lord Crewe and M. Sazonov at Crewe Hall, 29 September 1912; see also BD IX (1), pp. 759–61.

position until the collapse of the Tsarist régime in 1917.[61]

What did Russia want in Afghanistan? Sazonov, during his English visit, gave a number of examples of the Russian need for a more complex mechanism of Russo-Afghan relations.[62] There was, for example, the problem of the use of water for irrigation purposes from rivers which ran from Afghanistan into Russia. In recent years Afghan cultivation on the Murghab had been increasing, and the water supply from that river on the Russian side had been declining. Some Russo-Afghan agreement on the division of these waters was required. Could this be achieved without negotiations at Kabul, whither the Russians in 1907 had agreed not to send their agents?[63] Probably not. Again, Sazonov pointed to such matters as the spread of bubonic plague and locust swarms from Afghanistan into Russia, matters calling for a greater measure of discussion between the Russian and Afghan authorities than those permitted in 1907. Sazonov made no definite proposals about Afghanistan at this time; but the British suspected that what he was, in fact, seeking was something in the nature of a Russian sphere of interest in the northern and north-western portion of the country. The recent increase of Russian military strength in North-East Persia, for example the establishment of a Cossack post at Turbat-i-Shaikh Jam not far from Herat, and the Russian proposals for the construction of a railway along the Oxus to Termez on the Afghan border, pointed to such an ambition. To the Indian Government, which for nearly a century had been dedicated to the total exclusion of Tsarist influence from the Amir's realm, the implications of Sazonov's

[61] See, for example, PEF 1912/82, Memo. by Political Department, India Office, of August 1915 entitled *Revision of Anglo-Russian Convention of 1907*.

Some commentators have misunderstood the Russian position. E. B. Price, for example, in his *Russo-Japanese Treaties*, op. cit., p. 64, suggests that Sazonov did, in fact, give the British a free hand in Tibet in exchange for a British promise not to protest against Russian actions in Mongolia.

[62] For documents relating to the question of Russian interests in Afghanistan at this time, see the FO Confidential Print volume (Conf. 10295), *Correspondence respecting Russia and Central Asia 1912*.

[63] The 1907 agreement only permitted the Russians a measure of contact with local officials on the Afghan side of the frontier: it denied the right of any Russian representation at the capital.

remarks were hardly welcome; and it became far less eager to allow the Tibetan question to be subjected to Anglo-Russian discussion than was the Home Government in London. It did not, moreover, forget that the Amir had never given his assent to the Afghan section of the 1907 Convention, which, therefore, it could well be argued was invalid. What if the Russians, after fruitless talks with the British over Afghanistan, decided that they could legally ignore the restrictions imposed on them in this direction in 1907? Would the British be able, in fact, to protest with much force if the Russians did send an agent to Kabul, especially if it could be shown that the Indian Government was itself ignoring the 1907 Convention in relation to Tibet?

Could the British, perhaps, make concessions in Sinkiang rather than Afghanistan? From what Sazonov said to Lord Crewe there seemed to be scant grounds for optimism in this direction. As Lord Crewe recorded their conversation on 29 September:

> We did not discuss in detail the question of Chinese Turkestan, Hunza, &c., M. Sazonow saying that he wished to declare categorically that Russia had no wish to take over the administration of Chinese Turkestan. If there was ever a question of advancing in that region, it would only be in the immediate neighbourhood of its northern boundary, by Kulja and the Ili River, where the frontier was easy to cross and where incidents might occur on either side. But as to Kashgar and the Kashmir frontier, they were most inaccessible from Russian Turkestan, and they had no desire for any footing there. It was only the ill-treatment, of a barbarous sort, of Russian traders at Kashgar which had caused the increase of the force [of Cossack guards at the Russian Consulate], and there was no wish to leave it there. In any part of Chinese Turkestan there would be no question of a Russian move without informing us beforehand.[64]

It is unlikely that Crewe and his colleagues believed all this; but they could hardly avoid accepting Sazonov's word. Sinkiang was, therefore, for the present unusable as a British pawn to be exchanged, as it were, for the Tibetan bishop.

Sazonov had indicated that the Russians were not prepared

[64] BD IX (1), p. 760.

to accept a straight Mongolia-Tibet exchange, thus hampering British policy to the north of the Himalayan range: yet by the end of 1912 it was becoming apparent to many British observers that the very fact of the increase of Russian influence in Mongolia necessitated a closer British watch on the course of events in Tibet. In November 1912, as we have already seen, the Russians accepted, if only provisionally, Outer Mongolian independence from China.[65] A month earlier the *Tsongdu*, the Tibetan National Assembly, informed Lord Hardinge that Tibet had now broken off all connection with China and would like to see all Chinese officials and soldiers leave Tibet, words which recalled the Mongolian declaration of independence of December 1911.[66] In late 1912 Tibet and Outer Mongolia, now behaving as if they were fully independent states, began negotiations which culminated in the Tibeto-Mongol Treaty of 11 January 1913. The chief Tibetan delegate was Dorjiev, who then went straight on from Urga to St. Petersburg, bringing with him yet another letter from the Dalai Lama to the Tsar.[67] At about the same time a Mongolian mission also arrived at St. Petersburg to request the establishment of what amounted to a Russian embassy at Urga, the capital of the new state which was soon to be known as Outer Mongolia.[68] If the Russians agreed, then they would have acquired formally what they already in fact possessed, powerful influence at the centre of a state with unique treaty relations with Tibet. Since the Tibeto-Mongol treaty in its Third Article declared that 'both States, the Mongolian and the Tibetan, shall henceforth, for all time, afford each other aid against dangers from without and from within', it now appeared that Russia had acquired the theoretical means to intervene very actively indeed in Tibetan affairs. For example, were the Dalai Lama to ask for Mongol military help against the Chinese, what was there to prevent the Russians from training and equipping a Mongolian expeditionary force for Tibetan service, with all that that implied in terms

[65] See pp. 438–41 above and Appendix XIII.

[66] FO 535/15, no. 284, IO to FO, 11 November 1912.

[67] *The Times*, 6 January 1913; *Daily Telegraph*, 15 January 1913; FO 371/1609, no. 7222, Buchanan to Grey, 14 February 1913.

For text of the Tibeto-Mongol treaty, and for further references relating to it, see Appendix XIV.

[68] FO 371/1608, no. 2252, Buchanan to Grey, 13 January 1913.

of indirect Russian political influence in Tibet? It might be argued that at this time Mongolia was not actually in territorial contact with Tibet, being separated from it by Kansu and Sinkiang. In fact, however, the desolate tracts in question were no barrier. Nomad travel between Mongolia and north-eastern Tibet was frequent and quite beyond the Chinese power to control. Moreover, if Sinkiang did fall into Russian hands, even this flimsy membrane between Tibet and the Russian sphere of influence would have been punctured.

Sazonov told Buchanan that he considered the Tibeto-Mongol Treaty to be '*nul et non avenu*'.[69] Tibetan Ministers like the Lönchen Shatra were later to deny that Dorjiev had ever been authorised by the Dalai Lama to sign it. Yet British officials in London, India and Peking could not forget its implications. Even if invalid, there was nothing to prevent its subsequent validation. Moreover, a formal treaty was not necessary for Russian-sponsored Mongol intervention in Tibetan affairs. The political changes in Tibet and Mongolia since the outbreak of the Chinese Revolution in themselves created the opportunity for a Russian forward policy in Chinese Central Asia which would hardly have been possible in the days when Curzon was so alarmed by the first Dorjiev missions from Lhasa to St. Petersburg. Russian intervention in Tibet through Mongolia was something more than a theoretical possibility. The very head of the new Mongol state, the Urga Hutukhtu, so Jordan reported, was, in fact, a Tibetan and the son of a man in the Dalai Lama's service. A Mongol army of some 6,000 men was in process of being trained by Russian advisers. Russian

[69] FO 371/1608, no. 2600, Buchanan to Grey, 17 January 1913. Sazonov maintained that, as a Russian subject, Dorjiev could not possibly act in a diplomatic capacity on behalf of the Dalai Lama, a peculiar argument, to say the least. The British Foreign Office, at all events, thought that Sazonov's professions as to the innocence of Dorjiev's activities should be taken '*cum grano*'.

Modern commentators have been divided in their views as to the validity of the Tibeto-Mongol treaty. People like Bell have tended, at least in public, to dismiss it. W. K. Lee, in his *Tibet in Modern World Politics*, New York, 1931, p. 139, accepts it as a valid treaty. In a review of Lee's book, however, in the *Chinese Social and Political Science Review*, XVI, 1932–3, Shao Hsun-cheng denies that Dorjiev had any powers to make binding treaties of this kind; but then the Chinese patriots have always found it hard to accept treaties which Tibet made without Chinese participation.

firms were busy despatching Winchester rifles to Lhasa by way of their agents in Urga. The Russians had just posted two Buriats, who had completed training in Urga as Consular students, to Kumbum on the Kansu-Tibet border; and these men, Jordan thought, 'will now doubtless form a link of connection between Lhasa and the Russian agency at Urga'.[70] The Tibetan implications of the Mongolian situation simply could not be ignored; and by March 1913 some acute British observers appreciated that everything pointed to the need for a major revision of the Anglo-Russian Convention of 1907. Sir Eyre Crowe's opinion on this point has already been noted. It is interesting to see that the Tibeto-Mongol treaty also convinced Sir Arthur Nicolson, the actual negotiator with Isvolski of the 1907 agreements, that he had secured a less than perfect instrument. He had been largely responsible for the exclusion of Mongolia from the St. Petersburg agenda in 1906–7: by March 1913 he must have concluded that in this he had been mistaken. As he minuted:

> What I am anxious about are Russo-Tibetan relations via Mongolia, and how we can parry a large increase, even if indirect, of Russian influence in Tibet—which to my mind seems fairly imminent. The best means which occur to me in order to define at least, if we cannot counteract, the influence which Russia is evidently intent on establishing, would be by a frank discussion with her and either a complete revision of the existing Anglo-Russian Convention or the drafting of a new Convention. Since 1907 various very important events have occurred directly affecting Tibet. I need not enumerate them, but they distinctly alter the *status quo* in Tibet and both Russian and British relations towards Tibet. It would, I submit, be unwise to let Russia under cover of the [Urga] Hutukhtu have direct relations with Lhasa and the Dalai Lama. Our relations with Russia are at present very friendly, and long may they remain so, but conditions and friendships do undergo changes, and I think we should, if possible, provide for all contingencies.[71]

Sir Edward Grey agreed with Nicolson's reasoning; but, he minuted, 'I fear that if we ask directly for an alteration of the

[70] FO 371/1608, no. 13452, Jordan to Grey, 10 March 1913.
[71] FO 371/1610, no. 12462, Minute by Nicolson, 12 March 1913.

Anglo-Russian agreement about Tibet, they [the Russians] will ask for some improvement from their point of view about the Afghan agreement.' This had been his conclusion from the Sazonov talks of September 1912.[72] Were there other approaches to the Tibetan problem which did not involve decisions quite so drastic as the alteration of the position of Afghanistan in Anglo-Russian diplomacy, an issue which had led to two British wars in the Hindu Kush? Foreign Office and India Office memoranda of January 1913, which were submitted to the Cabinet for consideration on 27 January 1913, illustrate clearly the range of policies then available to the British.[73] One possibility was *not* considered seriously, namely the inauguration of some measure of joint Anglo-Russian intervention in Tibet, perhaps disguised as a scientific mission, as Rockhill had suggested in early 1911: the British were trying to keep the Russians out of Tibet and saw no advantage at all in providing them with a gratuitous foothold in that country. Some thought was given to helping the Chinese reoccupy Central Tibet in return for a Chinese settlement of the whole Indo-Tibetan and Sino-Burmese boundary alignment to the satisfaction of British requirements: but this would involve the abandonment of the potential advantages of a weak Tibet in exchange for Chinese promises of very doubtful value: the idea was only advanced, in fact, so that it could be rejected and got out of the way. Another possibility, and one which had been dear to some British strategists ever since the Curzon era, was the use of Nepal. Nepalese troops could drive the remaining Chinese forces out of Tibet and make sure that they did not return. The British could perhaps establish, through Katmandu, an indirect protectorate over the Dalai Lama against which the Russians would not find it so easy to protest. Such use of Nepal, however, ran counter to the prevailing trend of British policy towards that Himalayan kingdom which was aimed at limiting, not increasing, the freedom of action of the Durbar. Nepal,

[72] FO 371/1610, no. 12462, Minute by Grey, 12 March 1913.

[73] FO 371/1609, no. 4477, Foreign Office memorandum on Tibet, January 1913; PEF 1913/16, no. 3191/13, Tibet, memo. by Sir A. Hirtzl of the India Office, 27 January 1913.

See also PEF 1908/23, no. 252/13, IO minute of 27 January 1913; FO 371/1609, no. 2534, Viceroy to Secretary of State, 16 January 1913.

once unleashed into Tibet, might prove impossible to control; and Nepalese involvement in Central Asian military adventures would certainly drain off Gurkha recruits needed for the British service. The Gurkhas, so Sir Arthur Hirtzl of the India Office wrote, 'form the best fighting material of the Indian army'.[74] If the Nepalese forces were not used in Tibet, perhaps the British might employ their own troops, in the process completely ignoring the 1907 Convention. British intervention could take a number of forms, ranging from a full-scale expedition to Lhasa, through limited British expeditions into Chumbi and Zayul, to the supplying of the Tibetans with British weapons and military instructors. In its heart of hearts the Indian Government would probably have liked to do something along these lines, an extension, as it were, of the policy behind the Abor Expedition; but it knew that on both diplomatic and financial grounds such intervention was quite out of the question at this period of growing tension in Europe. Thus only the policy indicated in the memorandum of 17 August 1912 remained.

The memorandum of 17 August implied, in fact, not only Chinese but also Tibetan agreement. It was a compromise scheme of the kind which the British are said to be so clever in devising. British requirements were that Tibet should cease to be a threat to the Indian border, which meant the exclusion of both Chinese and Russian (or indirect Russian via Mongolia) influences, while at the same time its political status should not appear to be modified by British action in such a way as to invite Russian protests, invoking the 1907 Convention, and Russian demands for compensation in other sensitive portions of the Indian frontier zone like Afghanistan. To secure all this the Chinese would have to agree to surrender the realities of power, present and future, in Central Tibet, in exchange for a 'face-saving' recognition of their suzerainty there; and the Tibetans would have to abandon their pretensions to complete political independence in return for the guaranteed enjoyment of internal autonomy. Both sides, however, would gain real advantages by such an arrangement. China would get recognition of suzerainty, of however little practical value that status might be, in a Central Tibet which had slipped from her grasp and which, otherwise, might well leave the Chinese community

[74] PEF 1913/16, Tibet, memo. by Hirtzl, 27 January 1913.

altogether. Tibet would be relieved from the constant threat of Chinese counter-attacks from the Marches and from the fear that one day a strong China might regain what a weak China had lost in 1912. The British were very hopeful that a settlement on this pattern might be arrived at. The process, of course, would certainly involve a degree of British diplomatic contact with the Tibetans which might perhaps be interpreted as an infringement of the letter of the 1907 Convention with Russia. However, the diplomacy in question could well be secret; and this would, in the opinion of many British observers, satisfy the Russians. As Lord Crewe remarked to Grey, after having had some three months in which to digest the implications of his conversations with Sazonov, what the Russian Foreign Minister was really saying was 'that it does not matter what we do in Tibet, if only it is done *sub rosa*, but that he cannot face any modification of our pledges'.[75]

The compromise solution to the Tibetan problem, as Jordan, for one, appreciated, implied some form of tripartite agreement between the Tibetans, Chinese and British: this, in his view, was a logical development of the memorandum of 17 August 1912. For one thing, the settlement of Tibetan status involved the definition of the physical limits of the state ruled by the Dalai Lama and the establishment of his boundaries with the Chinese. The Chinese would have to accept an autonomous Tibet of such dimensions as to keep directly ruled Chinese territory from touching upon the sensitive tracts of the British Indian northern and north-eastern border. Only the British presence at the negotiations could ensure that this was properly done. In a telegram to Grey of 6 March 1913 he outlined a scheme for the solution of the Tibetan problem along these lines which was really a rough blue-print for the Simla Conference which opened in the autumn of that year. He said that

> these new facts—the elimination of Chinese influence [in Tibet] and the connection which Russia has established through Mongolia—seem to me to demand revision of our Tibetan policy and an abandonment of our disinterested attitude unless we are prepared to see Tibet, which cannot, I conceive, long stand alone, gravitate towards Russia. The

[75] FO 371/1609, no. 4477, Crewe to Grey, 22 January 1913.

first essential of such a change would be the establishment of closer relations with the Dalai Lama and a fuller knowledge of what arrangements the Tibetan Government are prepared to make. In return for a guarantee against Chinese encroachment on her eastern border, Tibet might be induced to authorise the reinstatement at Lhasa of a Chinese Amban with a suitable escort. A tripartite agreement between Great Britain, China and Tibet would probably be the best solution, and negotiations in India between the three parties would serve as a useful preliminary to such an agreement; even their failure would leave us in a better position to negotiate with Tibet independently of China.[76]

Jordan's tripartite conference and agreement, while it provided some goal towards which British policy-makers could strive, still did not eliminate the prospect of Anglo-Russian discussions: it merely postponed it. Any formal change in the status of Tibet or in the nature of British relations with that region, if it was to be of the slightest value to the Indian Government, still involved the removal of some of the prohibitions implicitly or explicitly contained in the Anglo-Russian Convention of 1907. Jordan's 'first essential', the 'establishment of closer relations with the Dalai Lama', simply could not be achieved without violating the 1907 agreement, in which the British had declared that they would have no political relations with the Dalai Lama, except through the Chinese, on questions other than those relating to trade and the trade marts specified in the 1890, 1904 and 1906 Conventions. This fact presented the British with three choices. Firstly, they could go ahead with their negotiations with the Dalai Lama and the establishment of their Resident, by whatever title he might be known, in Lhasa without consulting the Russians at all. This would amount, as Sazonov was to remark in 1914, to the 'tearing up' of the Anglo-Russian Convention. In view of the Anglo-Russian relationship in European affairs, such a step would hardly be in tune with the spirit of the times. Secondly, they could come to some tacit settlement of Tibet by tripartite talks between China, Britain and Tibet which yielded no valid agreement, a *de facto* but not *de jure* solution. But was it likely that any solution which was not *de jure* would also be stable and durable? Thirdly, they

[76] PEF 1913/40, no. 916/13, Jordan to Grey, 6 March 1913.

could seek Russian consent for a modification of the 1907 terms in respect to Tibet, thus running the very real risk that Russia would demand in return compensations in other Asian regions. Tibet would have to be balanced against Persia, Afghanistan and, perhaps, Sinkiang. By the end of 1917, with the collapse of the Tsarist régime in Russia, the British had still not fully made up their minds which choice they would take.

PART THREE
The Simla Conference and the
McMahon Line, 1913 to 1914

XXII

THE CHINESE AGREE TO ATTEND A CONFERENCE AT SIMLA

THE Chinese Government, as might have been expected, made no effort to volunteer a reply to Jordan's memorandum of 17 August 1912; and, until the Home Government had had time to reflect upon the implications of Sazonov's remarks and to arrive at some idea as to how its policy in Tibet could be related to that of Russia in Mongolia and Sinkiang, Jordan was not instructed to press the Chinese on this matter. It was clear, at all events, that Yuan Shih-k'ai's Government were not likely to produce an acceptable statement on Tibet without a great deal of argument backed by threats. Some of Yuan's colleagues, members of the Young China Party like Dr. Yen, the Vice-Minister for Foreign Affairs, were bitterly opposed to any surrender of the Chinese position in Tibet which the Manchus had acquired in 1910. They saw Tibet as a region whither China could export her excess population, and they announced in journals sympathetic to their views that if the British interfered with Chinese 'colonising projects on their frontier dominions, they [the Chinese] may be obliged to turn their attention to Australia and to convert it into an outlet for their surplus millions'.[1] Such men could hardly be expected to give up Tibet merely because the British asked them to do so.

On 3 December the India Office finally decided that the time had come for the Chinese to be made to answer the memorandum.[2] There was no longer any point in hoping for Russian co-operation. Moreover, the Chinese, who had been

[1] FO 535/15, no. 235, Jordan to Grey, 12 September 1912.
[2] FO 535/15, no. 296, IO to FO, 3 December 1912.

very active in Eastern Tibet in the late summer and autumn, going on with projects for the creation of Sikang Province, for example, and proposing to bring Zayul once more under direct Chinese administration, were now held up by the onset of winter. Before the opening of the new campaigning season in the spring of 1913 they should be made to agree to a clear limit to their territory in the Marches, so that never again would Chinese troops and officials have direct access to the British border in the Assam Himalayas.[3] The Chinese, so Lord Crewe felt, should also be forced now to accept a definition of the Sino-Burmese border along the line of the Salween-Irrawaddy divide and to abandon all claims to Pienma and Hkamtilong. If the withholding of British recognition of the Republic did not prove to be threat enough for the Chinese, then

> Sir J. Jordan should be instructed to inform them that unless they are prepared to negotiate on the lines indicated, and to carry the negotiations through within three months, His Majesty's Government will regard the Anglo-Chinese Convention of 1906 as no longer holding good, and will hold themselves free to enter into direct negotiations with Tibet. Moreover, should Chinese troops enter Tibet, they will be prepared to give active assistance to the Tibetans in resisting their advance and in establishing and maintaining Tibetan independence.

The last sentence, of course, served to emphasise the need for a definition of boundaries: at what point must the Chinese stop if they wished to avoid British military aid to the Dalai Lama? The Chinese, the India Office declared in conclusion, should reply to Jordan within fourteen days of receipt of his reminder, which should be, in fact, an ultimatum, of the 17 August memorandum.

[3] At this point Crewe and the India Office were inclined towards leaving far more territory in Chinese hands than the Indian Government were to propose. Crewe thought that Zayul should fall within the dominions of the Dalai Lama, but that De-ge and Chamdo, 'the districts the conquest of which she has shown herself able effectively to maintain', should continue under Chinese rule. It is a pity that the India Office did not adhere to this view. It was McMahon's insistence that the Chinese should surrender Chamdo, more than any other factor, which prevented the Chinese from signing the Simla Convention. See PEF 1912/29, no. 657/13, IO to FO, 3 December 1912.

Grey saw much merit in the India Office proposals, which he transmitted to Jordan for comment.[4] The Foreign Office, of course, realised that the threat of direct Anglo-Tibetan discussions and British military support for the Dalai Lama involved consideration of the 1907 Convention; and it was clear that the Russians, at this stage, would not make any Tibetan concessions without a *quid pro quo*, probably in Afghanistan; but Nicolson thought that they might not be so unreasonable if faced with a *fait accompli*. In any case, as the India Office had pointed out, it was unlikely that the Chinese could ignore the possibility of direct British dealings with the Dalai Lama on the analogy of recent Russian relations with the Mongols. To do so would be to provide an occasion for international recognition of Tibetan independence, which it had long been the object of Chinese policy, under both the Manchus and the Republic, to avoid. Grey, however, was not prepared to authorise an ultimatum of this kind until he had received the views of the Peking Legation and until the whole question of Tibet had been discussed in Cabinet.

Jordan agreed that the time had come to press harder on the Wai-chiao-pu;[5] but he did not approve of all the India Office proposals. In the first place, he saw no point in tying up at this stage the Sino-Burmese boundary with the Tibetan question. Nor did he entirely welcome the suggested threats to the Chinese. The Republic could be coerced to a certain degree with impunity; but too much force would only arouse widespread Chinese resentment. As Jordan pointed out, the British, with their enormous investment in China, could not afford to take the same kind of risks as the Russians. The most he was prepared to do, pending firm instructions from London, was to point out to the Wai-chiao-pu the wisdom of coming to an agreement along the lines of the memorandum of 17 August before the British changed their mind and demanded conditions far less favourable to the Republic.

On 14 December, presumably as the result of some quiet prompting from the British Legation, the Wai-chiao-pu requested an interview with Jordan to discuss the 17 August memorandum. Dr. Yen, the Vice-Minister whom Jordan thought

---

[4] FO 535/15, no. 303, Grey to Jordan, 12 December 1912.
[5] FO 535/15, no. 304a, Jordan to Grey, 13 December 1912.

'a very obstructive individual', argued that the memorandum was quite unjustified. The Chinese had the right to control all of Tibet as they saw fit. The British in the past had acknowledged that right. How could they defend their present attitude? Jordan countered with some observations on the real nature of Chinese power in Lhasa since 1888, when Lord Dufferin drove the Tibetans from Sikkim after the Chinese had shown themselves quite unable to influence their subjects, remarks which Dr. Yen 'did not appear to relish'. After much verbal thrust and parry, 'with good humour on both sides, but with very little result', Jordan concluded the interview by pointing out that

> the terms of the memorandum [of 17 August], which had been drawn up at a time when there was still some Chinese authority in Tibet, were far more favourable than China had now any right to expect, and I strongly urged their acceptance while the offer was still open.[6]

On 23 December the Wai-chiao-pu despatched a note to Jordan containing its formal reply to the 17 August memorandum and summarising the discussion of 14 December.[7] The Chinese had full power in Tibet, as witness the terms of the Anglo-Chinese Convention of 1906. There was no intention of converting Tibet into a Chinese province or provinces: what was proposed was 'to give effect to the unanimous desire of the nation and complete the union of the five races in one family— an end widely different from conversion into a province'. The Chinese wished, and had the treaty right, to police Tibet; 'but there has never been any idea of stationing an unlimited number of troops in Tibet'. The Wai-chiao-pu saw no need for a fresh treaty relating to Tibet: the agreements of 1906 and 1908 were still in force, and they served to meet all legitimate British interests, which were mainly commercial, to the north of the Himalayas. The Chinese then protested against the closing of the Indo-Tibetan border to them, declaring that

> according to international usage, unless a state of war exists the procedure of closing communications is not resorted to and China and Great Britain being friendly countries, such

[6] FO 371/1329, no. 55588, Jordan to Grey, 16 December 1912.
[7] FO 535/15, no. 314, Jordan to Grey, 26 December 1912.

action in the present circumstances is very unpleasing to the Chinese Government which earnestly hopes for its early discontinuance.

Finally, the Wai-chiao-pu remarked on the antiquity of commercial relations between Britain and China—presumably a veiled threat of Chinese restrictions on British trade—and declared that British recognition of the Republic would not only be a gesture of friendship but also lead to mutual prosperity. All these, when considered impartially, were reasonable points; and Jordan studied them with sympathy. They did not, however, in any way indicate an easy solution to the Tibetan problem.

On 30 January 1913, no doubt influenced by the state of affairs in Mongolia, the Chinese Minister for Foreign Affairs, Lu Cheng-hsiang, asked Jordan to discuss with him further the memorandum of 17 August.[8] He was now prepared to consider the memorandum seriously, but he objected, for a start, to the use of the term suzerainty to describe the Chinese position in Tibet. It had never been used in previous treaties. Jordan declined to comment on this argument, but observed that it was in any case pointless talking about Tibet without also attempting a definition of borders. Lu replied that the border question was extremely complex, and its consideration at this stage would only result in delay. What Lu had in mind, it seemed, was an agreement to limit Chinese power in Central Tibet to an Amban and escort, but to do so without limiting Chinese policy towards the Marches and in such matters as the creation of Sikang. Without a border definition, however, there was no way of telling quite what the Chinese understood by Central Tibet. Jordan suspected, and subsequent events were to prove him right, that Central Tibet in Chinese thinking did not extend very far east of Lhasa and that it excluded such areas of interest to the Indian Government as Pome and Zayul. On the question of the Amban and his escort, the Chinese position, it could be argued, was not very far removed from that of the British. We have seen that Chung Ying and Lu Hsing-chi had been struggling to persuade the Tibetans to retain this office in its pre-1910 state after the rest of the Chinese forces had been withdrawn.

[8] FO 371/1609, no. 4823, Jordan to Grey, 31 January 1913.

The Chinese, however, saw their Amban as the foundation upon which they would base their return in strength to Lhasa: the Indian Government saw him as no more than an historical curiosity, a reminder of a brief episode of Chinese domination which would never be repeated. The issue which symbolised the difference between these two attitudes was the boundary between Lhasa and Chinese-controlled territory. It was clear that the farther eastwards the Chinese boundary was pushed, the harder would a Chinese return to Lhasa be to accomplish.

In the first months of 1913 the British, always with the implications of the Mongolian situation in mind, proceeded to refine their Tibetan policy. It became an axiom that the Amban, if he should ever return to Lhasa, should have an escort of no more than 300 men, a figure which the Indian Government estimated to have applied in 1904 on the eve of the Young-husband Mission. The Tibet in which the Chinese should be denied all but these symbols of influence was defined by the Indian Government to include not only Lhasa and the west, but also Zayul, Markham, Draya, Chamdo, Gyade and Nagchuka. This meant that the Chinese frontier would be just west of Batang, where, it was thought, it had been fixed in the early eighteenth century. It also meant, however, that in accepting such a boundary the Chinese would have to surrender such districts as Chamdo, which they then held in some strength. Finally, as we have already seen, by February 1913 the British had come to the conclusion that in any serious negotiations with the Chinese over the memorandum of 17 August the Tibetans should be represented as well.

The idea of direct Tibetan participation in discussions of this kind, of course, was no novelty. It had been an object of British policy since at least the crisis of 1886, and it had resulted both in the Lhasa Convention of 1904 and in the attendance of a Tibetan delegate at the Trade Regulations negotiations of 1907–8.[9] The presence of Tibetan representatives had become all the more essential since the time of the Tibeto-Mongol treaty, which provided an entrée for Russian influence in Lhasa and which could be interpreted as an indication that the Dalai Lama now regarded himself as a sovereign ruler who was not prepared to see the affairs of his country decided by others

[9] See BCCA and Ch. III above.

over his head. How, for example, could the return to Lhasa of the Amban and his escort be secured without express Tibetan agreement? The opportunity for Tibetan entry into the arena of Sino-British negotiations lay conveniently to hand. At the same time as the British were attempting to obtain discussion of the 17 August memorandum, the Chinese were doing their best to by-pass the British in a direct Sino-Tibetan settlement. They had insisted, of course, that talks of this kind must have their venue either in Lhasa or in Eastern Tibet; and on this basis the Dalai Lama's Government had refused to commit itself. In early 1913, however, the Lama, perhaps fearing lest the Indian Government would ignore him altogether in coming to terms with Peking, agreed to open discussions with the Chinese provided they ceased their military pressure in the east and they accepted Darjeeling, on British soil, as the meeting-place.[10] The Dalai Lama's proposal offered the chance to convert two sets of bipartite discussions, Sino-Tibetan and Sino-British, into a single tripartite negotiation.

By February 1913 the concept of a settlement of the Tibetan problem through tripartite talks on British Indian territory, either at Darjeeling or Simla, was accepted as policy by the Indian Government. Recalling the fate of the Calcutta negotiations of 1905, and with much resentment at the way in which it felt Indian interests had been sacrificed in the Peking negotiations of early 1906, it expressed itself as very reluctant indeed to see a matter as important to its frontier security as was Tibet entrusted to the tender mercies of British diplomatists in London or Peking. It was able to point to one powerful precedent in the 1908 Trade Regulations negotiations in India, which the Tsarong Shape had attended as a Tibetan delegate. By the end of March the Home Government, while still fearing that such tripartite talks would be more vulnerable to Russian protest under the 1907 Convention than Sino-British discussions in Peking, accepted the Indian Government's view. Jordan was informed to this effect on 5 April.[11]

By this time, and here was an example of the direct influence of the Mongolian situation on British Tibetan policy, the India Office had more or less made up its mind that one of the terms

[10] FO 371/1609, no. 6124, Viceroy to Secretary of State, 4 February 1913.
[11] FO 535/16, no. 180, Grey to Jordan, 5 April 1913.

which these tripartite negotiations should secure was the British right to have a permanent representative in Lhasa. Lord Crewe did not think that the time was quite ripe for the British to exercise such a right—this depended, as did so many aspects of Central Asian policy at this time, upon a revision of the Anglo-Russian Convention of 1907—but to have the right accepted in principle was definitely worth while. Some of Crewe's permanent officials at the India Office were more forceful in their argument. Lionel Abrahams, for example, declared that

> the whole lesson of the last ten years, it may possibly be said, is that Tibet cannot stand alone; that it must be subject to some influence; and that we cannot allow that influence to be other than British; and that British influence can only be maintained by a British agency in some form or other at the capital.[12]

Younghusband would surely have enjoyed reading these words.

The Chinese, who saw the direction in which British policy was evolving, hastened to make some counter-move. Tibetan participation, they appreciated, would certainly damage their prestige and could hardly fail to provide the occasion for *some* direct Anglo-Tibetan negotiations, even if carried on in secret. On 27 March the Wai-chiao-pu informed Jordan that it was now authorised to propose a full discussion of the Tibetan question on the basis of the memorandum of 17 August, and that it was prepared to send a plenipotentiary to London for that purpose.[13] It suggested that Wen Tsung-yao would be a suitable person. Wen, it will be remembered, had been Lien Yü's assistant in Lhasa at the time of Chung Ying's entry with the flying column of Chao Erh-feng's troops.[14] He had thereupon resigned his post, because he felt the Chinese had gone back on promises made to the Tibetans. Wen was thought to be sympathetic to the Tibetan people. His proposed appointment was intended to bait the hook of the Chinese offer. In fact, it was likely that Wen, though perhaps more humane than Lien Yü, was as eager to retain a Chinese hold on Tibet as any other Chinese official. He was certainly a supporter of the policy of the union of the five races. The British would have been foolish

[12] FO 371/1610, no. 13816, IO to FO, 25 March 1913.
[13] FO 371/1610, no. 14001, Jordan to Grey, 27 March 1913.
[14] See pp. 271, 272 above.

indeed to expect that he would make any dramatic concessions. In the event, the British were not enticed. Grey instructed Jordan to inform the Wai-chiao-pu that Wen would be welcomed in Darjeeling by Tibetan and British representatives; but no discussions would be held in London.[15]

When the idea of Tibetan participation in the Sino-British negotiations was first discussed in London, Grey at the Foreign Office was of the opinion that the outcome should not be a tripartite treaty. The talks should be between the Tibetans and the Chinese, though following the general lines indicated in the memorandum of 17 August, and the British role should be limited to the offering of 'benevolent assistance'.[16] Otherwise, Grey thought, the Russians could accuse the British of violating the 1907 Convention, which forbade direct Anglo-Tibetan political discussion beyond the limits specified in the 1890, 1904 and 1906 Conventions. Jordan, however, was able to argue most convincingly against this view. On practical grounds, he said, British participation was essential not only in the discussions but also in the resultant agreement. Without it, for one thing, the negotiations might be prolonged indefinitely: the Chinese, after all, were probably the best diplomatic procrastinators in the world. Secondly, absence of a British signature to any instrument that might result would weaken its force in Chinese eyes. How could the British guarantee terms to which they were not a party? Thirdly, there were several aspects of the existing British treaty relations with and concerning Tibet which needed revision, like the 1908 Trade Regulations, for example; and here a treaty signed by the Indian Government was called for. Moreover, Jordan argued, the 1908 Trade Regulations had already established a precedent for such tripartite agreements which had aroused no Russian protest: hence, the Russians could not at this stage object to tripartite negotiations or agreements as such. Grey was impressed. As he minuted:[17]

It may fairly be argued that we are entitled to become a party to a Tripartite Agreement with China and Tibet without

[15] FO 535/16, no. 180, Grey to Jordan, 5 April 1913.
[16] FO 535/16, no. 155, Secretary of State to Viceroy, 19 March 1913.
[17] FO 371/1610, no. 16537, Jordan to Grey, 10 April 1913, with attached minute by Grey.

violating the Anglo-Russian Agreement. Under that Agreement (I have not got it by me to refer to) we are entitled to negotiate with China about Tibet and we are entitled to the fulfilment of our pre-1907 agreement with Tibet. We have therefore a *locus standi* for being a party to negotiations with China and Tibet.

He added, however, that:

We should have to be careful that under the tripartite agreement we acquire no rights and undertake no responsibilities that infringed the Anglo-Russian agreement. We should therefore be bound to explain to Russia what we are doing and the limits within which we intend to keep. I do not mean that we should be bound to inform Russia of all that passed, which affected only the relations of Tibet with China, but we should have to keep her informed of the scope of our action.

Thus the decision to make the proposed talks fully tripartite did not confer on the British unlimited freedom of action. The position, or at least the fiction that this was the position, would have to be maintained in which, as Lord Morley explained to the House of Lords on 28 July 1913,

China and Tibet will be, so to call them, the protagonists. Unless something arises we shall be the honest broker, but an honest broker who will keep his eyes open with regard to those interests which I have described to your Lordships [i.e. Lhasa Convention, &c.].[18]

The principles of the memorandum of 17 August 1912 had by the end of April 1913, when the Home Government reached full agreement on the tripartite nature of the Tibet negotiations, evolved a long way. Originally, the British had been hoping to force the Chinese to make some binding definition as to the status of Tibet and to the nature of Chinese rights and interests there. Now the British were acting, ostensibly, as mediators in a Sino-Tibetan dispute. This change had its disadvantages. Tibetan as well as Chinese agreement was now required for any

[18] *Parliamentary Debates*, 5th Series, Vol. XIV, House of Lords, Session of 1913, p. 1436.

This concept of the nature of the Simla Conference was to be embodied in the Commission appointing Sir H. McMahon the British plenipotentiary. See p. 478 below.

resultant treaty or other instrument. It also, however, had definite advantages. It was now possible, with both Tibet and China present, to bring about a drastic revision of the nature of British relations with, and influence in, Tibet such as Young-husband had failed to achieve. But here the Anglo-Russian Convention of 1907 intruded itself. Such revisions required Russian consent. Once the possibility of revision was admitted, however, would it not be wise to initiate immediately negotiations with Russia over the kind of advantages in Tibet which might now perhaps be obtained? As the India Office then saw it (30 April 1913), the British might perhaps acquire through the coming negotiations an exclusive Lhasa Residency, the right to reoccupy Chumbi, freedom to communicate directly with Tibetan authorities at all levels of government, and some rewards for the Nepalese such as rectification of the Tibeto-Nepalese border and compensation to Nepalese merchants for losses suffered during the Lhasa fighting in 1912.[19] Sir Edward Grey agreed that such matters as these required Russian consent; but he thought it would be rash to raise them in St. Petersburg until it was absolutely necessary to do so. All that was called for at present was to notify the Russian Government that tripartite negotiations were about to take place. Further Anglo-Russian discussion could well be postponed until the tripartite negotiations had borne some fruit.[20]

On 26 May 1913 Jordan informed the Wai-chiao-pu that its offer of 30 January to discuss the British memorandum of 17 August 1912 had now been accepted.[21] The Tibetans were to participate in these talks, which would take place in India, perhaps at Darjeeling. The Chinese were not amused. Moreover, at this moment they were once more on the offensive in the Marches and had some hope of much improving their Tibetan position without British help. Yuan Shih-k'ai's only apparent reply to Jordan's proposal was a Presidential Order that Szechuanese boundaries with Tibet should not lie west of Giamda, a town a bare 100 miles from Lhasa.[22] This was, Jordan thought, an oblique Chinese claim to sovereignty over

[19] FO 371/1610, no. 20005, IO to FO, 30 April 1913.
[20] PEF 1913/16, no. 1933/13, FO to IO, 15 May 1913.
[21] FO 371/1611, no. 24102, Jordan to Grey, 26 May 1913.
[22] FO 371/1611, no. 24103, Jordan to Grey, 26 May 1913.

large tracts of Tibet along the Assam Himalayas, including Zayul and Pome, which the Indian Government had determined should be freed from all Chinese influence. Chinese spirits had evidently been raised by reports of victory in the Marches, including the recapture of that perennial trouble spot, Hsiang-ch'eng.[23] On 5 June Jordan called on Yuan to protest in very strong terms against the implications of the Presidential Order, which Yuan promptly denied and which now looked like nothing more than a 'face-saving' gesture.[24] Under Jordan's pressure, Yuan's opposition to the tripartite conference in India seemed to collapse. He explained, however, that there could no longer be any question of Wen Tsung-yao as Chinese representative: Wen had refused to go to India, convinced that the Chinese would receive much better treatment in London. Yuan suggested Chang Yin-tang instead, perhaps as a final gesture of defiance. On Jordan's refusal to accept this official who had caused the Indian Government so much trouble between 1906 and 1908, Yuan proposed Chen I-fan, who had recently been Counsellor at the Chinese Legation in London, and who, but for the outbreak of the Chinese Revolution, would have taken part in Anglo-Chinese negotiations on the Yunnan-Burma border. Jordan promptly declared that Chen would be most welcome in India, a view which the Foreign Office in London shared. As Sir Walter Langley remarked:

> Ivan Chen was number two in the Chinese Legation for nine years and was well known to us. His appointment is the best there could be as he is very friendly to us, speaks English very well and is most intelligent.[25]

On the following day President Yuan formally announced that Chen I-fan would attend a tripartite conference in India.[26]

No sooner had Jordan been informed of Chen's appointment than the Indian Government set to work to arrange its end of the proposed conference. On 5 June Hardinge wrote to the Dalai Lama asking him to send a delegate to India:[27] this was

[23] FO 371/1611, no. 25452, Jordan to Grey, 4 June 1913.
[24] FO 371/1611, no. 25790, Jordan to Grey, 5 June 1913.
[25] Loc. cit., Langley's minute.
[26] FO 371/1611, no. 25809, Jordan to Grey, 6 June 1913.
[27] FO 535/16, no. 294, Hardinge to Dalai Lama, 5 June 1913.

certainly a 'political' letter of the kind prohibited in the 1907 Convention. A few days later the Viceroy appointed Sir Henry McMahon, the Indian Foreign Secretary, as the British representative, to be assisted by Charles Bell and, it was hoped, by a member of the China Consular Service.[28] Hardinge also proposed that the scene of the conference be moved from Darjeeling to Simla, where 'we could exercise much more effective control over the proceedings while the Tibetan delegates would not be so exposed to Chinese intrigues as at Darjeeling', which was a clear indication of the way in which the Indian Government intended to run the conference.[29] On 17 June Hardinge learned that the Dalai Lama had selected the Lönchen Shatra as his representative to what from now onwards would be known as the Simla Conference.

[28] FO 371/1611, no. 27640, IO to FO, 16 June 1913.

Archibald Rose, at one time acting British Consul at Tengyueh in Yunnan, was the Consular officer selected to advise the British delegation on Chinese affairs. Rose had obtained considerable experience of the Chinese attitude towards frontier matters during his contact with the disputed Yunnan-Burma border. In 1911 he made an extended tour of Chinese border tracts including a visit to Kashgaria, on the basis of which he proposed as a possible solution to the Burma border dispute that China be persuaded to abandon its claims to Pienma (Hpimaw) in Burma in exchange for a surrender by the Mir of Hunza of his rights in the Sarikol district (Taghdumbash Pamir) of Sinkiang. The Indian Government declared themselves in favour of the scheme; it gave them something they wanted in exchange for something which they really did not possess, the Mir of Hunza's position in Sarikol being tenuous to say the least: but Jordan pointed out that the Chinese would never agree, and the idea was forgotten. Rose had an outlook on political matters most congenial to the Indian Government; and he was to get along famously with McMahon and Bell.

See FO 371/1335, no. 7971, *Report on the Chinese Frontiers of India*, by A. Rose, Calcutta, 1911; A. Rose, 'The Chinese Frontiers of India', *Geographical Journal*, XXXIX, 1912; FO 535/15, no. 22, Viceroy to Secretary of State, 6 February 1912, and no. 83, Jordan to Grey, 14 May 1912.

[29] PEF 1913/17, no. 2376/13, Viceroy to Secretary of State, 15 June 1913.

The Tibetans accepted the change of venue from Darjeeling to Simla with some reluctance, pointing out that they possessed no cipher of their own, so that all their references to Lhasa would have to be by messenger. It took seven days for a letter to reach Lhasa from Darjeeling, and eleven from Simla; thus the move of the scene of the Conference from Darjeeling to Simla greatly increased the difficulty for the Tibetan delegation of keeping in touch with its own Government. It is probable that the Indian Government had concluded that this would make the Lönchen Shatra more amenable to the British point of view.

It would have been naïve of the British, of course, to suppose that once Yuan had named a delegate he would cease all attempts to turn the Conference into something rather more to the Chinese taste. A few days after Chen's appointment, for example, Yuan announced that there would be another Chinese delegate at the Conference, with equal status.[30] This was Hu Han-min, a former Governor of Canton who had recently quarrelled with the Central Government over the question of the Five Power Loan, and whom Yuan would have been very pleased to see out of China for a while. Hu was known to be extremely anti-British, and doubtless his presence at Simla would have more than offset Chen I-fan's charm and amiability. Alston, *chargé* during Jordan's absence from Peking on leave, lost no time in protesting against Hu's appointment, which was then cancelled. Yuan noted that Hu would probably have declined the post in any case.[31]

A more serious argument developed over the title of Chen's appointment. Yuan, by Presidential Order, appointed him 'Commissioner for the Pacification of Tibet' with the implication that he was dropping in at Simla, as it were, on the way to take up his duties at the Tibetan capital.[32] A precedent for this interpretation, of course, could be found in the appointment of T'ang Shao-yi to the Calcutta negotiations in 1905.[33] T'ang, too, was supposed to be visiting India *en route* for Tibet. The British found Chen's titles objectionable on two counts. Firstly, the Conference had yet to decide whether the Chinese could, in fact, send an official to Central Tibet, and Yuan was thought to be trying in this indirect way to anticipate its decisions.[34]

[30] *Morning Post*, 18 June 1913; FO 371/1611, no. 27967, Alston to Grey, 18 June 1913.

[31] FO 535/16, no. 298, Alston to Grey, 23 June 1913.

[32] FO 371/1611, no. 27650, Alston to Grey, 15 June 1913.

[33] See p. 36 above.

[34] At about this time Lu Hsing-chi was also trying to enter Tibet, informing the Dalai Lama that he had been appointed Amban in place of Chung Ying, who, in turn, had replaced Lien Yü. Thus it looked as if the Chinese were actually trying to establish at least two major posts in Central Tibet, those of the Amban and the Pacificator. The Indian Government took no notice of Lu's claims and was adamant in refusing him permission to cross the Tibetan border from British territory. See, for example, FO 371/1611, no. 31755, IO to FO, 10 July 1913.

Secondly, the term Pacificator had a definite implication of the Chinese intention to bring Tibet to terms by force. Alston duly protested. The Wai-chiao-pu replied that they only used the word Pacificator to indicate their peaceful intentions; and with this the British had to be content.

A yet more serious debate developed over the status of the Tibetan delegate to the Conference. As in the case of the Trade Regulations negotiations of 1907-8, the Chinese fought hard to deny the Tibetan representative equal status with the Chinese.[35] On that occasion the Chinese had the better of the argument. They now declared that the Lönchen Shatra should have the same status as did Tsarong Shape, suggesting some formula such as that he was the Tibetan representative signing any agreement which might arise from the Conference 'after and as adjoint to the Chinese representative', which Alston rejected.[36] The Wai-chiao-pu then came up with yet another plan. Why not have two distinct sets of negotiations? Chen would first deal with the Tibetans, and would then discuss the resultant agreement with the British. Something like this had also been suggested in 1907-8. Alston replied that the Conference must be truly tripartite or nothing.[37] Finally, the Wai-chiao-pu advanced the following formula: they would declare that

> it has become the duty of this Government of China to order the said Plenipotentiary to proceed to India, there to negotiate a provisional treaty jointly with the Plenipotentiary appointed by Great Britain and the Tibetan Plenipotentiary, and to sign articles which may be agreed on in order that all difficulties which have existed in the past may be dissolved.[38]

Alston decided that this was the best that he could hope for: it at least admitted in principle that the negotiations were tripartite and that there existed a Tibetan *plenipotentiary*. The reference to 'a provisional treaty' was certainly a bit ominous; but, perhaps, it meant no more than a treaty requiring ratification, which would certainly be the case with any instrument arising from the Simla Conference.

[35] See p. 146 above.
[36] FO 371/1611, no. 32442, Alston to Grey, 14 July 1913.
[37] FO 371/1612, no. 36258, Alston to Grey, 6 August 1913.
[38] FO 371/1612, no. 36932, Alston to Grey, 10 August 1913.

From this moment on the Chinese ceased to argue major points, but until the actual opening of the Conference in October they continued to procrastinate and prevaricate, raising minor issues. Chen appeared very reluctant to leave China. At one point he requested a postponement of the Conference for a few weeks so that he could outfit himself with new clothes in Shanghai.[39] It was only after Alston told Yuan on 25 August that the Simla Conference, which it had originally been planned to start on 1 July, would commence its work on 6 October whether Chen had arrived or not that the Chinese representative was authorised to set out.[40] Accompanied by Archibald Rose, the Consular officer appointed to advise the Indian Government during the Conference, Chen sailed from Shanghai on 3 September. He reached Simla on 5 October, a day before Alston's deadline was due to expire:[41] the Lönchen Shatra had already been in Simla for eleven days.[42] Chen arrived, moreover, in the company of one B. D. Bruce, an officer in the Chinese Customs whom Aglen, the Inspector-General of that service, seems to have deputed to assist the Chinese delegation at the Conference.[43] This last-minute attempt to increase the Chinese strength was vehemently opposed by the Indian Government, which had unhappy memories of the role played by European employees of the Chinese Customs at an earlier stage in the Tibetan question; and it in no way reinforced McMahon's belief in the Chinese willingness to reach a genuine settlement.

Once Yuan Shih-k'ai had accepted the idea of a conference the Indian Government expected that all Chinese military activity in the Marches would cease, at least for the duration of the Simla talks. In fact, however, the Szechuan authorities showed no sign of any intention to postpone their hopes for Tibetan conquest. Alston was instructed to warn President Yuan of some of the possible consequences of such activity: a significant Chinese advance in the Marches, he could say, might

[39] PEF 1913/18, no. 3601/13, Alston to Grey 30 August 1913.

[40] FO 371/1612, no. 39306, Alston to Grey, 25 August 1913.

[41] FO 371/1612, no. 45698, IO to FO, 7 October 1913.

[42] FO 535/16, no. 371, Viceroy to Secretary of State, 24 September 1913.

[43] For example, FO 371/1613, no. 48622, Alston to Grey, 26 October 1913.

result in the British breaking of negotiations with China. Grey, however, felt that it would not be wise to threaten, in such an event, direct Anglo-Tibetan discussions without the Chinese (because of the 1907 Convention), or active British support for the Tibetans (since 'His Majesty's Government would be well advised not to commit themselves in such a manner unless they were prepared, in the event of the threat proving ineffective, to proceed to support the Tibetans', which the Home Government was not).[44] Thus Alston's warning had little impact; and, in any case, it was unlikely, as the Foreign Office appreciated, that Yuan actually possessed the authority to frustrate the ambitions of a determined Szechuan Provincial Government. Throughout the Conference the situation in the Marches remained tense. The best the British could do was to station a Consular officer at Tachienlu, Louis King, to watch and report developments while the Conference was in progress.[45]

The Tibetans, in the months before the Conference finally assembled, also proved themselves troublesome in a number of ways. On 27 July they sent to Lord Hardinge an account of the kind of terms they were prepared to accept.[46] Tibet should be given complete control over its internal affairs. In foreign relations the British might be permitted a say in major matters, otherwise the Tibetans would make their own decisions. No Chinese officials and soldiers, not even the Amban and his small escort, would be permitted to return to Tibet, where the only Chinese to be tolerated would be bona-fide merchants. By Tibet the Dalai Lama understood the territory stretching eastwards all the way to Tachienlu. All this, with the exception, of course, of the reference to the British, was, so the Lhasa Government said, what the Tibetans had enjoyed in the seventeenth century in the days of the fifth Dalai Lama. Such terms, implying a virtually complete Tibetan independence and laying claim to thousands of square miles of territory which had been under Chinese control for more than a century, were quite unrealistic; and if the Tibetans insisted on them the Conference was certainly bound to fail to produce any useful agreement. There was evidence, moreover, that the Dalai Lama

[44] PEF 1913/17, no. 2296/13, FO to IO, 9 June 1913.
[45] FO 535/16, Alston to King, 4 September 1913.
[46] FO 371/1612, no. 34848, IO to FO, 28 July 1913.

still had doubts as to the wisdom of taking part in the Conference at all, and that there were times when he felt that he might do better by dealing with the Chinese without British participation. He was much tempted by the offers which the Chinese commander at Chamdo was making him through the Kalon Lama. On 10 August, for example, the Lönchen Shatra told Bell that if a Chinese delegate did not arrive in India in the very near future his Government would open negotiations in Eastern Tibet.[47] Finally, there was the problem of the Panchen Lama, who was clearly very anxious to be represented at the Conference, and who might otherwise try to make his own arrangements with the Chinese: but by now the Indian Government had concluded that it could safely ignore the Panchen Lama.[48] McMahon, however, could have been in little doubt that the complicated balance of Chinese and Tibetan compromises which were his own Government's objective at the Simla Conference would not be easily secured.

While the preliminaries of the Conference were being arranged the Foreign Office was careful to keep the Russians informed, though in somewhat general terms, of what was afoot. Sazonov made no attempt to exploit any of the technical, and sometimes rather more than technical, breaches of the 1907 Convention which the British were then committing—this seemed encouraging—but he did try to arrange for the Russian Consul-General at Calcutta to be at Simla throughout the Conference, a plan which Lord Hardinge refused to consider for a moment.[49] On the eve of the Conference, however, Simla abounded in spies of many nations, including Russia and Japan;[50] and the Indian Government appreciated that it was now performing on a far more public stage than had been the case, for instance, during the Calcutta negotiations of 1905 or the Trade Regulations negotiations of 1907–8. It certainly enjoyed in October 1913 nothing like the freedom of action which Younghusband had possessed in Lhasa in September 1904.

[47] FO 371/1612, no. 37622, IO to FO, 14 August 1913.
[48] FO 371/1612, no. 37245, IO to FO, 11 August 1913.
[49] FO 371/1612, no. 38578, FO to IO, 22 August 1913.
[50] FO 371/1612, no. 39760, IO to FO, 27 August 1913.

XXIII

THE FIRST ROUND OF THE CONFERENCE, OCTOBER 1913 TO JANUARY 1914

THE formal opening of the Simla Conference took place on 6 October and its first working meeting was held on 13 October, when Sir Henry McMahon was elected President of the Conference.[1] The British delegation to the Conference

[1] Jerome Ch'en has implied that it was not until the Simla Conference had begun and the Chinese had agreed to negotiate with a Tibetan plenipotentiary that the British were prepared to accord their recognition to the Chinese Republic. There is a case of sorts for this view: the Conference opened on 6 October; Britain recognised the Republic on 7 October: but, in fact, the case does not bear close examination.

Recognition involved all the Powers. Though the British had colluded with Russia and Japan in attempting to use recognition as a lever to gain concessions in Tibet, Mongolia and Manchuria, it must have been obvious that, once a number of other Powers had taken this step, Britain, Russia and Japan would have to follow suit.

The process of recognition began as follows: 9 April 1913, Brazil; 10 April, Peru; 2 May, the United States. Other Powers delayed until the formal election by the National Assembly of Yuan Shih-k'ai as President of the Republic, which took place on 6 October, and of Li Yuan-hung as Vice-President on the following day. On 7 October, acting on a Japanese proposal, thirteen Powers gave their recognition: Sweden, Spain, Belgium, Russia, Denmark, France, Portugal, Japan, Holland, Britain, Austria, Italy, Germany. On 8 October the Swiss followed, and then, on 9 October, the process was completed by Norway.

It seems more than probable, therefore, that the dates of the opening of the Simla Conference and of British recognition of the Republic have but a coincidental relationship to each other. See J. Ch'en, *Yuan Shih-k'ai 1859–1916*, London, 1961, p. 175; H. Cordier, *Histoire Générale de La Chine*, 4 vols., Paris, 1920, Vol. 4, p. 293; H. F. McNair and D. F. Lach, *Modern Far*

consisted of Sir Henry McMahon as plenipotentiary, assisted by Charles Bell as Tibetan adviser and Archibald Rose of the Consular Service, as Chinese adviser. The Tibetans sent as their plenipotentiary the Lönchen Shatra, the Chief Minister of the Dalai Lama's Government, who was well known to Bell as a result of his residence in India during 1910–12. The Chinese were represented by Chen I-fan (or Ivon Chen), a diplomat familiar with the English way of life and language. In theory the Conference had been assembled because, so McMahon's Commission put it, 'a state of war now exists between the Government of China and the Government of His Holiness the Dalai Lama, whereby . . . [the Anglo-Chinese Convention of 1906] . . . has been rendered of no effect', and because 'His Holiness the Dalai Lama has invoked our good offices to remove all causes of differences between his Government and that of China'.[2] The British role, again in theory, was to be very much that of the 'honest broker' mediating in a Sino-Tibetan dispute. It is not surprising, therefore, that McMahon proposed that the Conference should start with a clarification of Chinese and Tibetan positions.[3]

A written statement of Tibetan claims was presented to the Conference on 13 October. It protested against Chinese action in Tibet since 1910; declared that 'Tibet is an independent

[2] FO 371/1913, no. 31252, IO to FO, 7 July 1913, and McMahon's Commission, dated 31 July 1913.

[3] The most important source for the story of the Simla Conference is McMahon's *Final Memorandum*, enclosed in Lord Hardinge's despatch to Lord Crewe of 23 July 1914. This lengthy document can be found in FO 371/1931, no. 43390, IO to FO, 26 August 1914; in FO 535/17; and in PEF 1913/20. I will refer to it hereafter as *Memorandum*.

Many documents relating to the Simla Conference are to be found in *The Boundary Question Between China and Tibet*, Peking, 1940. This work, which appears to have been published under Japanese auspices, contains genuine documents from the British archives, marred only by occasional typographical errors. I have compared all its contents with the versions in the India Office and Foreign Office archives. I will hereafter refer to this work as *BQ*.

Eastern International Relations, 2nd ed., New York, 1955, p. 149; Chang Chung-fu *Chung Hua Min Kuo Wai Chiao Shih* (A Diplomatic History of the Chinese Republic), Vol 1, Chungking, 1943, pp. 37–54. I am indebted to my colleague Dr. Lo of the Australian National University for this last reference.

State and that the Precious Protector, the Dalai Lama, is the Ruler of Tibet, in all temporal as well as in spiritual affairs'; denied that the Anglo-Chinese Convention of 1906 had any validity in relation to Tibet; claimed that the Dalai Lama had the right to rule over not only Central Tibet but also all the Marches up to Tachienlu and the Kokonor territory; no Chinese officials of any description whatsoever, the statement continued, would now be allowed to enter Tibet; it was pointed out that Mongolia was in close diplomatic relations with Tibet; the statement concluded with a demand for cash compensation for the damage done in Lhasa during the fighting there in 1912, some of this money to be paid to the Nepalese and Ladakhis.[4]

The Chinese countered with their own statement on 30 October.[5] After recounting the long history of Chinese influence in Tibetan affairs, Chen proposed the following terms:

(1) Tibet should be recognised as 'an integral part of the territory of the Republic of China';

(2) the Chinese retained the right to appoint an Amban at Lhasa with an escort of 2,600 men, of whom 1,000 should be posted in Lhasa and the remainder wherever the Amban saw fit;[6]

(3) Tibet should have no relations with any foreign Power except through the Chinese, unless expressly provided for in the Lhasa Convention and the Anglo-Chinese Convention of 1906;

(4) the Tibetans should grant an amnesty to all those who

---

[4] *BQ*, p. 1.

It is interesting that in these claims the Tibetans took care to exclude the area of the Tsaidam swamp. Tsaidam, which McMahon had included within Tibet, the Lönchen Shatra refused to accept. McMahon thought this reluctance indicated a Tibetan desire to respect Mongol claims over Tsaidam; and here he detected further evidence of the existence of a Tibeto-Mongol agreement of some kind.

[5] *BQ*, p. 7.

[6] This figure was probably the Chinese strength in Central Tibet after Chung Ying had entered Lhasa in February 1910, a date which to the Chinese had something of the symbolic value which the British attached to the eve of the Younghusband Mission in 1904.

The term Amban, of course, is an anachronism after the fall of the Manchus. I have retained it here because it was still, in the period of the Simla Conference, part of the language which the British used in their discussion of Tibetan problems.

had sided with the Chinese since 1910, and who were now being punished by the Dalai Lama;

(5) if it should be found necessary to revise the 1908 Tibet Trade Regulations, this should be done by Anglo-Chinese discussion without Tibetan participation;

(6) the frontier between Tibet and China proper should be, as indicated on a map accompanying the statement, in the general region of Giamda, where Yuan Shih-k'ai had already announced it to be, just over 100 miles from Lhasa.

Having studied these two documents, McMahon summoned a meeting of the Conference on 18 November, when he explained to Chen and the Lönchen Shatra that it seemed to be futile to discuss other points of difference until the whereabouts of the boundary between the territories of the Chinese and the Dalai Lama had been settled.[7] Some compromise was clearly called for in view of the great distance which separated the lines in the two claims, for Giamda and Tachienlu must be about 1,000 miles apart (Maps no. 10 and no. 11). Chen felt he could not agree to such a proposal without instruction from Peking, since his orders were to decide the question of the political status of Tibet before discussing its physical limits. The Lönchen Shatra, however, said he would go along with McMahon; and, rather than risk bipartite talks, Peking on 23 November authorised Chen to take part as well.[8] The discussions were then transferred from Simla to Delhi, where it was not so cold and, moreover, where the Chinese and Tibetan delegates could be removed from 'the inconvenient curiosity shown in all their doings by members of the Japanese Consulate-General' in Calcutta, who had come to Simla for this purpose.

Once it had come to producing evidence in support of territorial claims, the Tibetans found themselves far more prepared than the Chinese.[9] Chen had with him little more than a pamphlet by Fu Sung-mu on the campaigns of Chao Erh-feng and a few European works on Tibet like those of Sir Thomas

[7] *Memorandum.*

[8] On hearing McMahon's proposal, Chen immediately took to his bed; and for a few days the British delegation thought that this marked the end of the Conference as far as the Chinese were concerned. It had not been forgotten that the Calcutta negotiations of 1905 had been to all intents and purposes terminated by T'ang Shao-yi's diplomatic illness.

[9] *Memorandum.*

Holdich. He telegraphed in desperation to the Chinese Legation in Paris for a copy of the official *Institutions of the Manchu Dynasty* which, rather optimistically, he hoped would supply him with some of the facts he needed. The Lönchen Shatra, on the other hand, had with him documents by the cartload, which he proceeded to lay before the Conference. These included the text of the Sino-Tibetan Treaty of A.D. 822, copies of monastery

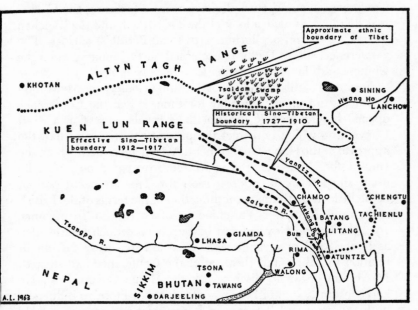

10   *Some historical Sino-Tibetan boundaries*

grants and letters of submission by tribal chiefs from districts as far to the east as Tachienlu. Some documents, McMahon reported, were 'delicate manuscripts in richly embroidered covers', and among them was 'the official history of Tibet, compiled by the fifth Dalai Lama and known as the *Golden Tree of the Index of the Sole Ornament of the World*, a work of great scope and colossal dimensions'. As the manuscripts piled up, Chen became increasingly annoyed (as, one suspects, Chinese diplomats became during the Sino-Indian boundary discussions of 1960–61, when the Indian side started quoting from Sanskrit epics). On 18 December he proposed that the time had come to call a halt to this search for papers of dubious relevance to the subjects under discussion. Both sides, he urged, should now draw up a detailed and consolidated statement of their territorial claims; and these alone, when ready, should be considered by the Conference. Chen, in any case, felt in sore need of reference to Peking. The Lönchen Shatra was persuaded to agree. It was decided that, once the claims were ready, McMahon should study them and propose some measure of arbitration. The Conference then adjourned. Chen went off, during the Christmas holidays, to have a look at the Taj Mahal, and the Lönchen Shatra set out on a pilgrimage to some Buddhist shrines. The Conference, still at Delhi, reassembled on 12 January, when the Chinese and Tibetan statements were duly tabled.

For much of this first phase of the Simla Conference McMahon was doing no more than play for time. When the Conference opened in October he did not have in his possession a draft Convention which both met the present situation and had the approval of the Home Government. A draft agreement which the India Office had prepared in March 1913 could no longer be used, since it made no provision for Tibetan participation, being little more than an amplification of the terms of the British memorandum of the Wai-chiao-pu of 17 August 1912. Since 1912 the Indian Government had evolved a much clearer idea as to the kind of arrangements it would like to see made in relation to Tibet; and these, after the Conference had started, McMahon began to discuss with the Home Government. He had constantly in mind the recent evidence of foreign influence, both Japanese and Russian, in Lhasa, and he was particularly concerned at the implications of the Tibeto-Mongol Treaty. Since 1912, he noted,

> the collapse of Chinese power in Tibet, and the activities of Russia in Mongolia, had caused . . . a complete change in the *status quo* in Tibet, which was clearly prejudicial to the interests of Great Britain, in spite of the fact that our geographical position and our extended frontier line forced upon us a closer relation with Tibet than could be claimed by any foreign Power.[10]

All this, McMahon argued, indicated the necessity for direct Anglo-Tibetan relations in the future, and the presence of a British representative at Lhasa. What about the Anglo-Russian

[10] Loc. cit.

482

Convention? McMahon felt that, in respect of Tibet, the Russians must be persuaded to agree to some modifications. He pointed out that the Russian denial of any equation between the Mongolian and Tibetan situations could not be sustained. By the Russo-Mongol and Tibeto-Mongol Treaties, McMahon demonstrated, Russia had

> obtained an open door for her trade across the northern frontier of Tibet, and the right for Russo-Mongolian subjects to take part in Tibetan industrial enterprise. She has indeed secured, by way of Mongolia, an actual, though indirect, method of overcoming the restrictions imposed upon her by Articles 3 and 4 of the Anglo-Russian Convention.[11]

The Foreign Office should point out to Sazonov that, Russia having already disregarded the Anglo-Russian Convention in this direction, the British could now feel free to follow suit.

The existing draft agreement, which the India Office had proposed on 7 March 1913 on the basis of the memorandum of 17 August 1912, read as follows:[12]

Article 1

The two Governments [China and Great Britain], recognising that Tibet is under the suzerainty, but not the sovereignty, of China, mutually engage to respect the territorial integrity of the country and to abstain from interference in its internal administration which shall remain in the hands of the Tibetan Government at Lhasa.

Article 2

The Government of China engages not to send troops into Tibet or to station civil or military officers or establish Chinese colonies in the country. Should any such troops, officials or colonists remain in Tibet at the date of signature of this agreement, they shall be withdrawn within a period not exceeding one month.

Article 3

The foregoing article shall not be held to preclude the continuance of the arrangement by which, in the past, a Chinese representative with suitable escort has been maintained at Lhasa, with authority to advise the Tibetans as to their foreign relations, but it is hereby provided that the said escort shall in no circumstances exceed 300 men.

[11] Loc. cit. [12] FO 371/1610, no. 10751, IO to FO, 7 March 1913.

Article 4

China is hereby released from engagements entered into by her under the Tibet trade regulations of the 20th April 1908; His Britannic Majesty's Government will hereafter hold the Tibetan Government responsible for the due fulfilment of the provisions of the aforesaid regulations in regard to the administration of the trade marts, the protection of trade routes, the regulation of commerce, &c.

Article 5

For the purposes of the present agreement, Tibet shall be held to include the districts of Za-yul, Mar-kham, Draya, Chiamdo, Gyade, and Nagchuka, and all country lying south and west of the Tang-la range.

The main departures here from the wording of the memorandum of 17 August 1912 were the reference to the proposed new Trade Regulations, whereby the Chinese were no longer to intervene in any way in the permitted areas of British relations with the Tibetans, and the attempt to define the geographical limits of that part of ethnic and cultural Tibet which was to be accepted as the domain of the Dalai Lama. This draft was far too mild to suit McMahon; and it differed in several significant respects from the final texts of the Simla Conventions of April and July 1914.

What McMahon had decided that he wanted by November 1913 was something along these lines:[13]

Article 1

The Governments of Great Britain and China, recognising that Tibet is under the suzerainty, but not the sovereignty, of China, mutually engage to respect the territorial integrity of the country, and to abstain from interference in its administration, which shall remain in the hands of the Tibetan Government at Lhasa.[14]

Should the Tibetan Government in the future decide to inaugurate changes in its administrative system, it undertakes not to seek or obtain advice or assistance from any Power, or subject of any Power, other than those which are parties to this treaty.

[13] FO 371/1613, no. 58681, Viceroy to Secretary of State, 12 November 1913; no. 58684, Hirtzl to Langley, 2 December 1913.

[14] The expression 'sovereignty', omitted from the memorandum of 17 August 1912, is now included here, as it was also in Article 1 of the India Office draft.

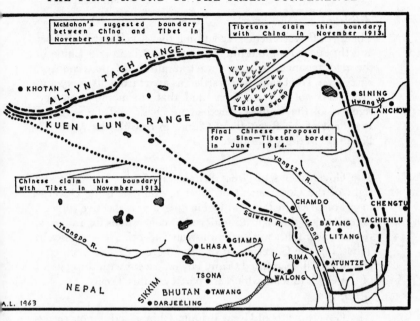

Simla Conference boundaries, November 1913

Article 2

(As in Article 2 of the India Office draft.)

Article 3

The foregoing article shall not be held to preclude the continuance of the arrangement by which, in the past, a Chinese representative with suitable escort has been maintained at Lhasa, but it is hereby provided that the said escort shall in no circumstances exceed 300 men.

The Government of Great Britain shall have the right to maintain in a similar manner a representative at Lhasa to discuss and settle with the Government of Tibet matters relating to their mutual interests.[15]

[15] There is a slight change in wording of the first paragraph of this article from Article 3 of the India Office draft: all reference to the Amban's right to have a say in Tibetan foreign relations is now omitted. McMahon argued that in the past the Amban could only claim to have a right to be concerned in Tibetan relations with Nepal, Bhutan and Sikkim, and it was British policy to put an end to any Chinese contact with these Himalayan States: hence it would be wise to make no mention of Tibetan foreign relations in this context. The proposed future conduct of Tibetan foreign relations was dealt with adequately enough in Article 6.

Article 4

The three Governments, recognising the special status of Tibet and the special mutual interest of Great Britain and China in the maintenance of peace and tranquillity in that country, agree that Tibet shall be regarded as apart from all party and provincial politics in China, and that the nomination and removal of the Chinese Resident in Lhasa shall lie with the President of the Republic of China, in consultation with His Britannic Majesty's Minister at Peking.[16]

Article 5

The Governments of Great Britain and China recognise the right of the Government of Tibet to grant (and the Governments of Great Britain and China and their respective subjects hereby enjoy the right to undertake) concessions for railways, roads, telegraphs, mining, industrial and other enterprises in Tibet, but the Government of Tibet agrees that no such concessions shall be granted to any Power, except with the consent of the Governments which are parties to this Treaty.[17]

Article 6

The Governments of Great Britain, China, and Tibet, recognising that Great Britain, by reason of her geographical position, has a special interest in the external relations of Tibet, hereby engage that Tibet shall not form the subject of any negotiations or agreement with any State without the consent of the Government of Great Britain.[18]

[16] McMahon's object in this Article was to ensure that Szechuan and Yunnan Provinces, far less subject to British diplomatic pressure than the Central Government, should have no say in the internal affairs of Tibet. Lord Hardinge disapproved of this Article, and especially of its second part dealing with the procedure for nominating and removing the Amban. It thereupon was abandoned.

[17] McMahon here was trying to counter the possible Russian exploitation of the Tibetan economy under cover of the Tibeto-Mongol Agreement. Lord Hardinge, who saw that the Article to all intents and purposes created a Sino-British commercial monopoly in Tibet, thought that these terms could not be reconciled with the Anglo-Russian Convention of 1907. The Article, as such, was thereupon dropped, British commercial interests in Tibet being left to a separate set of trade regulations to be negotiated in place of those of 1908.

[18] This was designed to control Tibetan relations with, in particular, China and Nepal. China is understood to belong to the category 'any State'. The Article was aimed at Article III of the Russo-Mongol Agreement of 1912: see Appendix XIII.

Article 7

China is hereby released from her rights and obligations under the Trade Regulations of 1893 and 1908, and also from her engagements under Article III of the Convention of 1890 to prevent acts of aggression from the Tibet side of the Sikkim-Tibet frontier.

The Government of India hereby acknowledges its responsibility for the fulfilment of the provisions of the aforesaid Trade Regulations of 1893 and 1908 in regard to maintenance of trade marts and protection of trade routes.

The Governments of Great Britain, China, and Tibet hereby reaffirm all the former agreements in regard to Tibet to which they have been parties, except in so far as those agreements may be modified by provisions of the present treaty.[19]

Article 8

For the purpose of the present Treaty Tibet shall be held to include all the territory shown within the frontier indicated in red on the map attached to this treaty.[20]

Article 9

The Government of China hereby agrees to pay to the Government of Tibet such compensation as may be justly due for losses incurred between the 1st January 1905 and the date of the present Treaty, by the Government and subjects of Tibet, and by Nepalese and Ladakhis in that country, in consequence of acts done by Chinese officials and soldiers. Similarly the Government of Tibet agrees to grant an amnesty to all those officials and subjects of Tibet who have been imprisoned by the Tibetan authorities by reason of their

[19] This Article was designed to sweep away much of the existing structure of British treaty relations with Tibet, and, in particular, to clear the way for a new set of trade regulations.

[20] The map in question was an outline map of Tibet and the Marches based on the Royal Geographical Society map of that region at a scale of 1 : 3,800,000. During the course of the Conference a proliferation of lines were drawn on these maps.

Lord Hardinge, at this early stage before December 1913, had already decided that 'in view of the possible dispute as to the correct boundary between Tibet and Bhutan and Nepal, we think it preferable to confine the Indo-Tibet boundary laid down by the agreement map to the Assam-Tibet boundary east of Bhutan and to the north-east salient of Burma'. This particular stretch of the British border with Tibet was to become known as the 'McMahon Line'.

sympathy for the Chinese, and also to restore them all the property which for some reason has been confiscated by the said authorities.[21]

Article 10

The usual clause regarding comparison of texts and agreement that the English text shall be authoritative.

The Home Government were not entirely happy about McMahon's draft and Lord Hardinge's general endorsement of it. India had been busy preparing drafts on the assumption that Russia would acquiesce to its terms 'without raising awkward questions elsewhere'. This was unrealistic. Both the India Office and the Foreign Office were now sure—indeed, had been sure since Sazonov's visit in September 1912—that any approach to the Russians for a modification of the 1907 Convention relating to Tibet would lead to Russian requests for compensation in Persia, Afghanistan or Sinkiang. Lord Hardinge had expressed himself as opposed to any change in the status of Afghanistan. He did not like the idea of giving the Russians a free hand in Sinkiang. Concessions in Persia also had their disadvantages. What other possibilities might there be? Lord Crewe suggested that

> we must consider the prospect of replacing the fourth article [of the Anglo-Russian Convention of 1907] by one dividing Tibet into British and Russian spheres of commercial influence, we undertaking not to seek concessions for ourselves nor to veto Russian concessions in the latter's sphere. Alternatively, the article might merely be so modified as to secure that no concessions would be sought or obtained by either Power in any part of Tibet unless the prior consent of the other Power were given.[22]

Lord Hardinge could well give thought to the kind of sphere India would require. It should certainly have Lhasa. Perhaps a

[21] Lord Hardinge regarded this Article as a means by which an assessment of the compensation to be paid by China could be arrived at, and he hoped that it would be dropped during the Conference. By April 1914 it has disappeared from the draft. The sum of compensation proposed during the Conference was Rs. 4,24,840.

[22] FO 535/16, no. 447a, Secretary of State to Viceroy, 3 December 1913; PEF 1913/18, no. 4619/13, IO minute of 3 December 1913.

strip of Tibet extending north for 200 miles along the Himalayas would be the answer. Without some such offer, Crewe believed, the Russians would be extremely unlikely to accept the kind of changes in the 1907 Convention which the Indian Government were proposing without demanding non-Tibetan compensations. In any case, the Russians would never accept McMahon's Article 5 with its implications of a British commercial monopoly. Moreover, the right for a British representative to go to Lhasa would undoubtedly cause trouble: Crewe would like to see it omitted.

Hardinge, as might be guessed, objected strongly to any idea of a Russian sphere in Tibet.[23] A major object of the present exercise was to keep Russia out of Tibet. McMahon's Article 5 was promptly dropped. The British Resident in Lhasa, however, Hardinge would not abandon at any price. He was absolutely essential to the success of the agreement, and without him the rest of the draft could be dismissed as mere academic phrases. He hoped that the Foreign Office would make another, and more determined, attempt to obtain Russian agreement to the Lhasa Residency as 'the price of our recognition of the Mongolian agreements, without discussion of other questions dealt with in the Anglo-Russian Convention being reopened'. Hardinge could still not bring himself to take Sazonov at his word. Lord Crewe and Sir Edward Grey were sufficiently impressed to allow the Lhasa Residency to stand, though perhaps with the mental reservation that its surrender might be used as a bargaining counter with the Russians at some later date.

In December 1913 McMahon himself proposed a significant modification of his own draft.[24] He had been much impressed by the way in which the Russians had recently settled with China the extremely difficult question of the status of that portion of Mongolia which had declared its independence in 1911 and with which the Russians had signed a treaty in 1912. In the Russo-Chinese Declaration of 23 October/5 November 1913 Mongolia was divided into two zones.[25] One zone, only implied in the Declaration, was Inner Mongolia. Here, again

[23] FO 535/16, no. 474, Viceroy to Secretary of State, 11 December 1913.
[24] *Memorandum.*
[25] See Appendix XV.

by implication, China was sovereign. The other zone was Outer Mongolia. This was

(1) under Chinese suzerainty,

(2) autonomous, and

(3) part of Chinese territory (this last point was made in notes exchanged at the same time as the Declaration was made). In Outer Mongolia the Chinese agreed to maintain no officials or soldiers beyond a 'Dignitary' and his escort. Provisions were made for future Russo-Chinese discussion of issues arising from the present status of Outer Mongolia. Provisions were also made for the definition of the boundaries of Outer Mongolia. It struck McMahon, while he was watching the Chinese and Tibetan delegations attempt to describe a Tibet of widely differing areas, that perhaps these conflicting claims might be reconciled by adopting the principle of the Mongolian Declaration. Why not suggest that Tibet in its widest sense, that is to say what the Tibetans were claiming, be partitioned (Map no. 12)? One zone, Inner Tibet, would be under some degree of Chinese sovereignty. The other zone, Outer Tibet, would be the autonomous domain of the Dalai Lama under Chinese suzerainty. The Sino-Tibetan argument would thereby be transformed. The Tibetan character of Tibet would no longer be challenged. The discussion would now be confined to which areas fell into which of the two zones. Partition along such lines would also bring with it a number of political dividends for the British. If properly managed, it should be possible to ensure that British territory nowhere along the border in the Assam Himalayas touched upon Inner, or Chinese-dominated, Tibet, thus preventing for the future Chinese penetration into the tribal hills. Moreover, the creation of Inner Tibet would bring into being a buffer of Chinese territory between autonomous Tibet and Mongolia which might possibly make more difficult the conduct of Tibeto-Mongol relations and their exploitation by the Russians. The narrow strip of Kansu separating Tibet in the Kokonor region from Outer Mongolia did not, in late 1913, appear to McMahon to be particularly secure in Chinese possession. Mongols lived in it. The definition of the borders of Outer Mongolia, while provided for in the Russo-Chinese Declaration, had not yet been made. It seemed quite likely that the Indian Government would wake up one day to find that

Outer Mongolia had swallowed this piece of China and had become a Tibetan neighbour.

The Home Government did not provide McMahon with its approved draft agreement until 20 February 1914; but it lost no time in authorising, on 6 January, the proposal to partition Tibet into Inner and Outer Zones.[26] On the face of it, McMahon's two zones were logical enough. They involved, however, a stricter interpretation of the analogy of the Mongolian and Tibetan situations than the facts of history would perhaps warrant. The distinction between Inner and Outer Mongols was one with precedents in Manchu practice dating back to the seventeenth and eighteenth centuries. The distinction between Inner and Outer Tibetans was new to the Chinese. Manchu Tibet was certainly divided up into a number of regions administered in different ways. In Eastern Tibet there existed a mosaic of feudal states and monastic domains owing allegiance to China through Szechuan, Yunnan and Kansu Provinces. In Central Tibet there was the Dalai Lama under the theoretical control of the Amban at Lhasa. But in Manchu thinking Central Tibet was probably rather less autonomous than some of the districts of Eastern Tibet. With the late Manchu period and the coming of the Republic the situation changed somewhat; and the division, if anything, would now be described as between Lhasa territory and China proper. To the Chinese in 1914 the acceptance of the concept of an Inner Tibet would mean the express renunciation, for example, of Sikang Province, that dream of Chao Erh-feng.

To the Dalai Lama's Government, also, the idea of partition was also not entirely welcome. While a stable division between the two zones would give Lhasa a secure eastern frontier with China, it would at the same time involve the surrender of Tibetan claims over a large tract of territory. Tibetan ideas of sovereignty certainly did not coincide with those of Western international lawyers of today. The distinction between political and religious subordination was in their minds somewhat vague. The complex traditional relationships between the states of the Tibetan Marches and China could well be accommodated with the Tibetan view of their place in the world. The Dalai Lama had greatly resented the changes of the Chao Erh-feng era not

[26] *Memorandum.*

491

so much because they affected the power of Lhasa in the east, which was certainly in most of the districts concerned rather slight, but because they broke with the pattern established in the days of K'ang Hsi and Ch'ien Lung; and these changes were given an implied legal standing by the concept of Inner and Outer Tibet. Inner Tibet might not be recognised as falling within the Chinese provincial structure, and Sikang might be declared invalid, but the region was still under some kind of Chinese sovereignty. It could hardly be under Tibetan sovereignty as well. Thus the Tibetans were obliged to face up to a situation which they would much rather have ignored. They were now, just as much as they had been by the formation of Sikang, being deprived of the symbols as well as the substance of control to the east. The Tibetans attached great importance to symbols in their political ideology.

As we shall see, the idea of the two zones, which seemed so rational and so attractive to Sir Henry McMahon, was to result in the failure of the Simla Conference to produce a valid tripartite agreement, a failure which has contributed greatly to the present instability of the Sino-Indian border.

XXIV

THE FIRST SIMLA CONVENTION,
27 APRIL 1914

THE Simla Conference, which was at this moment actually being held in Delhi reassembled after the Christmas holidays on 12 January 1914. Both Chen and the Lönchen Shatra had their detailed statements ready, the Tibetan's being a document of prodigious length with a staggering number of enclosures.[1] The Chinese statement was relatively short and betrayed Chen's lack of documents.[2] It claimed that Giamda marked the boundary point between Lhasa territory and the Marches, and that such districts as Chamdo, Zayul, Pome, Pemako and De-ge were all within the Chinese sphere. The Chinese right to Gyade was argued with some force; this meant the existence of a salient of Chinese territory thrusting towards Lhasa from the direction of Kokonor (or Chinghai), to which the Chinese also laid claim. The whole of Kokonor, it was said, was under the authority of a Chinese Amban stationed at Sining. It was inhabited by Mongols, twenty-nine banners in all, not Tibetans, who had been Chinese feudatories since early Manchu times.

The Tibetans in their statement adhered to the claim to a Tibet which extended all the way to Tachienlu on the Szechuan border; and they produced a mass of documents, ninety in all, to prove their point. It would have been the work of many months to sift through this material and arrive at some valid assessment of its relevance and force. Such a task, moreover, would have involved the services of experts in Tibetan constitutional history and law. McMahon had neither the experts

[1] *BQ*, pp. 23–87.   [2] *BQ*, pp. 14–22.

nor the time. He used the Tibetan statement as a useful definition of Tibet in its widest possible sense, which could then be divided, after the Mongolian model, into Inner and Outer Zones (Map no. 12). He put his proposals for Tibetan partition before the Conference on 17 February, when he tabled an outline map with two lines, one red and the other blue, drawn on it.[3] The red line showed Tibet 'as a geographical and

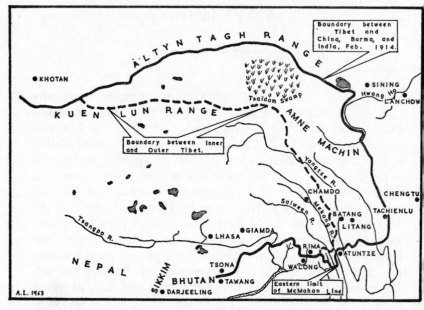

12 *Simla Conference boundaries, February 1914*

political unit' more or less as suggested by the Tibetan claim. The blue line divided Inner from Outer Tibet and its position was based on Chinese evidence, particularly on the boundary marker which the Manchus had erected in the eighteenth century in the neighbourhood of Batang. McMahon argued that this stone, on the Bum La between the Yangtze and Mekong valleys, indicated the true historical divide between Chinese sovereignty and Chinese suzerainty.[4] In theory,

[3] This was the basic outline map used throughout the Conference, and to which reference has already been made. See p. 487 above, note.

[4] The Bum La marker was erected by the Chinese in 1727 following their expulsion of the Zungars from Tibet. See Teichman, *Travels*, op. cit., p. 2.

McMahon implied, the territory to the east of the Bum La, Inner Tibet, was still Tibet; and the Chinese could only 're-establish such a measure of control in Inner Tibet as will restore and safeguard their historic position there, without in any way infringing the integrity of Tibet as a geographical and political entity'. In fact, of course, it was plain that the Chinese could do what they wanted in Inner Tibet provided they adhered to the fiction that it was part of a mystical Greater Tibet. Outer Tibet was to be autonomous, in fact as well as in theory; and here the Chinese could do no more than maintain an Amban and ceremonial escort.

To Chen this division was unacceptable. He felt it had no historical, legal or traditional justification. Moreover, it involved the Chinese surrender of territory to the west of the Yangtze-Mekong divide, the Chamdo district for example, which the Chinese then occupied. The most he seemed to be prepared to concede at this moment was a rather vague Tibetan autonomy in the countryside surrounding Lhasa. McMahon resolved to keep on arguing with Chen. The question of the two zones could be reconsidered by the Conference when it met again on 11 March. At this meeting, moreover, McMahon would be able to present a draft agreement, the text of which had at last arrived from London.[5]

The London draft was basically similar to that which McMahon had proposed in November 1913. It read as follows:[6]

Article 1

The Conventions specified in the present schedule to the present Convention shall, except in so far as they may have been modified by, or may be inconsistent with or repugnant to, any of the provisions of the present Convention, continue to be binding upon the High Contracting Parties.

Article 2

The Governments of Great Britain and China, recognising that Tibet is a State under the suzerainty, but not the sovereignty, of China, and recognising also the autonomy of Outer Tibet, engage to respect the territorial integrity of the country, and to abstain from interference in the administration of Outer Tibet (including the selection and appointment of the Dalai

[5] *Memorandum.*   [6] *BQ*, pp. 91–95.

Lama), which shall remain in the hands of the Tibetan Government at Lhasa.

The Government of China engages not to convert Tibet into a Chinese province and Tibet shall not be represented in the Chinese Parliament or any similar body. The Government of Great Britain engages not to annex Tibet or any portion of it.

Article 3

Recognising the special interest of Great Britain, in virtue of the geographical position of Tibet, in the existence of an effective Tibetan Government, and in the maintenance of peace and order in the neighbourhood of the frontiers of India and adjoining States, the Government of China engages, except as provided in Article 4 of this Convention, not to send troops into Outer Tibet, nor to station civil or military officers, or establish Chinese colonies in the country. Should any such troops, officials, or colonists, remain in Outer Tibet at the date of the signature of this agreement, they shall be withdrawn within a period not exceeding one month.

The Government of Great Britain engage not to station military or civil officers in Outer Tibet (except as provided in the Convention of 1904 between Great Britain and Tibet) or troops (except the Agent's escorts), or to establish colonies in that country.

Article 4

The foregoing Article shall not be held to preclude a Chinese representative with suitable escort from residing at some place in Tibet to be determined hereafter but it is hereby provided that the said escort shall in no circumstances exceed 300 men.

Article 5

The Governments of China and Tibet engage that they will not enter into any negotiations or agreements regarding Tibet with one another, or with any other Power, excepting such negotiations and agreements between Great Britain and Tibet as are provided for by the Convention between Great Britain and Tibet of September 7, 1904, and the Convention with China of April 27, 1906.

Article 6

Article III of the Anglo-Chinese Convention of 1906 is hereby cancelled, and it is understood that in Article IX (d) of the Anglo-Tibetan Convention of 1904 the term 'Foreign Power' does not include China.

Article 7

(a) The Trade Regulations of 1893 and 1908 are hereby cancelled.

(b) The Tibetan Government engages to negotiate with the British Government new Trade Regulations to give effect to Articles II, IV and V of the Convention of 1904, and to appoint duly authorised representatives for the purpose without delay; provided always that such Regulations shall in no way modify the present treaty except with the consent of the Chinese Government.

(c) The Government of China is hereby released from its engagements under Article III of the Convention of 1890 between Great Britain and China to prevent acts of aggression from the Tibetan side of the Tibet-Sikkim frontier.

Article 8

The British Agent who resides at a trade mart established under Article II of the Convention between Great Britain and Tibet of September 7, 1904, may visit Lhasa with his escort whenever it is necessary to consult with the Tibetan Government regarding matters arising out of that Convention, which it has been found impossible to settle by correspondence or otherwise.

Article 9

For the purpose of the present Convention the borders of Tibet, and the boundary between Outer and Inner Tibet, shall be as shown in red and blue respectively on the map attached hereto.

Nothing in the present Convention shall be held to prejudice the existing rights of the Tibetan Government in Inner Tibet, which include the power to select and appoint the high priests of monasteries, to retain full control of all matters affecting religious institutions, to issue appointment orders to chiefs and local officers, and to collect all customary rents and taxes.

Article 10

The Government of China hereby agrees to pay compensation amounting to Rs. 4,24,840 due for losses incurred by Nepalese and Ladakhis in Tibet in consequence of acts done by Chinese officials and soldiers in that country.

Article 11

The present Convention shall come into force on the date of

signature. The English, Chinese and Tibetan texts of this Convention have been carefully compared and, in the event of any question arising as to the interpretation of the Convention, the sense of the English text shall be held to be correct.

Schedule

1. Convention between Great Britain and China relating to Sikkim and Tibet, signed at Calcutta the 17th March 1890.

2. Convention between Great Britain and Tibet, signed at Lhasa the 7th September 1904.

3. Convention between the United Kingdom and China respecting Tibet, signed at Peking the 27th April 1906.

Both the proposals for the partition of Tibet and the terms of the draft agreement, McMahon thought, 'evidently stirred the Chinese to activity'.[7] Lu Hsing-chi, who had in the course of 1913 announced that he was both the Chinese Consul at Calcutta and the Chinese Amban at Lhasa (in which capacities the Indian Government had refused to recognise him), was now watching the Conference with close attention and reporting its progress to Peking by means of telegrams which the British duly intercepted, studied and filed away. Lu concluded that China was going to gain nothing at this time from tripartite discussion.[8] He argued that if China agreed to the kind of terms which McMahon was now proposing, the precedent might be exploited by the other Powers elsewhere along the borders of the Republic. Chen should walk out of the Conference, Lu advised President Yuan. The Chinese should then concentrate on keeping up the military pressure on the Tibetans in the Marches, aiming first to seize Pome and Gyade, and then to march to Lhasa as did Chung Ying in 1910. The British, of course, would protest; but they were unlikely to do much more. India was in a state of political unrest. The Indian Government was not going, at this juncture, to commit large forces to the barren wastes of the Tibetan plateau. Lu's advice brought about a marked stiffening in the Chinese attitude. The Wai-chiao-pu, for instance, declared categorically in early March that it would not consider for one moment a Chinese border farther east than Enta, a point on the upper Salween to the west of

[7] *Memorandum.*

[8] FO 535/17, no. 52, Viceroy to Secretary of State, 14 March 1914.

Chamdo: this was better than Giamda, but still a long way from the Mekong-Yangtze divide indicated as the Inner-Outer Tibet border by McMahon. The Indian Government considered deporting Lu Hsing-chi, but then decided not to, so as to avoid revealing to the Chinese that their telegrams were being monitored.[9]

On 20 March Chen called on McMahon to inform him that his Government had virtually rejected the entire draft agreement and had decided that if a Sino-Tibetan border of any kind had to be fixed at all, then it should be on the Salween and not at the point indicated on McMahon's map of 17 February.[10] At this moment it really looked as if the Conference, as far as the Chinese were concerned, was drawing to a close. McMahon replied, on 26 March, with what amounted to an ultimatum. The attitude of the Chinese, he said, 'appeared to indicate a lack of appreciation of the actual conditions existing in Tibet'. Every day it was becoming more difficult to restrain the Tibetans from launching their own offensive against the Chinese positions in the East (with, it was clearly implied, British aid); and, unless Chen was prepared to talk things over soon in a more reasonable frame of mind, then McMahon would 'have no alternative but to withdraw our present draft with the accompanying map, and to lay before the Conference proposals of a different nature'. All this was intended to convince Chen that unless he accepted McMahon's draft and map as the basis for discussion the British would come to an agreement with the Tibetans without Chinese participation. How seriously McMahon meant to implement this threat it is not easy to say. An Anglo-Tibetan agreement without China would certainly have involved the Anglo-Russian Convention; and the Indian Government could not be sure of diplomatic support in this respect from Sir Edward Grey. McMahon, at any rate, resolved to be prepared for the withdrawal of the Chinese delegation from the Conference; and on the same day that he put his threat to Chen he arranged for the draft agreement to be sent up to Lhasa for the Dalai Lama's approval. It would take roughly fourteen days for a Tibetan reply to reach Simla, where

[9] PEF 1913/19, no. 1021/14, IO minute on Viceroy to Secretary of State, 14 March 1914.

[10] *Memorandum.*

499

the Conference was now to move from Delhi.[11] Until 7 April, then, McMahon still had time to think about his next step.

On 7 April, at Simla, Chen called for a meeting of the Conference at which he could present what he described as his Government's final proposals.[12] The main issue remained the location of the Sino-Tibetan border, and Chen reported his Government's continued refusal to withdraw east of the Salween. After the meeting McMahon summoned Chen to a private interview during which he repeated, in stronger terms, the threats of 26 March. He told Chen that until the Chinese showed 'a more reasonable attitude' McMahon would 'suspend personal relations' with the Chinese plenipotentiary. On the next day Rose called on Chen to remind him that the Conference had now reached its sixth month without achieving anything, and to inform him that a meeting would be called by the British delegation on 14 April in which 'the proceedings would be of a conclusive nature'. Chen was now getting very worried. The possibility of a bilateral Anglo-Tibetan treaty was not at all to the Chinese taste, and there was no telling what his own fate at Yuan Shih-k'ai's hands would be if he permitted such an agreement to take place. Yet his Government appeared to be adamant on the boundary question. On 13 April Chen called at the Indian Foreign Office to ask whether the British might not offer some small modifications in the alignment of the Inner-Outer Tibet border, anything which would enable him to request his Government to agree to abandoning Enta on the Salween while at the same time saving 'face'. Rose proposed that Kokonor Lake, Tachienlu and Atuntze be excluded from Inner Tibet and placed in China proper. Chen thereupon requested a postponement of McMahon's deadline for a few days to enable him to consult Peking. He was given until 22 April.

On 15 April Chen again called at the Indian Foreign Office.[13] For the first time since the Conference began he seemed prepared to start serious negotiations. For ten hours Chen and the British delegation went through McMahon's draft, point by point; and in some areas a real measure of agreement was

[11] FO 535/17, no. 61, Viceroy to Secretary of State, 26 March 1914.
[12] *Memorandum.*
[13] *Memorandum*; *BQ*, pp. 101–14.

reached. Article I was accepted as it stood. In Article II Chen objected to the use of the term 'sovereignty', and McMahon agreed to leave 'suzerainty' unqualified, as it had been in the memorandum of 17 August 1912. Chen also felt that there should be some statement to the effect that Tibet was a portion of Chinese territory: McMahon agreed to insert such a phrase as a Note to the final agreement. Chen then asked that there should be a separate agreement between the British and the Chinese defining exactly what 'suzerainty' meant: McMahon refused and the matter was dropped. The references to the Dalai Lama and to the Chinese Parliament McMahon agreed at Chen's request to relegate to Notes, where they would not have quite the same psychological force as in the body of the agreement. In Article III McMahon accepted two minor modifications, the deletion of the word 'colonists' from the last sentence of Paragraph 1 and the extension of the period of grace for unauthorised Chinese in Outer Tibet from one to three months. The wording of Article IV was changed but slightly. Articles V and VI remained unchanged. After some discussion, McMahon agreed to relegate section (c) of Article VII to a Note. Chen clearly did not like the provision in Article VIII for a British representative to visit Lhasa, and wished the agreement to specify that the Trade Agent, while in the Tibetan capital, could only discuss commercial matters with the Tibetan authorities. McMahon refused to consider such qualifications, but did accept a Note limiting the size of the Trade Agent's escort to 75 per cent of the Amban's escort. On the vexed question of Article IX Chen was still unable to offer any modification of the Chinese stand on the Inner-Outer Tibet boundary: this subject was not pursued too hotly by McMahon on this occasion. The Article, of course, did no more than refer to a map, and a discussion of its wording in no way affected the boundary issue as such. Chen objected to the description of the nature of Tibetan rights in Inner Tibet; and McMahon agreed to delete the phrase 'to issue appointment orders to chiefs and local officers, and to collect all customary rents and taxes'. The resultant Article left Lhasa with nothing more than a religious concern in Inner Tibet, thus making Chinese temporal sovereignty there, in effect, unqualified. Article X, which provided for cash compensation to the Nepalese and Ladakhis, Chen refused to have at any price. Since it had only been inserted in the draft for purposes of bargaining, McMahon was quite willing to remove it. Chen offered in place of Article X the following:

> In case of differences between the Governments of China and Tibet in regard to questions arising out of this Convention, the aforesaid Governments engage to refer them to the British Government for equitable adjustment.

This was an important concession on Chen's part, which gave the British some measure of treaty right to intervene in future Sino-Tibetan relations; and McMahon accepted it gladly. As a result of this long discussion, Chen and McMahon arrived at a draft agreement which, with its seven attached notes, is to be found in Appendix XVII. The actual definition of the Inner-Outer Tibet boundary was not to be found in the text of the draft, but was to be marked on an attached map. Henceforward, therefore, the Simla Conference centred on the securing of agreement as to the whereabouts of a red line and a blue line on a skeleton map.

Though Chen had suddenly shown himself very reasonable indeed in his attitude towards the draft agreement, he was unable to report on the eve of the expiry of McMahon's ultimatum that his Government had modified significantly its views on the boundary question. The Chinese position was embodied in five main propositions:[14]

1. The border between Szechuan and Tibet (as the Chinese Government persisted in describing the Inner-Outer Tibet boundary) was the Salween.

2. To the east of the Salween the Chinese enjoyed full control, and their sovereignty was unqualified.

3. To the west of the Salween to Giamda, the former boundary point between Lhasa and Sikang, the Tibetans should acknowledge a status different from that of Lhasa territory even if they enjoyed effective autonomy here: this was a symbolic way of keeping the concept of Sikang alive.

4. The whole of the Kokonor region, Chinghai as the Chinese called, was now, as it long had been, under Chinese rule.

[14] FO 535/17, no. 70, Chinese Minister to Grey, 6 April 1914, contains a clear statement of these five points.

5. Gyade, also known as the region of the thirty-nine banners (or tribes), which was situated on the upper reaches of the Salween, should enjoy a special status, being under a traditional form of indirect Chinese rule which precluded the stationing there of Chinese magistrates: Gyade was important, of course, as the territorial connecting link between Kokonor (or Chinghai) and the Chinese-claimed boundary point on the Salween at Enta.

Because of the boundary question, Chen felt himself unable at the meeting (which McMahon had indicated would be the last) of the Simla Conference of 22 April to initial the draft agreement and its attached map.[15] The Lönchen Shatra, convinced that the Chinese were now going to leave the Conference, thereupon declared that, in view of the present attitude of the Chinese Government, his own Government were no longer prepared to accept an agreement which would commit them to the return to Lhasa of the Amban and the surrender to China of such districts as De-ge and Nyarong. Whether the Lönchen Shatra was acting in collusion with McMahon or not is not entirely clear. Probably he was not. At all events, the Lönchen Shatra's intervention enabled McMahon to demonstrate to Chen that the possibility of a settlement of the Tibetan problem between the British and the Tibetans on a bilateral basis was now very real indeed. McMahon ordered the draft agreement to be removed from the table 'with as much ceremony as possible'. Both the Lönchen Shatra and Chen were now very agitated, a condition revealed on their 'usually placid and inscrutable faces'. Chen's anxieties have already been indicated. The Lönchen Shatra probably realised that he was on the point of taking a step which might well earn him the displeasure of his master, the Dalai Lama. McMahon chose this moment to announce that he had decided to adjourn the final meeting of the Conference for five days, until 27 April, so that Chen could have another opportunity to consult his Government in Peking. Chen and the Lönchen Shatra both appeared much relieved.

On the evening of 26 April Chen received his final instructions from the Wai-chiao-pu, which were vague and indicated no real promise of a Chinese change of mind. He told McMahon

15 *Memorandum*; *BQ*, pp. 115–23.

that, in these circumstances, he could not possibly initial the draft and its attached map.[16] On the morning of 27 April, when the Conference again assembled, this was still Chen's position. McMahon said that Chen, unless he could bring himself to co-operate with the British and Tibetan delegates, should now withdraw from the conference-room. Moreover, any agreement which might be signed in Chen's absence would not contain the

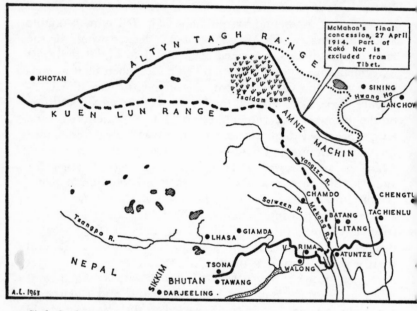

13   *Simla Conference boundaries, April 1914*

expression 'suzerainty' as a description of China's relationship to Tibet: the implication was clear; if Chen did not agree to the existing draft and map, the British would to all intents and purposes recognise Tibet as a fully independent state. Chen, very upset, thereupon removed himself to a neighbouring room, where he was joined by Rose. McMahon now resolved to attempt to arrange a final concession to the Chinese. Once Chen had gone he asked the Lönchen Shatra whether the Tibetan Government would be prepared to see some of the Kokonor territory, to which, he observed, 'the Chinese appeared to attach importance, although neither the Chinese nor the Tibetans had any definite

[16] Loc. cit.

information in regard to its nature or inhabitants', be shown on the map as in China rather than in Inner Tibet (Map no. 13). Moreover, he suggested that the Note attached to the draft, in which reference was made to the prohibition of Tibetan representatives from attending Chinese Parliaments, should be made applicable to Outer Tibet only. The Lönchen Shatra agreed to these changes, which were then put to Chen in another room. After some solitary reflection, Chen made up his mind. He would, he said, be willing to initial the draft and the map, 'but on the clear understanding that to initial and to sign them were two separate actions'. His initials could not possibly bind his Government, whose views he would now seek by telegraph. On this understanding Chen re-entered the conference-room and put his 'initials'—actually he wrote his name in full—on the draft and map. Sir Henry McMahon then congratulated the delegates on their good work and declared the meeting at an end: the Conference, however, remained in being, and would continue to do so until the Chinese endorsement of Chen's action had been received.

On 29 April the Wai-chiao-pu, acting on the advice of Lu Hsing-chi, whose spies at Simla had reported to him the latest developments, repudiated Chen's action: China could not possibly hold herself bound by his initials.[17] On 30 April Dr. Wellington Koo from the Wai-chiao-pu called on Jordan in Peking to protest strongly against the way in which Chen had been made to agree to a document so contrary to Chinese official policy. He hinted that if the Indian Government tried to insist on the validity of this agreement (the Simla Convention as it was to become known), British commercial interests in the Yangtze valley might suffer.[18] On 1 May the Chinese Minister in London, Lew Yuk-lin, protested to Grey; and on that day Jordan reported that the Wai-chiao-pu had now proposed that, since the Simla talks had broken down, negotiations between Britain and China over Tibet should forthwith be transferred to London or Peking.[19]

By the end of April 1914, therefore, the Simla Conference had failed to produce a valid tripartite agreement. It had,

[17] FO 535/17, no. 104, Viceroy to Secretary of State, 29 April 1914.
[18] FO 371/1930, no. 22150, Jordan to Grey, 30 April 1914.
[19] FO 371/1929, no. 19289, Chinese Minister to Grey, 1 May 1914.

however, secured the British a number of other advantages which must have convinced McMahon that he had not wasted the last six months. Firstly, while in Delhi between January and March the British and Tibetans, without consulting the Chinese, had reached an agreement on the alignment of the Indo-Tibetan border in the Assam Himalayas. The result, the McMahon Line, will be considered later. Secondly, the Lönchen Shatra had been persuaded to accept a new set of Tibet trade regulations in place of those of 1908 and 1893.[20] The new regulations, in the negotiation of which the Chinese took no part, transformed the conditions of British commercial activity to the north of the Himalayas. The trade marts were turned into something very like the Chinese Treaty Ports, with the British Trade Agents possessing extraterritorial powers.[21] The British were guaranteed complete control over the lines of communication between the marts and the Indian border. The Tibetans agreed to give up their love for the creation of commercial monopolies. British merchants could carry on their business throughout the country, and the British Trade Agents could talk or correspond with whatever Tibetan officials they chose. Indian tea, though only by implication, was now permitted a sale in Tibet. The trade marts were not specified by name; hence, by implication again, it was possible for the Indian Government to consider the existence of marts other than those at Gartok, Gyantse and Yatung. The 1914 trade regulations would have brought joy to the hearts of nineteenth-century British 'pioneers of commerce', but they did not, it must be admitted, go far towards a solution of the political problem of the Indian northern frontier.

[20] See Appendix XVIII.

[21] But Treaty Ports which were open to British trade only. The Indian Government was most anxious that the Tibetan trade marts should not acquire the same international status as the Treaty Ports of China proper: if they did, it would not be easy to keep the Russians out of them. The preservation of the exclusive British position in the trade marts was a strong argument against any policy which might lead to the acknowledgment of Chinese *sovereignty* in Tibet.

XXV

THE SECOND SIMLA
CONVENTION, 3 JULY 1914

THE moment that the Peking Government had repudiated Chen's initialling of the draft Convention, as McMahon had more than suspected it would, the British were faced with the prospect of either letting the Simla Conference come to an inconclusive end or making some bipartite arrangement with the Tibetans. There was always a chance, of course, that rather than see the Lhasa Government behave in such a sovereign manner the Republic would change its mind about the draft: but no one on the British side could have been very optimistic in this respect. From the outset, as we have seen, the British had appreciated that the proceedings of the Simla Conference would have at some stage to be communicated to St. Petersburg for Russian acceptance: this was an apparently inescapable consequence of the 1907 Convention. It had been decided, however, to obtain agreement at Simla first, and then talk with the Russians. Now, with a direct Anglo-Tibetan treaty becoming more than an academic possibility, Grey at the Foreign Office concluded that Anglo-Russian consultation could no longer be postponed.

It had been clear ever since Sazonov's visit to England in 1912 that the Russians were perfectly willing to give the British a free hand in Tibet in exchange for a suitable *quid pro quo*. In British minds the obvious *quid pro quo* was the recognition of Russian interests in Mongolia; but Sazonov had declared that the Tibetan and Mongolian questions could not be related, because Mongolia had not been dealt with in the 1907 Convention. Mongolia and Tibet, as Sazonov said on a later occasion, 'have nothing to do with each other, and ought not to be mentioned in the same breath'.[1] But could not Tibet and Mongolia be made, on grounds other than the 1907 Convention, to have something to do with each other? This was a question which the Foreign Office had been examining since the time of the Russo-Mongol Agreement of November 1912. One possibility emerged from the Russo-Chinese Declaration of November 1913, which confirmed the Russian commercial position in Mongolia outlined in the Urga Protocol appended to the Russo-Mongol Agreement of 1912. Outer Mongolia was now brought within the general framework of the China trade. Could not the British press for their own commercial rights in Outer Mongolia? The Mongolian trade, of course, was of minimal interest to the British at that time. Only two British, or part British, firms were actually doing business in Urga in 1913, the British American Tobacco Company and Price's Candle Company;[2] but they would certainly suffer some loss through preferential treatment to Russian merchants. Perhaps the time was now ripe for the British to start their own diplomatic overtures towards the Outer Mongolian authorities, seeking an 'open door' for British merchants there.[3] Perhaps, in order to keep British diplomacy out of Urga, where it would compete with that of the Russians in a way possibly as irritating to St. Petersburg as the presence of Dorjiev in Tibet had been to the Indian Government, Sazonov might change his mind about the connection between the Mongolian and Tibetan questions.

In February and March 1914 Buchanan, the British Ambassador in St. Petersburg, had a number of talks with Sazonov on this point.[4] The Russian Foreign Minister, however, was not impressed. He could not take British concern for the future of the Mongolian trade very seriously. He pointed out that traders

[1] FO 371/1937, op. 5785, Buchanan to Grey, 3 February 1914.

[2] FO 371/1608, no. 46463, Alston to Grey, 20 September 1913. For the texts of the Mongolian agreements of 1912 and 1913, see Appendices XIV and XV.

[3] PEF 1913/41, no. 4614/13, FO to IO, 7 November 1913.

[4] FO 371/1937, no. 2684, Grey to Buchanan, 24 January 1914; no. 4563, Buchanan to Grey, 1 February 1914; no. 5785, Buchanan to Grey, 3 February 1914; no. 7516, Grey to Buchanan, 27 February 1914; no. 10334, Buchanan to Grey, 4 March 1914. See also BD X, Pt. 2, p. 775.

in Mongolia experienced great difficulty in getting paid, and remarked that the British would be well advised to avoid this profitless field of commercial enterprise. In any case, the Russians by their treaties of 1862 and 1881 had special rights in the land trade with China, rights similar to those which the British enjoyed, for example, on the Sino-Burmese border. Would the British, he implied, agree to combine these two regions, Yunnan and Mongolia, in a single set of negotiations? The British certainly would not. The commercial approach to the Mongolian problem was fraught with dangers. In any case, it was difficult to answer Sazonov's point that if the British really wanted to export their goods to Outer Mongolia, why did they not do so via Russia, where they would enjoy the communication benefits of the Trans-Siberian Railway? The British continued, from time to time, to ponder the Mongolian problem, considering, for instance, the desirability of establishing a Consulate in Urga:[5] but by April 1914 it was clear that they had failed to find a way to link Mongolia to Tibet within the framework of Anglo-Russian treaty relations. Any request to St. Petersburg, therefore, for a relaxation of the provisions of the 1907 Convention affecting Tibet would imply, as it had since September 1912, British concessions in Persia, Afghanistan and, perhaps, Sinkiang. Grey had no illusions about this when he instructed Buchanan in early May 1914 to start talking once more with Sazonov about Tibet.[6]

Buchanan, who was to be assisted by R. T. Nugent,[7] a young attaché at the Foreign Office who had been dealing with the papers on Tibet since 1912, was authorised on 4 May to show to Sazonov the following documents:[8]

(1) the draft Convention, as initialled on 27 April 1914;

(2) the draft text of the new trade regulations;

(3) the notes relating to the McMahon Line (which will be discussed in detail elsewhere), but not the *maps* attached to these notes, and,

(4) the map showing the Inner-Outer Tibet boundaries which was to be attached to the Simla Convention.

[5] FO 371/1937, no. 28145, Jordan to Grey, 5 June 1914.
[6] FO 371/1929, no. 18917, Grey to Buchanan, 4 May 1914.
[7] FO 371/1929, no. 19135, Minute by Nicolson, 1 May 1914.
[8] FO 535/17, no. 112, Grey to Buchanan, 4 May 1914.

Russian assent for the draft Convention was required on two main points; the commercial provisions of Article 6, and Article 8, which permitted the British Trade Agent to visit Lhasa. Buchanan was authorised, if he saw fit, to offer to replace Article 10, with its implied British control over Tibetan foreign relations, by something less controversial. On the question of the McMahon Line, Buchanan was to explain to Sazonov that its definition had only become possible because of recent exploration, and that

> the line chosen follows the main geographical features approximating to the traditional border between Tibet and the semi-independent tribes under the control of the Government of India, and . . . as far as possible it divides exactly the territory occupied by people of Tibetan origin from that inhabited by the Miris, Abors, Daphlas, and the other tribes within the British sphere of influence.

It was not suggested that Sazonov be told that by the McMahon Line notes the British had, in fact, acquired Tibetan territory of considerably greater extent than the Chumbi Valley. Grey urged Buchanan to bring Sazonov to terms as quickly as possible: the Lönchen Shatra was growing impatient and longing to get back to Lhasa, and once he went the Simla Conference would be well and truly dead.

On this basis Buchanan began discussions with Sazonov on 17 May.[9] The Russian Foreign Minister was not very helpful. Though he made no objection at this time about the proposed new commercial arrangements, he protested against Articles 8 and 10 of the draft Convention. Article 10, which Sazonov thought gave the British a protectorate over Tibet, would have to be replaced, as, indeed, Grey had already concluded. Article 8, the right of a British official to go to Lhasa on political business, would only be accepted by Russia in exchange for the right of a Russian political agent, perhaps a non-European, to visit Herat in Afghanistan. As Sazonov put it, unless he could show some diplomatic gain of this magnitude, he could not hope to survive the attacks of his enemies in the Imperial Government who would certainly accuse him of treasonable weakness to the British. Buchanan endeavoured to argue that,

[9] FO 371/1930, no. 21986, Buchanan to Grey, 17 May 1914.

in fact, Article 8 of the draft was really a fair price for British acceptance of recent Russian activities in Persia, the bombardment of Meshed, the attempts to purchase large portions of Azerbaijan, the stationing of more than 12,000 troops—only 6,000, said Sazonov—in the northern part of the country; in all of which, the British Ambassador claimed, Russia had certainly departed from the spirit of the 1907 agreement. Sazonov was unmoved.

Buchanan concluded that Sazonov was indifferent to what the British actually *did* in Tibet, as long as they kept their actions secret, an interpretation of the Russian's attitude which Crewe had already arrived at in late 1912. What mattered were appearances. In a second interview with Sazonov, on 18 May, this point became clearer.[10] The Russian Foreign Minister said that he would certainly accept Article 8 if the British were willing to present a note giving Russia, too, the right to send a representative to Lhasa. Russia would then sign a *secret* agreement to the effect that she would never try to send such an agent there. Buchanan looked upset, whereupon Sazonov suggested another approach. If the British would present a note on Article 8 to the effect that the British representative would not go to Lhasa without Russian approval, then the Russians would make a secret engagement that such approval would not be withheld. A similar formula, Sazonov hinted, might also be applied to Article 6. If Russia were given the right in the Convention to seek commercial concessions in Tibet, then she would promise, again in secret, never to avail herself of that right. In addition, Sazonov still required positive Russian gains elsewhere, in Afghanistan and Persia, as a weapon against his enemies in the Government, the Nationalists, notably M. Krivoshein, who were reported to be seeking his downfall.[11]

In Afghanistan, Sazonov wanted the right for Russia to station a native agent in Herat, to deal with irrigation problems and to make sure that no railways were built in that part of the country in competition with lines planned by the Russians. In other words, not only was there to be a Russian agent but also it was to be accepted that the Herat region was to all intents

[10] FO 371/1930, no. 22413, Buchanan to Grey, 18 May 1914.
[11] FO 535/17, no. 132, Buchanan to Grey, 19 May 1914.

and purposes within the Russian sphere of influence. In Persia the Russian demands were not quite so urgent, but Sazonov made it plain to Buchanan that he would shortly be seeking a British note recognising 'more fully Russia's predominant interest in North Persia so that we [the British] should not in future be always bringing complaints about the doings of Russian Consuls there'. This was not, Sazonov said, a condition of agreement on Tibet, it was a 'sequence' to such agreement.[12]

Grey was prepared to consider seriously the greater part of Sazonov's conditions, though he could certainly not agree to give Russia the explicit right to have a political agency in Herat—Indian protests would have been deafening.[13] He told Buchanan to offer Sazonov public British notes on Articles 6 and 8, along the lines already indicated, in exchange for secret Russian ones, and to propose the replacement of Article 10 by some innocuous words about the comparison of texts. It was hoped that on this basis the Convention could be signed. Meanwhile Buchanan would begin discussions with Sazonov on the Afghan issue, which could hardly be settled overnight. The Indian Government, however, were not satisfied at this turn of events.[14] How could Article 10, which already formed part of an initialled draft, be changed without completely invalidating a document of already dubious validity? But Grey insisted, after Buchanan had again consulted Sazonov, that Article 10 must go.

On India Office advice, Grey decided that the Afghan discussions must result in precise geographical definition of the area concerned.[15] Also, the Afghan agreement, in whatever form it might take, should be kept secret: otherwise the Afghans could hardly fail to conclude that their country had been partitioned into spheres of influence on the Persian pattern. Lord Hardinge, with a more immediate practical concern for Afghan attitudes, urged that no geographical definition be made at all, since, secret or public, news of it would most probably leak out to give the Amir the impression that his country was being divided up. Moreover, Hardinge thought it essential to

[12] Loc cit.
[13] FO 371/1930, no. 22567, Grey to Buchanan, 22 May 1914.
[14] FO 371/1930, no. 22959, Viceroy to Secretary of State, 21 May 1914.
[15] FO 371/1930, no. 22567, Minute by Political Department, India Office.

talk things over in Kabul before starting any negotiations about Afghanistan in St. Petersburg.[16] Indian opinions, however, were disregarded by both Crewe and Grey.

If Grey had really believed that he could obtain Russian agreement on the draft Simla Convention before the precise shape of the Afghan concession had been decided, he was being extremely optimistic. Not only did Sazonov insist that the Afghan agreement should be public—after all, he was seeking to satisfy Russian opinion—but it should be settled before the Simla Convention was signed.[17] On 6 June Grey told Buchanan to go ahead with the Afghan discussions.[18] He was to make no mention of the Russian agent at Herat, but, in a somewhat oblique manner, offer British recognition that the Russians had special interests in the northern part of Afghanistan adjacent to their border. These interests did not entitle Russia to anything like a protectorate or even a sphere of influence in the region in question; but they did mean that Russia could expect an assurance that no other Power (i.e. the British) would attempt to establish its influence or its interests there. Northern Afghanistan was to be, as it were, a sphere of British non-influence or non-interest, a strangely negative concept which was to be embodied in a British Note along these lines:

> The Russian Government reaffirms its adherence to the principle that Afghanistan is outside the sphere of Russian political influence.
>
> The British Government engages that it will not support any application by British subjects for irrigation works, railways or preferential rights for commercial or industrial enterprises in Northern Afghanistan.

This was to be public. There would also be a secret agreement defining 'Northern Afghanistan' as bounded by a line running from Ishkashan on Ab-i-Panja to Zebak, to Munjan Pass, to Doshi via Sinjitak and Badak Passes, to Tarkuch on Band-i-Amir, to Daulat Yar, then along the crest of Koh-i-Baba and

[16] FO 535/17, no. 148, Viceroy to Secretary of State, 28 May 1914. Mr. W. Hale of the Australian National University is at present working on this period of Anglo-Afghan relations; and I am indebted to him for information on the Indian attitude towards these discussions.

[17] FO 535/17, no. 138, Buchanan to Grey, 25 May 1914.

[18] FO 371/1930, no. 24729, Grey to Buchanan, 6 June 1914.

Siyah Baba ranges to the point where the Hari Rud enters Russian territory at Zulfikar, words which were carefully chosen to exclude Herat and the plain of the Afghan Hari Rud (Map no. 14).

On 10 June Sazonov commented on the British proposals.[19] In the first place, he insisted that any definition of Northern Afghanistan should be made public; after all, his main concern was to persuade Russian public opinion that he had not betrayed the national interest in helping the British with their Tibetan problem. In the second place, he pointed out that the Hari Rud, as far as Russian irrigation was concerned, was by far the most important Afghan river; and any definition of Northern Afghanistan must include all its valley. He suggested, therefore, that the British definition should be modified so that from Daulat Yar the boundary should run south of the river along the Safed Kuh range, instead of along the crests of the ranges on the northern side, as Buchanan had been empowered to propose (Map no. 14). Sazonov also, at this juncture, introduced a quite new concession which he now felt he needed to justify relaxing the Tibetan clauses of the 1907 Convention. He asked the Indian Government to allow Russian subjects who were on pilgrimage to Buddhist holy places to enter Tibet from British India. A number of such persons had arrived in India in February and March 1914 and been refused by the Indian Government permits to cross the Indo-Tibetan border, leading to protests by the Russian Consul-General at Calcutta.[20]

The Indian Government, of course, would not hear of the Russians being granted an easier access to Central Tibet than that already provided for in the 1907 Convention. If Russian Buddhist pilgrims wanted to go to Lhasa or Tashilhumpo, then they should do so by way of Mongolia and China. As for the Russian proposal that Herat should be included within 'Northern Afghanistan', the British were prepared to come to a measure of compromise on this point.[21] Perhaps, in addition to the definition outlined in the proposed British note, there should be a second zone, the Herat region, in which the British would deny their right to any concessions relating to irrigation, but not to such

[19] FO 535/17, no. 164, Buchanan to Grey, 10 June 1914.
[20] FO 371/1931, no. 32062, IO to FO, 14 July 1914.
[21] FO 371/1930, no. 26285, Buchanan to Grey, 11 June 1914.

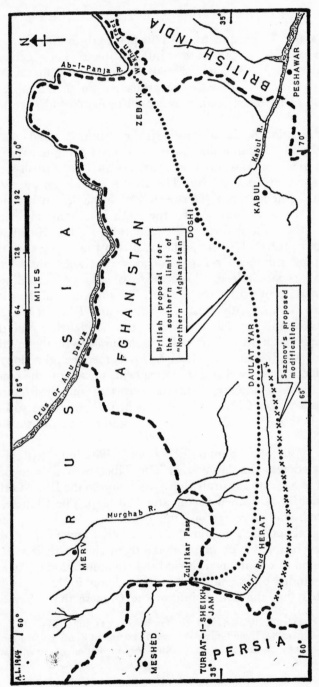

14 *Anglo-Russian proposals for the definition of 'Northern Afghanistan', May–June 1914*

matters as railways and trade. This proposal, in effect, would reserve to Russia certain limited interests in a region which was otherwise, as it were, unassigned. Buchanan felt that if the Russians were not offered some protection for their supply of water from the Hari Rud, they would probably 'take the law into their own hands'.[22]

At this point the discussions in St. Petersburg petered out. It was clear to Buchanan that Sazonov was not going to agree to the draft Simla Convention at a price which the British were particularly anxious to pay. The British would not agree to publish the definition of 'Northern Afghanistan', which would certainly be misunderstood by the Amir in Kabul; and they clung to their reservations on Herat and the Afghan Hari Rud. To both British and Russian diplomatists in June 1914, with the developing European crisis, Central Asian issues must have seemed trivial indeed. Their discussion was accordingly adjourned until early 1915, when the British and Russian positions in Persia, Afghanistan, Sinkiang and Tibet were again considered, this time in relation to the Dardanelles and the possible Russian acquisition of Constantinople.[23] By the middle of June 1914, therefore, the Indian Government could no longer hope for a speedy Russian agreement to adapt the 1907 Convention to accommodate the terms of the draft Simla Convention. Yet Chen and the Lönchen Shatra were still in Simla, both eager to go home. Some rapid decision was called for.

The position at Simla since Chen's initialling had been repudiated was simple enough. The Tibetans had been persuaded to agree to the draft Convention and to the Inner-Outer Tibet border as defined on the attached map. The Chinese, it appeared, had accepted all the draft, and were now only arguing about the lines on the map. Were any further concessions possible which might make them change their mind? McMahon at one moment hoped that the alteration of Article 10, demanded by Sazonov, might be exploited in this sense. He suggested that the British inform the Chinese that 'they are

[22] FO 371/1930, no. 26746, Buchanan to Grey, 11 June 1914.
[23] PEF 1912/82, India Office, Political Department Confidential Memorandum C.142, Revision of Anglo-Russian Convention of 1907, dated August 1915.

ready to defer to China's susceptibilities so far as to modify Article 10 . . . with a view to removing any undue suggestions of British tutelage from the Convention', a plan which, Grey thought, 'is too clever and yet not so clever that the Chinese will not find it out and laugh at it'.[24] No further use could be made of Article 10.

Another concession was suggested by Jordan after his threats and arguments, during the first two weeks of June, had failed to move the Wai-chiao-pu.[25] The idea emerged from a conversation on 16 June with the Chinese Foreign Minister, Sun Pao-ch'i, who remarked that the real border between China and Northern Tibet was not the Altyn Tagh range but the Kun Lun range. After searching through narratives of Tibetan exploration by Rockhill, Welby, Sven Hedin, Bonvalot, and Prince Henri d'Orleans, Jordan concluded that Sun might have a point. If not Chinese, the tracts north of the Kun Lun, usually called the Chang Tang, were quite barren, a veritable no-man's-land. Why not pull the Tibetan border south to the Kun Lun, and give the Chang Tang to China (Map no. 15)? On 23 June McMahon approved a concession along these lines; but Jordan then discovered that it in no way impressed the Wai-chiao-pu.[26] The Chinese had absolutely no intention of giving up Chamdo or any other of their advanced positions in the Marches.

What could the British now do? One possibility, of transferring the discussions to Peking or London and excluding the Tibetans from them, the Indian Government would not have at any price. On the other hand, to sign the Convention without the Chinese would perhaps be a rather too flagrant violation of the 1907 Convention. Moreover, if the British made a bipartite agreement with Tibet they would, in effect, be acknowledging an independent Tibetan state which they might soon be called upon to defend. A Sino-British conflict in Central Asia was unthinkable in the light of the mounting international tension in Europe. There seemed but one possible course of action, which,

[24] FO 371/1930, no. 23928, Viceroy to Secretary of State, 28 May 1914, with minute by Grey.
[25] FO 535/17, no. 187, Jordan to Grey, 16 June 1914.
[26] FO 371/1930, no. 28677, Viceroy to Secretary of State, 23 June 1914; FO 535/17, no. 188, Wai-chiao-pu to Jordan, 27 June 1914.

no doubt, was the subject of some self-congratulation in London as being another example of the British genius for compromise. The Convention would be signed by no one; but the British and Tibetan delegates would sign a declaration to the effect that they agreed to be bound by the terms of the Convention, and that the rights and privileges which it gave to China would be held in suspension, as it were, until Peking had

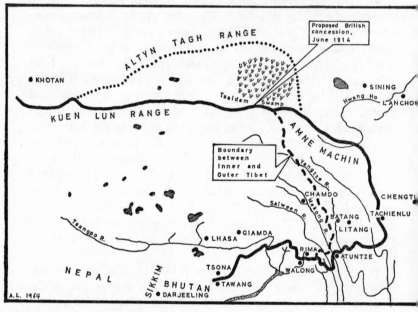

15　*Simla Conference boundaries, June 1914*

also signed.[27] This device would oblige the Tibetans to agree to the return to Lhasa of the Amban and his escort and to accept Chinese suzerainty should the Convention ever become tripartite. It would also enable the new Tibet trade regulations, which did not require Chinese signature, to come into operation; and, as we shall see, it would add some extra force to the secret Tibeto-British agreement on the boundary in the Assam Himalayas.

McMahon, there can be no doubt, would have preferred to have the Tibetans sign the Convention; and on 2 July, when

[27] *Memorandum.*

he called a final meeting of the Simla Conference for the following day, he apparently still thought seriously of doing so. However, he could hardly ignore the urgent telegram from Lord Crewe, of 3 July, which told him that 'His Majesty's Government cannot authorise separate signature with Tibetans'.[28] Thus the Conference ended in a charade. After a last plea to Chen to change his mind, McMahon and the Lönchen Shatra proceeded to sign a joint Anglo-Tibetan declaration that the two signatories would hold the draft Convention, which they then initialled, to be binding, and, also, to sign the new Tibet trade regulations. All this was done in Chen's presence; but, McMahon reported with some satisfaction, 'the nature of the documents executed at the meeting is not known to the Chinese plenipotentiary, who, I am now given to understand, believes the Convention *was* signed. This impression I have not thought it necessary to correct.' Chen was told that

> the Agreements now concluded between the Lönchen Shatra and myself [McMahon] were final in character and that no alterations in them would now be possible. I was able to assure him, however, after consultation with my Tibetan colleague, that we were both prepared to leave open the way to Chinese participation, should he be in a position to attach his signature to the Convention before our departure from India.[29]

Chen promised to inform his Government of this fact. The final meeting of the Simla Conference was then brought to a close.[30]

[28] FO 371/1931, no. 30825, Secretary of State to Viceroy, 3 July 1914.
[29] *Memorandum.*
[30] Some confusion exists, which McMahon's attempts to mislead the Chinese have not served to clarify, as to exactly what was *signed* on this occasion. Some recent authorities have stated that the Simla Convention was signed. See, for example, International Commission of Jurists, *Tibet and the Rule of Law*, Geneva, 1959, p. 86, and *Tibet and the Chinese People's Republic*, Geneva, 1960, p. 140; Tibet Society, *Tibet and Freedom*, London, 1961, p. 18; Great Britain, Foreign Office, *Tibet*, Peace Handbook No. 70, London, 1920, p. 42; Great Britain, Central Office of Information, *Tibet*, London, 1958, p. 5; Z. Ahmad, *China and Tibet, 1708–1959*, Chatham House Memorandum, London, 1960, p. 21. It should be clear from the account given in this book that, unless McMahon disobeyed instructions and did not inform London of the fact, the text of the Convention was only *initialled* by McMahon and the Lönchen Shatra. However, the British and Tibetan

The Simla Convention which McMahon had obtained was the same as the draft which Chen had initialled on 27 April with the exception of Articles 10 and 11. Article 10, as we have seen, had been deleted; and in its place had been inserted the second paragraph of Article 11, relating to the comparison of texts. The Convention had been signed by no one. The Russians had not accepted it. What was it worth? A great deal, McMahon thought. During its negotiation new trade regulations had been secured and the Assam Himalayan border had been defined. The Chinese, he argued, would come to their senses and sign one day, thus producing a final settlement to the Tibetan question. Meanwhile, the British had obtained the freedom of direct communication with the Lhasa Government and would no longer have to face the nightmare of seeking the solution of local border problems through Chinese mediation.

What was the next step? Before leaving Simla for a well-earned leave in England, McMahon made a number of proposals concerning 'the measures necessary to render the Conference effective in the interests of Tibet and ourselves'.[31] Obviously something would have to be done about the Lhasa Residency, the key to the maintenance of British influence in Tibet; but the simple implementation of Article 8 was probably ruled out for the time being by Sazonov's attitude. Hence McMahon suggested a rather devious approach. In Note 7

[31] Loc. cit.

---

plenipotentiaries appear to have *signed* and *sealed* the map attached to the Convention. They also signed a declaration that they would abide by the terms of the Convention and also the text of the new Trade Regulations. The *signing* of the map is probably a fact of some significance. This was the one part of the Convention which the Chinese would not accept at any price. The implication of McMahon's act, it would seem, was to make it possible for the Chinese to adhere to the Convention at some later date only if they also agreed to accept the boundary between Inner and Outer Tibet as it was shown on the map of 3 July 1914. Any modification of the map, it could perhaps be argued, would involve a fresh round of Anglo-Tibetan negotiations. Could it be that McMahon had it in mind to prevent Sir John Jordan or some other employee of the Foreign Office in London, at some future date, from making any fresh concessions to the Chinese? A facsimile of the map in question has been reproduced in India, Ministry of External Affairs, *Atlas of the Northern Frontier of India*, New Delhi, 1961, and in *Royal Central Asian Journal*, July–October 1963.

attached to the Convention it was agreed that, once all Chinese troops and officials had withdrawn from Outer Tibet, the Amban and his escort could make their way to Lhasa.[32] The Chinese evacuation, the Note continued, was to be carried out 'to the satisfaction of the three signatories to this Convention, who will investigate and report without delay'. McMahon took these words to imply the right of a British mission to visit the Inner-Outer Tibet frontier; and he now proposed that Rose, accompanied by a small survey detachment and under the auspices of the Tibetan authorities, should return to China by way of Lhasa, Chamdo and Tachienlu. Thus would the British presence be manifested on the actual front line of Sino-Tibetan hostilities, and a lesson would perhaps be read by the Szechuan Provincial Government. The plan was overruled by London on the grounds that

> the Anglo-Russian Agreement limits the right of direct com-
> munication with Tibet, and that until an agreement has been
> reached with the Russian Government, in this as in other
> respects . . . [the Indian Government] . . . can only act
> upon the initialled Convention so far as it does not violate the
> 1907 Agreement.[33]

McMahon also thought that now was the time to augment both the strength and the importance of the Gyantse Trade Agency. The size of its escort should be increased.[34] It should be a post upgraded in seniority (McMahon wanted Bell to take it over). The Trade Agent's housing should be improved. In other words, the Gyantse Trade Agency should be turned into something like a British Residency in exile, as it were, waiting for transfer to Lhasa. In principle this was approved by the Home Government. Another of McMahon's proposals was the opening of a new trade mart at Chamdo, where Louis King could perhaps be the first Trade Agent. The new trade regula-tions contained no reference to the permitted number of trade marts in Tibet, and the Dalai Lama would certainly welcome one at Chamdo, a place which was still firmly in Chinese hands. The Chamdo mart would enable the British to observe and frustrate Chinese plans in the Marches and to prevent anything

[32] See Appendix XVII.
[33] FO 371/1931, no. 30835, FO to IO, 14 July 1914.
[34] *Memorandum.*

like the repetition of Chao Erh-feng's advance to Lhasa in 1910. The Home Government experienced no difficulty in rejecting this particular scheme, though it agreed, as an alternative, that King should remain for a while longer at his Tachienlu observation post.

McMahon was convinced that, until the Chinese at last saw the light and signed the Convention—which he still thought they might do one day—there existed a continuing threat to the Dalai Lama's Government from the Szechuan forces in the Marches. The Kalon Lama might soon find himself hard pressed, a temptation for him to come to terms with his local Chinese adversaries as he had been contemplating since 1913. There seemed, therefore, to be a sound case for helping the Tibetans increase their military strength. A powerful Tibet was far less likely to heed Chinese overtures. McMahon advised that Tibet be given between 3,000 and 5,000 rifles, some 500,000 rounds of ammunition, and the services of a few British military instructors who would not only put backbone into the Lhasa army but also compete with the Japanese and the Russian Buriats already employed in training Tibetan troops. These instructors, therefore, should be European rather than Indian. Not only should the Tibetan army benefit from British advice, but so also should other aspects of the Tibetan administration. The Dalai Lama should be lent British surveyors, geologists and doctors; and young Tibetans should be encouraged to come to India for specialised training. All this aid would greatly strengthen a Tibet which was, whatever the unsigned Convention might say to the contrary, to all intents and purposes an independent state on the British border. Some of these proposals were approved in London; and by September 1914 arms, ammunition and supplies were on their way to Lhasa.[35] The Dalai Lama was

[35] Immediately after the close of the Simla Conference the British adopted a far more helpful attitude towards Tibetan projects for the acquisition of modern arms. In the summer of 1914, for example, the Dalai Lama had placed an order with Armstrong Whitworth for a number of mountain guns. While the Simla Conference was still in progress Armstrong Whitworth were prevented from tendering by the India Office; but the moment the 3 July Declaration was signed they were allowed to do so, with the implicit understanding that the guns in question would be delivered to Tibet through British territory. See FO 371/1931, no. 30077, Armstrong Whitworth to IO, 1 July 1914, and FO to IO, 6 July 1914.

so grateful that he offered the Indian Government all the help, moral and material, which it lay in his power to give to the British Empire in its conflict with the Central Powers.[36]

As a permanent settlement of the Tibetan problem, the Simla Conference can hardly be described as a complete success. It produced new trade regulations and the McMahon Line, which went far to satisfy British administrative requirements along the Himalayan border, but it yielded no final definition of Tibetan status in international law. The existence of the unsigned Simla Convention seems to have prevented the Indian Government between 1914 and 1947 from ever expressly recognising Tibetan independence. The British representative who, from the late 1930s onwards, permanently resided in Lhasa, was never given any formal diplomatic title. Though the British, *de facto*, came eventually to deal with Tibet as if it were a sovereign state, still *de jure* they felt themselves unable to deny Chinese suzerainty there, whatever that expression might mean. When the Chinese in 1950, under a Communist régime, were at last in a position to implement their Tibetan suzerainty, it was not easy to maintain that thereby they were committing an act of aggression. In 1954, in the Sino-Indian Agreement of 29 April, Chinese rights in what was described as the 'Tibet region of China' were recognised: no attempt was made to draw any subtle distinctions between sovereignty and suzerainty.[37]

The Chinese would possibly have signed the Simla Convention had it not been for the alignment of the boundary between Inner and Outer Tibet which McMahon had proposed. Even when McMahon had made a number of concessions, the Chinese were still faced with the prospect of abandoning territory which they then held and from which, it then seemed, the Tibetans were unlikely to dislodge them. Yuan Shih-k'ai, for example, could not possibly in 1914 have approved the Chinese evacuation of Chamdo. General P'eng Jih-sheng, and his Szechuan superiors, would never have obeyed Yuan's orders in this respect. The Chinese withdrawal from Chamdo, therefore, would have involved a Tibetan offensive backed by British military assistance; and by agreeing to it the Chinese Central

[36] Bell, *Tibet*, op. cit., p. 160.
[37] *Foreign Policy of India: Texts of Documents*, Lok Sabha Secretariat, New Delhi, October 1958, for the text of this agreement. See Appendix XX.

Government would, in effect, have also agreed to British military intervention in Outer Tibet. McMahon had no great sympathy for the Chinese and very little understanding of the history of Chinese rule in Central Asia: as Sir Walter Langley told Jordan after meeting McMahon on his return to England, 'It is no doubt difficult to convince anyone from India that there is a Chinese point of view which deserves consideration.'[38] McMahon had failed to appreciate, so Jordan noted, that '*Inner Tibet* is a new geographical expression to Chinese ears and that the arrangement will sound like the surrender of Chinese territory'.[39] The proposed Tibetan partition not only required a total Chinese withdrawal from Outer Tibet but a theoretical Chinese surrender of claims to full sovereignty—however little this might mean in practice—over places like Batang and Litang in Inner Tibet, which were viewed in Peking as being just as Chinese as, say, Szechuan Province. At the moment when McMahon was suggesting that Batang and Litang were in Inner Tibet, Louis King, the British Consular officer stationed at Tachienlu for the duration of the Simla Conference, was actually asking the Szechuan authorities for Chinese passports to visit these places.

Jordan, from his position in Peking, was not particularly happy at the way in which the Simla Conference had been conducted. In late June 1914, on the eve of the Conference's final meeting, he summed up his views in a private letter to his friend Sir Walter Langley at the Foreign Office:

> Whether China signs or refuses to sign the Convention, the future outlook seems to me very unsatisfactory. If she signs, she will do so with bad grace and with very little intention of observing it. If she refuses to sign, the position will be more acute and perhaps call for more immediate action. The Indian Government are pledged to Tibet, and doubtless the threat has been made after fully considering all the consequences it may entail. Apart altogether from the effect such a step would have on our vast commercial and industrial interests in China, I do not myself see how it is practicable. We can scarcely, I imagine, contemplate marching British troops

[38] Jordan Papers (in the Foreign Office Library), Langley to Jordan, 18 November 1914.
[39] Jordan Papers, Jordan to Langley, 17 September 1914.

across Tibet, and we can hardly propose to take an indirect part in a border warfare in which the vanquished usually pay the penalty of being skinned alive. However, all this is beyond my province.

I wish the frontier negotiations had not been so abruptly closed and that we could have reached a settlement which would have given some hope of permanency. I know very well the immense difficulty of Sir Henry McMahon's task and have had as much experience as most people of the provoking delays and disappointments connected with all Chinese negotiations.

It may possibly be due to the late and imperfect information which reached us, but somehow the Delhi negotiations [January to March 1914] conveyed to us an impression of lack of reality. It looked as if the British and Tibetan Representatives knew each others' cards throughout, and as if Ivan Chen was not too loyal to his own Government. The methods of the Government of India are similar to those which Russia and Japan have tried out but have found of so little service that they have seen fit to abandon them.[40]

Jordan's hinted accusation of Anglo-Tibetan collusion against the Chinese needs to be taken very seriously. McMahon was throughout the Conference far closer to the Tibetans than to the Chinese. The Lönchen Shatra, there can be little doubt, looked on McMahon much as a defendant in a legal action looks on his Counsel. McMahon, as it were, had the Tibetan brief and was making the best case of it he could. There were times during the Conference when the Lönchen Shatra was actually represented by Rose, a member of the British delegation. In return for British advocacy, the Tibetans gave McMahon the frontier alignment in the Assam Himalayas with which his name has become permanently associated, and the new trade regulations. McMahon was probably far more interested in obtaining his fee than in winning his case. Were he to use certain arguments, effective though they might be in the conference-room, he would gain his point, that is to say, obtain Chinese signature to the Convention, but would in the process lose his clients. The proposed Tibetan partition into Inner and Outer zones, as we have seen, involved the surrender of cherished rights and attitudes by the Tibetans as well as by the Chinese. There were

[40] Jordan Papers, Jordan to Langley, 28 June 1914.

some surrenders, however, to which the Tibetans would simply not agree. They clung to their claim, for example, to Chamdo, a town which Chao Erh-feng had captured on the eve of his advance to Lhasa, and which the Chinese had only retained in 1912 after the great Chamdo monastery had been destroyed by P'eng Jih-sheng. If settlement with China involved giving up Chamdo, then the Tibetans would probably have preferred to come to terms with the Chinese without British participation. They would have thus avoided the new trade regulations, which in some respects they resented and which, subsequently, they endeavoured to ignore;[41] and they would have escaped the theoretical loss of territory implied in the McMahon Line agreement. In years to come the Tibetans were to argue that they only made such concessions to the Indian Government in return for a guaranteed eastern frontier with China. McMahon, therefore, probably could not afford to offer more than a limited number of concessions to the Chinese if he also wished to obtain any useful, and, from the point of view of Indian frontier policy, vital gains from the Tibetans.

Given the diplomatic circumstances in which the Simla Convention took place, McMahon probably took a sensible enough course. The new trade regulations offered vastly improved arrangements for Anglo-Tibetan communication which needed no longer to be confined to commercial matters. The McMahon Line provided at least a temporary solution to the problem of the British border in the Assam Himalayas and would enable the Indian Government to expand that influence among the hill tribes which it had established during the period of the Abor Expedition. These were concrete gains. If they had been secured at the cost of a Simla Convention not signed by China, the price might not be regarded as excessive. The Simla Convention, once signed, would still require Russian approval, which, so the discussions with Sazonov had indicated clearly enough, would most probably in turn require British concessions over the treaty status of Afghanistan. Was the Simla Convention as such worth this? McMahon, we can be sure, thought not.

Could McMahon have obtained a Convention acceptable to

[41] After the Simla Conference, for example, the Tibetans persisted in their practice of granting to individuals the monopoly of important segments of Tibetan trade.

the Chinese while at the same time keeping the Tibetans on his side? It seems likely that he could had he not embarked upon his scheme for the partition of Tibet. In the Russian agreements on Outer Mongolia, of November 1913 and June 1915, the negotiators faced problems of geographical definition similar to those which confronted McMahon during the Simla Conference.[42] In the 1913 agreement, however, Outer Mongolia was not defined with great precision. Its limits were stated in terms of the Chinese jurisdictions which it replaced, but

> inasmuch as there are no detailed maps of Mongolia, and as the boundaries of the administrative divisions are uncertain, it is agreed that the exact boundaries of Outer Mongolia, as well as the boundary between the district of Kobdo and the district of Altai, shall be the subject of subsequent conferences provided for in Article V of the Declaration.

The 1915 agreement used similar, though slightly more detailed, language, specifying delimitation on the ground at some future date. In fact, the Sino-Mongolian border was not finally settled until the 1960s. The Russians concentrated on the political objectives and left the question of geography until later. Since in so many ways the Mongolian agreements resemble the Simla Convention, it may well be asked why McMahon did not adopt an analogous approach to the problem of the Inner-Outer Tibet boundary. He could, perhaps, have injected into the Conference the principle of partition without demanding that the zones thus produced be marked out at that time on a map. The Chinese would probably have signed a Simla Convention without a map. McMahon would still have obtained his Line and the new trade regulations.

Why, then, did McMahon not do this? It is probable that he found himself unable to avoid the discussion of a detailed partition the moment that he allowed the Conference to open with the presentation of Chinese and Tibetan territorial claims, a result, for the most part, of his inability at that stage to produce a draft agreement. McMahon, moreover, was perhaps unduly impressed by the theoretical implications of the Tibeto-Mongol treaty of January 1913, in which he saw the creation of a route for Russian influence right into the political centre of Tibet.

[42] See Appendices XV and XIX.

One objective of the zonal division of Tibet was to create a buffer of Chinese-controlled, but not, as it were, Chinese-owned, territory between Mongolia and Tibet. The international recognition of the limits of Inner Tibet would have made it impossible for China, in some future negotiations with Russia or Russian-sponsored Outer Mongolia, to alienate this buffer. In the event, by his last proposed concession of June 1914, McMahon himself transferred most of the tract in question from Inner Tibet to China. Had the Chinese signed the Convention on 3 July, the Indian Government would have acquired no added security in this respect.

The Chinese have often been criticised for refusing to sign the Convention. It has been pointed out that the Chamdo region, which they clung to with such determination during the Conference, was, in fact, taken from them by the forces of the Kalon Lama in 1918. They nearly lost Tachienlu as well. The Sino-Tibetan truce of Rongbatsa which was patched up in October 1918, under the supervision of Eric Teichman, created a provisional border, a cease-fire line, more or less along the Mekong-Yangtze watershed where it had been indicated on McMahon's map. No Chinese statesman in 1914, however, could have anticipated the developments of 1918, when China, torn by civil war and demoralised by Japanese pressure, collapsed in the Marches. Even in 1918, moreover, the Chinese adhered to their claims to a degree of influence throughout Tibet which they would have had to renounce had they ever signed the Convention. It is hard to see what benefits the Chinese would, in fact, have derived from signature. They would have got the Amban, or his equivalent, back to Lhasa; but there is no reason to suppose that his presence would have added much to the means of diplomatic contact with the Tibetan authorities which they already possessed. The absence of an Amban, moreover, was more than compensated for by the absence of a permanent British Resident. They would have acquired recognition of their suzerainty in Tibet; but they were never particularly attached to this word, and, in any case, the British both by the unsigned Convention and by earlier treaties were still obliged to recognise some special Chinese status in Tibet, even if they refused it any practical effect. Between 1914 and 1950 it was not easy to challenge Chinese suzerainty, even though the Chinese had not signed the Convention. Finally, by refusing to sign, the Chinese had escaped according any recognition to the validity of either the 1914 trade regulations or the McMahon Line.

Yuan Shih-k'ai must have in his heart of hearts been extremely glad when the Simla Conference ended; and his chief regret was, perhaps, that Chen had been weak enough to allow himself to be persuaded (Yuan might have used to himself the word 'blackmailed') into putting his initials on the draft of 27 April. Acceptance of the Simla Convention would not have been popular in China, where it was widely regarded as another example of those 'unequal treaties' by which the foreigners had plundered the Middle Kingdom. It is likely that many Chinese of impeccably reactionary views would not, had it been put to them in 1914, have disagreed fundamentally with the following picture of the Simla Conference which the Chinese Communists presented in 1959:

> After the outbreak of the 1911 Revolution in China to overthrow Manchu rule, the British imperialists lost no time in inciting their protégés, the reactionaries of the upper social strata in Tibet, to stage a revolt. . . . The next step taken by the British imperialists was to put their plot in motion in the diplomatic field. Hand in glove with the Tibetan reactionaries, they engineered the Simla Conference in 1913–14 . . . at which they brought pressure to bear upon the then warlord government of China. At the Conference, the British terms were deliberately designed to annex Tibet and extend its colonial rule there through its colonial government in India. This aroused the indignation of the Chinese people, the Tibetans in particular. The Chinese representative to the Simla Conference refused to sign the treaty and the treaty was never recognised by the Chinese Government.[43]

[43] *Concerning the Question of Tibet*, Foreign Languages Press, Peking, 1959, pp. 199–200.

XXVI

THE McMAHON LINE

THE Simla Convention, even if the Chinese had signed it, would not in itself have provided a final solution to the problem of the British border in the Assam Himalayas. The Inner-Outer Tibet partition, it is true, would on paper have kept the Chinese from direct territorial contact with the tribal hills; but it offered no guarantee that the Tibetans would not in the future raise claims, with Chinese support, to rights and influence in regions which since 1910 the Indian Government thought ought to be firmly located within the British sphere. Since 1910, mainly as a result of the Abor Expedition and its offshoots, the Indian Government had acquired a fairly clear idea of where its border in the Assam Himalayas ought to be. What it now needed, in addition to the guarantee of the exclusion of Chinese power from Outer Tibet, was some treaty definition of this boundary alignment; and such a document was one of the prizes which Hardinge and McMahon hoped to win during the Simla Conference. The Assam border, however, was a subject which, for reasons already noted, the Indian Government had decided it did not want to discuss with China: there were good grounds, therefore, for not placing it on the Simla agenda. It seemed wiser to use the Simla Conference as the occasion for direct Anglo-Tibetan discussions on the border, without Chinese participation, the results of which might, if the opportunity presented itself, be confirmed, though perhaps indirectly, in the final tripartite agreement. As we shall see, by an exchange of notes on 24/25 March 1914 McMahon obtained Tibetan agreement to a boundary alignment which has since become famous as the McMahon Line; and by the judicious use of a little extra red ink in prolonging the frontier of greater Tibet on the map attached to the draft Simla Conventions, McMahon endeavoured to obtain Chinese acknowledgment of his Line.

Since the deterioration in Sino-Indian relations in the 1950s Indian officials have maintained that the McMahon Line notes merely 'formalised the natural, traditional, ethnic and administrative boundary in the area'.[1] The tribal tracts in the Assam Himalayas, it has been stated, were already under Indian administration in the eighth century A.D. when the *Yogini Purana* was written; and have been continuously so from that date to the present time. As one Indian writer has put it:

> The entire tribal area up to the McMahon Line has been under continuous Ahom and, later, British administration. Under the latter, from the outset, the tribal areas were under the jurisdiction of the Political Agents or Deputy Commissioners of the adjoining districts. . . . No boundary in the world can claim to have been as free from disputes and as well established by tradition, treaty and administration as the India-China boundary.[2]

Unfortunately, it cannot be said that this picture of the administrative history of the Assam Himalayas, however much it might suit the demands of modern Indian diplomacy, is a true one. At the time of the Chinese occupation of Lhasa in early 1910 Tibetan administration, either directly or indirectly, extended in the Tawang Tract right down to the edge of the Assam plains. At that time the British had made but the most superficial penetration in the Assam Himalayas except in the Lohit Valley, where a number of British and other European travellers had recognised the location of the Tibetan frontier in the neighbourhood of Walong; and even on the Lohit it could not at that time be said that the Mishmi tribes had in any legally binding way come under British sovereignty. The McMahon Line which was defined in the Anglo-Tibetan notes of 24 and 25 March 1914 and in the map referred to in those notes was not an ancient Indian border. It was a new frontier alignment designed to replace the old Outer Line along the foothills. It was not based on traditions

[1] *White Paper II*, p. 40, Nehru to Chou En-lai, 26 September 1959.

[2] K. Gopalachari, 'The India-China Boundary Question', *International Studies*, V, nos. 1–2, July–October 1963, p. 42.

See also P. C. Chakravarti, *India's China Policy*, Bloomington, Indiana, 1962, p. 137.

of great age, but was the result of active British survey work following Williamson's murder by Abor tribesmen in early 1911.

The genesis of the McMahon Line as an Indian frontier alignment is to be found in Lord Minto's telegram of 23 October 1910, to which reference has already been made.[3] On this occasion, as a result of the evidence which had come to light of Chinese interest in the Mishmi country along the Lohit, Minto proposed 'to gain a buffer' between British and Chinese territory by advancing northward the Outer Line: he suggested that the new boundary should follow the general line of the crests of the Assam Himalayan range from the eastern edge of the Tawang Tract to the Irrawaddy-Salween divide. The Tawang Tract in 1910 was still regarded by the Indian Government as so firmly Tibetan, all the way down to the foothills, that it was not proposed then to bring it within British India as a result of the new boundary. The 1910 proposals were extremely vague. Geographical information about the Assam Himalayas, with the exception of the Lohit Valley, was meagre indeed. British officials, again with the exception of the Lohit, had only penetrated into the hills north of the Outer Line for a depth of a very few miles in a small number of places. In these circumstances the Home Government felt itself unable to make any decision on Minto's proposal, and the issue was postponed.

On 21 September 1911, after Williamson's murder had had time to make its impact felt on Indian frontier policy, Lord Hardinge repeated Lord Minto's suggested alignment for a new Indo-Tibetan border in Assam as part of his recommended policy of 'loose political control'. Lord Crewe, while questioning some of the implications of 'loose political control', agreed that a new frontier of this general type seemed to be called for; and it was decided that one of the objects of the Abor Expedition and its related ventures, the Miri Mission and the Mishmi Mission, would be to determine the most suitable alignment for the new boundary, which was to keep the Chinese as far away from the Indian plains as could possibly be reconciled with the facts of Tibetan occupation. By the end of 1913 the Indian Government was in possession of sufficient information to enable it to describe the proposed alignment in considerable detail. There were stretches, of course, which were still un-

[3] See p. 336 above.

explored; but the crest of the Assam Himalayas was no longer the *terra incognita* it had been to the Indian Foreign Department in October 1910.

The obvious principle upon which to base the new frontier alignment was, as many Indian observers have pointed out during the course of the Sino-Indian dispute, the watershed between rivers flowing into Assam and those flowing into Tibet. Unfortunately, the Assam Himalayas do not lend themselves particularly well to a uniform application of the watershed concept of boundary making. The range is cut through by the Tsangpo-Brahmaputra, one of the great rivers of Asia flowing through thousands of miles of undoubted Tibetan territory from its source not far from the sources of the Indus. The true watershed between the Indian plains and Central Asia would lie north of the Tsangpo and its tributaries; and a boundary following this line would include Lhasa, Shigatse and Gyantse and most of the towns of Central Tibet within India. As exploration of the Assam Himalayas proceeded it was discovered that the Tsangpo-Brahmaputra was by no means the only river which would have to be crossed by the proposed new boundary. On the extreme east, where Burma meets Tibet, the upper reaches of the Taron, a tributary of the Nmaihka branch of the Irrawaddy, ran through a region of Tibetan population. The Lohit, as had long been known, north of Walong became the Zayul Chu in the Tibetan district of Zayul. To the west of the Tsangpo-Brahmaputra valley in the Assam Himalayas the Subansiri and its tributary the Chayul Chu were found to have sources well within undoubted Tibetan territory, as also did the Nyamjang Chu, the river which passed from Tibet through the northern part of the Tawang Tract into Eastern Bhutan. It was clear, therefore, that, unless the new boundary was going to result in the British annexation of a great deal of Tibet, it would have to run across at least six major rivers. The McMahon Line, the final form of this boundary, therefore, did not, in fact, follow the main India-Central Asia watershed. Rather, it was drawn along a series of watersheds between the valleys of the major rivers which had their sources to the north of the line of the highest peaks of the Himalayan range. In several sections of the alignment McMahon and his advisers were obliged to decide between two or more watershed-lines. There was nothing inevitable about the definition of the McMahon line in detail: this was as much the result of a series of British decisions as of the clear dictates of tradition and ethnology.

In selecting a satisfactory new boundary the Indian Government faced particular difficulties in the Tawang Tract (Map no. 16). Here, as has already been remarked, Tibetan territory was considered to extend from the crest of the range right down to the foot of the hills a few miles north of Udalguri. Neither in Minto's proposals of 23 October 1910 nor those of Hardinge of 21 September 1911 was there any suggestion that the boundary between British India and the Tawang Tract should be modified. To do so, it must have been thought, would involve the annexation of Tibetan territory, a step contrary to the letter of the Anglo-Russian Convention of 1907. The Tawang Tract, however, could not be ignored. It constituted a salient under Tibetan (and hence, potential Chinese) control which cut right through the barrier of the Himalayas. As a weak point in the British defences Tawang was far more serious than the Chumbi Valley farther to the west. By June 1912, therefore, the Indian General Staff had decided that, notwithstanding the terms of the 1907 British agreement with Russia, something should be done about Tawang. It noted that:

> The demarcation of the frontier line about Tawang requires careful consideration. The present boundary (demarcated)[4] is south of Tawang, running westwards along the foothills from near Udalgiri to the southern Bhutan border, and thus a dangerous wedge is thrust between the Miri country and Bhutan. A comparatively easy and much used trade route traverses this wedge from north to south, by which the Chinese would be able to exert influence or pressure on Bhutan, while we have no approach to this salient from a flank, as we have in the case of the Chumbi salient. A rectification of the boundary here is therefore imperative, and an ideal line would appear to be one from the knot of mountains near Long. 93°, Lat. 28° 20', to the Bhutan border north of Chona Dzong [Tsöna] in a direct east and west line with the northern frontier of Bhutan. There appears to be a convenient water shed for it to follow.[5]

[4] A reference to Major Graham's demarcation of the foothill line in the 1870s. See p. 301 above.

[5] PEF 1910/14, no. 3057/12, General Staff Note on the N.E. Frontier, 1 June 1912.

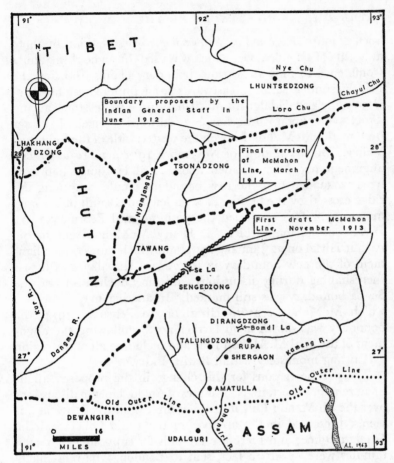

16 *McMahon Line proposals along the Tawang Tract*

The proposed boundary modification implied in this view of the Indian General Staff was extreme indeed, involving the British occupation of not only Tawang and the Mönpa inhabited districts to the south but also the Tibetan administrative centre of Tsöna Dzong. The Indian Government, while becoming convinced of the need to take over some of the Tawang Tract, evidently concluded that a more southerly alignment would meet its requirements. In a memorandum of 28 October 1913 McMahon indicated that the Indian Government was still bound to abide by a foothill border in the Tawang area; and he enclosed the skeleton map, based on the Royal Geographical

Society map, *Tibet and the Surrounding Regions*, edition of 1906, at a scale of 1 : 3,800,000, which was used throughout the Simla Conference to indicate various boundary claims, showing the British frontier running eastwards from Bhutan just north of Dewangiri and Udalguri until it had quite passed the Tawang Tract, whereupon it ran sharply northward to meet what later became the McMahon Line on the western side of the Subansiri Valley.[6] By the middle of November 1913 a more advanced alignment had been decided upon. Lord Hardinge had now been persuaded that the new boundary should run along the ridge crossed by the Se La (Pass), a few miles south of Tawang monastery.[7] This remained the position until February 1914. In an outline map which Sir Henry McMahon sent to Sir Arthur Hirtzl on 22 January 1914, and which showed the alignment of the new boundary in the Assam Himalayas as it was then shaping during discussions with the Lönchen Shatra, the Se La boundary was still marked.[8] In another map, however, which McMahon sent to Hirtzl on 19 February 1914, the boundary was shown a bit farther north, following the alignment of the final McMahon Line and including all of the region of Tawang monastery within British India.[9]

The precise reasons for this change in the proposed alignment remain uncertain. No minutes of Anglo-Tibetan discussions over the McMahon Line in the first three months of 1914 are, it seems, preserved in the archives of the India Office and the Foreign Office; and there are grounds for supposing that such minutes were never, in fact, sent to London. The most likely explanation for the inclusion of Tawang monastery within British territory is, perhaps, that in late 1913 McMahon had at his disposal accurate and up-to-date information about the Tawang Tract from Bailey and Morshead, who came down through Tawang on their return from the adventurous journey along the Tsangpo Valley, and who arrived in Simla to report to McMahon on 26 November 1913.[10] Bailey, in his report,

[6] PEF 1913/18, no. 4692/13, Memo. by McMahon, 28 October 1913.
[7] PEF 1913/18, no. 4790/13, Viceroy to Secretary of State, 21 November 1913.
[8] PEF 1913/19, no. 461/14, McMahon to Hirtzl, 22 January 1914.
[9] PEF 1913/19, no. 893/14, McMahon to Hirtzl, 19 February 1914.
[10] FO 535/16, no. 449, Viceroy to Secretary of State, 26 November 1913.

showed that Tawang monastery played a crucial role in the administration of the Mönpa tribes south of the Se La; and it probably seemed to McMahon, after due reflection, that any future British administration south of the Se La would be made easier by some measure of British control over the Tawang monks.[11] Moreover, McMahon seems to have had some hope that with the advance northwards of the British border the old trade route between Tibet and Assam through Tawang would revive.[12] From Bailey's report he may well have concluded that the Tawang monks, if left to their own devices, would probably place all manner of obstacles in the way of traders following the Tawang road.

To the east of the Tawang Tract there was a stretch of the new boundary alignment which crossed the Subansiri (known in Tibet as the Tsari Chu) and its tributary the Chayul Chu (Map no. 7). It had been the intention of the Miri Mission to visit this region; but the hostile attitude of the tribesmen on the upper Kamla tributary of the Subansiri had forced Kerwood and his party to turn back long before they had reached the southern limits of Tibet. On this remote tract Bailey and Morshead, who had reached the upper Subansiri from the Tibetan side, were able to provide the first reliable information. They noted that on the Subansiri, or Tsari Chu, Migyitun marked the southern limit of Tibetan occupation, and that below that point lay *Lopa* (tribal) territory. However, they discovered that the Tibetans were in the habit of making pilgrimages at twelve-yearly intervals down the Subansiri well south of Migyitun, bribing the *Lopa* tribesmen heavily with salt and other goods to dissuade them from massacring the devout travellers.[13] On Bailey's advice, McMahon seems to have decided that the new boundary should run just below Migyitun, but with the understanding that some small modifications might have to be made here to meet Tibetan religious susceptibilities.

East of the Subansiri was the valley of the Tsangpo-Brahmaputra where that great river had carved its way through the Himalayan massif (Map no. 17). Here the determination of a satisfactory alignment for the boundary involved several

[11] Bailey, *Report*, op. cit., pp. 13–14.
[12] *Memorandum.*
[13] Bailey, *Report*, op. cit., pp. 10–12. See also p. 322 above.

difficult decisions. Firstly, on the upper reaches of the Siyom tributary of the Tsangpo-Brahmaputra there were settled Buddhist populations who had, it seemed, come under the feudal control of the great Lhalu family of Tibet and who paid dues of some kind to the Tibetan authorities of Kongbo district. Secondly, along the Tsangpo-Brahmaputra Valley itself it was by no means easy to draw a sharp dividing line between Abor and Tibetan or Tibetan-influenced settlement. There were Abor villages farther upstream than the lowest Tibetan villages, and into the region through which the McMahon Line was to be drawn Bhutanese had migrated during the nineteenth century, settlers who still in 1913 considered themselves to be the subjects of the Tongsa Penlop. Relations between the Abors and the Tibetans and Mönpas (a term used here to cover both people from the Tawang area and from Eastern Bhutan) had been far from peaceful. Past campaigns had imposed on Abor villages not far north of the old Outer Line the obligation to render various forms of tribute to the Tibetan authorities in Pome and Kongbo. As a result of British survey and exploration during 1912 and 1913 it had become apparent that up to Korbo the Dihang (or Siang) Valley was predominantly settled by Abors, who, though in many cases in some kind of relationship with Tibet, could not on cultural or linguistic grounds be classified as Tibetans. North of Korbo to the point where the Nyalam and Chimdru rivers flowed into the Tsangpo-Siang, in the district sometimes known as Pemakoichen, there was a mixed population with, perhaps, Tibetans and Mönpas in the majority. North of the Nyalam-Chimdru line the settled popula-tion was predominantly Tibetan, though Abor (or *Lopa*) groups came here from time to time for purposes of trade. The Tibetan and Mönpa villages in Pemakoichen, however, had been established fairly recently, none being more than a century old, at the expense of the Abors. Dundas and Nevill, in the light of all the available information, proposed in October 1913 two possible boundary alignments across the Dihang Valley.[14] One, which included Pemakoichen, ran as far north as the Nam La and the recently discovered peak, Namche Barwa, over 25,000 feet high. This would bring into British territory a number of

[14] FO 535/16, no. 422, Assam to India, 17 October 1913. See also Bailey, *Report*, op. cit.

Tibetans and Mönpas, but it could be justified on the grounds that Pemakoichen had once been Abor country. Another alignment crossed the Siang farther south between the villages of Korbo and Mongku. It excluded country where the Abors were now in a minority, and it was probably far easier to administer. This alignment the Indian Government resolved to adopt.

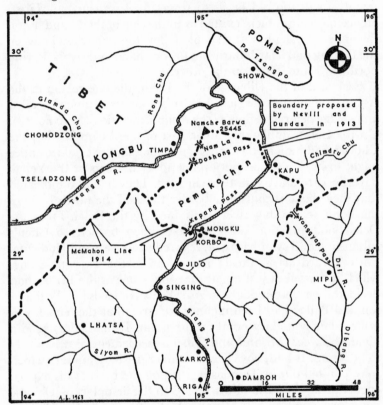

17   *McMahon Line proposals on the Dihang-Siang*

To the east of the Dihang Valley lay the basin of the Dibang, which had been visited in 1912 and 1913 by parties branching off from the Mishmi Mission up the Lohit.[15] At the head of the Dibang Valley, on the Dri, Andra and Yongyap tributaries,

[15] Bailey, *Report*, op. cit.; Bailey, *No Passport*, op. cit.; C. P. Gunter, *Report of the Mishmi Exploration Survey Detachment, 1912–13*, in S. G. Burrard, *Records of the Survey of India IV*, Calcutta, 1914.

Tibetans had been settling during the first decade of the twentieth century. They were seeking, it seemed, a holy place with a mountain made entirely of glass of which a Tibetan prophet had once spoken. These settlers had come into conflict with the Mishmi tribesmen of the region, and by 1913 they had found local resistance too much for them, and all but a few, mainly those too old or ill to travel, had returned to Tibet. Hence no real problem existed as to the line of the boundary on the upper Dibang basin: it should follow the watershed between the Dibang and its tributaries on the one hand and rivers flowing northward into Tibet on the other.

Eastward of the Dibang lay the Lohit, the one region in the Assam Himalayas of which the British possessed much detailed knowledge before the days of the Abor Expedition (Map no. 18). On the Lohit, unlike any other part of the Assam border, the Chinese had indicated exactly where they thought their frontier ought to be. They had put up boundary markers at the Yepak River in 1910 and again twice in 1912. They had also indicated that they thought that their border touched the north bank of the Lohit where that river was joined by the Delei. From the Delei-Lohit junction the Chinese-claimed border, so Chen's submission of November 1913, referred to above, would indicate, ran eastward across the Dibang basin to the Tsangpo-Siang, which it crossed at just about the same place as the British had decided their border ought to go.[16] British officials like Williamson and Bailey had been inclined to agree that the Yepak was quite a fair boundary point on the Lohit. It marked as good a divide between Mishmi and Tibetan settlement as was likely to be found. It had, however, a number of disadvantages which were pointed out by Dundas in 1913 on the basis of his experiences during the Mishmi Mission.[17] In the first place, a Chinese boundary point at the Yepak which also implied a Chinese boundary point at the Delei-Lohit junction was quite out of the question. A Chinese, or, for that matter, a Tibetan, post at the point where the Delei flowed into the Lohit would be situated deep in Mishmi country and astride the route from Sadiya to the proposed British frontier post at Menilkrai near the Yepak. This fact alone was sufficient to suggest that the

[16] FO 371/1613, no. 53461, IO to FO, 24 November 1913.
[17] FO 535/16, no. 422, Assam to India, 17 September 1913.

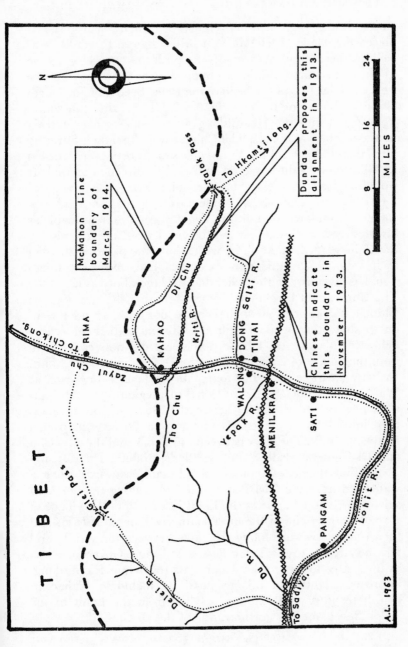

18 *McMahon Line proposals on the upper Lohit*

entire frontier alignment here should be shifted north so that it placed the whole Delei Valley in British hands. It would be as well, in these circumstances, also to push the boundary up the Lohit. Firstly, there would be obtained an easier watershed line from the Glei Pass at the head of the Delei. Secondly, just north of the Yepak, along the Di Chu and Sal Ti streams, ran routes from Zayul into the Hkamtilong district of Northern Burma by way of the Talok Pass. The Chinese were already infiltrating into Hkamtilong from the Yunnanese side. If they ever returned to Tibet they might try to do so from this direction as well. It would be prudent to close this particular door while the opportunity existed. Dundas was able to argue that the Chinese-claimed boundary point on the Yepak was not so reasonable as his predecessor Williamson had believed. 'Just the one visit of the Chinese to Menilkrai', he wrote, 'and the planting there of their flags, which indicate no boundary line, and the notification, has given rise to the belief that the land above as far as the Tho Chu cannot be claimed by us.' Ignoring the fact that the Chinese had thrice visited the Yepak, not once, Dundas went on to show that while significant Mishmi settlement ceased below the Yepak, yet Tibetan settlement did not really begin until the village of Kahao, where the Di Chu joined the Lohit. In between there were but four Tibetan houses (one each at Walong and Tinne and two at Dong) in a region where Mishmis were accustomed to graze their cattle. Some of the Tibetans here, indeed, Dundas said, were actually employed as herdsmen by the Mishmis. The tract between the Yepak and the Tho Chu and Di Chu was really 'Tom Tiddler's ground'. Dundas suggested that the new boundary should run eastwards along a watershed from the Glei Pass to the Lohit along the northern side of the Tho Chu, cross the Lohit just south of the village of Kahao (in his opinion the most southerly Tibetan *village*), and then run on eastward along the ridge between the Kri Ti and Di Chu streams to the Talok Pass. The Indian Government, so as the better to secure the Talok Pass route into Hkamtilong, improved slightly on this proposal by including Kahao in British territory and running the line from the Lohit to the Talok Pass along the northern side of the Di Chu.[18]

[18] PEF 1913/18, no. 4790/13, Viceroy to Secretary of State, 21 November 1913.

In February 1914, before the Tibetans had even accepted the new boundary, the proposed alignment across the Lohit was enforced by British administrative action.[19] On 1 January 1914 T. P. M. O'Callaghan, Dundas's assistant with responsibility for the Mishmi tribal areas, with an escort of thirty-nine Gurkhas, set out from Sadiya on a tour up the Lohit. At the beginning of February he reached the Yepak, where he saw traces of the Manchu Chinese boundary markers of 1910 and early 1912, as well as a new marker put up in June 1912 by officials of the Chinese Republic after the Mishmi Mission had withdrawn from Menilkrai. O'Callaghan uprooted all the markers he could find and took them with him upstream to Kahao where he hid them in the undergrowth. He justified this action on the grounds that

> it is possible in after years an attempt would be made to misinterpret our omission as a tacit admission of Chinese and Tibetan claims, had we allowed them to remain, and by my action in removing them and leaving them near Kahao we have acknowledged no claims.[20]

From Kahao O'Callaghan went on to Rima, where he was warmly welcomed by the local Tibetan authorities, who asked how the Simla Conference was progressing and who assured him that they believed Tibetan interests were safe in British hands. He could detect no remaining trace of Chinese influence in Zayul. At the time when O'Callaghan moved the Chinese markers there is evidence that the Indian Government had not yet made up its mind to bring the boundary north of Kahao, which was beyond doubt a Tibetan settlement. O'Callaghan's action, however, endorsed by Sir Archdale Earle, the Chief Commissioner for Assam, decided the question once and for all.[21] Kahao became British and the boundary was run north of the Di Chu.

East of the Lohit lay British Burma. Here also was an undefined border with Tibet which could not be ignored if the eastern flank of the new boundary, the McMahon Line, were not to be left in the air (Map no. 19). It was necessary to create

---

[19] PEF 1913/28, no. 1918/14, O'Callaghan's Tour Diary, 7 March 1914.
[20] Loc. cit.
[21] Reid, *Assam Frontier*, op. cit., p. 250.

some link between the Talok Pass, the new Tibet–India–Burma trijunction, and the Isu Razi Pass on the Salween-Irrawaddy divide which the British claimed was their border with Yunnan Province.[22] Here there existed the problem of the Taron, a tributary of the Nmaihka branch of the Irrawaddy with its sources near the Tibetan towns of Drowa and Menkong. Its highest reaches were certainly inhabited by a few Tibetans, and across its upper basin ran the main road linking Zayul, Pome and Kongbo to Yunnan via Menkong and Atuntze. A true watershed line around the Taron, therefore, would result in a British intrusion into undoubted Tibetan territory, and at the point, moreover, where the Inner-Outer Tibet border of the Simla Convention map had its origin. In the winter of 1912–13 the Taron Valley was explored by Captains Pritchard and Waterfield, thus adding greatly to information which Pritchard and Bailey had acquired in 1911–12.[23] This venture, which was to cost Pritchard his life, demonstrated that the ideal line for the British border was one which crossed the Taron at latitude

[22] In the period of the Assam Himalayan explorations following Williamson's death the British came to regard the Talok (or Diphu) Pass as one of the fixed points in their universe, marking the divide between the Brahmaputra river system in India and the Irrawaddy system in Burma. The Talok or Diphu Pass, however, was also seen to be a potential gateway into the extreme north-west of Burma from Tibet, a gateway which the Indian Government resolved to deny to China should the Chinese ever again be in a position to exploit it. The decision to run the McMahon Line along the north of the Di Chu stream was a product of this resolve. It also meant that the McMahon Line did not, in fact, actually run through the summit of the Talok or Diphu Pass but followed a crest a few miles northwards. In the Sino-Burmese border agreement of 1 October 1960 the Diphu Pass was accepted as being actually on the boundary line and was the western extremity of the line as then agreed upon (though the Chinese refused to admit that this meant that in their view the Diphu or Talok Pass was the China–India–Burma trijunction point—to do so, of course, would have implied some acceptance of the McMahon Line as a Sino-Indian boundary). The Indian Government delivered a number of protests against the location of the new Sino-Burmese border at the Talok or Diphu Pass, protests which the Chinese had no difficulty in dismissing. See *White Paper*, V, p. 20, Indian note of 30 December 1960.

[23] B. E. A. Pritchard and F. C. Waterfield, *Report on a Journey . . . on the North-East Frontier*, 1912–13, Simla, 1913. See also Bailey, *China, Tibet, Assam*, op. cit., and B. E. A. Pritchard, 'A journey from Myitkyina to Sadiya via the N'maikha and Hkamti Long', *Geographical Journal*, XLIII, 1914.

27° 40'. North of this point the inhabitants had never paid any tribute to the chiefs of Hkamtilong and regarded themselves as Tibetan subjects. The military authorities also agreed that the British should not assume any responsibility for the defence of the northern Taron Valley. The suggestion of Pritchard and Waterfield was accepted by the Indian Government and embodied in the McMahon Line.[24]

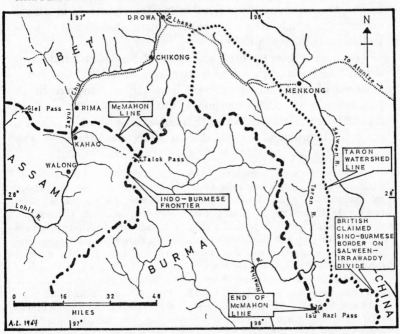

19   *McMahon Line proposals on the Taron*

Once the Indian Government had decided upon the detailed alignment of its new boundary, 850 miles long, in the Assam Himalayas, it had to arrange for Tibetan acceptance of proposals involving, in fact, the British annexation of some 2,000 square miles of territory which, hitherto, the Dalai Lama had looked upon as part of his dominions. This was achieved between January and March 1914, while the Simla Conference was in Delhi, through discussion between Charles Bell and the Lönchen

[24] PEF 1913/18, no. 4790/13, Viceroy to Secretary of State, 21 November 1913.

545

Shatra. The result was the Anglo-Tibetan exchange of secret notes of 24/25 March 1914.[25] The texts of the notes were first published in 1929, and from them we can derive some picture of what went on in the talks which gave rise to them.[26] Unfortunately, the Indian Government does not appear to have seen fit to communicate with London the minutes of the Bell-Lönchen Shatra negotiations; and it is unlikely that the present Indian Government will reveal in the immediate future these documents which touch so closely upon the modern Sino-Indian boundary dispute.[27]

The information on the geography of the Assam Himalayas which had been acquired since 1911 was embodied in a map, at a scale of eight miles to the inch, in two sheets, entitled 'North East Frontier of India, Provisional'. On this map, which was still far from perfect, though better than anything hitherto available, the new boundary, the McMahon Line, was drawn.[28] The

[25] Appendix XVI.

[26] The notes were first published in the 1929 edition of Aitchison's *Treaties*. At least, this is what is generally said. Mr. John Addis, however, informs me that there were two versions of the 1929 Aitchison's *Treaties*, one containing the text of the McMahon Line notes and the Simla Convention, and the other without these documents. Mr. Addis believes that these texts were inserted into the Aitchison collection at a date later than 1929, and that a new volume was substituted for the original volume which omitted these texts. The original 1929 volume, of which Mr. Addis saw a copy at Harvard University, not only leaves out the texts of the McMahon Line notes and the Simla Convention, but also states that the Simla Conference produced no valid agreements. In the revised volume, which is to be found in most English libraries, there is a clear implication that the McMahon Line notes and the July text of the Simla Convention are agreements binding in international law. Mr. Addis has discussed this question at length in his *The India-China Border Question*, privately circulated by the Centre for International Affairs, Harvard University, in February 1963. I am much indebted to Mr. Addis both for sending me a copy of this fascinating work and for allowing me to make a reference to it here.

[27] The only account of the McMahon Line negotiations which I could find in the Foreign Office and India Office archives was a memorandum by McMahon of 28 March 1914, which he later incorporated in his *Memorandum*. See FO 535/17, no. 91. This document has very little information on what actually took place during the Bell-Lönchen Shatra discussions.

[28] A slightly earlier version of the map *North East Frontier of India*, Provisional Issue, General Staff India, SDO no. 741, than that on which the McMahon Line was drawn can be seen in the Foreign Office Map Room, no. 17144. This is dated August 1913 for Sheets I and II and Septem-

Lönchen Shatra had now to be persuaded to accept the Line. Lacking the minutes, it is not easy to say exactly how this feat was accomplished; but some general conclusions are possible. It seems most probable, in the first place, that the Lönchen Shatra saw the McMahon Line as part of a greater bargain: so at least the Tibetans were to argue at a later date. Tibet would agree to a boundary with the British to the taste of the Indian Government. The British would guarantee a Tibetan boundary with China more to the taste of the Dalai Lama than anything he could hope to secure unaided. Such a bargain, if it were ever made, implicitly or explicitly, would go far to explain McMahon's reluctance to make concessions to the Chinese over the alignment of the Inner-Outer Tibet boundary. If so, then the McMahon Line contributed to the failure of the Simla Conference, which in turn, ironically, was a factor in the eventual failure of the McMahon Line as a final solution to the problem of the security of the Assam Himalayas.

In the second place, it is clear from the few available documents that the Lönchen Shatra did not surrender unconditionally Tibetan claims and rights south of the McMahon Line. In the Tawang Tract he secured the retention of what he

---

ber 1913 for Sheets III and IV (which do not relate to the McMahon Line, covering Eastern Tibet), while the McMahon Line map is dated February 1914. Between these two issues an appreciable amount of fresh information has been added. The contrast, moreover, between the earliest edition of SDO no. 741 and previous maps in respect of detail and accuracy is astounding. See, for example *The North East Frontier of India*, SDO no. 81 of July 1911, at a somewhat smaller scale to SDO no. 741 (FO Map Room no. 17090); *The North East Frontier of India*, specially prepared for the Chief of General Staff, and published under the direction of Colonel S. G. Burrard, R.E., F.R.S., Offg. Surveyor-General of India, 1910, at a scale of thirty-two miles to the inch (FO Map Room no. 17024); *Map of China*, GSGS no. 2631a, War Office, August 1908 (in FO 371/620, no. 886); *Tibet and the Surrounding Regions*, published by the Royal Geographical Society, corrected 1906, at a scale of sixty miles to the inch (FO Map Room no. 17016). All these maps not only compare most unfavourably in detail and accuracy with SDO no. 741, but also show boundaries in the Assam Himalayas following very different alignments from the McMahon Line. None include the Tawang Tract within India, and the War Office map GSGS no. 2631a shows the old Outer Line foothill boundary. It cannot be maintained, after a careful study of British maps of the period 1904–14, that the McMahon Line had become a cartographical feature before the Simla Conference.

must have considered tax-collecting rights, albeit disguised under the term 'certain dues now collected by the Tibetan Government . . . from the Mönpas and Lopas for articles sold'. A similar condition was applied to the Siang and Lohit valleys. The estates of the Lhalu family on the upper Siyom, moreover, the Lönchen Shatra appears to have insisted would not be disturbed in any way. Finally, on the upper reaches of the Subansiri the Tibetan pilgrimages would go on as before, with no British interference. To these conditions McMahon appears to have agreed—such is the most logical interpretation of his note to the Lönchen Shatra of 24 March 1914. He also agreed that the Tibetans, if they felt they were suffering other losses or difficulties through the McMahon Line, should have the right to reopen discussions on the subject with Charles Bell. The McMahon Line, therefore, was to some extent provisional and experimental, as McMahon indicated rather obliquely to Hardinge and Crewe when he wrote that

> the Tibetan Government at Lhasa has fully considered this frontier question and agrees with the Tibetan plenipotentiary in recognising the line now defined as the correct boundary between India and Tibet. They have shown a great desire throughout the course of our discussions regarding our mutual frontier to show a reasonable and just attitude. Should it be found desirable in the light of more detailed knowledge which the Tibetan Government and ourselves may acquire in the future to modify the course of the boundary line at any place, we shall doubtless endeavour to show a similar attitude in regard to Tibetan interests, although no obligation to do so has been mentioned in the agreement.[29]

The McMahon Line, on this analysis, has rather strange constitutional implications. Areas like the Tawang Tract, the upper Siang and Siyom valleys, and the Lohit between the Yepak and Kahao, were brought within the territorial limits of the British Indian Empire. Yet they were not to become British-administered territory. They were, in fact, more like British-protected regions on the analogy of Bhutan, with internal autonomy. Bhutan, however, was a political unit in its own right. Bhutanese administered it. Regions like Tawang, on the

[29] FO 535/17, no. 91, Memo. by McMahon, 28 March 1914.

other hand, were administered by officials appointed from without the British Empire in its widest sense and responsible to a foreign government. Thus it could be argued that portions of Tibet, such as Tawang, had passed into the British sphere of interest, and the McMahon Line here was less an international boundary than a line below which the Indian Government would not tolerate the influence of any Power (i.e. China) other than Tibet; and Tibetan influence would only be accepted if it were unobtrusive. To this view, the only interpretation which the Tibetans were likely to accept, McMahon was also to a great extent committed by the policy of 'loose political control'. Even on the Lohit, for example, where Lord Crewe had accepted in principle the need for an advanced British outpost, British troops were not permitted to be stationed north of the Yepak where the Chinese had placed their boundary markers.

The McMahon Line boundary involved, as we have seen, the nominal transfer of territory from Tibet to India. Since this transaction took place at the very moment when British, Tibetan and Chinese delegates were discussing the signature of a convention declaring that Tibet was under Chinese suzerainty and that it formed part of the territory of China, McMahon must have concluded that it would be as well to obtain some kind of Chinese approval for his Line. The Assam Himalayan border, however, was not on the agenda of the Conference; and the British had no wish to discuss it with the Chinese, whom, they held, it did not concern. It would not be easy, therefore, to secure Chinese approval for an agreement of which they were not informed (the Anglo-Tibetan notes of 24/25 March) on a subject which was not formally mentioned to them; but McMahon attempted to do just this. His instrument was the skeleton map, at a scale of 1 : 3,800,000, on which boundaries were continually being drawn throughout the course of the Conference. On this map McMahon indicated what he thought should be the proper limits of Inner and Outer Tibet. The boundary of 'greater' Tibet, that is to say of the region to be partitioned, was indicated by a red line. The boundary between Inner and Outer Tibet, that is to say, between Chinese and autonomous Tibetan territory, was shown by means of a blue line. Since, in theory, the Conference was only concerned with Sino-Tibetan border issues, the red line on McMahon's skeleton map was not carried all the way round 'greater' Tibet. It began suddenly on the Karakash River in the extreme north-west and ended equally abruptly just above Tawang on the south-east. From the Karakash River to the Burma–Tibet–China trijunction at the Isu Razi Pass the red line separated Tibet from China: from the Izu Razi Pass onwards to Tawang the red line divided Tibet from British India. The Chinese, if they ever agreed to the limits of Inner and Outer Tibet so indicated, would also find that they had accepted the McMahon Line: unless, of course, they discovered in time what McMahon was up to and demanded that the Isu Razi Pass-Tawang stretch of the red line be removed. Ivan Chen, probably no better at maps than the average Indian diplomat who has argued his country's case during the present Sino-Indian boundary dispute, appears not to have detected McMahon's sleight of hand: or, if he did spot something, to have been too intimidated by the overpowering British delegation to protest. He duly initialled on 27 April 1914 a map on which the McMahon Line was shown, an action which the Chinese have never been allowed to forget.

Why, one may well ask, did not the Indian Government, when it had the opportunity, secure some definition of the entire Tibetan border? Why leave unsettled the stretch between Tawang and the Karakash? There are several reasons why the red line stopped at Tawang and on the Karakash. Firstly, as we have already noted, the Indian Government did not want to embark upon a discussion of the Tibeto-Nepalese and Tibeto-Bhutanese boundaries.[30] Neither of these had been satisfactorily defined. Each would provide the raw material for a great deal of argument, and neither could really be considered without inviting to the Conference representatives from the states concerned. McMahon certainly did not want to bring Nepal and Bhutan into the Simla Conference in any way. The Sikkim-Tibet frontier had already been defined by treaty in 1890, and there was no need to consider it further. To the west of Nepal lay long stretches of the Indo-Tibetan border which were the subject of minor disputes, such as those in the neighbourhood of the Shipki Pass and elsewhere along the border in what are now East Punjab, Himachal Pradesh and Uttar Pradesh, and those along the Tibet-Ladakh border as at Khurnak, Nyagzu, and

[30] See p. 487, note, above.

Demchok. No doubt a full discussion with the Lönchen Shatra of issues such as these would have consumed much time for very little gain.[31] Moreover, the added prolongation of the red line on McMahon's map would almost certainly bring into the Conference the question of the alignment of the British as well as the Chinese border with Tibet; and once the British border was being discussed, McMahon's Line in the Assam Himalayas could hardly remain unnoticed.

It is a fact which has received surprisingly little comment in recent years that the Chinese, during the course of the Simla Conference, did raise a number of specific claims to territory to the south of the McMahon Line. Chen I-fan, when stating the Chinese case on 12 January 1914, implied that Chao Erh-feng, in 1911, had brought some of the hill tribes of Zayul, a term which appeared to cover Abor and Miri as well as Mishmi territory, under the protection of the Manchu Dynasty.[32] At various times during the Conference, when Chen was drawing on the skeleton map his ideas of the Inner-Outer Tibet boundary, the Chinese line always started below Walong at the Yepak tributary to the Lohit, ran westwards to touch the Lohit again at the Lohit-Delei junction, and then cut north-westwards across the Dibang basin to meet the Dihang-Siang at a point a little below the McMahon alignment.[33] From the Dihang-Siang Chen's line continued north-westerly to Giamda in Tibet, which the Chinese delegation maintained was a town on the Sino-Tibetan border. When Chen withdrew the Inner-Outer Tibetan boundary to the Salween, it might be argued that he then abandoned all claims to Assam Himalayan territory. This Chinese concession, however, was not accepted by the Conference, with the result, we may suppose, that the Chinese reverted to their Giamda boundary claim with all that it implied in the tribal hills of Assam. Why, then, did Chen initial

[31] Bell and the Lönchen Shatra seem to have had *some* discussion on other sections of the Indo-Tibetan border after the McMahon Line notes had been exchanged. See India, Ministry of External Affairs, *Report of the Officials of the Governments of India and the People's Republic of China on the Boundary Question*, New Delhi, 1961, p. 84.

[32] *BQ*, pp. 17–18.

[33] FO 371/1613, no. 53461, IO to FO, 24 November 1913; PEF 1913/18, no. 4768/13, Memo. by McMahon, 6 November 1913; FO 371/1929, no. 6603, IO to FO, 12 February 1914.

the map attached to the Simla Convention, which showed the McMahon Line in such conflict with Chinese ideas which he, himself, had expressed? Two possible answers suggest themselves. First, Chen must have realised that his actions would be repudiated by his own Government, so it did not really matter what he initialled. Second, in view of the intense moral pressure to which he was subjected before he agreed to initial, it is very unlikely that he gave much thought to the little appendix to the red line marking the Tibetan border on the Convention map which has since become famous as the McMahon Line.

There can be no doubt that McMahon was being less than straightforward in his scheme for obtaining Chinese approval for his Line. Had the Chinese actually signed the Convention, they would certainly have found it hard to deny some degree of validity to the definition of the Indo-Tibetan boundary in the Assam Himalayas. However, the Chinese did not sign, and by 1929, when the Anglo-Tibetan notes of 24/25 March were first published—if not much earlier—they surely perceived that they had been the intended victims of a British trick, which would go far to explain the Chinese loathing for the 'illegal' McMahon Line. Ironically, however, the Chinese never seem to have understood that McMahon was also trying to hoodwink them into accepting a change in the status of that baleful tract on the extreme north-eastern frontier of Ladakh now familiar to the proverbial schoolboy, Aksai Chin. The Chinese, when they raised claims to Aksai Chin in the 1950s, do not appear to have realised that the same Simla Convention map which implied Chinese acceptance of the McMahon Line, also implied British (and hence, Indian) acceptance of Tibetan (and hence, Chinese) possession of a part at least of Aksai Chin.

In March 1899 Sir Claude Macdonald presented a note to the Tsungli Yamen in which Chinese rights to a portion of Aksai Chin were recognised.[34] The Chinese never replied formally to the note, but the British in the first decade of the twentieth century felt that they were bound by it. With the increasing possibility that the Russians might take over Sinkiang, the Aksai Chin plateau, desolate and unpopulated as it was, acquired in the eyes of British strategists a certain importance

[34] The text of this note, along with some account of its history and consequences, is to be found in Lamb, *China-India Border*, op. cit.

as a buffer between potential Russian territory and the passes leading from the Karakoram to the Indian plains. Hence it was argued that it would be as well to do something about Aksai Chin. By virtue of the 1899 note, it would be hard to claim it as British. Why not make it Tibetan? This, at all events, was the view of the Indian Foreign Department under Sir Louis Dane in 1907.[35] In 1912, with the Sinkiang situation becoming more critical, Lord Hardinge urged that Aksai Chin, in any readjustment of the Kashgaria-Kashmir border which might be arranged as a precondition for recognition of a Russian protectorate or annexation of Sinkiang, should be kept out of Russian hands. The Simla Conference provided an admirable occasion for achieving such an objective. McMahon almost certainly saw its possibilities. The red line on his map was carried to the north-west to a point on the north bank of the Karakash River so as to outflank Aksai Chin. Since the red line was defined as 'the frontiers of Tibet', and since Tibet here lay south of the red line, then it could only follow that some at least of Aksai Chin was shown as being Tibetan. The point is one difficult to express in words. The position can, perhaps, best be appreciated through maps. Map 20 shows the red line on the Simla Convention map. Map 22 shows the fluctuation of borders in Aksai Chin between 1899 and 1947. Map 21 shows how the extreme western end of the red line on the Simla Convention map follows the same course as does part of the present Indian-claimed border in the Aksai Chin region.[36]

---

[35] PEF 1912/82, no. 1227/07, Dane to Ritchie, 3 April 1907.

[36] Some of these points, and the first drafts of these maps, were presented to the Asian History Conference of September 1964 at the University of Hong Kong in a paper by Alastair Lamb entitled *A note on a problem of boundary definition in Ladakh*.

It is interesting that here, as in the case of the McMahon Line, some of the Chinese boundaries advanced during the Simla Conference ran south of the extremity of the red line. The early Chinese claim line, for example, crosses the Karakash below Kizil Jilga, implying that Sinkiang territory extended to that point and that south of it lay Tibet. The adjustment on the final Convention map, therefore, is tantamount to a transfer of some of Sinkiang Aksai Chin to Tibet; which, it has been suggested, was indeed the intention of the British delegation at the Conference. See PEF 1913/20, no. 2653/14, Jordan to Grey, 16 June 1914, with attached a sketch map showing various boundary alignments proposed during the course of the Simla Conference.

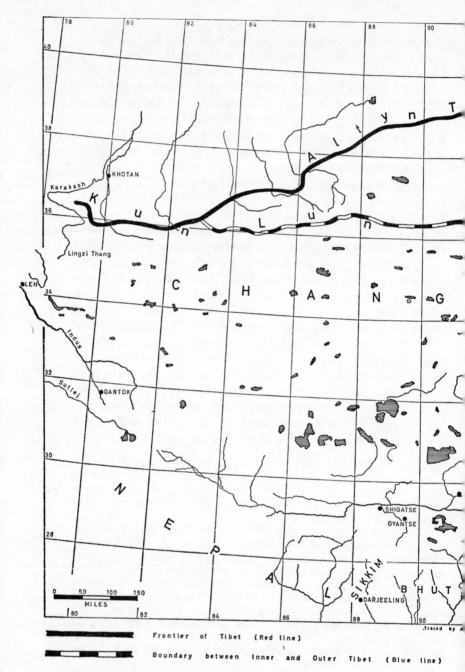

20 *Slightly simplified tracing of the map appended to the Simla Convention (both texts)*

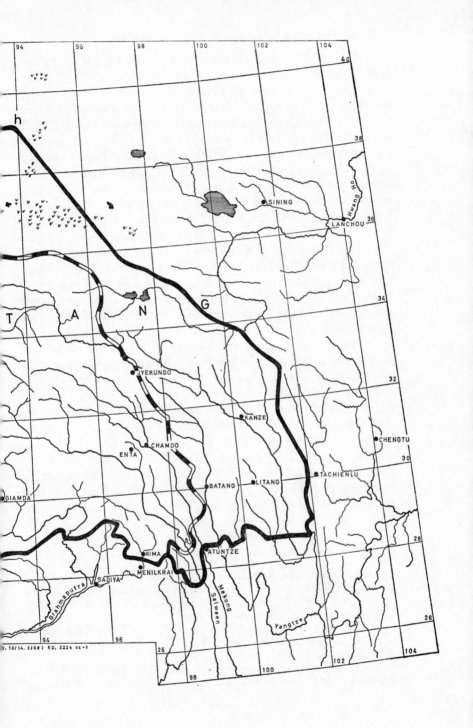

The validity of the McMahon Line has been defended by the Indian Government of late on three main grounds.[37] First, it has been argued that this particular alignment was really the traditional and established boundary between India and Tibet which dated back to antiquity. The weakness of this approach has already been demonstrated in this book, and requires no further comment here. Second, that the Anglo-Tibetan notes of 24/25 March 1914 are a binding and valid agreement in international law. This can hardly be maintained with much conviction. By the 1906 Convention the British had recognised China's right to conduct Tibetan foreign relations and had denied that they could themselves negotiate with Tibet, beyond the scope of the Lhasa Convention and the trade regulations, except through the Chinese. The Simla Conference was summoned to consider whether the nature of Anglo-Tibetan relations could be modified; but when the McMahon Line notes were exchanged the Conference had as yet failed to produce an agreed draft Convention, let alone a signed and sealed instrument. In March 1914, there can be no doubt, the British did not possess the treaty right to come to a bipartite agreement with the Tibetans. Third, that the McMahon Line, whatever the standing of the notes of 24/25 March, was confirmed by the Chinese when Chen on 27 April initialled the draft Convention and the attached map. It has further been pointed out by observant Indians and their supporters, Sir Olaf Caroe for instance, that Chen, though he said he *initialled* the map, actually *signed* it.[38] The original map has been produced in evidence. But this is really semantic horseplay. Initialling is a technical term with implications understood by diplomatists; and, diplomatically speaking, Chen *initialled*. His action, both with respect to the draft Convention and to the map, was promptly repudiated by his Government, as Chen warned

[37] See, for example, K. K. Rao, 'The Sino-Indian Boundary Question and International Law', *International and Comparative Law Quarterly*, April 1962; L. C. Green, 'Legal Aspects of the Sino-Indian Border Dispute', *China Quarterly*, no. 3, July–September 1960.

[38] Sir O. Caroe, 'The Sino-Indian question', *Royal Central Asian Journal*, July–October 1963; Sir O. Caroe, 'The Sino-Indian Frontier Dispute', *Asian Review*, April 1963.

The map in question has been published in India, Ministry of External Affairs, *Atlas of the Northern Frontier of India*, New Delhi, 1961.

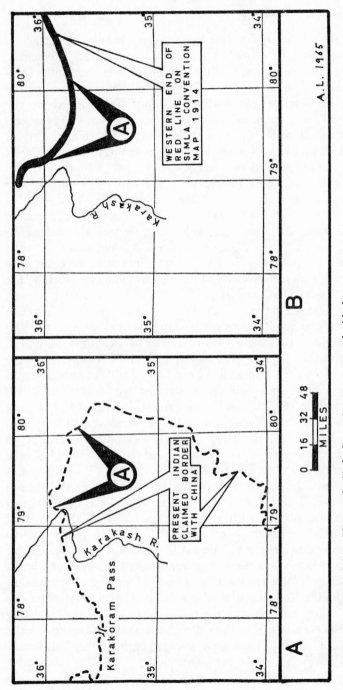

21 The western end of the red line on the Simla Convention map compared with the present boundary claimed by India in the Aksai Chin region

McMahon it would be. It is hard to see what validity in international law can be attributed to these proceedings. The Indian Government certainly had no illusions about the Simla Convention, which, it wrote to Charles Bell some time after the Simla Conference had ended, 'has not been signed by the Chinese Government or accepted by the Russian Government, and is therefore for the present invalid'.[39] The Chinese never signed it, and the Russians never accepted it, so presumably it has remained invalid ever since.

Sazonov was kept informed of the general nature of the McMahon Line negotiations; but it is certain that no one told him that the cession of Tibetan territory was involved. Despite complicated, and generally misleading, arguments to the contrary in recent years, there can be no real doubt that until 1914 Tawang north of the Se La was as Tibetan as was, say, the Chumbi Valley. It was administered by Tibetan officials, the Tsöna Dzongpons, and it paid revenue to the Dalai Lama's treasury. South of the Se La the position was less clear; but even here the case for Tibetan ownership was very strong. Tawang as brought within British India by the McMahon Line was in area considerably greater than the Chumbi Valley. Had the implications of its annexation been made public, Sazonov could no more have accepted them than he could have a British reoccupation of Chumbi. There can be little doubt, therefore, that by acquiring Tawang the Indian Government had acted in total disregard of the 1907 Anglo-Russian Convention. It is unlikely that Grey and Crewe quite understood what was happening in this part of the Assam Himalayas. They did not, it seems, have the opportunity to study the minutes of the meetings between Bell and Lönchen Shatra at which Tawang was discussed; and they had little detailed knowledge of the extent of Tibetan influence south of the McMahon Line. As we have seen, ever since the Abor Expedition the Indian Government had been rather less than open and above board about what it was doing in the Assam Himalayas. Members of Parliament were unable to find out if an extension of British territory was being contemplated, or merely a consolidation of existing British possessions. Had the truth about Tawang become public in 1914, Grey could not have avoided putting the facts before

[39] FO 535/18, no. 44.

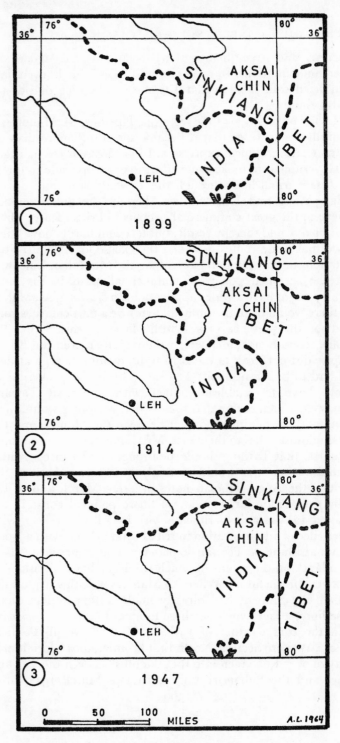

22   *Boundary changes in the Aksai Chin area, 1899–1947*

Sazonov, thus strengthening the Russian case for Afghan and other compensations. In these circumstances it might even have been decided in London that Tawang was best left outside the British Empire.

Having obtained his Line from the Tibetans, McMahon was naturally eager to see that it became something more than an abstract cartographical expression. In his *Memorandum* he urged his Government to make some effort to open up trade routes in the Assam tribal hills, through the Tawang Tract and up the Dihang-Siang and Lohit valleys. Perhaps he did not really believe in the great commercial benefits to British India which he argued would thereby result; but he could hardly have failed to see that trade routes provided the excuse for official British visitations in the remote regions along the McMahon Line, and that the accepted policy of 'commercial' posts in the Abor country might have a wider application. In Tawang, McMahon felt there would be in the immediate future a particularly strong need for the presence of a British officer to ensure that the implied conditions under which the region entered the British Empire did not work to the British disadvantage. A great deal still had to be learnt about Tawang. The Indian Government would have to establish contact with the great Tawang monastery which dominated the district. Measures would have to be taken to minimise conflict between the Mönpas and the non-Buddhist tribes to their east. McMahon was not proposing, of course, that Tawang should be brought under direct British administration: this would certainly be contrary both to the spirit of the Anglo-Tibetan notes of 24/25 March and to the India Office's declared policy of 'loose political control'. All he asked for was an experimental visit by a British officer 'with experience of administration in tribal country' and with a 'good native assistant of Tibetan experience and a native medical attendant', on the results of which would be based decisions as to policy for the future. When McMahon made this request the Indian Government had already made an experiment along these lines, a fact which he chose to ignore in his *Memorandum*.

In the cold weather of 1913–14 Captain Nevill, Political Officer, Western Section, North East Frontier, took a formidable party of over 1,000 men into the Aka hills between the Tawang Tract and the Subansiri Valley. In late March 1914, after an armed clash with hostile Dafla tribesmen, Nevill and his companion Captain Kennedy, a doctor, made their way towards the Tawang Tract. They reached Dirangdzong on 23 March; and on 1 April they arrived at Tawang town, where they were met by the two Tsöna Dzongpons, the Tibetan officials in charge of the government of the region. Nevill was in no doubt that Tawang, at least 'the country north of the Saila [Se La]' belonged to the Tibetan Government and was 'under Tsöna administration'. South of the Se La, with the exception of the village of Sengedzong, lay the domain of the great Tawang monastery with its more than 500 inhabitants, a daughter house of Drebung monastery at Lhasa. The Tawang officials, both monastic and lay, suspected that Nevill's visit indicated an active British interest in a portion of the Assam Himalayas which hitherto had been virtually neglected by the Indian Government—Morshead and Bailey, in 1913, had been the first Europeans to visit Tawang—and they seemed eager to talk political matters with the new British arrivals. Nevill refused to depart from polite generalities. Though at this time Tawang had been, at least on paper, British for about one week, he made no attempt to inform the Tawang and Tsöna authorities of this fact: indeed, no mention of the Britishness of Tawang was ever made there by an Indian Government official until the 1930s. Nevill, on his return, urged the appointment of some permanent British representative in Tawang; but his views were not even formally transmitted to Simla.[40] With the coming of the First World War the Indian Government were not prepared to contemplate any extension whatsoever of their responsibilities into remote border tracts.[41] Thus nothing was done immediately

[40] Reid, *Assam Frontier*, op. cit., pp. 283–7; PEF 1913/28, no. 3461/14, Nevill to Assam, 21 June 1914, enclosing diary of a visit to Tawang.

[41] During the course of the first nine months or so of 1914 the Assam Government made a number of proposals for administrative activities in the Assam Himalayas right up to the new McMahon Line. Apart from Nevill's ideas about Tawang, there were Dundas's plans to push posts up the Dihang-Siang as far, eventually, as Karko, and there was the project for a post up the Lohit at Menilkrai linked to Sadiya by a carriage road. On 12 November 1914, however, Hardinge informed the Assam Government that he had 'decided to take no further action on your proposals until the grave preoccupations of the war have passed'. PEF 1913/28, no. 4745/14, India to Assam, 12 November 1914, and IO minute, 7 December 1914.

after the birth of the McMahon Line to indicate to the Lönchen Shatra and the Tibetan Government that they were mistaken in believing that Tawang, though in theory British, remained for all practical purposes a Tibetan district. A similar British inactivity was similarly interpreted in Lhasa in relation to those other sections of the Assam Himalayas where the Tibetans felt they possessed territorial rights.

The Chinese objection to the McMahon Line, which was already being given expression on Chinese maps in Kuomintang times, was based less on the belief that the Line involved the British annexation of large tracts of Tibetan (and hence Chinese) territory than on the conviction that the British and Tibetans had no right to agree about Lines at all. Wherever the McMahon Line might have run, so long as its treaty basis was found in the events of the Simla Conference, the Chinese would certainly have rejected it. This is a point which Mr. Nehru and his advisers, some of whom should certainly have known better, appear to have failed to appreciate. As a boundary alignment, once the McMahon implications had been removed the 1914 Line had much to recommend it. The annexation by India of Tawang proper was probably a mistake; and it would have been better, from the point of view of securing Tibetan co-operation over the years, if the Line had been kept at the Se La alignment. The advance northwards from the Yepak to beyond the Di Chu on the Lohit was also, perhaps, rather ill advised. The Chinese, after all, had in both late Manchu and early Republican times made a claim to the Yepak boundary, where they had erected boundary markers and proclamations on the extent of Chinese sovereignty; and it was perhaps foolish of McMahon to dismiss these without comment. O'Callaghan's removal of the Chinese markers from the Yepak can hardly be described as a particularly friendly act. In some ways it was a foolish one, for it removed proof that the Chinese believed that their boundary should run far north of the old Outer Line. Elsewhere along the alignment, however, on the Subansiri, the Siang-Dihang (or Tsangpo-Brahmaputra), the Dibang and the Taron, the British showed considerable moderation in selecting their boundary.

Once it was admitted that the non-Buddhist hill tribes, the Mishmis, Abors, Miris, Akas, Daflas and so on, were not Tibetans and had never been, in any legally significant way,

Tibetan subjects, then the McMahon Line except in Tawang and on the Lohit provided as reasonable a divide between Tibetan and non-Tibetan populations as could be devised. It was inevitable that there should be some Tibetans south of the Line, as on the upper Siyom and Siang valleys, and there were a few non-Tibetan groups north of the Line in Pemakoichen on the Tsangpo. It is rarely possible in practice to devise a perfect ethnic divide. Had there ever been a genuine attempt at a negotiated Anglo-Chinese boundary settlement, or had the Assam boundary problem been submitted to arbitration, then the result, except in Tawang and on the Lohit, would certainly have been something very like the boundary which McMahon decided upon. This boundary, it should be noted, was essentially an ethnic one, based on the division between Tibetan and non-Tibetan populations. Only in Tawang and on the Lohit, where the ethnic principle was departed from, did it assume the characteristics of a boundary based on geographical features selected for strategic reasons. Apart from these two regions, the argument behind the alignment was not, in fact, that the *traditional* Indian border followed the crest of the Himalayan range; it was that the non-Tibetan or non-Buddhist Assam hill tribes, not being under Tibetan sovereignty, should be incorporated within the Indian Empire.

The present Indian Government has failed, or refused, to see this point. It has reiterated that the *traditional* boundary in the Assam Himalayas is also the one which follows the main Himalayan *watershed*. The McMahon Line, India has declared, is a watershed alignment. In fact, the watershed principle was nowhere mentioned in the Anglo-Tibetan notes of 24/25 March 1914. The principle only appears in the language of Sino-Indian boundary treaties in the Sikkim-Tibet Convention of 1890, where a short length of boundary is defined as a water parting between two named river systems: but here there was no attempt to create a general watershed principle for all Himalayan borders.[42] As we have seen, the McMahon Line did not

[42] The British members of the Kashmir Boundary Commissions of 1846 and 1847 appear to have considered the watershed principle as valuable in boundary making in mountainous tracts; but it must be admitted that they achieved no great success in creating a watershed boundary in what has now become known as the Western Sector of the Sino-Indian boundary dispute. See BCCA, p. 81.

follow the main watershed between rivers flowing into the Bay of Bengal and the Arabian Sea on the one hand, and those flowing into the Central Asian deserts and into China and South-East Asia on the other. The only general geographical description which can be given to the McMahon Line is this: it is a boundary more or less following the line of the highest peaks in the Assam Himalayas, these peaks, where possible, being linked by watersheds. This description, however, is by no means comprehensive. A number of the highest peaks, like Namche Barwa on the Tsangpo, lie north of the line. There is nothing inevitable about the watersheds followed. As we have seen, the Indian Government had to choose between a number of possible watershed systems. At intervals the Line departs entirely from the watershed concept to cross a major river like the Nyamjang, the Subansiri, the Siang-Dihang, the Lohit and the Taron. The watershed, really, is here less a universal principle of boundary making than a convenient way to separate populations inhabiting mountain valleys.

The presence or absence of the watershed principle acquires considerable importance when it is appreciated that the McMahon Line is not a perfectly surveyed alignment. By 1914 many of the tracts through which the Line was to run had been surveyed with varying degrees of accuracy; but by no means all the Line had been surveyed. The stretch from the Dihang-Siang to the Bhutanese border was most imperfectly known, the area having been only partially surveyed from the northern side by Bailey and Morshead in 1913, whose work here supplemented the few facts acquired previously by native explorers (Pundits) of the Indian Survey. Thus there inevitably exist errors in the map on which the Line was first drawn. Had the Chinese accepted the McMahon Line as a valid boundary, there would still have been room for a great deal of argument during the process of joint demarcation on the ground. The present Indian Government, when it began in the 1950s to establish posts right on the McMahon Line, found in several places that the alignment, as indicated by the co-ordinates of the 1914 map, did not, in fact, follow the watersheds which seemed to India to be appropriate. The result, ironically, has been that India has laid claim to territory to the *north* of the McMahon Line, in Tawang, for example. Here the Chinese have managed to show most convincingly that the Line and Indian claims do not agree. The Chinese, while in no way accepting the validity of the Line, have taken some delight in pointing out that, even if they did, they still would not be in complete agreement with Indian ideas on the border. India has replied that where the 1914 map does not agree with the watersheds as they exist on the ground it is the watersheds and not the map which should be followed.[43] This is a not entirely satisfactory line of argument, and it has led the Legal Adviser of the Indian Ministry of External Affairs to call on precedents from Latin America and from arguments between the Dutch and Portuguese, not to mention the Dutch and Americans, relating to the limits of colonial empires in South-East Asia.[44] The Chinese, which is hardly surprising, have not been impressed.

Had McMahon ever intended his Line to be anything more than a rather nebulous private arrangement between the Indian Government and the Tibetans, he might well have inserted, as did the negotiators of the Sikkim-Tibet Convention of 1890, some reference to the watershed principle into the text of the agreement by which the Line was defined. He did not, however, do so. If the analysis given earlier on in this chapter of the constitutional basis, as it were, of the McMahon Line is correct, McMahon never anticipated significant Indian administration right up to the Line and never believed that there would be any need for the precise demarcation of the Line on the ground. All he really wanted was a definition of the *theoretical* limits of British territory. The Line was based on the assumption that its northern side would be in the hands of a weak Tibetan Government whose frontier violations would constitute no significant threat to Indian security. His Line was not designed to keep

[43] *White Paper*, VIII, pp. 10–17, Nehru to Chou En-lai, 14 November 1962 and annexure.

[44] K. K. Rao, 'The Sino-Indian Boundary Question and International Law', *International and Comparative Law Quarterly*, 1962, pp. 405 *et seq*. Mr. Rao states that 'it is universally accepted that, where a mountain range forms the boundary, the watershed constitutes the frontier, failing special treaty arrangements'. This may well be so: but, in the case of the Assam Himalayas, the question remains which watershed? Excessive emphasis on the abstract watershed principle, to which Indian observers tend, would seem rather to obscure the issues.

the Chinese out. The main anti-Chinese barrier was not the McMahon Line; it was the boundary between Inner and Outer Tibet. This barrier, of course, was in the long run destroyed by the Chinese refusal to sign the Simla Convention. It did not stop the Chinese from 'liberating' Outer Tibet in the 1950s and, in the process, subjecting the McMahon Line to stresses which it was never designed to withstand.

XXVII

CONCLUSIONS AND AN EPILOGUE

T HE unsigned Simla Convention, the new Tibet trade
regulations and the McMahon Line, these were the
dividends which the Indian Government received from the
Simla Conference, the return for a decade of negotiation,
argument and anxiety since the Younghusband Mission. British
officials like Charles Bell and Henry McMahon, who had
become deeply involved in the Tibetan question, declared that
they were now content and compiled lists of the benefits accru-
ing to the British from the various agreements concluded at
Simla and Delhi in 1914. In fact, however, even Bell could
hardly have failed to appreciate that, lacking Chinese signature
and Russian agreement to the Simla Convention the legal
position of Tibet still remained very much up in the air. The
Indian Government could perhaps now deal more easily with
the Tibetan authorities than it had been able to up to 1912;
but this facility derived less from the 1914 agreements than
from the fact that one consequence of the outbreak of the
Chinese Revolution had been the temporary collapse of Chinese
power and influence in Lhasa. Tibet was still under Chinese
suzerainty: it had not been declared by the Powers to be an
independent state even though its own rulers from time to time
might make claims to this effect. The Chinese, indeed, after
1914 possessed as good arguments in support of their right to
reoccupy Central Tibet as they had in 1910.[1] On paper,

[1] It has often been said, particularly by recent Indian apologists like
K. Krishna Rao (*International and Comparative Law Quarterly*, 1962), that in
1913 Tibet declared her independence. The Tibetans, indeed, might have
wished to do so; and their opening statement at the Simla Conference could
well be construed as such a declaration; but by agreeing, on 3 July 1914,
to abide by the terms of the draft Simla Convention, even though unsigned

nothing had changed since the days of the Anglo-Chinese Convention of 1906. When the Chinese proceeded to 'peacefully liberate' Tibet in the 1950s those nations sympathetic to the Tibetan cause found themselves unable to offer even a convincing legal defence for the Dalai Lama, who fled to India as his predecessor, in similar circumstances, had done in 1910.

What happened to the Simla Convention, the treaty which, had Peking accepted it, would have limited China's freedom of military action in Outer Tibet? Once the Chinese had become convinced that the Simla Conference had really ended and was not merely going to be transferred to Peking or London, they increased their efforts to come to some terms with the Tibetans through negotiations at Chamdo with the Kalon Lama, and they began to think about sending a mission from the Marches to Lhasa. In the spring of 1915 they managed to entice a Tibetan deputation to talks at Tachienlu. These overtures, however, did not seem particularly promising; and in the summer of 1915 the Wai-chiao-pu once more approached Jordan on the possibility of China being offered a suitably modified Simla Convention. The Chinese were now far more reasonable about the Inner-Outer Tibet boundary than they had been in 1914: they would, for example, agree to evacuate Chamdo within a year of signature. In return they asked for a few small changes in the wording of the text to emphasise China's suzerainty, and they sought the right to station Chinese Trade Agents at Chamdo, Gyantse, Shigatse, Yatung, Gartok and any other places which might in future be opened to British trade. The

---

by China, they acknowledged Chinese suzerainty (Article 2) and the fact that 'Tibet forms part of Chinese territory' (Note 1). This last admission, which Indian commentators have tended to overlook, is probably of crucial importance in any legalistic attempt to evaluate Tibetan treaty-making powers. Take the case of the McMahon Line. Could Tibet, whatever her status, alienate Tibetan, and hence by the definition in Note 1, Chinese territory without first obtaining Chinese consent? The British acquisition of Tawang immediately raises this question, to which, in all probability, an impartial tribunal would give the answer 'No'. A prominent American international lawyer, writing in 1941, gave this definition of the post-Simla Conference status of Tibet: '*De jure* Tibet is still part of China with a high degree of autonomy, but *de facto* it enjoys independence in close relations with Great Britain.' See Q. Wright, H. Lauterpacht, E. M. Borchard, P. Morrison, *Legal Problems in the Far Eastern Conflict*, London, 1941.

Chinese Trade Agents would be equal in rank and status to their British opposite numbers and have escorts of the same size. Jordan refused to reopen the Tibetan question at this stage.

In 1916 Yuan Shih-k'ai died while attempting to restore the Chinese monarchy. There followed a reaffirmation of the Republic under a new constitution, a process which was tantamount to a change of régime. Would Yuan's successors feel themselves in any way bound by the initials of Yuan's representative at the Simla Conference? Jordan thought not. He urged the negotiation of a fresh tripartite agreement, based on the Simla Convention, but incorporating the Chinese proposals of 1915. The British Government were still thinking about Jordan's suggestions when, in the latter part of 1917, civil war broke out in Yunnan and Szechuan with disastrous consequences for the Chinese forces in the Tibetan Marches.[2] The Kalon Lama appears to have been reluctant to take advantage of the Chinese when they were down; but he was given little choice when at the very end of 1917 General P'eng Jih-sheng, in desperation, attempted to launch an offensive from Chamdo towards Lhasa. The Kalon Lama counter-attacked and the Chinese collapsed. In April 1918 Chamdo surrendered and P'eng and more than 2,000 Chinese troops fell into Tibetan hands. They were surprisingly well treated and eventually evacuated to China by way of India, Burma and Yunnan. By the early summer the Tibetans were threatening Batang and appeared to be on the verge of an advance which might carry them all the way to Tachienlu. At this point Szechuanese officials sought the help of Eric Teichman, a British Consular officer stationed at Chengtu. In October 1918 Teichman secured the truce of Rongbatsa between the Chinese and the Kalon Lama, which stabilised the Sino-Tibetan border along the Mekong-Yangtze divide more or less where it had been shown on the map attached to the draft Simla Convention which Ivan Chen had initialled. These events made Peking eager to come to some final settlement of the Tibetan question, anxious lest the Rongbatsa truce be broken and the Tibetans advance even farther eastwards. In early 1919, it seems, they again proposed to sign the Simla Convention with the modifications they

[2] By far the best available account of Sino-Tibetan relations between 1914 and 1918 is to be found in Teichman, *Eastern Tibet*, op. cit.

had advanced in 1915: but by now neither the Tibetans, who had won against the Chinese and might well win again, nor the Indian Government saw any point in accepting the Chinese proposals which thereupon were forgotten.[3] In 1919, therefore, the Simla Convention to all intents and purposes disappeared. No more would probably have been heard of it had the Indian Government not seen fit to publish its text (without the map) in the 1929 edition of Aitchison's *Treaties* along with the 24/25 March 1914 notes on the McMahon Line.[3a]

Up to 1917 the Indian Government, when it was able to take time enough from the war to give thought to Tibet, felt that it could not establish too overt a relationship with the Dalai Lama until it had obtained Russian sanction for the principles of the Simla Convention. Anglo-Russian negotiations on the subject were held in 1915 when the whole Central Asian situation was considered in the light of a new Asian partition in which Russia was to get, among other areas, Constantinople and European Turkey. The discussions seem to have been related to the Dardanelles campaign, and with the final evacuation they came to an abrupt end. The possibility still existed, however, that a wide redistribution of spheres of influence would follow the Allied victory, in which Russia would demand her share; and it would perhaps be as well for the British not to commit themselves too deeply with Tibet and thereby reduce their postwar bargaining power. Thus Whitehall in 1916 and 1917 refused permission for British officers to visit Lhasa, even though invited to do so by the Dalai Lama, fearing Russian protest on the basis of the 1907 Convention. Article 8 of the Simla Convention, which allowed such visits in certain circumstances, was thus a dead letter. It was not until the permanent collapse of a Russian Government likely to be friendly to the Allies had become certain that the Indian Government was finally allowed to think seriously about British missions to Lhasa. Sir Charles Bell arrived at the Tibetan capital on a mission in November 1920,[4] creating a precedent

[3] M. E. Willoughby, 'The relation of Tibet to China', *Journal of the Central Asian Society*, XI, 1924.

[3a] See above, Ch. XXVI, note 26.

[4] Sir C. Bell, 'The Dalai Lama; Lhasa 1921', *Journal of the Central Asian Society*, XI, 1924.

which was followed from time to time by successive Political Officers for Sikkim. When the Gould Mission left Lhasa in February 1937,[5] moreover, one of its members remained behind. Thus, rather obscurely, Younghusband's dream of a permanent British representative in the Tibetan capital was finally achieved. After Indian independence and following the Chinese 'liberation' of Tibet in 1950–2, this post, to which no formal title appears to have been given, was transformed into the Indian Consulate-General at Lhasa.

From the time of the Bell Mission to Lhasa of 1920 the Indian Government evidently considered itself free to have such diplomatic relations with the Dalai Lama's Government as it saw fit. What, at this period, did the British consider the international status of Tibet to be? They had never formally repudiated the recognition of Chinese suzerainty which they had offered during the Simla Conference. Tibet was certainly, in the eyes of London and Simla, *de jure* part of the Chinese political world, albeit a remote and highly autonomous one. *De facto*, however, Tibet was considered to have as much freedom of action as the British wished to allow her; and the Indian Government ceased to be much concerned about the Chinese point of view. The British saw no reason why they should consult Peking before assisting in the training of Tibetan soldiers and technicians, or before they sent Laden La to Lhasa in 1922 to persuade the Dalai Lama to adopt a more friendly attitude towards Nepal and to help reorganise the Tibetan police force. The Indian Government lent the Dalai Lama the services of a geologist, Sir Henry Hayden, to initiate a survey of Tibetan mineral resources, it procured on behalf of the Tibetan Government hydro-electric generating equipment, and it assisted in the establishment of an English school in Gyantse, all of this without seeking the approval of the *de jure* suzerain power. The British, moreover, had no hesitation in interfering with what might well be interpreted as Tibetan internal affairs, applying pressure, for example, to prevent the Dalai Lama from putting small duties on certain categories of exports to India.

[5] For some account of the Gould mission to Lhasa of 1936–37, see Gould, *Jewel in the Lotus*, op. cit.; F. S. Chapman, *Lhasa: the Holy City*, London, 1938; P. Neame, 'Tibet and the 1936 Lhasa Mission', *Journal of the Royal Central Asian Society*, XXVI, 1939.

The Chinese, who never for one moment abandoned their hope that Tibet would again be brought back into the bosom of the family of the five races, no doubt interpreted British policy in Tibet as directed towards the establishment of a protectorate. In fact, however, the Indian Government between the two world wars was at pains to limit its Tibetan commitments as far as it could. Tibet by this time was something which the British Empire could not possibly hope to swallow. The Indian Government certainly acquired a real influence in Lhasa, but it never resembled the predominant British influence in Nepal. The Tibetans never broke off all relations with the Chinese, probably realising that the Indian Government would be no more prepared to defend them against attack from the east in the 1920s and 1930s than it had been in 1910. Following the Panchen Lama's flight to China in 1923 the Chinese managed to build up a nucleus of support in the centre of Tibetan politics. The story of the impact of Chinese and British influence in Tibet between the wars, and of the conflicts between progressive and conservative Tibetan factions, has been adequately related by H. E. Richardson, and it need not be discussed in detail here.[6] Suffice it to say that the basic Tibetan policy was to maintain the Religious State in being and to avoid either too rapid economic and political development or too close involvement with both China and British India. There were times when the British influence was in the ascendant, and there were periods when Chinese influence was waxing; but neither influence could ever have been said to have dominated Lhasa. This was not the political history of a British protectorate.

If anything, Tibet after the Simla Conference became what today would be called a neutral state, steering a difficult course between the interests of powerful neighbours of conflicting outlook. Its neutrality, however, was guaranteed by no international agreement, no equivalent of a Geneva Conference. The Simla Convention, which might perhaps have achieved this end, had by the 1920s passed into oblivion. Without such guarantees, Tibetan neutrality was extremely unstable. The

[6] Richardson, *Tibet*, op. cit. This book, while it leans perhaps a trifle too much towards the Tibetan point of view, is still far and away the best short account of the history of modern Tibet yet to have appeared.

British would not, and probably could not, protect it; and the Chinese respected it only so long as they were not in possession of sufficient military power to undertake the effective revival of Chao Erh-feng's policy. With the Communist victory in China, Tibetan neutrality was doomed; but it would probably have been equally threatened had the Kuomintang managed to crush the Communists. Once the Chinese People's Republic undertook the 'peaceful liberation' of what it now called 'the Tibet Region of China', there was nothing that the outside world could have done, even if such a body as the United Nations had been presented with any *de jure* case for intervention. No such case, however, could really be substantiated. Richardson has been very critical of the British delegation at the United Nations for declining to champion the Tibetan cause in 1950; but, on any objective assessment, it must be acknowledged that the British had then even less formal grounds for opposing a Chinese domination of Tibet than they had possessed in 1910. Here, perhaps, may be seen the ultimate significance of the failure of the Simla Conference; though it is extremely unlikely that the Simla Convention, even with a valid Chinese signature, would have turned out to be a particularly strong defence against 'liberation' from Peking.

During the years when the Simla Convention became increasingly a document of no more than antiquarian interest, the McMahon Line also appeared to be bound for oblivion. The very mild administrative measures which McMahon had recommended along the trade routes through the Assam Himalayas were rejected by his superiors. Some of the more ambitious proposals of the Abor Expedition period, the military post at Menilkrai and the road up the Lohit, for example, proposals which had won Lord Crewe's approval as inescapable consequences of the policy of 'loose political control', were quietly forgotten. By the end of the First World War the Indian Government, in fact, possessed far less direct influence in the tribal hills than it had enjoyed in 1912–13. Until the mid-1930s no British official ventured near the McMahon Line in the Tawang Tract, up the Dihang-Siang or up the Lohit. On the Subansiri British officials as late as 1947 had not yet been all the way up to the Line, the point where the Miri Mission was turned back in early 1912 still marking the farthest British

573

penetration; though the Line had been visited here from the Tibetan side.[7]

British frontier officers in the 1920s and early 1930s, of course, did not fail to point out to their superiors the need to do something about the country between the old Outer Line and the McMahon Line of 1914. Nevill, who was then in charge of the Balipara Frontier Tract (the western end of the Assam Himalayas), wrote in his 1927–8 report, for instance, that,

> discussing this frontier, I have often heard it expressed that the country is worth nothing and is not worth the expenses of Administration. This is not altogether true for there are very large areas of extremely rich country, the only thing wanting to develop it is settled conditions and a just administration.

What might be economically profitable, Nevill went on, was also highly desirable on political grounds. He declared, in this same report, that

> there is no doubt that as soon as China settles down this Tibetan frontier will become of great importance. China still has its eyes on Tibet and on Lhasa, the pro-Chinese party is growing in influence, and should China gain control of Tibet, the Tawang country is particularly adapted for a secret and easy entrance into India. Russia is also trying to establish her influence in Tibet, and if successful, could safely and secretly send her emissaries into India by this route.[8]

These words failed to cause even a ripple on the surface of the Viceregal calm of Simla.

By the mid-1930s, however, the British were finding it harder to ignore the McMahon Line, the validity of which the Kuomintang Government of China had begun to deny in unmistakable terms, its existence having come to their notice following the British publication of the 24 and 25 March 1914 Anglo-Tibetan notes (but not the map that accompanied the notes) in the 1929 edition of Aitchison's *Treaties*.[8a] The position was clearly

[7] For a short account of the McMahon Line after 1914, see Lamb, *China-India Border*, op. cit.

[8] Reid, *Assam Frontier*, op. cit., pp. 291–3.

[8a] See above, Ch. XXVI, note 26.

described in a long letter from the Assam Government in September 1936, which, in view of the impression the Indian Government has recently tried to create that the McMahon Line was a fully administered border of some antiquity, deserves quotation at length.

The Tibet Conference of 1914 resulted in the delimitation of the Indo-Tibetan frontier from the eastern frontier of Bhutan to the Isu Razi pass on the Irrawaddy-Salween water parting. The line, which was accepted by the Government of Tibet, was demarcated on maps then specially prepared, and is known as the McMahon Line. Sir Henry McMahon recommended in his memorandum that while great care should be taken to avoid friction with the Tibetan Government and the vested interests of the Tawang monastery, an experienced British officer should proceed to the western part of the area south of the Line to settle its future administration.

The 1914 Convention was never published, mainly because the Chinese Government failed to ratify it, and nothing was done to give effect to Sir Henry McMahon's recommendation for an extension of administration into the Tawang area. Another consequence is that many published maps still show the frontier of India along the administered border of Assam. . . . An important point to note is that the latest Chinese atlases show almost the whole of the tribal area south of the McMahon Line up to the administered border of Assam as included in China. It amounts to this, that while the Chinese already claim a large stretch of Indian territory east of Tawang as part of Sikang Province of China, the Tibetan Government, over whom the Chinese claim suzerainty, are collecting revenue and exercising jurisdiction in the Tawang area many miles south of the international frontier.

The Government of India consider that some effective steps should be taken to challenge activities which may be extended to a claim on behalf of China for Tawang itself, or even Bhutan and Sikkim. They therefore propose to demand from the Tibetan Government, which has recently reaffirmed the McMahon Line, that collection of revenue for the latter Government in the Tawang area should be discontinued, and the question whether it will be necessary to introduce Indian administration to replace Tibetan officials in that area has been left for further consideration in the light of Mr. Gould's report on the conclusion of his mission to Lhasa. The suggestion which has now been made to this Government [Assam] is that it is highly desirable to emphasise the interest of British India in the Tawang area either by *actual tours* or by *collecting the revenue ourselves*, since the mere reproduction of the McMahon Line on Survey of India maps would be insufficient to correct the false impressions which have gained ground in the years since 1914. The continued exercise of jurisdiction by Tibet in Tawang and the area south of Tawang might enable China, or still worse, might enable any other power which may in future be in a position to assert authority over Tibet [i.e. Soviet Russia!] to claim prescriptive rights over a part of the territory recognised as within India by the 1914 Convention. In taking any steps of the nature contemplated it would be necessary to make it very clear that there is no intention to interfere with the purely monastic collection of the Tawang monastery.[9]

The renewed interest in the McMahon Line indicated in the interesting document just quoted was to a great extent the product of the British response to Chinese claims reinforced by a rising Chinese influence in Lhasa following the death of the thirteenth Dalai Lama in 1933. In 1935 the Kuomintang proposed to bring the Panchen Lama back to Tibet in the midst of a Chinese army. British diplomatic protests in Nanking were ignored. The Indian Government, alarmed at this turn of events, sent F. W. Williamson, Political Officer for Sikkim, up to Lhasa to see if some truce could be patched up between the Lhasa authorities and the Chinese-supported Panchen Lama. Shortly after he reached the Tibetan capital, Williamson died. In his place, and at the request of the Tibetans, Basil Gould, the new Political Officer for Sikkim, continued the Lhasa mission, adding to his staff a British soldier of rank, Brigadier P. Neame, to advise the Tibetans on military questions. Gould discussed with the *Kashak*, the Tibetan Cabinet, many aspects of Tibetan foreign relations, including the McMahon Line and Tawang. On Tawang, Gould discovered that the Tibetan attitude was that

(1) up to 1914 Tawang had undoubtedly been Tibetan,

[9] Ibid., pp. 294–5, Assam Chief Secretary to Captain Lightfoot, 17 September 1936.

(2) they regarded the adjustment of the Tibet-Indian boundary as part and parcel of the general adjustment and determination of boundaries contemplated in the 1914 Convention. If they could, with our [British] help, secure a definitive Sino-Tibetan boundary they would of course be glad to observe the Indo-Tibetan border as defined in 1914, (3) they had been encouraged in thinking that His Majesty's Government and the Government of India sympathised with this way of regarding the matter owing to the fact that at no time since the Convention and Declaration of 1914 had the Indian Government taken steps to question Tibetan, or assert British, authority in the Tawang area.[10]

The Indian Government resolved to show the Tibetans that they had come to quite the wrong conclusion about Tawang and the McMahon Line. Captain Lightfoot, Political Officer for the Balipara Frontier Tract, should go up to Tawang, inform the inhabitants that they were now British subjects and collect, in demonstration of the fact, a symbolic tax.

In April 1938 Lightfoot reached Tawang, the first British official to do so while on duty, it would seem, since Nevill's visit of 1914. His presence was not welcomed by the local Tibetan authorities, who asked him to withdraw and who, while refusing to help him collect taxes, were at considerable pains to collect Tibetan taxes before his very eyes. Lhasa was promptly informed of Lightfoot's presence; and the Tibetan Government hastened to protest against it to Gould, who replied categorically that Tawang was British. Lightfoot, on his return to Assam, advised that the British now reorganise Tawang administration and undertake some form of permanent occupation there. His views, however, were not accepted in New Delhi.[11] The Tawang Tract south of the Se La was eventually brought under direct British authority in 1945–7; but Tawang itself still remained in 1947 as Tibetan as it had been in 1914, Lightfoot's visit having made no discernible impression on the Tibetans. Some Indian authorities of late have interpreted these transactions as implying a Tibetan 'confirmation' of the

[10] Ibid., p. 296, Sir R. Reid to Lightfoot, 27 May 1937.

[11] Ibid. pp. 297–300, Assam to India, 7 September 1938, and India to Assam, 20 April 1939.

McMahon Line;[12] but, on the basis of the few available documents, it looks far more like an express Tibetan repudiation of the Line as a valid boundary.

During the years following the Simla Conference when Tawang was so ignored by the Indian Government, the British could hardly be described as active elsewhere in the Assam Himalayas. On the Subansiri up to 1944 they did practically nothing at all; and by 1947 no British officer had yet travelled all the way from the plains to the McMahon Line. On the Dihang-Siang the Tibetan authorities in Kongbo and Pome continued to exert their power as far downstream as Karko and Simong. Here, in the late 1920s, there was a minor Tibetan civil war, fought on territory which was in theory British, when a chieftain from Pome fled south of the McMahon Line after refusing to pay taxes to Lhasa.[13] It was not until early 1939 that R. W. Godfrey, Political Officer for the Sadiya Frontier Tract, began patrolling for any distance up the Dihang-Siang Valley; and permanent outposts were located at Karko and Riga in the winter of 1940–1, thus finally ending the prohibition

[12] See, for example, K. Krishna Rao, op. cit., p. 403, whose source, *White Paper, III*, seems to put the question in a light not justified by the facts. The document in question, a note from India to China of 12 February 1960, has this to say about the confirmation of the McMahon Line:

> The Tibetans never protested against the Indo-Tibetan boundary as agreed upon in 1914. On more than one occasion they acknowledged its existence and affirmed that they had no wish to dispute its validity. When the McMahon Line was verbally reaffirmed by the British representative in 1936 and 1938, the Tibetan Government replied that they were fully aware of the terms of the 1914 Agreement. It is the Government of India which protested in 1943 against illegal penetration by the Tibetans into Indian territory. Similar protests were made by the Indian Government whenever the Tibetans sought to take advantage of Indian preoccupations in order to levy illegal dues in Indian territory.

There are several ways of making protests; and from this passage it would seem that, while verbally acquiescent, the Tibetans were certainly protesting against the McMahon Line by actions rather than words. The documents printed by Sir Robert Reid do not convey the impression that the Tibetans were ever reconciled to the loss of tracts like Tawang, the consequence of a British attempt to enforce the McMahon Line agreement of 1914 by its letter rather than its spirit.

[13] Ibid., p. 257.

CONCLUSIONS AND AN EPILOGUE

against permanent police posts in the Abor hills which Lord
Crewe had imposed in 1912–13.[14] Like the Dihang-Siang, the
Lohit, too, was ignored during the 1920s and early 1930s. In
1937, as part of the revived interest in the McMahon Line
which we have already noted in connection with Tawang, the
Assam Government proposed that work on the road from
Sadiya up the Lohit to Tibetan Zayul should be started again.
The Government of India rejected the proposal; but from then
onwards British Political Officers became more active in the
Mishmi country. In 1940 Godfrey travelled all the way up to
the McMahon Line, which he then crossed to pay a visit to the
Tibetan authorities at Rima. He was the first British official to
do this since O'Callaghan's tour in 1914.[15]

With the outbreak of war in the Far East the Indian Government again shelved projects for extending British administration right up to the McMahon Line. However, as a result of the
lessons learnt during the Japanese occupation of Burma, which
demonstrated the vulnerability of remote hill and jungle tracts
on the Indian border, a new attack on the problem of the
Assam Himalayas was authorised in 1943 and entrusted to the
general supervision of J. P. Mills.[16] For the first time the British
were to undertake something like a systematic penetration into
the tribal hills, with an anthropological approach to the
problem of bringing peoples of diverse and highly specialised
cultures under modern administration. The work of Mills and
Betts in Balipara (the Tawang Tract), of Fürer-Haimendorf and
Betts in the Subansiri, of Mainprice on the Lohit, all contributed
towards a transformation of the political situation in the Assam
Himalayas.[17] By the end of British rule in 1947 the Tawang

14 Ibid., p. 262.
15 Ibid., p. 265.
16 J. P. Mills, 'Problems of the Assam-Tibet Frontier', *Royal Central Asian
Journal*, 1950.
17 J. P. Mills, 'Tours in the Balipara Frontier Tract, Assam', *Man in
India*, 27, 1947; J. P. Mills, 'Mishmis of the Lohit Valley, Assam', *Journal
of the Royal Anthropological Institute*, 82, 1952; U. G. Bower (Mrs. Betts),
'The Daflas of the Subansiri Area', *Royal Central Asian Journal*, 1949;
U. G. Bower, *The Hidden Land*, London, 1953; C. von Fürer-Haimendorf,
Ethnographic Notes on the Tribes of the Subansiri Region, Shillong, 1947; C. von
Fürer-Haimendorf, *Exploration in the Eastern Himalayas*, Shillong, 1947;
C. von Fürer-Haimendorf, 'The Tribes of the Subansiri Region', *Royal
Central Asian Journal*, 1948; C. von Fürer-Haimendorf, 'Anthropology and

Tract up to the Se La, but not Tawang itself, had been brought under administration. Posts had been established right up to the McMahon Line on the Dihang-Siang. The lower and middle sections of the Subansiri basin had been visited by British anthropologists and political officers. The Mishmi tribes had been contacted and projects were once more being discussed for the road to Rima. Long stretches of the McMahon Line alignment, however, had yet in 1947 to have been visited from the Indian side; and the Tibetans had still not been persuaded to accept the permanence of the 1914 boundary settlement. Just before the transfer of power Lhasa asked the Indian Government whether the McMahon Line would die along with the British *raj*, and in late 1947 a Tibetan note to the newly independent Indian Ministry of External Affairs laid Tibetan claim not only to Tibetan districts south of the McMahon Line but also to all the Himalayan regions to which, in the course of her long history, Tibet had ever felt herself to have a valid claim. Thus Sikkim, the Darjeeling District, Bhutan and the whole of Ladakh were declared to be Tibetan property at this time.[18] These claims the Chinese inherited in 1950–1.

Shortly after the Chinese Communists had established themselves in Tibet the independent Indian Government began to take a far more active interest in the Assam Himalayas than had ever its British predecessor. In early 1951 Tawang proper was taken under direct Indian administration,[19] some thirty-seven years after the Tibetans, by the McMahon Line notes, had ceded it to India. The entire tract of the Assam Himalayas was subjected to a considerable measure of administrative reorganisation to create the North-East Frontier Agency (NEFA) of today, an independent administrative unit under the Indian Ministry of External Affairs though nominally headed by the Governor of Assam. In 1956 the Indian Frontier Administrative Service was created to staff NEFA. By the late 1950s Indian

---

[18] *White Paper*, II, p. 39, Nehru to Chou En-lai, 26 September 1959.
[19] Johri, *Where India, China and Burma Meet*, op. cit., p. 105.

Administration in the Tribal Areas of the North-East Frontier', *Eastern Anthropologist*, 1949; C. von Fürer-Haimendorf, *Himalayan Barbary*, London, 1955; C. von Fürer-Haimendorf, *The Apa Tanis and their Neighbours*, London, 1963.

posts had been established at many points along the McMahon
Line, such as Longju on the upper Subansiri, where the British
had never reached. This activity, combined with Chinese consolidation in Tibet, was bound to accentuate the defects of the
McMahon Line as a Sino-Indian boundary. The Chinese began
to send patrols across portions of the Line, which they did not
acknowledge in any way as a valid border. The first such
crossing appears to have been on the upper Lohit where, in
October 1957, a Chinese party made its way down to Walong,
just north of the Chinese boundary markers of 1910–12.[20] In
June 1959 the Chinese protested against the establishment of
an Indian post at Longju on the upper Subansiri.[21] In August
1959 a Chinese patrol, so the Indians protested, crossed the
McMahon Line at Khinzemane in the Tawang region.[22] Later
in the same month an armed clash developed between Indian
and Chinese patrols at Longju just south of Migyitun.[23] There

[20] *White Paper*, p. 33, Informal note from Indian External Affairs
Ministry to Chinese Embassy, New Delhi, 17 January 1959.

[21] Loc. cit., p. 34, Note from Chinese Foreign Office to Indian Embassy,
Peking, 23 June 1959.

[22] Loc. cit., p. 41, Note from Indian Embassy, Peking, to Chinese Foreign
Office, 11 August 1959.

The position of Khinzemane raises an interesting point. According to the
original McMahon Line map, in two sheets, which both the Chinese and
Indians have published at a reduced scale, in this part of Tawang the
McMahon Line does not run north of lat. 27° 45′ N.; yet the Indians
protested against a Chinese violation of the Line which took place at
lat. 27° 46′ N. How could the Chinese violate the McMahon Line at a
point north of the McMahon Line, that is to say on the Chinese side of it?
The Indians, invoking the watershed principle, claimed that the Line at
this point was clearly intended to follow the nearest watershed to the
co-ordinates indicated in the 1914 map, that is to say along the Thagla
Ridge. The Chinese have published an enlargement of the relevant portion
of the 1914 map which does make this contention seem to be a trifle absurd.
At this point the McMahon Line is just about to cross the Nyamjang River,
and hence could hardly be following the main watershed. There appear to
be available a number of watersheds between streams flowing into the
Nyamjang, none indicated in the 1914 map which is here less than detailed,
which the Line could follow. Here is another demonstration of the need in
which the McMahon Line stood, even had the Chinese accepted it, of being
jointly demarcated on the ground. See *Atlas of the Northern Frontier of India*,
op. cit., and *Peking Review*, nos. 47 and 48, 30 November 1962.

[23] *White Paper*, p. 43, Note from Chinese Foreign Office to Indian
Embassy, Peking, 27 August 1959.

could be no doubt that the Chinese did not consider the McMahon Line to be anything like as sacrosanct as it was regarded in New Delhi.

Chinese challenges to the McMahon Line, expressed on Chinese maps as well as by the activities of Chinese patrols, much distressed Mr. Nehru, who believed that he had already reached some agreement with China on this boundary alignment in 1956. As he wrote to Chou En-lai on 14 December 1958:[24]

> Towards the end of 1956, you [Chou En-lai] did us the honour of paying a visit to India and we had the pleasure of having you in our midst for many days. . . . We had long talks and discussed many international issues. . . . In the course of these talks you referred to the Sino-Burmese border. . . . It was in this connection that you mentioned to me the Sino-Indian border, and more especially the so-called McMahon Line. This McMahon Line covered a part of the Sino-Burmese border and a large part of the Chinese border with India. I remember your telling me that you did not approve of this border being called the McMahon Line and I replied that I did not like that name either. But for facility of reference we referred to it as such.
>
> You told me that you had accepted this McMahon Line border with Burma and whatever might have happened long ago, in view of the friendly relations which existed between China and India, you proposed to recognise this border with India also. You added that you would like to consult the authorities of the Tibetan region of China and you proposed to do so.
>
> Immediately after our talk, I had written a minute so that we might have a record of this talk for our personal and confidential use. I am giving below a quotation from this minute:
>
> > Premier Chou referred to the McMahon Line and again said that he had never heard of this before though of course the then Chinese Government had dealt with this matter and not accepted that line. He had gone into this matter in connection with the border dispute with Burma. Although he thought that this line, established by British Imperialists, was not fair, nevertheless, because it was an accomplished

[24] Loc. cit., pp. 49–50.

fact and because of the friendly relations which existed between China and the countries concerned, namely, India and Burma, the Chinese Government were of the opinion that they should give recognition to this McMahon Line. They had, however, not consulted the Tibetan authorities about it yet. They proposed to do so.

When the Chinese continued to show NEFA as part of their territory in their maps Mr. Nehru felt that Chou En-lai had broken his promise.

Nehru, however, probably misunderstood, as so often happens at summit meetings, what Chou En-lai had actually said. That the question of the McMahon Line arose in connection with the Sino-Burmese border issue is probably significant in this respect. What the Chinese were in the process of doing with Burma was to renegotiate the entire boundary alignment. The fact that the end result was very like the border in British days did not mean that the Chinese had accepted the Imperialist boundary as such: it merely showed that the real boundary, jointly decided by the free governments of Burma and China, turned out to be similar to the boundary which the Imperialists had tried to impose. The legal basis for the boundary, however, was no application of *uti possidetis*;[25] it was to be found in post-Imperialist treaty-making. Probably all Chou En-lai meant in his private talks with Nehru in 1956 was that, in a free, post-Imperialist, Sino-Indian boundary negotiation the Chinese would be prepared to accept a boundary not unlike the McMahon Line: if so, however, it

[25] This doctrine of *uti possidetis* was first evolved in Latin America, where it was decided that the boundaries of the Republics should be based on those of the Spanish Provinces which the Republics replaced. Generally the year 1810 was adopted as a point for which the boundaries had to be established. I feel that there is a very close analogy between the situation in respect to the Latin American Republics and that in respect to independent States formerly part of colonial empires. The strongest, legally speaking, Indian claim to a boundary would be based on a demonstration that the boundary in question had been established during the period of British rule. To argue this in relation to the McMahon Line would be to argue that the Chinese were bound by the McMahon Line notes of 1914. One could hardly expect Chou En-lai to agree.

For a brief account of the doctrine of *uti possidetis*, see N. Hill, *Claims to Territory in International Law and Relations*, London, 1945.

by no means followed that the Chinese would accept the McMahon Line as such. On 23 January 1959 Chou En-lai explained his position to Mr. Nehru. 'The Sino-Indian boundary', he said, 'has never been formally delimitated'; and 'historically no treaty or agreement' concerning it 'has ever been concluded between the Chinese Central Government and the Indian Government'. Chou En-lai was evidently prepared to begin negotiations for some general Sino-Indian boundary agreement; but he would not do so on the basis of the Indian claim that the boundary alignment had been already settled in Imperialist days. 'As you are aware,' he wrote to Mr. Nehru, 'the "McMahon Line" was a product of the British policy of aggression against the Tibet Region of China. . . . Juridically, too, it cannot be considered legal.'[26] How could China accept such a border? The Indians refused to see the Chinese point of view. They insisted that, as the McMahon Line and other stretches of the border were extant as established boundary alignments, there could be no possible ground for a fresh round of negotiation. China, they declared, in all justice could only accept the border as the Indians described it. The Chinese declined to do so; and the state of Sino-Indian relations deteriorated to the point, in late 1962, when the Chinese launched their military demonstrations in Ladakh and across the McMahon Line.

It has often been said by Indian and Western observers that the Chinese have been carrying out since the 1950s a policy of aggression along their borders, exploiting every claim however remote or far fetched to territory beyond their legitimate frontiers. In fact, from an analysis of recent Chinese boundary agreements with Burma, Nepal and Pakistan it would seem that China under the Communists has been rather more moderate than was the China of the Manchus or the Republic. In the Sino-Pakistani boundary agreement of 2 March 1963 the Chinese surrendered their claims to suzerainty over the state of Hunza, claims to which the Manchus had adhered with some tenacity.[27] In the Sino-Nepalese boundary agreement of 5 October 1961 there is no mention of Nepalese political

[26] *White Paper*, pp. 52–53, Chou En-lai to Nehru, 23 January 1959.
[27] The full text of the Sino-Pakistani agreement of 2 March 1963 is to be found in *Peking Review*, nos. 10 and 11, 15 March 1963.

dependence on China such as both the Manchus and the Republic had persisted in declaring.[28] In the Sino-Burmese boundary agreement of 1 October 1960 the Chinese, while securing recognised possession at last of Hpimaw, abandoned claims of considerable extent over territory to the west of the Salween-Irrawaddy divide.[29] This divide, which both the Manchus and the Government of Yuan Shih-k'ai could not bring themselves to accept as a border, the Chinese Communists now agreed to, with a few minor exceptions, in explicit terms. They also accepted part of the McMahon Line; but they did so, they said, because it seemed a good frontier line, not because it *was* the McMahon Line. Here are remarkable surrenders of Chinese claims which would surely have astonished Sir John Jordan. The cynic might say that they were made so as to embarrass the Indians. No doubt the Chinese appreciated that their border agreements with India's neighbours would have this effect; but it seems unlikely that the baiting of Mr. Nehru was in itself sufficient motive for the abandonment of traditional Chinese territorial claims. It is more likely that the Chinese genuinely wanted a settled border if it were presented to them in terms which they could accept and without any argument as to the validity of Imperialist treaties. The first Article of the 1963 Sino-Pakistani agreement is perhaps significant in this respect. It reads:

> In view of the fact that the boundary between China's Sinkiang and the contiguous areas the defence of which is under the actual control of Pakistan has never been formally delimited, the two Parties agree to delimit it on the basis of the traditional customary boundary line including natural features and in a spirit of equality, mutual benefit and friendly co-operation.[30]

Had China really wished to annoy India, she would surely not have used the expression 'the contiguous areas the defence of

[28] The full text of the Sino-Nepalese agreement of 5 October 1961 is to be found in *Peking Review*, no. 41, 13 October 1961.

[29] The full text of the Sino-Burmese agreement of 1 October 1960 is to be found in *Peking Review*, no. 40, 4 October 1960.

See also D. Woodman, *The Making of Burma*, London, 1962; D. Whittam, 'The Sino-Burmese boundary treaty', *Pacific Affairs*, 34, 1961.

[30] *Peking Review*, nos. 10 and 11, 15 March 1963, p. 67.

which is under the actual control of Pakistan': she would have used 'Pakistani Kashmir' or some such term.[31]

Could the British have done anything to prevent the Himalayan border crisis which their independent Indian successors had to face? Short of guaranteeing the permanent exclusion of China from Central Tibet, which, as has been suggested, it lay well beyond their power to do, there was probably no way in which a Sino-Indian crisis of some kind could have been avoided; but it might well have been far less serious. Two possible approaches to the Assam Himalayan boundary problem, for example, both rejected or postponed by the Indian Government, might have been more successful than the course actually followed. First, the Indian Government might have negotiated the McMahon Line with China. Had McMahon been able to secure Chinese signature to the Simla Convention, which would have meant concessions on the Inner-Outer Tibet border alignment which the Dalai Lama might well have refused to accept, it might perhaps have been possible to follow up the Convention with a supplementary Anglo-Chinese agreement on the Assam border. The history of the Simla Conference, of course, made such a settlement impossible for both the Chinese and the British; and so long as Mr. Nehru and his advisers clung to the validity of the proceedings at Simla and Delhi between October 1913 and July 1914, a settlement of this kind continued to be out of the question between independent India and Communist China.[32] Secondly, the Indian Government, having secured the McMahon Line, could have hastened to convert it into something rather more than a red line on a not particularly accurate map (in two sheets). If by 1950 all the Assam Himalayas were as actively under Indian administration as were the mountain tracts

---

[31] Despite this cautious phrase, the Indians did not deny themselves the luxury of a protest, arguing that Pakistan did not have a frontier with China and, therefore, could not participate in a Sino-Pakistani boundary agreement. See *White Paper*, IX, pp. 2–3, Note from Indian Ministry of External Affairs to Chinese Embassy, New Delhi, 2 March 1963.

See also A. Lamb, 'The Sino-Pakistani Boundary Agreement of 2 March 1963', *Australian Outlook*, December 1964.

[32] For an admirable summary of the Chinese point of view on the Sino-Indian boundary question, see Joan Robinson, 'The Chinese point of view', *International Affairs*, April 1964.

around Simla and Almora, for example, then the McMahon Line dispute might perhaps have been confined in practice, whatever theoretical claims were raised to the contrary, to minor adjustments of the border as has turned out to be the case in the Middle Sector of the Sino-Indian boundary dispute. There appears to be a relationship in inverse ratio, as one might indeed have expected, between the actual extent of disputed border territory occupied by the Chinese and the degree of effective administration previously established by the Indian Government there. The Aksai Chin area, which India did not, as far as can be determined from the available evidence, administer in any way at all, has now passed completely into Chinese hands. Along the rest of the border, where in varying degrees Indian administration existed, the Chinese have been more moderate in their physical occupation of, or penetrations into, Indian-claimed territory.

In the British failure to 'make good' the McMahon Line in sufficient time we can perhaps detect the underlying theme running through the events described in this book. It was clearly absurd, as Sir Edward Grey pointed out in 1911–12, to make theoretical claims to territory without the intention to extend administration there. Yet, by the time that the Chinese entered Lhasa in 1910, the British Empire in India had passed its zenith. The British were no longer an expanding power: they were attempting to hold and consolidate what they had against threats more from within than without. Ever since the days of Pitt's India Act the British had been wont to declare that they had no wish to acquire more territory in the Indian subcontinent than they actually possessed. Each fresh annexation was justified, and with much conviction, on the grounds of self-defence. The Mahratha threat, the Burmese threat, the Sikh threat, the Russian threat and the French threat, such explanations as these were put forward each time the Indian Government found itself in possession of yet another province or embarked upon a fresh frontier war. By the 1890s, with the delimiting of the Durand line between India and Afghanistan and the acquisition of Hunza, Chitral and a British border touching on the Pamir Knot, the Indian Empire had reached its optimum extent at the very moment when native Indian opinion was beginning its long agitation for a measure of self-government.

Curzon, on this analysis, was an anachronism. Devices like the Younghusband Mission were, by the opening of the twentieth century, bound to fail. They only made sense if they were backed by a determination to maintain a lasting British power in remote areas beyond what had been accepted as the natural boundaries of the Indian subcontinent. The British, after 1900, could no more have established a meaningful protectorate over Tibet than they could have taken Afghanistan under direct British administration. Hence the policy behind the Anglo-Russian Convention of 1907 accorded far better with the spirit of the times than did any of Curzon's forward proposals, however elegant and lucid might be the language in which he expressed them. But Grey and Morley, in some ways, were as blind to the realities of the situation as was Curzon. The Anglo-Russian Convention of 1907 was a measure of consolidation rather than of advance; but it was an extremely general measure requiring much amplification in detail. It implied that the great era of Anglo-Russian rivalry was over, and probably rightly so, since Tsarist Russia, too, was approaching, if she had not quite yet reached, the end of her expansionist phase. It did not, however, contain detailed and precise solutions to the many problems arising from the presence of buffer zones between the two great empires now in maturity. Once Tibet had been neutralised as far as Britain and Russia were concerned, there were but two really important Tibetan problems facing the Indian Government. The first was the nature of the Chinese position in Tibet, and the second was the determination of the exact alignment of the Indo-Tibetan border. The Indian Government, of course, did not see the choices in quite such simple terms, because it could not bring itself to believe that, after 1907, the Russians had, in fact, abandoned their Tibetan schemes. From 1912 to 1914, when it should have been concentrating on the Chinese problem, it was still busy seeking ways to keep the Russians out of Tibet. It is hard, from the standpoint of the 1960s, not to feel that Hardinge and McMahon were in this respect tilting at windmills.

Given the fact, fundamental to the whole concept of the Anglo-Russian Convention of 1907, that neither the British nor the Russians would, even if they could, in any circumstances establish anything like a protectorate over Tibet, then it was highly unrealistic to believe that Tibet could remain indefinitely as anything but a part of China. Hence, the long-term British interest was the securing of as favourable an Anglo-Chinese settlement of the Tibetan question as possible: and, moreover, that any settlement was probably better than none. Perhaps, had the Chinese Revolution not provided such a tempting moment of Chinese weakness, the Indian Government would have come to this conclusion which was certainly understood by diplomatists like Sir John Jordan. Unfortunately, in 1912 Lord Hardinge, who really should have known better, allowed himself to be persuaded that the Chinese might now be excluded permanently from contact with the British northeast frontier.[33] The Simla Conference, instead of being directed towards the acquisition of as friendly a Chinese neighbour as possible, aimed at having no Chinese neighbour at all.

Without a Chinese neighbour there was clearly no point in obtaining a Chinese-accepted Himalayan border. The device of the McMahon Line on the Simla Convention map was really nothing more than an added bonus of doubtful value. McMahon can hardly have believed that it would bind the Chinese, even if they did sign the Convention. Looking back from the vantage-point of the 1960s, we can see that the Simla Conference was really something of a disaster. Here was a weak China and a Tibet peculiarly vulnerable to British pressure both at the same conference table on British territory. This was the most favourable opportunity the Indian Government would ever have to settle the Himalayan border. The British allowed the opportunity to pass, and let the Conference break down over the issue, really quite academic as far as the basic British interests were concerned, of the alignment of the Inner-Outer Tibet border. They did so in great part because of their reaction to the Chinese policy on the Assam border during 1910 and 1911 and their inability, in this frame of mind, to overlook the

[33] As Owen Lattimore has shrewdly perceived, the British Imperial Government could never really reconcile itself to the idea of a successful Asian power as its neighbour. The lesson of the possibility of Asian self-rule might be only too well learnt by Britain's Indian subjects. Hence the idea of confirming the Chinese in possession of Tibet, whatever its practical advantages, was too alien to the mind of the Indian Government to receive very serious consideration. See Owen Lattimore, *Inner Asian Frontiers of China*, New York, 1951, pp. 236–7.

immediate possibilities of the Chinese collapse in Lhasa. The moment when the British decided to ignore the logic of Morley's policy of non-interference in Tibet was without doubt, we now can see, one of the great turning-points in Asian history: from it evolved the present Sino-Indian crisis. There is a certain irony in the way in which the independent Indian Government has clung to the illusory gains of the period 1912–14, apparently unaware that in them lie the roots of their present dilemma. Why Mr. Nehru, while declaring himself committed to a policy of friendship, of peaceful coexistence, with Communist China, should have adhered with such tenacity to those symbols, at least in Chinese eyes, of British Imperialism, the Simla Convention and the McMahon Line notes, is one of the mysteries of the twentieth century. If this book does no more than suggest that there is indeed a mystery here requiring solution, then it will have achieved its purpose.

APPENDICES

APPENDIX VIII

An agreement entered into by Changjoi Satrajah, Sreng Satrajah, Cheeng Dundoo Satrajah, of Naregoon and Tong Dabee Rajah, Cheng Dundoo Bramee, Poonjai Bramee, of Takhal Tooroom, dated 24 Maug 1250 B.S.—1844[1]

It having been ordered by His Lordship the Governor-General in Council that we should be allowed annually one-third of the whole of the proceeds of Koreeahpara Dwar, *viz.*, 5,000 Rupees, we voluntarily pledge ourselves to adhere to the following terms most strictly:

1st.—We pledge ourselves to be satisfied, now and for ever, with the above-mentioned sum of 5,000 Rupees, and relinquish all right over any proceeds that may accrue from the Dwar.

2nd.—In our traffic we pledge ourselves to confine our dealings to the established market places at Oodalgooree and Mungle Dye, and never interfere with the ryots, neither will we allow any of our Booteahs to commit any acts of oppression.

3rd.—We have relinquished all power in the Dwar, and can no longer levy any rent from the ryots.

4th.—We agree to apply to the British Courts at Mungle Dye for redress in all our grievances in their Territories.

5th.—Should we ever infringe any of the foregoing terms, we shall forfeit our right to the above pension.

FRANS JENKINS,
Agent, Governor-General.

[1] Aitchison, *Treaties*, op. cit., XIV (1929), p. 90.

It is not clear who the six named chiefs were; but it seems more than probable that the three *Satrajahs* were Sherdukpen from Shergaon (? Naregoon). Takhal Tooroom may possibly be Talungdzong.

It is hard to see how this agreement can be taken to mean that the chiefs in question have accepted British protection: all they say is that they agree to take Rs. 5,000 per annum in exchange for the surrender to the British of their rights in the Kariapara Duar, and that when in British territory they will abide by British law.

APPENDIX IX

Treaty signed by Captains Reid and Campbell and Chang-dandoo Namang Leden and Dao Nurhoo, Bhutia Rajas, on 28 January 1853, at Kurreahparah, Zillah Darrung[1]

We, Changdandoo Raja Namang Leden, Raja Dao Nurhoo Raja, being deputed by the Deba Rajas to carry letters of friendship to the Agent, Governor-General, North-East Frontier, desiring that the former friendly relations which existed between the Government of India and our Lhassa Government (lately disturbed by the mis-behaviour of one of our Gellings) should be again resumed, and being ourselves desirous above all things that peace should exist between our Government and that of India, do (now that we are assured the Government of India do not intend to invade our country) hereby solemnly declare that all military force in excess of what is required to maintain order in our own country shall be immediately withdrawn, and the soldiers sent to their houses, and should the peace be ever broken by us, we shall consider that all claims to the Rs. 5,000 hitherto paid yearly to our Government by the Government of India shall be forfeited, and that our trade with the people of the plains shall be put a stop to.

All this we of our own good will agree to and swear to in the presence of Captains Reid and Campbell, signing the agreement as copied out in Bhutia language from the Bengali copy made by Tuchka Mahomed Darogah.

And moreover, with regard to the followers and others of the Gelling who have come down to the plains for protection, we promise not to molest them, but hope, with the good help of the Agent, Governor-General, to make friends with them and persuade them to return to their own country.

[1] Aitchison, *Treaties*, op. cit., XII (1931), p. 154.

The signatories of this agreement were acting on behalf of the Deba Rajas of Tawang. Who were the Deba Rajas? They were either the authorities of Tawang monastery or, perhaps more probably, the two Dzongpön of the Tibetan district of Tsöna.

It is hard to see how this treaty can be read to mean that the Tawang authorities had acknowledged that they had come under British sovereignty.

APPENDIX X

Agreement entered into by the Meyong Abors on 5 November 1862[1]

Whereas it is expedient to adopt measures for maintaining the integrity of the British territory in the District of Luckhimpoor, Upper Assam, on the Meyong Abor Frontier, and for preserving peace and tranquillity, and whereas by virtue of a letter No. 11 of 11th October 1862, from the Officiating Commissioner of Assam, transmitting orders from the Government of Bengal conveyed in a letter No. 265-T., dated 8th August 1862, from the Officiating Junior Secretary to the Government of Bengal, the Deputy Commissioner of Luckhimpoor has been authorized to proceed in this matter, an Engagement to the following effect has been entered into with the Meyong Abors this 5th day of November A.D. 1862 at Camp Lalee Mookh:

Article 1

Offences committed by the Meyong Abors in a time of hostility towards the British Government, and for which the assembled heads of villages have sued for pardon, are overlooked and peace is re-established.

Article 2

The limit of the British territory which extends to the foot of the hills is recognized by the Meyong Abors, who hereby engage to respect it.

Article 3

The British Government will take up positions on the frontier in the plains, will establish stations, post guards, or construct forts, or open roads, as may be deemed expedient, and the Meyong Abors will not take umbrage at such arrangements, or have any voice in such matters.

Article 4

The Meyong Abors recognize all persons residing in the plains in the vicinity of the Meyong Hills as British subjects.

[1] Aitchison, *Treaties*, op. cit., XII (1931), pp. 156–9.

Article 5
The Meyong Abors engage not to molest or to cross the frontier for the purpose of molesting residents in the British territory.

Article 6
The communications across the frontier will be free both for the Meyong Abors and for any persons British subjects, going to the Meyong villages for the purpose of trading or other friendly dealings.

Article 7
The Meyong Abors shall have access to markets and places of trade which they may think fit to resort to; and on such occasions they engage not to come armed with their spears and bow and arrows, but merely carry their daos.

Article 8
Any Meyong Abors desiring to settle in or occupy lands in the British territory engage to pay such revenue to Government as may be fixed upon by the Deputy Commissioner; the demand, in the first instance, to be light.

Article 9
The Meyong Abors engage not to cultivate opium in the British territory or to import it.

Article 10
In the event of any grievance arising or any dispute taking place between the Meyong Abors and the British territory, the Abors will refrain from taking the law into their own hands, but they will appeal to the Deputy Commissioner for redress and abide by his decision.

Article 11
To enable the Meyong Abors of the eight khels or communities, who submit to this engagement, to keep up a Police for preventing any marauders from resorting to the plains for sinister purposes, and to enable them to take measures for arresting any offenders, the Deputy Commissioner on behalf of the British Government, agrees that the communities referred to shall receive yearly the following articles:

100 Iron hoes
80 Bottles of rum
30 Maunds of salt
2 Seers of Abkaree opium
2 Maunds of tobacco

Article 12
The articles referred to above, which will be delivered for the first year on the signing of this enagement, will hereafter be delivered

from year to year to the representatives of the eight khels or communities of the Meyong Abors as aforesaid on their meeting the Deputy Commissioner at Lalee Mookh or at any other convenient place on the Meyong Doar side.

Article 13

On the occasion of meeting the Deputy Commissioner, the Meyong Abors in earnest of their continued friendly feeling, engage to make a tribute offering of a mithun, pigs, and fowls, in exchange for which they will obtain usual suitable acknowledgements.

Article 14

In the event of Meyong Abors infringing or failing to act up to any of the provisions of this engagement, it will be considered null and void, and will no longer have effect.

Article 15

The original of the above engagement, which is drawn up in English, will remain with the Deputy Commissioner of Luckhimpoor, Upper Assam, and a counterpart or copy will be furnished to the subscribing Meyong Abors.

Article 16

In ratification of the above engagement contained in fifteen paragraphs the Deputy Commissioner of Luckhimpoor, Assam, on behalf of the British Government, puts his hand and seal, and the recognised headmen or Chiefs of the eight khels or communities of the Meyong Abors affix their signatures or marks, this 5th day of November A.D. 1862.

H. S. BIVAR, MAJOR,
*Depy. Commr., 1st Class, Luckhimpoor,
and Agent, Govr.-Genl., North-East Frontier.*

On behalf of the community of Munkoo	Lomjur Gham, his mark
	Taukoor ,, ,, ,,
	Yabang ,, ,, ,,
	Chapeur ,, ,, ,,
	Taying ,, ,, ,,
On behalf of the community of Ramkong	Pooruding Gham, his mark
	Azragi ,, ,, ,,
	Kakoh ,, ,, ,,
	Koling ,, ,, ,,
	Goling ,, ,, ,,
	Daling ,, ,, ,,

On behalf of the community of Bokoong	Moozung Gham, his mark
	Sootam ,, ,, ,,
	Gandal ,, ,, ,,
	Bidoo ,, ,, ,,
	Takoor ,, ,, ,,
	Yaleng ,, ,, ,,
On behalf of the community of Padamneh	Kerie Gham, his mark
	Taddang ,, ,, ,,
	Tuttoo ,, ,, ,,
On behalf of the community of Kemi	Tassee Gham, his mark
	Somuing ,, ,, ,,
	Takokh ,, ,, ,,
	Taneeh ,, ,, ,,
	Takoom ,, ,, ,,
	Takor ,, ,, ,,
	Loling ,, ,, ,,
	Lomeh ,, ,, ,,
On behalf of the community of Lekang	Basing Gham, his mark
On behalf of the village of Galong	Taming Gham, his mark
	Takir ,, ,, ,,
	Tussif ,, ,, ,,
	Dookang ,, ,, ,,
On behalf of the village of Ledoom	Looking Gham, his mark
	Taying ,, ,, ,,

Note. Very similar agreements were entered into with other Abor groups in 1862 and 1863. In each case the clear distinction was made between British territory 'which extends to the foot of the hills' and the territory of the tribes. There can be no doubt that the frontier following this foothills alignment was the British international boundary in the sense that the British sovereignty stopped there.

These agreements were directed to controlling the Abors while they were on British territory and to preventing them from unsettling the frontier. As far as their internal affairs were concerned, these treaties permitted the British no concern provided British territory was not affected.

There is nothing, in fact, in these agreements which would forbid the Abor communities concerned to enter into treaty relations with the Tibetans or Chinese or, for that matter, any other Power.

APPENDIX XI

Tom Browns from Central Asia

The arrival at Rugby in 1913 of four Tibetan youths is one of the more unexpected by-products of the Chinese Revolution and its consequences on the Tibetan plateau. The whole episode, moreover, provides an admirable example of the political complexities which could face the British in their dealings with their Tibetan neighbours; and, as such, it deserves relating.

The idea of providing a Western education for a number of carefully selected youths was not particularly novel. The Indian Government had been thinking, since at least the days of the Younghusband Mission, about starting training projects in India for young Tibetans. The matter had been discussed with the Panchen Lama in 1905–6, and there can be no doubt that Bell explored its possibilities in great detail with the Dalai Lama during the latter's residence in Darjeeling in 1910–12. There was evidence that Tibetans were already going off for training in both Russia and Japan; and it seemed reasonable enough that in these circumstances a class of British-trained Tibetans should be created. Thus when, after returning to Tibet, the Dalai Lama in August 1912 proposed that 'some energetic and clever sons of respectable families' in Tibet be sent to England, the Indian Government was prepared to co-operate. In early 1913 the youths selected turned up at the British Trade Agency at Gyantse, where their companion, a Tibetan official called Lungshar, presented Gould with a request from the Dalai Lama for 'four first-class educations at Oxford College, London'.[1]

At this time Basil Gould was about to go to England on leave. The Indian Government, therefore, decided that he should guide the four Tibetans through the difficult first few weeks of their journey away from the 'roof of the world'. The boys were also to be accompanied on their trip by Lungshar and his wife and by the Sikkimese policeman Laden La, whose son, Sonam Topge, was also going to the United Kingdom for his schooling. The four boys were Mondo, who was a monk and aged 17, Kyipup, aged 16, Gongkar, also 16, and Rinchengang, 11 years old. Their party included two Tibetan

[1] Gould, *Jewel in the Lotus*, op. cit., p. 27.

599

servants. Gould and his charges reached England in April 1913. The Tibetan boys settled down at 'The Warren', Heath End, Farnham, where they began to learn English under the supervision of the Berlitz School of Languages while their future movements were being considered.[2]

From the outset the British found Lungshar something of a nuisance. In theory no more than the official escort for the boys, in fact Lungshar regarded himself (and may well have been so regarded by the Dalai Lama) as a Tibetan ambassador at large. Before leaving India he had been detected in intrigues with Japanese agents in Calcutta, who hoped, it seemed, that the boys could be diverted to Japan for their education—a further piece of evidence that Japan was developing very wide Central Asian interests.[3] No sooner in England than Lungshar began to talk about going to Germany, to the United States and to other countries, including, by implication, Russia. He also demanded formal interviews with King George V and with members of the British Cabinet. Lungshar tried to set up his own house, a kind of Tibetan Embassy, in London, away from Laden La, whose task it was to keep the Tibetan official under close supervision.[4] Lungshar's popularity with the India Office, who were responsible for the Tibetans' welfare in England, was not increased when his wife undertook, with considerable success, the seduction of one of the Tibetan boys. Lungshar could not be confined to Farnham for ever. He was able to visit London on occasions, when his movements were closely watched by the Special Branch of Scotland Yard, who found him meeting one Mukandi Lal, an Indian undergraduate at Hertford College, Oxford, with 'advanced views'.[5] Lungshar also established relations with the Chinese Legation in London, but the India Office were unable to find out why. Within three months of Lungshar's arrival in England the India Office were trying to get the Indian Government to persuade the Dalai Lama to recall this troublesome Tibetan. The Dalai Lama, who seems to have attached some importance to Lungshar's mission, and who, many years later, was to make Lungshar one of his most trusted and influential advisers, refused.[6] Lungshar, therefore, was able to remain in Europe until mid-1914.

[2] FO 535/16, no. 223, Gould to Bell, 9 April 1913, and Gould to IO, 30 April 1913.

[3] FO 535/16, no. 223, Gould to Bell, 9 April 1913.

[4] PEF 1913/76, no. 1937/13, Gould to IO, 14 May 1913.

[5] PEF 1913/76, Scotland Yard to IO, 31 January 1914.

[6] FO 371/1612, no. 35182, IO to FO, 29 July 1913.

For more about Lungshar's subsequent career, see Richardson, *Tibet*, op. cit.

The British would have liked to deny that Lungshar possessed any diplomatic status at all. They did not trust him, and they were worried lest his presence should lead to Russian protests under the 1907 Convention. However, it was appreciated that the Russians, in early 1913, had rather weakened their case in this particular respect, when they allowed Dorjiev to bring from Tibet fifteen boys to be educated in Russian schools. Dorjiev had also brought with him letters and presents from the Dalai Lama to the Tsar, which the latter had accepted.[7] Hence there were precedents, as well as good political reasons, for Lungshar's communication of gifts and messages from the Lama to King George.[8] On 28 June 1913, therefore, Lungshar was received by the King at Buckingham Palace.[9] The Dalai Lama's gifts were handed over. They were valued at £1,000. In return, King George presented to the Lama gifts worth £1,127 19s. 4d., including photographs of the King and Queen, paintings of Buckingham Palace and the Houses of Parliament, a set of the coins of the United Kingdom, a telescope (rather a cheap one, costing £22 5s., which Dollonds thought was quite good enough for a Tibetan Lama), a set of the *Encyclopaedia Britannica*, a silk scarf from Liberty's, a carriage and harness, a pair of sporting guns, some Irish table linen, and a pair of gold lions on marble pedestals. What the Dalai Lama thought of this assemblage is not recorded.

When Lungshar and the four boys reached England no decision had yet been made as to the place of their schooling. Gould records that, after a discussion between Sir A. Hirtzl, J. E. Shuckburgh and Gould, Harrow, Eton and Wellington were rejected and Rugby decided upon as just the place to educate Tibetans.[10] This story is not entirely borne out by the archives, which suggest that the first school considered was Cheltenham.[11] This was rejected only when it was discovered that three sons of President Yuan Shih-k'ai and a son of the Chinese Minister in London were also down for this establishment. The India Office asked the Foreign Office whether the headmaster of Cheltenham might be persuaded to refuse the Chinese boys; but the Foreign Office opinion that Yuan's sons were certainly a more prestigious addition to the school enrolment than four Tibetans ended this official attempt to meddle in public school politics. Rugby was then decided upon. Thus there was never a

---

[7] FO 371/1609, no. 7570, Buchanan to Grey, 13 February 1913.

[8] FO 371/1611, no. 26551, Minute by Gregory, 10 June 1913.

[9] FO 371/1613, no. 48043, Secretary of State to Viceroy, 17 October 1913.

[10] Gould, *Jewel in the Lotus*, op. cit., p. 29.

[11] See correspondence in FO 371/1612, nos. 40328 and 40329.

chance that the OE or OH tie would have turned out to be a passport to Tibet.[12]

Rinchengang, the youngest of the four boys, after Rugby went on to the Universities of London and Birmingham, where he studied electrical engineering. Gongkar went on to a short period of officer training with the Indian Army; but his death of pneumonia in 1917 deprived the Tibetan armed forces of the benefit of his experience.[13] The other boys all returned to Tibet, where they were effectively sidetracked by the Tibetan establishment.[14] By the 1940s, when Heinrich Harrer made his way to Lhasa, only one of them was still alive.[15]

The episode of the Tibetan boys had clear political implications. Lord Hardinge justified the venture on the grounds that 'in our opinion the success of the experiment is most important; the education of Tibetan youths will otherwise be entrusted to the Russians or Japanese'.[16] Both the Chinese and Japanese made attempts to 'get at' Lungshar and his charges while they were in Calcutta. Lungshar's audience with King George V, and his presentation of gifts from the Dalai Lama to Lord Crewe, Sir Edward Grey, and the Lord High Commissioner for Education as well, was a direct parallel to the activities of Dorjiev in St. Petersburg. The British discovered, however, that the establishment of such relations with the Tibetans was not an unmixed blessing. In the first place, there remained the risk of Russian protest. As was clear from at least 1907, the British could not really use Dorjiev as an excuse for their own contacts with the Dalai Lama. Somehow, Dorjiev was always engaged upon purely 'religious' business such as was authorised by the 1907 Convention: no one could claim that Lungshar was solely concerned with religious matters. In the second place, once a Tibetan envoy like Lungshar reached England, it was very difficult to stop him attempting to open up relations with Powers other than the British. This sort of diplomacy, far from securing British influence in Tibet, seemed to involve the risk of widening Tibetan international

[12] David Macdonald has it that two of the boys went to Harrow; but he is in error. See D. Macdonald, *Twenty Years in Tibet*, London, 1932, p. 218.

[13] Gongkar is said to have fallen in love with and tried to marry an English girl, but to have been refused permission for such a match by the Dalai Lama. Macdonald, *Twenty Years*, op. cit., p. 219.

[14] Gould, *Jewel in the Lotus*, op. cit., pp. 29–30: see also Bell, *Dalai Lama*, op. cit., p. 203.

[15] H. Harrer, *Seven Years in Tibet*, London, 1953.

[16] FO 535/16, no. 135, Viceroy to Secretary of State, 6 March 1913.

[17] FO 535/16, no. 223, Gould to IO, 30 April 1913.

relations to an undesirable degree. All this reinforced the British conclusion that the best status for Tibet was not full independence; rather, Tibet chained to a nominal Chinese suzerainty was a Tibet which would be forced to confine its quest for foreign assistance to British India.

The experiment of the education in England of the four Tibetan boys can hardly be described as a success. The boys made no significant contribution in later life to the development of Tibet; and they certainly made the Tibetans no more pro-British than would have been the case had they remained at home. The experiment was not repeated during the remaining period of British rule in the Indian subcontinent.

APPENDIX XII

Sir John Jordan's Memorandum to the Wai-chiao-pu, dated Peking, 17 August 1912[1]

In a conversation with His Excellency Yuan Shih-kai on the 23rd of June His Britannic Majesty's Minister referred to the Chinese Military Expedition which was being organised against Tibet and gave His Excellency clearly to understand that the Tibetan question could be easily settled by friendly negotiation at a later date but that the use of force at that time would seriously prejudice an amicable arrangement. His Excellency Yuan Shih-kai assured Sir John Jordan that there was no intention of incorporating Tibet in China and that the Treaties would be scrupulously observed.

On June 29 His Majesty's Minister informed Mr. Lu Chenghsiang that His Majesty's Government would not tolerate any attempt to reduce Tibet, who had independent Treaty relations with Great Britain, to the condition of a Province of China and he warned the Chinese Government that grave complications might ensue if the Chinese expedition crossed the frontier into Tibet.

In consequence of a visit paid to him in a few days previously by the Vice-Minister for Foreign Affairs, His Majesty's Minister again saw His Excellency Yuan Shih-kai on the 16th instant and, in reply to his enquiry, received the most emphatic assurances that there was no intention either of ordering the expedition to cross the frontier into Tibet or of incorporating that country in the Provinces of China. These assurances have been noted and duly reported to His Majesty's Government who will doubtless welcome them as indicating China's intention scrupulously to observe Treaty engagements. At the same time His Majesty's Government consider it to be in the interest of harmonious relations that they should now state clearly their policy in regard to Tibet. His Majesty's Minister had the honour to inform His Excellency Yuan Shih-kai that a communication in this respect would shortly be submitted to the Chinese Government and he now begs, under instructions from Sir Edward Grey, to make the following definite statement of that policy.

(1) His Majesty's Government, while they have formally recog-

[1] PEF 1912/69, no. 3460/12, Jordan to Grey, 17 August 1912.

nised the 'suzerain rights' of China in Tibet, have never recognised, and are not prepared to recognise, the right of China to intervene actively in the internal administration of Tibet which should remain, as contemplated by the Treaties, in the hands of the Tibetan Authorities, subject to the right of Great Britain and China, under Article I of the Convention of April 27, 1906, to take such steps as may be necessary to secure the due fulfilment of Treaty stipulations.

(2) On these grounds His Majesty's Government must demur altogether to the conduct of Chinese officers in Tibet during the last two years in assuming all administrative power in the country and to the doctrine propounded in Yuan Shih-kai's Presidental Order of the 21st of April 1912 that Tibet is to be 'regarded as on an equal footing with the Provinces of China Proper', and that 'all administrative matters' connected with that country 'will come within the sphere of internal administration'.

His Majesty's Government formally decline to accept such a definition of the political status of Tibet and they must warn the Chinese Republic against any repetition by Chinese officers of the conduct to which exception has been taken.

(3) While the right of China to station a representative, with a suitable escort, at Lhasa, with authority to advise the Tibetans as to their foreign relations, is not disputed, His Majesty's Government are not prepared to acquiesce in the maintenance of an unlimited number of Chinese troops either at Lhasa or in Tibet generally.

(4) His Majesty's Government must press for the conclusion of a written agreement on the foregoing lines as a condition precedent to extending their recognition to the Chinese Republic.

(5) In the meantime all communication with Tibet via India must be regarded as absolutely closed to the Chinese and will only be reopened on such conditions as His Majesty's Government may see fit to impose when an Agreement has been concluded on the lines indicated above.

This does not apply to the withdrawal of the present Chinese garrison at Lhasa, who, as Yuan Shih-kai has already been informed, are at liberty to return to China via India if they wish to do so.

Sir John Jordan has the honour to request the Wai Chiao Pu to favour him with a reply to this Memorandum.

(Signed) J. N. JORDAN.

APPENDIX XIII

Russo-Mongol Agreement of 21 October/3 November 1912, and the attached Protocol concerning Russian trade in Mongolia[1]

A. *The Agreement*

IN accordance with the desire unanimously expressed by the Mongolians to maintain the national and historic constitution of their country, the Chinese troops and authorities were obliged to evacuate Mongolian territory, and Djebzoun Damba-Khutukhta was proclaimed Ruler of the Mongolian people. The old relations between Mongolia and China thus came to an end.

At the present moment, taking into consideration the facts stated above, as well as the mutual friendship which has always existed between the Russian and Mongolian nations, and in view of the necessity of defining exactly the system regulating trade between Russia and Mongolia:

The actual State Councillor Jean Korostovetz, duly authorised for the purpose by the Imperial Russian Government; and

The protector of the ten thousand doctrines Sain-noin Khan Namnan-Souroun, President of the Council of Ministers of Mongolia;

The plenipotentiary Tchin-souzouktou Tzin-van Lama Tzerin-Tchimet, Minister of the Interior;

The plenipotentiary Daitzin-van Handa-dorji, of the rank of Khan-erdeni, Minister for Foreign Affairs:

The plenipotentiary Erdeni Dalai Tzun-van Gombo-Souroun, Minister of War;

The plenipotentiary Touchetou Tzun-van Tchakdorjab, Minister of Finance; and

The plenipotentiary Erdeni Tzun-van Namsarai, Minister of Justice;

Duly authorised by the Ruler of the Mongolian nation, by the Mongolian Government and by the ruling Princes, have agreed as follows:

ARTICLE 1—The Imperial Russian Government shall assist Mongolia to maintain the autonomous régime which she has

[1] MacMurray, *China Treaties*, op. cit., Vol. II, pp. 992–6.

established, as also the right to have her national army, and to admit neither the presence of Chinese troops on her territory nor the colonisation of her land by the Chinese.

ARTICLE 2—The Ruler of Mongolia and the Mongolian Government shall grant, as in the past, to Russian subjects and trade the enjoyment in their possessions of the rights and privileges enumerated in the protocol annexed hereto.

It is well understood that there shall not be granted to other foreign subjects in Mongolia rights not enjoyed there by Russian subjects.

ARTICLE 3—If the Mongolian Government finds it necessary to conclude a separate treaty with China or another foreign Power, the new treaty shall in no case either infringe the clauses of the present agreement and of the protocol annexed thereto, or modify them without the consent of the Imperial Russian Government.

ARTICLE 4—The present amicable agreement shall come into force from the date of its signature.

In witness whereof the respective plenipotentiaries, having compared the two texts, Russian and Mongolian, of the present agreement, made in duplicate, and having found the two texts to correspond, have signed them, have affixed thereto their seals, and have exchanged texts.

Done at Urga on the 21st October, 1912, corresponding to the 24th day of the last autumn month of the 2nd year of the reign of the Unanimously Proclaimed, according to the Mongolian calendar (November 3, 1912).

B. *The Protocol annexed to the Agreement*

BY virtue of the enactment of the second article of the agreement, signed on this date between Actual State Councillor, Ivan Korostovetz, Plenipotentiary of the Imperial Russian Government, and the President of the Council of Ministers of Mongolia, Sain-noin Khan Namman-Souroun, the Protector of ten thousand doctrines; the Plenipotentiary and Minister of the Interior, Tchin-souzouk-tou Tzin-van Lama Tzerin-Tchimet; the Plenipotentiary and Minister for Foreign Affairs, Daitzin-van Handa-dorji of the rank of Khanerdeni; the Plenipotentiary and Minister of War, Erdeni Dalai Tzun-van Gombo-Souroun; the Plenipotentiary and Minister of Finance, Touchetou Tzun-van Tchakdorjab; and the Plenipotentiary and Minister of Justice, Erdeni Tzun-van Namsarai, on the authority of the Ruler of Mongolia, the Mongolian Government, and the Ruling Princes; the above-named Plenipotentiaries have come to an agreement respecting the following articles, in which are set forth the rights and privileges of Russian subjects in Mongolia, some of which they already enjoy, and the rights and privileges of Mongolian subjects in Russia:

ARTICLE 1—Russian subjects, as formerly, shall enjoy the right to reside and move freely from one place to another throughout Mongolia; to engage there in every kind of commercial, industrial, and other business; and to enter into agreements of various kinds, whether with individuals, or firms, or institutions, official or private, Russian, Mongolian, Chinese, or foreign.

ARTICLE 2—Russian subjects, as formerly, shall enjoy the right at all times to import and export, without payment of import and export dues, every kind of product of the soil and industry of Russia, Mongolia and China, and other countries, and to trade freely in it without payment of any duties, taxes, or other dues.

The enactments of this (2nd) article shall not extend to combined Russo-Chinese undertakings, or to Russian subjects falsely declaring themselves to be owners of wares not their property.

ARTICLE 3—Russian credit institutions shall have the right to open branches in Mongolia, and to transact all kinds of financial and other business, whether with individuals, institutions, or companies.

ARTICLE 4—Russian subjects may conclude purchases and sales in cash or by an exchange of wares (barter), and they may conclude agreements on credit. Neither 'khoshuns' nor the Mongolian Treasury shall be held responsible for the debts of private individuals.

ARTICLE 5—The Mongolian authorities shall not preclude Mongolians or Chinese from completing any kind of commercial agreement with Russian subjects, from entering into their personal service, or into commercial and industrial undertakings formed by them. No rights of monopoly as regards commerce or industry shall be granted to any official or private companies, institutions, or individuals in Mongolia. It is, of course, understood that companies and individuals who have already received such monopolies from the Mongolian Government previous to the conclusion of this agreement shall retain their rights and privileges until the expiry of the period fixed.

ARTICLE 6—Russian subjects shall be everywhere granted the right, whether in towns or 'khoshuns', to hold allotments on lease, or to acquire them as their own property for the purpose of organising commercial industrial establishments, and also for the purpose of constructing houses, shops, and stores. In addition, Russian subjects shall have the right to lease vacant lands for cultivation. It is, of course, understood that these allotments shall be obtained and leased for the above-specified purposes, and not for speculative aims. These allotments shall be assigned by agreement with the Mongolian Government in accordance with existing laws of Mongolia, everywhere excepting in sacred places and pasture lands.

ARTICLE 7—Russian subjects shall be empowered to enter into agreements with the Mongolian Government respecting the working of minerals and timber, fisheries, &c.

ARTICLE 8—The Russian Government shall have the right, in agreement with the Government of Mongolia, to appoint consuls in those parts of Mongolia it shall deem necessary.

Similarly, the Mongolian Government shall be empowered to have Government agents at those frontier parts of the Empire where, by mutual agreement, it shall be found necessary.

ARTICLE 9—At points where there are Russian consulates, as also in other localities of importance for Russian trade, there shall be allotted, by mutual agreement between Russian consuls and the Mongolian Government, special 'factories' for various branches of industry and the residence of Russian subjects. These 'factories' shall be under the exclusive control of the above-mentioned consuls, or of the heads of Russian commercial companies if there be no Russian consul.

ARTICLE 10—Russian subjects, in agreement with the Mongolian Government, shall retain the right to institute, at their own cost, a postal service for the dispatch of letters and the transit of wares between various localities in Mongolia and also between specified localities and points on the Russian frontier. In the event of the construction of 'stages' and other necessary buildings, the regulations set forth in article 6 of this protocol must be duly observed.

ARTICLE 11—Russian consuls in Mongolia, in case of need, shall avail themselves of Mongolian Government postal establishments and messengers for the dispatch of official correspondence, and for other official requirements, provided that the gratuitous requisition for this purpose shall not exceed one hundred horses and thirty camels per month. On every occasion, a courier's passport must be obtained from the Government of Mongolia. When travelling, Russian consuls, and Russian officials in general, shall avail themselves of the same establishments upon payment. The right to avail themselves of Mongolian Government 'stages' shall be extended to private individuals, who are Russian subjects, upon payment for the use of such 'stages' of amounts which shall be determined in agreement with the Mongolian Government.

ARTICLE 12—Russian subjects shall be granted the right to sail their own merchant-vessels on, and to trade with the inhabitants along the banks of, those rivers and their tributaries which, running first through Mongolia, subsequently enter Russian territory. The Russian Government shall afford the Government of Mongolia assistance in the improvement of navigation on these rivers, the establishment of the necessary beacons, &c. The Mongolian Government authorities shall assign on these rivers places for the berthing of vessels, for the construction of wharves and warehouses, for the preparation of fuel, &c., being guided on these occasions by the enactments of article 6 of the present protocol.

ARTICLE 13—Russian subjects shall have the right to avail themselves of all land and water routes for the carriage of wares and the droving of cattle, and, upon agreement with the Mongolian authorities, they may construct, at their own cost, bridges, ferries, &c., with the right to exact a special due from persons crossing over.

ARTICLE 14—Travelling cattle, the property of Russian subjects, may stop for the purpose of resting and feeding. In the event of prolonged halts being necessary, the local authorities shall assign proper pasturage areas along travelling cattle routes, and at cattle markets. Fees shall be exacted for the use of these pasturing areas for periods exceeding three months.

ARTICLE 15—The established usage of the Russian frontier population harvesting (hay), as also hunting and fishing, across the Mongolian border shall remain in force in the future without any alteration.

ARTICLE 16—Agreements between Russian subjects and institutions on the one side and Mongolians and Chinese on the other may be concluded verbally or in writing, and the contracting parties may present the agreement concluded to the local Government authorities for certification. Should the latter see any objection to certifying the contract, they must immediately notify the fact to a Russian consul, and the misunderstanding which has arisen shall be settled in agreement with him.

It is hereby laid down that contracts respecting real estate must be in written form, and presented for certification and confirmation to the proper Mongolian Government authorities and a Russian consul. Documents bestowing rights to exploit natural resources require the confirmation of the Government of Mongolia.

In the event of disputes arising over agreements concluded verbally or in writing, the parties may settle the matter amicably with the assistance of arbitrators selected by each party. Should no settlement be reached by this method, the matter shall be decided by a mixed legal commission.

There shall be both permanent and temporary mixed legal commissions. Permanent commissions shall be instituted at the places of residence of Russian consuls, and shall consist of the consul, or his representative, and a delegate of the Mongolian authorities of corresponding rank. Temporary commissions shall be instituted at places other than those already specified, as cases arise, and shall consist of representatives of a Russian consul and the prince of that 'khoshun' to which the defendant belongs or in which he resides. Mixed commissions shall be empowered to call in as experts persons with a knowledge of the case from among Russian subjects, Mongolians, and Chinese. The decisions of mixed legal commissions shall be put into execution without delay, in the case of Russian subjects through a Russian consul, and in the case of Mongolians and Chinese through the prince of the 'khoshun' to which the defendant belongs or in which he is resident.

ARTICLE 17—The present protocol shall come into force from the date of its signature.

In witness whereof, the respective plenipotentiaries, finding, upon comparison of the two parallel texts of the present protocol—Russian and Mongol—drawn up in duplicate, that the texts correspond, have signed each of them, affixed their seals, and exchanged texts.

Executed at Urga, the 21st October, 1912 (o.s.), and by the Mongolian calendar, on the twenty-fourth day of the last autumn moon, in the second year of the administration of the 'Unanimously Proclaimed'.

In the original follow the signature of M. Korostovetz, Minister Plenipotentiary; and in the Mongol language the signatures of the President of the Mongolian Council of Ministers, and the Plenipotentiaries, the Ministers of the Interior, Foreign Affairs, Finance, and of Justice.

APPENDIX XIV

Treaty between Tibet and Mongolia, said to have been signed at Urga on 11 January 1913[1]

Whereas Mongolia and Tibet, having freed themselves from the Manchu Dynasty and separated themselves from China, have become independent States, and whereas the two States have always professed one and the same religion, and to the end that their ancient mutual friendships may be strengthened: on the part of the Government of the Sovereign of the Mongolian people—Nikta Biliktu Da Lama Rabdan, acting Minister of Foreign Affairs and Assistant Minister General and Manlai Caatyr Bei-Tzu Damdinsurun; on the part of the Dalai Lama, ruler of Tibet—Gujir Tsanshib Kanchen Lubsan-Agwan, Donir Agwan Choinzin Tschichamtso, manager of the bank, and Gendun-Galsan, secretary, have agreed on the following:

Article I

The Dalai Lama, Sovereign of Tibet, approves of and acknowledges the formation of an independent Mongolian State, and the proclamation on the 9th day of the 11th month of the year of the Pig, of the master of the Yellow Faith Je-tsun Dampa Lama as the Sovereign of the land.

Article II

The Sovereign of the Mongolian people Je-tsun Dampa Lama approves and acknowledges the formation of an independent State and the proclamation of the Dalai Lama as Sovereign of Tibet.

[1] H. G. C. Perry-Ayscough and R. B. Otter-Barry, *With the Russians in Mongolia*, London, 1913, pp. 10–13.

The Tibetan representative who signed this document is said to have been Dorjiev. There exist some doubts as to the validity of this treaty. See Bell, *Tibet*, op. cit., pp. 150–1.

For reports of this treaty, see the *Daily Telegraph*, 15 January 1913, and *The Times*, 10 February 1913.

Sazonov, the Russian Foreign Minister, reported the signing of this treaty to Sir G. Buchanan, the British Ambassador at St. Petersburg. Sazonov said the treaty, in his opinion, was not valid: it was '*nul et non avenu*'. See FO 371/1608, Buchanan to Grey, 17 January 1913.

Article III

Both States shall take measures, after mutual consideration, for the prosperity of the Buddhist faith.

Article IV

Both States, the Mongolian and the Tibetan, shall henceforth, for all time, afford each other aid against dangers from without and from within.

Article V

Both States, each on its own territory, shall afford mutual aid to their subjects, travelling officially and privately on religious or State business.

Article VI

Both States, the Mongolian and the Tibetan, shall, as formerly, carry on mutual trade in the produce of their lands—in goods, cattle, &c., and likewise open industrial institutions.

Article VII

Henceforth transactions on credit shall be allowed only with the knowledge and permission of official institutions; without such permission no claims shall be examined by Government Institutions.

Should such agreements have been entered into before the conclusion of the present treaty, and should the parties thereto be unable to settle matters amicably, while the loss suffered is great, the payment of such debts may be enforced by the said institutions, but in no case shall the debts concern the *Shabinars* and *Hoshuns*.[2]

Article VIII

Should it be necessary to supplement the articles of this treaty, the Mongolian and Tibetan Governments shall appoint special Plenipotentiaries, who shall come to an agreement according to the circumstances then existing.

Article IX

The present treaty shall come into force on the date of the signature thereof.

Plenipotentiaries of the Mongolian Government: Acting Minister of Foreign Affairs Biliktu Da Lama Rabdan and Assistant Minister General and Manlai Caatyr Bei-Tzu Damdinsurun.

[2] Perry-Ayscough and Otter-Barry give the following explanation of these terms: '*Shabinars*—people who depend from the Court of Hu-tuk-tu and pay taxes to the Court Department. *Hoshun*—principality'.

Plenipotentiaries of the Dalai Lama, Sovereign of Tibet: Gujir Tsanshib Kanchen Lubsan-Agwan, Donir Agwan Choinzin Tschimastso, manager of the bank of Tibet, and Gendun-Glasan, secretary.

According to the Mongolian chronology, on the 4th day of the 12th month of the second year of 'Him who is exalted by all'.

According to the chronology of Tibet, in the year of the Water-Mouse, on the same month and day.

APPENDIX XV

*Russo-Chinese Declaration and exchange of notes regarding
Outer Mongolia, 23 October/5 November 1913*[1]

A. *Declaration*

The Imperial Government of Russia having formulated the
principles which it took as the basis of its relations with China as
regards Outer Mongolia, and the Government of the Chinese
Republic having stated its approval of the said principles, the two
governments have agreed upon the following:

I.—Russia recognizes that Outer Mongolia is under the
suzerainty of China.

II.—China recognizes the autonomy of Outer Mongolia.

III.—Recognizing the exclusive right of the Mongols of Outer
Mongolia to provide, themselves, for the internal administration of Autonomous Mongolia and to settle all questions
of a commercial and industrial nature relating to that
country. China binds itself not to intervene in these matters
and consequently will not send troops into Outer Mongolia, nor will it keep any civil or military official there,
and it will abstain from colonizing in that country. It is
understood, however, that a Dignitary sent by the Chinese
Government may reside at Urga, accompanied by the
necessary subordinates and an escort. The Chinese Government may, moreover, in case of need, keep in certain
localities of Outer Mongolia, to be determined in the
course of the conferences provided for in Article V of the
present agreement, agents for the protection of the interests
of its subjects.

Russia, on its side, binds itself not to keep troops in
Outer Mongolia, with the exception of consular guards,
and not to intervene in any branch of the administration
of this country, and to abstain from colonizing.

IV.—China declares itself ready to accept the good offices of

[1] MacMurray, *China Treaties*, op. cit., Vol. II, pp. 1066–7.

Russia for the establishment of its relations with Outer Mongolia, in conformity with the principles above set forth and with the stipulations of the Russo-Mongolian Commercial Protocol of October 21, 1912 (November 3, 1912).

V.—Questions pertaining to the interests of Russia and of China in Outer Mongolia and resulting from the new state of affairs in this country will be the subject of subsequent conferences.

In faith whereof the undersigned, duly authorized to this effect, have signed the present Declaration and have affixed their seals thereto.

Done at Peking, in duplicate, October 23/November 5, nineteen hundred and thirteen, corresponding to the fifth day of the eleventh month of the second year of the Chinese Republic.

(Signed) SUN PAO-CHI.
(Signed) B. KROUPENSKY.

B. *Note from the Russian Minister at Peking to the Chinese Minister of Foreign Affairs, 23 October/5 November 1913*[2]

In proceeding to the signature of the Declaration under to-day's date relating to Outer Mongolia, the undersigned Envoy Extraordinary and Minister Plenipotentiary of His Majesty the Emperor of all the Russias, duly authorized to this effect, has the honor to declare, in the name of his government, to His Excellency Mr. Sun Pao-Chi, Minister of Foreign Affairs of the Chinese Republic, the following:

1.—Russia recognizes that the territory of Outer Mongolia forms a part of the territory of China.

2.—As regards questions of a political and territorial nature, the Chinese Government shall come to an agreement with the Russian Government through negotiations in which the authorities of Outer Mongolia shall take part.

3.—The conferences provided for in Article V of the Declaration shall take place between the three interested parties, who shall designate for this purpose a place where their delegates shall meet.

[2] The Chinese Minister for Foreign Affairs simultaneously addressed to the Russian Minister a Note embodying, word for word, the four numbered paragraphs set forth in the Note printed here.

4.—Autonomous Outer Mongolia shall comprise the regions which have been under the jurisdiction of the Chinese Amban of Urga, of the Tartar General of Uliassutai, and of the Chinese Amban of Kobdo. Inasmuch as there are no detailed maps of Mongolia and as the boundaries of the administrative divisions of this country are uncertain, it is agreed that the exact boundaries of Outer Mongolia, as well as the boundary between the district of Kobdo and the district of Altai, shall be the subject of the subsequent conferences provided for in Article V of the Declaration.

The undersigned takes advantage of this opportunity to renew to His Excellency Mr. Sun Pao-chi the assurances of his very high consideration.

(Signed) B. KROUPENSKY.

APPENDIX XVI

The McMahon Line Notes, March 1914[1]

A. *McMahon to the Lönchen Shatra, 24 March 1914*

To
   Lönchen Shatra
      Tibetan Plenipotentiary.

In February last you accepted the India-Tibet frontier from the Isu Razi Pass to the Bhutan frontier, as given in the map[2] (two sheets), of which two copies are herewith attached, subject to the confirmation of your Government and the following conditions:

(a) The Tibetan ownership of private estates on the British side of the frontier will not be disturbed.

(b) If the sacred places of Tso Karpo and Tsari Sarpa fall within a day's march of the British side of the frontier, they will be included in Tibetan territory and the frontier modified accordingly.

I understand that your Government have now agreed to this frontier subject to the above two conditions.

You wished to know whether certain dues now collected by the Tibetan Government at Tsöna Jong and in Kongbu and Kham from the Monpas and Lopas for articles sold may still be collected. Mr Bell has informed you that such details will be settled in a friendly spirit, when you have furnished him with the further information, which you promised.

The final settlement of this India-Tiber frontier will help to prevent causes of future dispute and thus cannot fail to be of great advantage to both Governments.

Delhi   (Signed) A. H. McMahon,
                              British Plenipotentiary.

---

[1] Aitchison, *Treaties*, XIV (1929), pp. 34–35.

[2] This map (the original scale was eight miles to the inch) was first published in *An Atlas of the Northern Frontier of India*, Government of India, Ministry of External Affairs, New Delhi, 1960.

618

B. *The Lönchen Shatra to McMahon, 25 March 1914* (Translation)

To

Sir Henry McMahon,
British Plenipotentiary to the China-Tibet Conference.

As it was feared that there might be friction in future unless the boundary between India and Tibet is clearly defined, I submitted the map, which you sent me in February last, to Lhasa for orders. I have now received orders from Lhasa, and I accordingly agree to the boundary as marked in red in the two copies of the maps signed by you subject to the conditions, mentioned in your letter, dated the 24th March, sent to me through Mr Bell. I have signed and sealed the two copies of the maps. I have kept one copy here and return herewith the other.

Sent on the 29th day of the 1st Month of the Wood-Tiger year (25th March 1914) by Lönchen Shatra, the Tibetan Plenipotentiary.

Seal of the
Lönchen Shatra.

APPENDIX XVII

Convention between Great Britain, China and Tibet, initialled at Simla, 27 April 1914[1]

His Majesty the King of Great Britain and Ireland and of the British Dominions beyond the Seas, Emperor of India, His Excellency the President of the Republic of China, and His Holiness the Dalai Lama of Tibet, being sincerely desirous to settle by mutual agreement various questions concerning the interests of their several States on the Continent of Asia, and further to regulate the relations of their several Governments, have resolved to conclude a Convention on this subject and have nominated for this purpose their respective plenipotentiaries, that is to say:

His Majesty the King of Great Britain and Ireland and of the British Dominions beyond the Seas, Emperor of India, the Hon'ble Sir Arthur Henry McMahon, Knight Grand Cross of the Royal Victorian Order, Knight Commander of the Most Eminent Order of the Indian Empire, Companion of the Most Exalted Order of the Star of India, Secretary to the Government of India, Foreign and Political Department;

---

[1] This text is printed in *The Boundary Question between China and Tibet*, Peking, 1940, pp. 133–9, but with the date and the ratification clause omitted.

The text of the Simla Convention of 27 April 1914, which was initialled by the Chinese plenipotentiary, Chen I-fan, is not quite the same as the text of 3 July, which the Tibetan and British plenipotentiaries declared to be binding, and which Chen I-fan refused to initial or sign.

The differences between the two texts are stated here in notes, which also make reference to an earlier draft of the Convention which was presented to the Simla Conference on 17 February 1914.

Article IX of both texts of the Convention refers to a map. This is a fairly small-scale map of Tibet, and parts of India and China, which should not be confused with the map (in two sheets) which is mentioned in the McMahon-Lönchen Shatra Notes of 24–25 March 1914. The map which accompanied the 27 April text, as well as that for the 3 July text (which is slightly different in its markings), has been printed in *An Atlas of the Northern Frontier of India*, Government of India, Ministry of External Affairs, New Delhi, 1960.

His Excellency the President of the Republic of China, Monsieur Ivan Chen, Officer of the Order of the Chia Ho;

His Holiness the Dalai Lama of Tibet, Lönchen Ga-den Shatra Pal-jor Dorje; who having communicated to each other their respective full powers and finding them to be in good and due form have agreed upon and concluded the following Convention in eleven Articles:

Article I

The Conventions specified in the Schedule to the present Convention shall, except in so far as they may have been modified by, or may be inconsistent with or repugnant to, any of the provisions of the present Convention, continue to be binding upon the High Contracting Parties.

Article II

The Governments of Great Britain and China recognizing that Tibet is under the suzerainty of China, and recognizing also the autonomy of Outer Tibet, engage to respect the territorial integrity of the country, and to abstain from all interference in the administration of Outer Tibet (including the selection and installation of the Dalai Lama), which shall remain in the hands of the Tibetan Government at Lhasa.

The Government of China engages not to convert Tibet into a Chinese province. The Government of Great Britain engages not to annex Tibet or any portion of it.

Article III

Recognising the special interest of Great Britain, in virtue of the geographical position of Tibet, in the existence of an effective Tibetan Government, and in the maintenance of peace and order in the neighbourhood of the frontiers of India and adjoining States, the Government of China engages, except as provided in Article 4 of this Convention, not to send troops into Outer Tibet, nor to station civil or military officers, nor to establish Chinese colonies in the country. Should any such troops or officials remain in Outer Tibet at the date of the signature of this Convention, they shall be withdrawn within a period not exceeding three months.

The Government of Great Britain engages not to station military or civil officers in Tibet (except as provided in the Convention of September 7, 1904, between Great Britain and Tibet) nor troops (except the Agents' escorts), nor to establish colonies in that country.

Article IV

The foregoing Article shall not be held to preclude the continuance of the arrangement by which, in the past, a Chinese high official with suitable escort has been maintained at Lhasa, but it is hereby provided that the said escort shall in no circumstances exceed 300 men.

Article V

The Governments of China and Tibet engage that they will not enter into any negotiations of agreements regarding Tibet with one another, or with any other Power, excepting such negotiations and agreements between Great Britain and Tibet as are provided for by the Convention of September 7, 1904, between Great Britain and Tibet and the Convention of April 27, 1906, between Great Britain and China.

Article VI

Article III of the Convention of April 27, 1906, between Great Britain and China is hereby cancelled, and it is understood that in Article IX(d) of the Convention of September 7, 1904, between Great Britain and Tibet the term 'Foreign Power' does not include China.

No less favourable treatment shall be accorded to British commerce than to the commerce of China or the most favoured nation.

Article VII

(a) The Tibet Trade Regulations of 1893 and 1908 are hereby cancelled.

(b) The Tibetan Government engages to negotiate with the British Government new Trade Regulations for Outer Tibet to give effect to Articles II, IV and V of the Convention of September 7, 1904, between Great Britain and Tibet without delay; provided always that such Regulations shall in no way modify the present Convention except with the consent of the Chinese Government.[2]

Article VIII

The British Agent who resides at Gyantse may visit Lhasa with his escort whenever it is necessary to consult with the Tibetan Government regarding matters arising out of the Convention of September 7, 1904, between Great Britain and Tibet, which it has been found impossible to settle at Gyantse by correspondence or otherwise.

[2] In an earlier draft, put before the Conference on 17 February 1914, the following was added to this Article:
'(c). The Government of China is hereby released from its engagements under Article III of the Convention of 1890 between Great Britain and China to prevent acts of aggression from the Tibetan side of the Tibet-Sikkim frontier.'

Article IX

For the purpose of the present Convention the borders of Tibet, and the boundary between Outer and Inner Tibet, shall be shown in red and blue respectively on the map attached hereto.[3]

Nothing in the present Convention shall be held to prejudice the existing rights of the Tibetan Government in Inner Tibet, which include the power to select and appoint the high priests of monasteries and to retain full control in all matters affecting religious institutions.[4]

Article X

In case of differences between the Governments of China and Tibet in regard to questions arising out of this Convention the aforesaid Governments engage to refer them to the British Government for equitable adjustment.[5]

Article XI

The present Convention will take effect from the date of signature.

The English, Chinese and Tibetan texts of the present Convention have been carefully examined and found to correspond, but in the event of there being any difference of meaning between them the English text shall be authoritative.[6]

In token whereof the respective Plenipotentiaries have signed and sealed this Convention, three copies in English, three in Chinese and three in Tibetan.

[3] See Map no. 20 on pp. 554–5 for these boundaries. This map, on a small scale, contains the only indication of the McMahon Line to emerge formally from the Simla Conference in its tripartite form.

[4] The 17 February 1914 draft had this phrase to end the last sentence: 'to issue appointment orders to chiefs and local officers, and to collect all customary rents and taxes.'

[5] In the 17 February draft this article read as follows:

'The Government of China hereby agrees to pay compensation amounting to Rs. 4,28,840 due for losses incurred by Nepalese and Ladakhis in Tibet in consequence of acts done by Chinese soldiers and officials in that country.'

In the 3 July version of the Convention, Article X, at the request of the Russian Government, was removed: the Russians argued that it in effect conferred upon the British a protectorate over Tibet. It was replaced by the second paragraph of Article XI relating to the comparison of texts. The 3 July text is the one usually printed, e.g. in Richardson, *Tibet*, op. cit., pp. 268–72, and in Aitchison, *Treaties*, op. cit., Vol. XIV (1929), pp. 35–38. It should be remembered, however, that it was the 27 April text which the Chinese representative to the Simla Conference, Chen I-fan, actually initialled.

[6] The second paragraph of Article XI was used to replace Article X in the 3 July text.

Done at Simla this 27th day of April, A.D. one thousand nine hundred and fourteen.[7]

Initials and seals of Sir H. McMahon,
Chen I-fan,[8]
The Lönchen Shatra.

Schedule

1. Convention between Great Britain and China relating to Sikkim and Tibet, signed at Calcutta the 17th March 1890.

2. Convention between Great Britain and Tibet, signed at Lhasa the 7th September 1904.

3. Convention between Great Britain and China respecting Tibet, signed at Peking the 27th April 1906.

The notes exchanged are to the following effect:

1. It is understood by the High Contracting Parties that Tibet forms part of Chinese territory.

2. After the selection and installation of the Dalai Lama by the Tibetan Government, the latter will notify the installation to the Chinese Government, whose representative at Lhasa will then formally communicate to His Holiness the titles consistent with his dignity, which have been conferred by the Chinese Government.

3. It is also understood that the selection and appointment of all officers in Outer Tibet will rest with the Tibetan Government.

4. Outer Tibet shall not be represented in the Chinese Parliament or in any other similar body.

5. It is understood that the escorts attached to the British Trade Agencies in Tibet shall not exceed seventy-five per centum of the escort of the Chinese Representative at Lhasa.

6. The Government of China is hereby released from its engagements under Article III of the Convention of March 17, 1890, between Great Britain and China, to prevent acts of aggression from the Tibetan side of the Tibet-Sikkim frontier.[9]

7. The Chinese high official referred to in Article IV will be free to enter Tibet as soon as the terms of Article III have been fulfilled to the satisfaction of representatives of the three signatories to this Convention, who will investigate and report without delay.

Initials and seals of Sir H. McMahon,
Chen I-fan,[10]
The Lönchen Shatra.

[7] The text printed in *Boundary Question*, op. cit., does not include the section relating to dates. The wording here is taken from the printed 3 July text; hence the omission of the Chinese and Tibetan dates.

[8] Chen I-fan, of course, did not initial the 3 July text.

[9] In the 17 February draft this was included as part of Article VII.

[10] Chen I-fan did not, of course, initial the 3 July text.

Declaration appended to the 3 July 1914 text of the
Simla Convention[11]

We, the Plenipotentiaries of Great Britain and Tibet, hereby record the following Declaration to the effect that we acknowledge the annexed Convention as initialled to be binding on the Governments of Great Britain and Tibet, and we agree that so long as the Government of China withholds signature to the aforesaid Convention, she will be debarred from the enjoyment of all privileges acruing therefrom.

In token whereof we have signed and sealed this Declaration, two copies in English and two in Tibetan.

Done at Simla this third day of July, A.D. one thousand nine hundred and fourteen, corresponding with the Tibetan date, the tenth day of the fifth month of the Wood-Tiger year.

Seal of the
Dalai Lama
    (Signed)   A. HENRY McMAHON,
                British Plenipotentiary

Signature and seal
of the Lönchen Shatra   Seal of the British
                    Plenipotentiary

Seal of the   Seal of the   Seal of the   Seal of the
Drepung Monastery Sera Monastery Gaden Monastery National
                                    Assembly

[11] FO 371/1931, IO to FO, 26 August 1914, enclosing McMahon's *Memorandum of the Tibet Conference.*

APPENDIX XVIII
Anglo-Tibet Trade Regulations, 1914[1]

Whereas by Article 7 of the Convention concluded between the Governments of Great Britain, China and Tibet on the 3rd day of July, A.D. 1914, the Trade Regulations of 1893 and 1908 were cancelled and the Tibetan Government engaged to negotiate with the British Government new Trade Regulations for Outer Tibet to give effect to Articles II, IV and V of the Convention of 1904;

His Majesty the King of the United Kingdom of Great Britain and Ireland, and of the British Dominions beyond the Seas, Emperor of India, and His Holiness the Dalai Lama of Tibet have for this purpose named as their Plenipotentiaries, that is to say:

His Majesty the King of Great Britain and Ireland and of the British Dominions beyond the Seas, Emperor of India, Sir A. H. McMahon, G.C.V.O., K.C.I.E., C.S.I.;

His Holiness the Dalai Lama of Tibet, Lönchen Ga-den Shatra Pal-jor Dorje;

And whereas Sir A. H. McMahon and Lönchen Ga-den Shatra Pal-jor Dorje have communicated to each other since their respective full powers and have found them to be in good and true form, the following regulations have been agreed upon:

I. The area falling within a radius of three miles from the British Trade Agency site will be considered as the area of such Trade Mart.

It is agreed that British subjects may lease lands for the building of houses and godowns at such Marts. This arrangement shall not be held to prejudice the right of British subjects to rent houses and godowns outside the Marts for their own accommodation and the storage of their goods. British subjects desiring to lease building sites shall apply through the British Trade Agent to the Tibetan Trade Agent. In consultation with the British Trade Agent the Tibetan Trade Agent will assign such or other suitable building sites without unnecessary delay. They shall fix the terms of leases in conformity with the existing laws and rates.

---

[1] Aitchison, *Treaties*, XIV (1929), pp. 39–41.

II. The administration of the Trade Marts shall remain with the Tibetan authorities, with the exception of the British Trade Agency sites and compounds of the rest-houses, which will be under the exclusive control of the British Trade Agents.

The Trade Agents at the Marts and the Frontier Officers shall be of suitable rank, and shall hold personal intercourse and correspondence with one another on terms of mutual respect and friendly treatment.

III. In the event of disputes arising at the Marts or on the routes to the Marts between British subjects and subjects of other nationalities, they shall be enquired into and settled in personal conference between the British and Tibetan Trade Agents at the nearest Mart. Where there is a divergence of view the law of the country to which the defendant belongs shall guide.

All questions in regard to rights, whether of property or person, arising between British subjects, shall be subject to the jurisdiction of the British Authorities.

British subjects, who may commit any crime at the Marts or on the routes to the Marts, shall be handed over by the Local Authorities to the British Trade Agent at the Mart nearest the scene of offence, to be tried and punished according to the laws of India, but such British subjects shall not be subjected by the Local Authorities to any ill-usage in excess of necessary restraint.

Tibetan subjects, who may be guilty of any criminal act towards British subjects, shall be arrested and punished by the Tibetan Authorities according to law.

Should it happen that a Tibetan subject or subjects bring a criminal complaint against a British subject or subjects before the British Trade Agent, the Tibetan Authorities shall have the right to send a representative or representatives of suitable rank to attend the trial in the British Trade Agent's Court. Similarly in cases in which a British subject or subjects have reason to complain against a Tibetan subject or subjects, the British Trade Agent shall have the right to send a representative or representatives to the Tibetan Trade Agent's Court to attend the trial.

IV. The Government of India shall retain the right to maintain the telegraph lines from the Indian frontier to the Marts. Tibetan messages will be duly received and transmitted by these lines. The Tibetan Authorities shall be responsible for the protection of the telegraph lines from the Marts to the Indian frontier, and it is agreed that all persons damaging the lines or interfering with them in any way or with the officials engaged in the inspection and maintenance thereof shall at once be severely punished.

V. The British Trade Agents at the various Trade Marts now or hereafter to be established in Tibet may make arrangements for the carriage and transport of their posts to and fro from the frontier of India. The couriers employed in conveying these posts shall receive all possible assistance from the Local Authorities, whose districts they traverse, and shall be accorded the same protection and facilities as the persons employed in carrying the despatches of the Tibetan Government.

No restrictions whatever shall be placed on the employment by British officers and traders of Tibetan subjects in any lawful capacity. The persons so employed shall not be exposed to any kind of molestation or suffer any loss of civil rights, to which they may be entitled as Tibetan subjects, but they shall not be exempted from lawful taxation. If they be guilty of any criminal act, they shall be dealt with by the Local Authorities according to law without any attempt on the part of their employers to screen them.

VI. No rights of monopoly as regards commerce or industry shall be granted to any official or private company, institution, or individual in Tibet. It is of course understood that companies or individuals, who have already received such monopolies from the Tibetan Government previous to the conclusion of this agreement, shall retain their rights and privileges until the expiry of the period fixed.

VII. British subjects shall be at liberty to deal in kind or money, to sell their goods to whomsoever they please, to hire transport of any kind, and to conduct in general their business transactions in conformity with local usage and without any vexations, restrictions or oppressive exactions whatever. The Tibetan Authorities will not hinder the British Trade Agents or other British subjects from holding personal intercourse or correspondence with the inhabitants of the country.

It being the duty of the police and Local Authorities to afford efficient protection at all times to the persons and property of the British subjects at the Marts and along the routes to the Marts, Tibet engages to arrange effective Police measures at the Marts and along the routes to the Marts.

VIII. Import and export of the following articles:

> arms, ammunition, military stores, liquors and intoxicating or narcotic drugs

may at the option of either Government be entirely prohibited, or permitted only as either Government on their own side may think fit to impose.

IX. The present Regulations shall be in force for a period of ten years reckoned from the date of signature by the two Plenipotentiaries; but, if no demand for revision be made on either side within six months after the end of the first ten years the Regulations shall remain in force for another ten years from the end of the first ten years; and so it shall be at the end of each successive ten years.

X. The English and Tibetan texts of the present Regulations have been carefully compared, but in the event of their being any difference of meaning between them the English text shall be authoritative.

XI. The present Regulations shall come into force from the date of signature.

Done at Simla this third day of July, A.D., one thousand nine hundred and fourteen, corresponding with the Tibetan date, the tenth day of the fifth month of the Wood-Tiger year.

> Seal of the
> Dalai Lama.

> Signature of the
> Lönchen Shatra   (Signed) A. HENRY MCMAHON,
> *British Plenipotentiary*

> Seal of the
> Lönchen Shatra   Seal of the
>   British Plenipotentiary

Seal of the   Seal of the   Seal of the   Seal of the
Drebung Monastery Sera Monastery Gaden Monastery National
                                                      Assembly

Note. What effect did the Trade Regulations of 1908 and 1914 have on the Indo-Tibetan trade? The figures for the Bengal-Tibet trade over the period 1902–18 rather suggest that the Trade Regulations had a surprisingly small impact. The highest figures during this period are for 1907–8, when the 1908 Regulations could hardly have had time to take effect. Only by 1917–18 was the Bengal-Tibet trade again approaching the value it had attained in 1907–8. These figures show, however, a direct relationship between the value of the trade and the political stability of the frontier. The lowest figures, for 1903–4, are in the period when the Younghusband Mission was in progress, first at Khambajong and then on the road to Lhasa. With the advance of Chao Erh-feng's troops towards Lhasa there is another dramatic drop in the trade figures, which then begin to rise again from 1914, when the probability of a Chinese reconquest of Central Tibet was clearly decreasing.

The Bengal figures do not by any means represent the entire Indo-Tibetan trade. In 1914–15, for example, the total value of trade between India and Tibet has been valued at Rs. 50,56,000, of which the Bengal component represented just over a half. Of the rest, by far the most important single element was the import of shawl wool from Western Tibet to Ladakh and to the Panjab. The Gartok trade mart, which was intended to bring about a vast increase both in the size and the profitability of the trade in shawl wool, proved to be rather a disappointment. The Indian Government were never, in the period covered by this book, able to secure the removal of the ancient restrictions on trade in this region, such as the Tibetan duties on goods passing through frontier points like Rudok and Demchok.

The trade between Bengal and Tibet by way of Gyantse and Yatung was considerable less in value than the trade between Tibet and China passing through Tachienlu. For example, in 1913 the Tachienlu trade was valued at £265,313, while the Bengal-Tibet trade for the same period was worth c. £134,000.

PEF 1912/22, no. 2493/13, Bell to India, 13 May 1913; no. 2283/14, Gould to India, 8 May 1914; no. 2285/15, Bell to India, 3 April 1915; no. 2236/16, Bell to India, 21 April 1916; no. 3444/18, Campbell to India, 7 April 1918: Great Britain, Foreign Office, *Tibet*, Peace Handbook no. 70, London, 1920, p. 64.

Figures for the Bengal-Tibet Trade, 1902–18

Year	Exports from Bengal	Imports to Bengal	Export from Bengal of treasure	Import to Bengal of treasure	Total
1902–3	8,10,677	9,63,165	37,765	95,225	19,06,833
1903–4	3,92,361	3,56,822	64,544	23,220	8,36,947
1904–5	7,38,946	4,10,794	83,400	2,02,054	14,35,194
1905–6	13,52,508	11,27,488	3,47,372	2,01,010	30,28,378
1906–7	9,47,628	11,53,226	1,84,190	1,72,494	24,57,538
1907–8	11,86,276	17,41,943	2,63,425	6,48,840	38,40,484
1908–9	13,36,853	12,53,683	8,260	4,78,790	30,77,586
1909–10	7,48,362	5,36,433	55,700	1,97,587	15,38,082
1910–11	8,25,141	9,56,214	10,550	2,26,935	20,18,840
1911–12	6,71,382	12,45,283	17,844	2,12,446	21,46,955
1912–13	8,61,554	8,30,745	2,000	1,91,480	18,85,779
1913–14	6,82,906	7,99,678	12,276	2,46,453	17,41,313
1914–15	11,09,357	11,77,183	1,33,000	1,95,245	26,14,785
1915–16	11,62,257	15,30,885	87,618	3,55,240	31,36,000
1916–17	11,33,723	17,09,577	59,000	3,15,085	32,17,585
1917–18	11,86,488	21,05,435	5,000	2,68,958	35,66,881

APPENDIX XIX

Tripartite Agreement between Russia, Mongolia and China relating to Outer Mongolia, signed at Kiachta 25 May/ 7 June 1915[1]

A. The Agreement

The President of the Republic of China,

His Imperial Majesty, the Emperor of all the Russias, and

His Holiness the Bogdo (Great) Cheptsun (Venerable) Damba (Sacred) Hut'ukht'u (Reincarnated) Khan (Ruler) of Outer Mongolia,

Animated by a sincere desire to settle by mutual agreement various questions created by a new state of things in Outer Mongolia, have named for that purpose their Plenipotentiary Delegates, that is to say:

The President of the Republic of China, General Pi Kuei-fang and Monsieur Ch'ên Lu, Envoy Extraordinary and Minister Plenipotentiary of China to Mexico;

His Imperial Majesty the Emperor of all the Russias, His Councillor of State Alexandre Miller, Diplomatic Agent and Consul General in Mongolia; and

His Holiness the Bogdo Cheptsun Damba Hut'ukht'u Khan of Outer Mongolia, E'êrh-tê-ni Cho-nang Pei-tzu Sê-lêng-tan, Vice-Chief of Justice, and T'uhsieh-t'u Ch'in Wang Ch'a-K'o-tu-êrh-cha-pu, Chief of Finance,

Who having verified their respective full powers found in good and due form, have agreed upon the following:

ARTICLE I—Outer Mongolia recognises the Sino-Russian Declaration and the Notes exchanged between China and Russia of the 5th day of the 11th month of the 2nd year of the Republic of China (23 October 1913).[2]

ARTICLE II—Outer Mongolia recognises China's suzerainty, China and Russia recognise the autonomy of Outer Mongolia forming part of Chinese territory.

[1] MacMurray, *China Treaties*, op. cit., Vol. II, pp. 1239–44.
[2] 5 November 1913, new style. See Appendix XV.

ARTICLE III—Autonomous Mongolia has no right to conclude international treaties with foreign powers respecting political and territorial questions.

As respects questions of a political and territorial nature in Outer Mongolia, the Chinese Government engages to conform to Article II of the Note exchanged between China and Russia on the 5th day of the 11th month of the 2nd Year of the Republic of China (23rd October 1913).

ARTICLE IV—The title: 'Bogdo Cheptsun Damba Kut'ukht'u Khan of Outer Mongolia' is conferred by the President of the Republic of China. The calendar of the Republic as well as the Mongol calendar of cyclical signs are to be used in official documents.

ARTICLE V—China and Russia, conformably to Articles II and III of the Sino-Russian Declaration of the 5th day of the 11th month of the 2nd year of the Republic of China (23rd October 1913), recognise the exclusive right of the Autonomous Government of Outer Mongolia to attend to all the affairs of its internal administration and to conclude with foreign powers international treaties and agreements respecting all questions of a commercial and industrial nature concerning autonomous Mongolia.

ARTICLE VI—Conformably to the same Article III of the Declaration, China and Russia engage not to interfere in the system of autonomous internal administration existing in Outer Mongolia.

ARTICLE VII—The military escort of the Chinese Dignitary at Urga provided for by Article III of the above-mentioned Declaration is not to exceed two hundred men. The military escorts of his Assistants at Uliassutai, at Kobdo, and at Mongolian-Kiachta are not to exceed fifty men each. If, by agreement with the Autonomous Government of Outer Mongolia, Assistants of the Chinese Dignitary are appointed in other localities of Outer Mongolia, their military escorts are not to exceed fifty men each.

ARTICLE VIII—The Imperial Government of Russia is not to send more than one hundred and fifty men as consular guard for its representative at Urga. The military escorts of the Imperial consulates and vice-consulates of Russia, which have already been established or which may be established by agreement with the Autonomous Government of Outer Mongolia, are not to exceed fifty men each.

ARTICLE IX—On all ceremonial or official occasions the first place of honor is due to the Chinese Dignitary. He has the right, if necessary, to present himself in private audience with His Holiness Bogdo Cheptsun Damba Hut'ukht'u Khan of Outer Mongolia.

The Imperial representative of Russia enjoys the same right of private audience.

ARTICLE X—The Chinese Dignitary at Urga and his Assistants in the different localities of Outer Mongolia provided for by Article VII of this agreement are to exercise general control lest the acts of the autonomous Government of Outer Mongolia and its subordinate authorities may impair the suzerain rights and the interests of China and her subjects in Autonomous Mongolia.

ARTICLE XI—Conformably to Article IV of the Notes exchanged between China and Russia on the 5th day of the 11th month of the 2nd Year of the Republic of China (23rd October 1913), the territory of autonomous Outer Mongolia comprises the regions which were under the jurisdiction of the Chinese Amban at Urga, of the Tartar-General at Uliassutai and of the Chinese Amban at Kobdo; and connects with the boundary of China by the limits of the banners of the four aimaks of Khalka and of the district of Kobdo, bounded by the district of Houlounbouir (*i.e.* Hailar) on the East, by Inner Mongolia on the South, by the Province of Sinkiang on the South-West, and by the district of Altai on the West.

The formal delimitation between China and autonomous Mongolia is to be carried out by a special commission of delegates of China, Russia and autonomous Outer Mongolia, which shall set itself to the work of delimitation within a period of two years from the date of signature of the present Agreement.

ARTICLE XII—It is understood that customs duties are not to be established for goods of whatever origin they may be, imported by Chinese merchants into autonomous Outer Mongolia. Nevertheless, Chinese merchants shall pay all the taxes on internal trade which have been established in autonomous Outer Mongolia and which may be established therein in the future, payable by the Mongols of autonomous Outer Mongolia. Similarly the merchants of autonomous Outer Mongolia, when importing any kind of goods of local production into Inner China, shall pay all the taxes on trade which have been established in 'Inner China' and which may be established therein in the future, payable by Chinese merchants. Goods of foreign origin imported from autonomous Outer Mongolia into 'Inner China' shall be subject to the customs duties stipulated in the Regulations for land trade of the 7th year of the Reign of Kuang-Hsu (1881).

ARTICLE XIII—Civil and criminal actions arising between Chinese subjects residing in autonomous Outer Mongolia are to be examined and adjudicated by the Chinese Dignitary at Urga and by his Assistants in the other localities of autonomous Outer Mongolia.

ARTICLE XIV—Civil and criminal actions arising between Mongols of autonomous Outer Mongolia and Chinese subjects residing therein are to be examined and adjudicated conjointly by the Chinese Dignitary at Urga and his Assistants in the other localities of autonomous Outer Mongolia, or their delegates, and the Mongolian Authorities. If the defendant or the accused is a Chinese subject and the claimant or the complainant is a Mongol of autonomous Outer Mongolia, the joint examination and decision of the case are to be held at the Chinese Dignitary's place at Urga and at that of his Assistants in the other localities of autonomous Outer Mongolia; if the defendant or the accused is a Mongol of autonomous Outer Mongolia and the claimant or the complainant is a Chinese subject, the case is to be examined and decided in the same manner in the Mongolian yamen. The guilty are to be punished according to their own laws. The interested parties are free to arrange their disputes amicably by means of arbiters chosen by themselves.

ARTICLE XV—Civil and criminal actions arising between Mongols of autonomous Outer Mongolia and Russian subjects residing therein are to be examined and decided conformably to the stipulations of Article XVI of the Russo-Mongolian Commercial Protocol of 21st October 1912.[3]

ARTICLE XVI—All civil and criminal actions arising between Chinese and Russian subjects in Autonomous Outer Mongolia are to be examined and decided in the following manner; in an action wherein the claimant or the complainant is a Russian subject and the defendant or the accused is a Chinese subject, the Russian Consul personally or through his delegate participates in the judicial trial, enjoying the same rights as the Chinese Dignitary at Urga or his delegate or his Assistants in the other localities of Autonomous Outer Mongolia. The Russian Consul or his delegate proceeds to the hearing of the claimant and the Russian witnesses in the court in session, and interrogates the defendant and the Chinese witnesses through the medium of the Chinese Dignitary at Urga or his delegate or of his Assistants in the other localities of Autonomous Outer Mongolia; the Russian Consul or his delegate examines the evidence presented, demands security for 'revindica-

[3] 3 November 1912, new style. See Appendix XIII.

tions' and has recourse to the opinion of experts, if he considers such expert opinion necessary for the elucidation of the rights of the parties, etc.; he takes part in deciding and in the drafting of the judgment, which he signs with the Chinese Dignitary at Urga or his delegate or his Assistants in the other localities of Autonomous Outer Mongolia. The execution of the judgment constitutes a duty of the Chinese authorities.

The Chinese Dignitary at Urga and his Assistants in the other localities of Autonomous Outer Mongolia may likewise personally or through their delegates be present at the hearing of an action in the Consulates of Russia wherein the defendant or the accused is a Russian subject and the claimant or the complainant is a Chinese subject. The execution of the judgment constitutes a duty of the Russian authorities.

ARTICLE XVII—Since a section of the Kiachta-Urga-Kalgan telegraph line lies in the territory of Autonomous Outer Mongolia, it is agreed that the said section of the said telegraph line constitutes the complete property of the Autonomous Government of Outer Mongolia.

The details respecting the establishment on the borders of that country and Inner Mongolia of a station to be administered by Chinese and Mongolian employees for the transmission of telegrams, as well as the questions of the tariff for telegrams transmitted and of the apportionment of the receipts, etc., are to be examined and settled by a special commission of technical delegates of China, Russia and Autonomous Outer Mongolia.

ARTICLE XVIII—The Chinese postal institutions at Urga and Mongolian-Kiachta remain in force on the old basis.

ARTICLE XIX—The Autonomous Government of Outer Mongolia will place at the disposal of the Chinese Dignitary at Urga and of his Assistants at Uliassutai, Kobdo and Mongolian-Kiachta as well as of their staff the necessary houses, which are to constitute the complete property of the Government of the Republic of China. Similarly necessary grounds in the vicinity of the residence of the said staff are to be granted for their escorts.

ARTICLE XX—The Chinese Dignitary at Urga and his Assistants in the other localities of Autonomous Outer Mongolia and also their staffs are to enjoy the right to use the courier stations of the Autonomous Mongolian Government conformably to the stipulation of Article XI of the Russo-Mongolian Protocol of 21 October 1912.

ARTICLE XXI—The stipulations of the Sino-Russian Declaration and the Notes exchanged between China and Russia of the 5th day of the 11th month of the 2nd year of the Republic of China (23 October 1913), as well as those of the Russo-Mongolian Commercial Protocol of the 21 October 1912, remain in full force.

ARTICLE XXII—The present Agreement drawn up in triplicate in Chinese, Russian, Mongolian and French comes into force from the day of its signature. Of the four texts which have been duly compared and found to agree, the French text shall be authoritative in the interpretation of the Present Agreement.

Done at Kiachta the 7th day of the Sixth Month of the Fourth Year of the Republic of China corresponding to the Twenty-Fifth of May (Seventh of June), One Thousand Nine Hundred Fifteen.

B. *Notes exchanged*

1. *A. Miller to General Pi Kuei Fang and Ch'ên Lu, Chinese Delegates Plenipotentiary, 25 May/7 June 1915*

Kiachta, May 24/June 7, 1915.

The undersigned Delegate Plenipotentiary of Russia to the tripartite negotiations at Kiachta has the honor to acknowledge to their Excellencies Messieurs Pi Kuei-Fang and Ch'ên Lu, Delegates Plenipotentiary of the Republic of China to the tripartite negotiations at Kiachta, the receipt of the following note of this day's date:

'The undersigned Delegates Plenipotentiary of the Republic of China to the Tripartite negotiations at Kiachta, duly authorized for this purpose, have the honor, on proceeding to sign the tripartite agreement of this day's date relating to Autonomous Outer Mongolia, to declare in the name of their Government to His Excellency, Mr Miller, Imperial Delegate Plenipotentiary of Russia to the tripartite negotiations at Kiachta, as follows: From the day of signature of the present Sino-Russo-Mongolian agreement the Government of the Republic of China grants a full amnesty to all the Mongols who submitted to the Autonomous Government of Outer Mongolia; it leaves to all the Mongols of Outer Mongolia as of Inner Mongolia the freedom as before of residence and travel in the said regions. The Government of the Republic of China will not place any restraint upon Mongols going in pilgrimage to Urga to testify their veneration to His Holiness Bogdo Cheptsun Damba Hut'ukht'u Khan of Outer Mongolia.'

The undersigned seizes this occasion to renew to the Delegates Plenipotentiary of the Republic of China the assurances of his very high consideration.

(Signed) A. MILLER.

2. *A. Miller to General Pi Kuei Fang and Ch'ên Lu, Chinese Delegates Plenipotentiary, 25 May/7 June 1915* (Translation)

Kiachta, May 25/June 7, 1915.

The undersigned Imperial Delegate Plenipotentiary of Russia to the tripartite negotiations at Kiachta, duly authorized for this purpose, has the honor, on proceeding to sign the tripartite agreement of this day's date relating to Autonomous Outer Mongolia, to declare in the name of his Government to their Excellencies Messieurs Pi Kuei-Fang and Ch'ên-Lu, Delegates Plenipotentiary of the Republic of China to the tripartite negotiations at Kiachta as follows:

It is agreed that all the telegraph offices which are situated along that section of the Kalgan-Urga-Kiachta line which lies within Outer Mongolia and of which mention is made in Article XVII of the Agreement of Kiachta, are to be handed over by the Chinese officials to the Mongolian officials within a period at most of six months after the signing of the Agreement; and that the point of junction of the Chinese and Mongolian lines is to be fixed by the Technical Commission provided for in the aforesaid article.

The above is at the same time brought to the knowledge of the Delegates Plenipotentiary of the Autonomous Government of Outer Mongolia.

The undersigned seizes this occasion to renew to the Delegates Plenipotentiary of the Republic of China the assurances of his very high consideration.

(Signed) A. MILLER.[4]

[4] A note of identical tenor was simultaneously addressed to the Mongolian delegates; and replies embodying the same declaration were addressed by both Chinese and Mongolian delegates to the Russian delegate under the same date.

APPENDIX XX

(A) *Agreement between the Republic of India and the People's Republic of China on Trade and Intercourse between Tibet Region of China and India, signed at Peking on 29 April 1954*[1]

The Government of the Republic of India and the Central People's Government of the People's Republic of China,

Being desirous of promoting trade and cultural intercourse between Tibet Region of China and India and of facilitating pilgrimage and travel by the peoples of China and India,

Have resolved to enter into the present Agreement based on the following principles:

(1) mutual respect for each other's territorial integrity and sovereignty,

(2) mutual non-aggression,

(3) mutual non-interference in each other's internal affairs,

(4) equality and mutual benefit, and

(5) peaceful co-existence.

And for this purpose have appointed as their respective Plenipotentiaries:

The Government of the Republic of India, H.E. Nedyam Raghavan, Ambassador Extraordinary and Plenipotentiary of India accredited to the People's Republic of China; the Central People's Government of the People's Republic of China, H.E. Chang Han-fu, Vice-Minister of Foreign Affairs of the Central People's Government, who, having examined each other's credentials and finding them in good and due form, have agreed upon the following:

Article I

The High Contracting Parties mutually agree to establish Trade Agencies:

(1) The Government of India agrees that the Government of China may establish Trade Agencies at New Delhi, Calcutta and Kalimpong.

[1] *White Paper* I, op. cit., pp. 98–105.

638

(2) The Government of China agrees that the Government of India may establish Trade Agencies at Yatung, Gyantse and Gartok.

The Trade Agencies of both Parties shall be accorded the same status and same treatment. The Trade Agents of both Parties shall enjoy freedom from arrest while exercising their functions, and shall enjoy in respect of themselves, their wives and children who are dependent on them for livelihood freedom from search.

The Trade Agencies of both Parties shall enjoy the privileges and immunities for couriers, mail-bags and communications in code.

Article II

The High Contracting Parties agree that traders of both countries known to be customarily and specifically engaged in trade between Tibet Region of China and India may trade at the following places:

(1) The Government of China agrees to specify (1) Yatung, (2) Gyantse and (3) Phari as markets for trade. The Government of India agrees that trade may be carried on in India, including places like (1) Kalimpong, (2) Siliguri and (3) Calcutta, according to customary practice.

(2) The Government of China agrees to specify (1) Gartok, (2) Pulanchung (Taklakot), (3) Gyanima-Khargo, (4) Gyanima-Chakra, (5) Rampura, (6) Dongbra, (7) Puling-Sumdo, (8) Nabra, (9) Shangtse and (10) Tashigong as markets for trade; the Government of India agrees that in future, when in accordance with the development and need of trade between the Ari District of Tibet Region of China and India, it has become necessary to specify markets for trade in the corresponding district in India adjacent to the Ari District of Tibet Region of China, it will be prepared to consider on the basis of equality and reciprocity to do so.

Article III

The High Contracting Parties agree that pilgrimage by religious believers of the two countries shall be carried on in accordance with the following provisions:—

(1) Pilgrims from India of Lamaist, Hindu and Buddhist faiths may visit Kang Rimpoche (Kailas) and Mavam Tso (Manasarovar) in Tibet Region of China in accordance with custom.

(2) Pilgrims from Tibet Region of China of Lamaist and Buddhist faiths may visit Banaras, Sarnath, Gaya and Sanchi in India in accordance with custom.

(3) Pilgrims customarily visiting Lhasa may continue to do so in accordance with custom.

Article IV

Traders and pilgrims of both countries may travel by the following passes and route:

(1) Shipki La pass, (2) Mana pass, (3) Niti pass, (4) Kungri Bingri pass, (5) Darma pass, and (6) Lipu Lekh pass.

Also, the customary route leading to Tashigong along the valley of the Shangatsangpu (Indus) River may continue to be traversed in accordance with custom.

Article V

For travelling across the border, the High Contracting Parties agree that diplomatic personnel, officials and nationals of the two countries shall hold passports issued by their own respective countries and visaed by the other Party except as provided in Paragraphs 1, 2, 3 and 4 of this Article.

(1) Traders of both countries known to be customarily and specifically engaged in trade between Tibet Region of China and India, their wives and children who are dependent on them for livelihood and their attendants will be allowed entry for purposes of trade into India or Tibet Region of China, as the case may be, in accordance with custom on the production of certificates duly issued by the local government of their own country or by its duly authorised agents and examined by the border checkposts of the other Party.

(2) Inhabitants of the border districts of the two countries who cross the border to carry on petty trade or to visit friends and relatives may proceed to the border districts of the other Party as they have customarily done heretofore and need not be restricted to the passes and route specified in Article IV above and shall not be required to hold passports, visas or permits.

(3) Porters and mule-team drivers of the two countries who cross the border to perform necessary transportation services need not hold passports issued by their own country, but shall only hold certificates good for a definite period of time (three months, half a year or one year) duly issued by the local government of their own country or by its duly authorised agents and produce them for registration at the border checkposts of the other Party.

(4) Pilgrims of both countries need not carry documents of certification but shall register at the border checkposts of the other Party and receive a permit for pilgrimage.

(5) Notwithstanding the provisions of the foregoing paragraphs of this Article, either Government may refuse entry to any particular person.

(6) Persons who enter the territory of the other Party in accordance with the foregoing paragraphs of this Article may stay within its territory only after complying with the procedures specified by the other Party.

Article VI

The present Agreement shall come into effect upon ratification by both Governments and shall remain in force for eight (8) years. Extension of the present Agreement may be negotiated by the two Parties if either Party requests for it six (6) months prior to the expiry of the Agreement and the request is agreed to by the other Party.

Done in duplicate in Peking on the twentyninth day of April, 1954, in the Hindi, Chinese and English languages, all texts being equally valid.

(Signed) NEDYAM RAGHAVAN,
    Plenipotentiary of the
    Government of the
    Republic of India.

(Signed) CHANG HAN-FU,
    Plenipotentiary of the
    Central People's
    Government, People's
    Republic of China.

Note. It is interesting that in this Agreement there is no mention of any of the British treaties relating to Tibet. The question of the Trade Marts, for instance, is discussed without any reference to British precedents. There is a definite implication that the 1954 Sino-Indian Agreement not only replaced the British treaties relating to Tibet but cancelled them as well.

(B) *Notes Exchanged*

Indian Note
                                 Peking, April 29, 1954

Your Excellency Mr. Vice-Foreign Minister,

In the course of our discussions regarding the Agreement on Trade and Intercourse Between Tibet Region of China and India, which has been happily concluded today, the Delegation of the Government of the Republic of India and the Delegation of the Government of the People's Republic of China agreed that certain matters be regulated by an exchange of notes. In pursuance of this understanding, it is hereby agreed between the two Governments as follows:

(1) The Government of India will be pleased to withdraw completely within six (6) months from date of exchange of the present

notes the military escorts now stationed at Yatung and Gyantse in Tibet Region of China. The Government of China will render facilities and assistance in such withdrawal.

(2) The Government of India will be pleased to hand over to the Government of China at a reasonable price the postal, telegraph and public telephone services together with their equipment operated by the Government of India in Tibet Region of China. The concrete measures in this regard will be decided upon through further negotiations between the Indian Embassy in China and the Foreign Ministry of China, which shall start immediately after the exchange of the present notes.

(3) The Government of India will be pleased to hand over to the Government of China at a reasonable price the twelve (12) rest houses of the Government of India in Tibet Region of China. The concrete measures in this regard will be decided upon through further negotiations between the Indian Embassy in China and the Foreign Ministry of China, which shall start immediately after the exchange of the present notes. The Government of China agrees that they shall continue as rest houses.

(4) The Government of China agrees that all buildings within the compound walls of the Trade Agencies of the Government of India at Yatung and Gyantse in Tibet Region of China may be retained by the Government of India. The Government of India may continue to lease the land within its Agency compound walls from the Chinese side. And the Government of India agrees that the Trade Agencies of the Government of China at Kalimpong and Calcutta may lease lands from the Indian side for the use of the Agencies and construct buildings thereon. The Government of China will render every possible assistance for housing the Indian Trade Agency at Gartok. The Government of India will also render every possible assistance for housing the Chinese Trade Agency at New Delhi.

(5) The Government of India will be pleased to return to the Government of China all lands used or occupied by the Government of India other than the lands within its Trade Agency compound walls at Yatung.

If there are godowns and buildings of the Government of India on the above-mentioned lands used or occupied and to be returned by the Government of India and if Indian traders have stores, godowns or buildings on the above-mentioned lands so that there is a need to continue leasing lands, the Government of China agrees to sign contracts with the Government of India or Indian traders, as the case may be, for leasing to them those parts of the land occupied by the said godowns, buildings or stores and pertaining thereto.

(6) The Trade Agents of both Parties may, in accordance with the laws and regulations of the local governments, have access to their nationals involved in civil or criminal cases.

(7) The Trade Agents and traders of both countries may hire employees in the locality.

(8) The hospitals of the Indian Trade Agencies at Gyantse and Yatung will continue to serve personnel of the Indian Trade Agencies.

(9) Each Government shall protect the person and property of the traders and pilgrims of the other country.

(10) The Government of China agrees, so far as possible, to construct rest houses for the use of pilgrims along the route from Pulanchung (Taklakot) to Kang Rimpoche (Kailas) and Mavam Tso (Manasarovar); and the Government of India agrees to place all possible facilities in India at the disposal of pilgrims.

(11) Traders and pilgrims of both countries shall have the facility of hiring means of transportation at normal and reasonable rates.

(12) The three Trade Agencies of each Party may function throughout the year.

(13) Traders of each country may rent buildings and godowns in accordance with local regulations in places under the jurisdiction of the other Party.

(14) Traders of both countries may carry on normal trade in accordance with local regulations at places as provided in Article II of the Agreement.

(15) Disputes between traders of both countries over debts and claims shall be handled in accordance with local laws and regulations.

On behalf of the Government of the Republic of India I hereby agree that the present Note along with Your Excellency's reply shall become an agreement between our two Governments which shall come into force upon the exchange of the present Notes.

I avail myself of this opportunity to express to Your Excellency Mr. Vice-Foreign Minister, the assurances of my highest consideration.

(Signed) N. RAGHAVAN,
*Ambassador Extraordinary
and Plenipotentiary of the
Republic of India.*

HIS EXCELLENCY MR. CHANG HAN-FU,
*Vice-Minister of Foreign Affairs,
Central People's Government,
People's Republic of China.*

Chinese Note

Peking, April 29, 1954

Your Excellency Mr. Ambassador,

I have the honour to receive your note dated April 29, 1954, which reads:

'* * * * * * *
* * * * * * *
* * * * * * *'

On behalf of the Central People's Government of the People's Republic of China, I hereby agree to Your Excellency's note, and your note along with the present note in reply shall become an agreement between our two Governments, which shall come into force upon the exchange of the present notes.

I avail myself of this opportunity to express to Your Excellency, Mr. Ambassador, the assurances of my highest consideration.

     (Signed) CHANG HAN-FU,
     Vice-Minister,
     Ministry of Foreign Affairs.
     People's Republic of China.

H. E. NEDYAM RAGHAVAN,
Ambassador Extraordinary and Plenipotentiary,
Republic of India.

BIBLIOGRAPHY

UNPUBLISHED SOURCES

This work is mainly based on the archives of the India Office and the Foreign Office. The India Office material is to be found in the India Office Library. The Foreign Office archives can be examined in the Public Record Office, London, and there are papers of great interest in the Foreign Office Library in Cornwall House. The main India Office documentary series consulted was *Political External Files* (PEF). Up to the end of 1905 the main Foreign Office series relating to Central Asia are FO 65 (Russia) and FO 17 (China). After 1905 the basic political series of Foreign Office archives is FO 371. For the period covered in this book a great deal of the documentary sources has been printed in the Foreign Office Confidential Print series 'Affairs of Tibet' and 'Affairs of Tibet and Mongolia'. These are to be found in the Public Record Office as FO 535. These Prints are extremely useful, but in most cases they omit minutes.

A number of collections of papers were also consulted. In the India Office Library: the Curzon-Hamilton correspondence, the Ampthill papers, the Morley-Minto correspondence. In the Foreign Office Library: the Nicolson papers, the Grey papers, the Jordan-Langley correspondence.

The following Blue Books were consulted:

Further Correspondence relating to Tibet, 1905, Cmd. 2370;

Further Correspondence Relating to Tibet, 1910, Cmd. 5240;

East India (North-East Frontier), Operations against the Abors, 1911, Cmd. 5961.

Considerable use was made of the cartographical riches of the Map Rooms of the India Office Library, the Foreign Office Library and the Library of the Royal Geographical Society.

Facsimiles (transcripts, translations) which appear in this book of Crown-copyright records in the Public Record Office appear by permission of the Controller of H.M. Stationery Office.

SECONDARY WORKS

The following list is not intended to be a comprehensive bibliography.

Abbreviations

CQ   *China Quarterly.*

GJ   *Geographical Journal.*

HJ   *Himalayan Journal.*

IA   *International Affairs.*

RCAJ *Royal Central Asian Journal; Journal of the Central Asian Society; Journal of the Royal Central Asian Society.*

Addis, J. M., *The India-China Border Question*, circulated privately by the Centre for International Affairs, Harvard University (Cambridge, Mass., 1963).

Ahmad, N., 'China's Himalayan Frontiers: Pakistan's Attitude', *IA* (October 1962).

Ahmad, Z., *China and Tibet, 1708–1959*, Chatham House Memo. (London, 1960).

Aitchison, C. U., *Collection of Engagements, Treaties and Sanads* (Calcutta), Vol. 2 of 1909 ed., and Vols. 12 and 14 of 1929 ed.

Alder, G. J., 'British policy on the "Roof of the World" with special reference to the Anglo-Russian Agreement of 1895', unpublished thesis, Bristol University (1959).

British India's Northern Frontier 1865–1895 (London, 1963).

Allen, B. C., *Census of India 1901*, Vol. IV, *Assam*, Pt. I (Shillong, 1902).

Assam District Gazetteers, V: Darrang (Allahabad, 1905).

Assam District Gazetteers VIII: Lakhimpur (Calcutta, 1905).

Ancel, J., *Les Frontières* (Paris, 1938).

Anon., *The Boundary Question between China and Tibet* (Peking, 1940).

'Eastern Bhutan', *HJ* VII (1935).

'Peking and Delhi', *Times Literary Supplement* (2 January 1964).

'The sources of the Subansiri and Siyom', *HJ*, IX (1937), and X (1948).

Bacot, J., *Le Tibet Revolté* (Paris, 1912).

'L'Angleterre et la Chine au Tibet', *L'Asie Francaise*, XI (January 1911).

'La question du Tibet', *L'Asie Francaise*, XII (September 1912).

Introduction à L'Histoire du Tibet (Paris, 1962).

Bailey, F. M., 'Exploration on the Tsangpo or Upper Brahmaputra' *GJ*, 44 (1914).

Report of an Exploration on the North-East Frontier, 1913 (Simla, 1914).

China, Tibet, Assam: a journey, 1911 (London, 1945).

No Passport for Tibet (London, 1957).

Bains, J. S., *India's International Disputes* (London, 1962).

Baruah, T. K. M., *The Idu Mishmis* (Shillong, 1960).

Bell, Sir C., 'The Dalai Lama; Lhasa 1921', *RCAJ*, XI (1924).
Tibet Past and Present (Oxford, 1924).
'The North-Eastern Frontier of India', *RCAJ*, XVII (1930).
The People of Tibet (Oxford, 1928).
The Religion of Tibet (Oxford, 1931).
Portrait of the Dalai Lama (London, 1946).

Bhargava, G. S., *The Battle for NEFA* (New Delhi 1964).

Bhuyan, S. K., *Anglo-Assamese Relations 1771–1826*, Gauhati, 1949.

Boggs, S. W., *International Boundaries: a study of boundary functions and problems* (New York, 1940).

Bonin, C. E., 'Les tribus de frontière et la pénétration Anglaise du Haut-Assam', *L'Asie Francaise*, XI (June 1911).
'L'expédition Anglaise du Haut-Assam', *L'Asie Francaise*, XI (December 1911).
'L'exploration du Haut-Assam', *L'Asie Francaise*, XII (June 1912).

Bower, U. Graham, 'The Daflas of the Subansiri area', *RCAJ* (1949).
The Hidden Land (London, 1953).

Brierly, J. L., *The Law of Nations* (Oxford, 1955).

Buchan, J., *Lord Minto: a memoir* (London, 1924).

Burrard, S. G., *Records of the Survey of India IV: Explorations on the North-East Frontier of India during 1911–12–13* (Calcutta, 1914).

Candler, E., *The Unveiling of Lhasa* (London, 1905).

Caroe, Sir O., 'The geography and ethnics of India's Northern Frontiers', *GJ*, 126 (1960).
'The Indian-Chinese Boundary Dispute', *GJ*, 127 (1961).
'The Sino-Indian Question', *RCAJ*, 50 (1963).
'The Sino-Indian Frontier Dispute', *Asian Review* (April 1963).
'India and Pakistan', *RCAJ*, 51 (1964).
'The India-China Frontiers', *GJ*, 130 (1964).

Carrasco, P., *Land and Polity in Tibet* (Seattle, 1959).

Carruthers, D., *Unknown Mongolia*, 2 vols. (London, 1913).

Chakravarti, P. C., *India's China Policy* (Bloomington, Indiana, 1962).
China-India Relations (Calcutta, 1961).

Chakravorty, B. C., *British Relations with the Hill Tribes of Assam since 1858* (Calcutta 1964).

Chang, Chung-fu, *Chung Hua Min Kuo Wai Chiao Shih* (A diplomatic history of the Chinese Republic), Vol. 1 (Chungking, 1943).

Chang, Y. C., 'The organization of the Waichiaopu', *Chinese Social and Political Science Review*, 1 (1916).

Chapman, F. Spencer, *Lhasa: the Holy City* (London, 1938).

Ch'en, J., *Yuan Shih-k'ai 1859–1916* (London, 1961).

Chen, T. F., *A History of Sino-Russian Relations* (Washington, D.C., 1957).

China, Foreign Languages Press, *Concerning the Question of Tibet* (Peking, 1959).

China, *Peking Review*, no. 40 of 1960, no. 41 of 1961, nos. 47 and 48 of 1962, nos. 10 and 11 of 1963.

Chu, W.-D., 'Tso Tsung-t'ang's role in the recovery of Sinkiang', *Tsing Hua Journal of Chinese Studies*, NS 1, no. 3 (Taipei, September 1958).

Churchill, R. P., *The Anglo-Russian Convention of 1907* (Cedar Rapids, Iowa, 1939).

Clark, G., *Tibet, China and Great Britain* (Peking, 1924).

Cooper, T. T., *The Mishmee Hills* (London, 1873).

Cordier, H., *Histoire Générale de la Chine*, Vol. 4 (Paris, 1920).

Curzon, Lord, *Frontiers* (Oxford, 1907).

Dallin, D. J., *The Rise of Russia in Asia* (London, 1950).

Dalton, E. T., *Descriptive Ethnology of Bengal* (Calcutta, 1872).

Das, T., *British Expansion in Tibet* (Calcutta, 1927).

Dunbar, G., *Frontiers* (London, 1932).

Other Men's Lives (London, 1938).

Durand, Sir H. M., 'Sir Alfred Lyall and the Understanding with Russia', *RCAJ* (1914).

Eekelen, W. F. van, *Indian Frontier Policy and the Border Dispute with China* (The Hague, 1964).

Elwin, V., *India's North-East Frontier in the Nineteenth Century* (Bombay, 1959).

'The Dalai Lama comes to India', *Geographical Magazine* (August 1959).

A Philosophy for NEFA (Shillong, 1960).

Fairbank, J. K., 'Tributary Trade and China's Relations with the West', *Far Eastern Quarterly*, 1 (1942).

Fairbank, J. K., and Teng, S. Y., 'On the Ch'ing Tributary System', *Harvard Journal of Asiatic Studies*, 6 (1941).

Fawcett, C. B., *Frontiers, a study in political geography* (Oxford, 1918).

Fisher, M. W., Rose, L. E., and Huttenback, R.A., *Himalayan Battleground; Sino-Indian Rivalry in Ladakh* (London, 1963).

Fitzgerald, C. P., *The Chinese View of their Place in the World* (London, 1964).

Fleming, P., *Bayonets to Lhasa* (London, 1961).

Fraser, D., *The Marches of Hindustan* (London, 1907).

Fraser-Tyler, Sir W. K., *Afghanistan* (Oxford, 1953).

Friters, G. M., *Outer Mongolia and its International Position* (London, 1951).

Fürer-Haimendorf, C. von, *Ethnographic notes on the tribes of the Subansiri region* (Shillong, 1947).

'The tribes of the Subansiri region', *RCAJ* (1948).

'Anthropology and Administration in the Tribal Areas of the North-East Frontier', *Eastern Anthropologist* (1949).

Himalayan Barbary (London, 1955).

The Apa Tanis and their Neighbours (London, 1963).

Gait, Sir E., *A History of Assam* (Calcutta, 1926).

Gooch, G. P., and Temperley, H. (ed.), *British Documents on the Origins of the War 1898–1914*: Vol. IV, *The Anglo-Russian Rapprochement* (London, 1953; first published 1929).

Vol. IX, Pt. 1, *The Balkan Wars* (London, 1933).

Vol. X, Pt. 2, *The Last Years of Peace* (London, 1938).

Gopalachari, K., 'The India-China Boundary Question', *International Studies*, V, nos. 1–2 (1963).

Great Britain, Central Office of Information, *Tibet* (London, 1958).

Foreign Office, *Tibet*, Peace Handbook no. 70 (London, 1920).

Green, L. C., 'Legal Aspects of the Sino-Indian Border Dispute', *CQ*, no. 3 (1960).

Greene, F., *The Wall has Two Sides* (London, 1963).

Grey of Fallodon, Viscount, *Twenty-Five Years 1892–1916*, 2 vols. (London, 1928).

Grierson, G. A., *Linguistic Survey of India*, III (Calcutta, 1909).

Griffith, W., 'Visit to the Mishmee Hills', *Journal of the Asiatic Society of Bengal*, VI (1837).

Gunter, C. P., *Report of the Mishmi Exploration Survey Detachment, 1912–13*, see Burrard, S. G.

Gupta, K., 'Review of *Where India, China and Burma Meet* by Sitaram Johri', *India Quarterly*, XIX, no. 3 (1963).

Gwynn, S. (ed.), *The Letters and Friendships of Sir Cecil Spring Rice: a Record*, 2 vols. (New York, 1929).

Hamilton, A., *In Abor Jungles* (London, 1912).

Hamilton, W., *A Geographical, Statistical and Historical Description of Hindostan*, 2 vols. (London, 1820).

East India Gazetteer (London, 1815).

Hardinge of Penshurst, Lord, *Old Diplomacy* (London, 1947).

Harrer, H., *Seven Years in Tibet* (London, 1953).

Hassenstein, D., *Some Contributions to the Geographical and Cartographical Literature of the Indo-Chinese Frontier Territories* (London, 1882).

Haushofer, K., *Grenzen in ihrer geographischen und politischen bedeutung* (Berlin, 1939).

Hedin, S., *Trans-Himalaya: discoveries and adventure in Tibet*, 2 vols. (London, 1910).

Hertslet, G. E. P., *Treaties, etc., between Great Britain and China; and between China and Foreign Powers, etc.*, 2 vols. (London, 1908).

Hill, N., *Claims to Territory in International Law and Relations* (London, 1945).

Holdich, Sir T., *Tibet the Mysterious* (London, 1908).

Political Frontiers and Boundary Making (London, 1916).

Hopkinson, A. J., 'The Position of Tibet', *RCAJ* (1950).

Hudson, G. F., 'The Frontier of China and Assam', *CQ*, no. 12 (1962).

'The Aksai Chin', *St Antony's Papers 14* (London, 1963).

Hunter, W., *A Statistical Account of Assam*, 2 vols. (London, 1879).

India, Bengal Secretariat Press, *Political Missions to Bootan* (Calcutta, 1865).

Selection of Papers regarding the Hill Tracts between Assam and Burmah and on the Upper Brahmaputra (Calcutta, 1873).

General Staff, *Military Report on the Bhareli River Area and Tawang, 1920* (Calcutta, 1921).

Lok Sabha Secretariat, *Foreign Policy of India; Texts and Documents* (New Delhi, 1958).

Ministry of External Affairs, *An Atlas of the Northern Frontier of India* (New Delhi, 1960).

Report of the Officials of the Governments of India and of the Chinese People's Republic on the Boundary Question (New Delhi, 1961).

Notes, Memoranda and Letters exchanged and Agreements signed between the Governments of India and China 1954–1959, White Paper (New Delhi, 1959).

Notes, Memoranda and Letters exchanged between the Governments of India and China, September–November 1959, and a Note on the Historical Background of the Himalayan Frontier of India, White Paper no. II (New Delhi, 1959).

Notes, Memoranda and Letters exchanged between the Governments of India and China, November 1959–March 1960, White Paper no. III (New Delhi, 1960).

Notes, Memoranda and Letters exchanged between the Governments of India and China, March 1960–November 1960, White Paper no. IV (New Delhi, 1960).

Notes, Memoranda and Letters exchanged between the Governments of India and China, November 1960–November 1961, White Paper no. V (New Delhi, 1961).

Notes, Memoranda and Letters exchanged between the Governments of India and China, November 1961–July 1962, White Paper no. VI (New Delhi, 1962).

Notes, Memoranda and Letters exchanged between the Governments of India and China, July 1962–October 1962, White Paper no. VII (New Delhi, 1962).

Notes, Memoranda and Letters exchanged between the Governments of India and China, October 1962–January 1963, White Paper no. VIII (New Delhi, 1963).

Notes, Memoranda and Letters exchanged between the Governments of India and China, January 1963–July 1963, White Paper no. IX (New Delhi, 1963).

Notes, Memoranda and Letters exchanged between the Governments of India and China, July 1963–January 1964, White Paper no. X (New Delhi, 1964).

Inlow, E. B., 'The McMahon Line', *Journal of Geography*, LXIII, No. 6 (1964).

International Commission of Jurists, *Tibet and the Rule of Law* (Geneva, 1959).

Tibet and the Chinese People's Republic (Geneva, 1960).

Jackson, W. A. D., *Russo-Chinese Borderlands* (Princeton, 1962).

Jain, G., *India meets China in Nepal* (Bombay, 1959).

Johri, S., *Where India, China and Burma Meet* (Calcutta, 1962).

Jones, P. H. M., 'Passes and Impasses', *Far Eastern Economic Review* (28 February 1963).

Jones, S. B., *Boundary-making, a handbook for statesmen* (Washington, D.C., 1945).

Karan, P. P., 'Geopolitical structure of Bhutan', *India Quarterly*, XIX, no. 3 (1963).

Karan, P. P., and Jenkins, W. M., jun., *The Himalayan Kingdoms: Bhutan, Sikkim, and Nepal* (Princeton, New Jersey, 1963).

Karnik, V. B., ed., *China Invades India* (Bombay, 1963).

Kaulback, R., 'Zayul and the Eastern Tibet Border Country', *RCAJ* (1934).

Tibetan Trek (London, 1936).

Kennedy, R. S., *Ethnological Report on Akas, Khoas, Mijis and Monbas of Tawang* (Shillong, 1914).

Kirk, W., 'The Sino–Indian Frontier Dispute', *Scottish Geographical Magazine*, 76 (1960).

'The Inner Asian Frontier of India', *Transactions of the Institute of British Geographers* (1962).

Korostovetz, J. J., *Pre-War Diplomacy* (London, 1920).

Von Cinggis Khan zur Sowjetrepublik (Berlin and Leipzig, 1926).

Kozloff, P. K., 'The Mongolia–Szechuan Expedition of the Imperial Geographical Society', *GJ*, XXXIV (1909).

651

Lamb, A., 'Some notes on Russian intrigue in Tibet', *RCAJ* (1959).
'The Spiti Valley Today', *RCAJ* (1956).
'Tibet in Anglo-Chinese Relations, 1767–1842', *Journal of the Royal Asiatic Society* (1957 and 1958).
'The Indo–Tibetan border', *Australian Journal of Politics and History*, VI (May 1960).
Britain and Chinese Central Asia: the road to Lhasa 1767–1905 (London, 1960).
'A problem of boundary definition in Ladakh', *Asian History Conference*, Paper no. 58 (Hong Kong, September 1964).
The China–India Border: the origins of the disputed boundaries (London, 1964).
'China's Land Borders', *Australia's Neighbours* (Sept.–Oct. 1964).
'The Sino-Pakistani Boundary Agreement of 2 March 1963', *Australian Outlook* (December 1964).
Communication to *Far Eastern Economic Review*, 125, (1965).
Landon, P., *Lhasa* (London, 1905).
Lattimore, O., *Inner Asian Frontiers of China* (London, 1951).
Pivot of Asia (London, 1952).
Lee, W. K., *Tibet in Modern World Politics* (New York, 1931).
Li, C. N., *The Political History of China, 1840–1928*, trans. and ed. by Teng, S.Y., and Ingalls, J. (Princeton, New Jersey, 1956).
Li, T. T., *The Historical Status of Tibet* (New York, 1956).
Little, W. R., *Report on the Abor Expedition, 1894* (Simla, 1895).
Lloyd, G. T., *Census of India 1921*, III, Pt. 1, *Assam* (Shillong, 1923).
Lobanov-Rostovsky, Prince A., *Russia and Asia* (New York, 1933).
Ludlow, F., 'The sources of the Subansiri and Siyom', *HJ*, X (1938).
M'Cosh, J., *Topography of Assam* (Calcutta, 1837).
Macdonald, D., *The Land of the Lama* (London, 1928).
Twenty Years in Tibet (London, 1932).
McGovern, W. M., *To Lhasa in Disguise* (London, 1924).
MacGregor, C. M., *A Military Report on the Country of Bhutan* (Calcutta, 1873).
Mackenzie, A., *History of the Relations of the Government with the Hill Tribes of the North-East Frontier* (Calcutta, 1884).
McMahon, Sir H., 'International Boundaries', *Journal of the Royal Society of Arts*, 84 (1935–6).
MacMurray, J. V. A., *Treaties and Agreements with and concerning China 1894–1919*, 2 vols. (New York, 1921).
McNair, H. F., and Lach, D. F., *Modern Far Eastern International Relations*, 2nd ed. (New York, 1955).
McSwiney, J., *Census of India 1911*, Vol. III, *Assam*, Pt. I (Shillong, 1912).

Majumdar, D. N., *Races and Cultures of India* (London, 1961).

Mason, K., *Abode of Snow* (London, 1955).

Mehra, P. L., 'The Younghusband Expedition, an interpretation', *Journal of Indian History*, 33 (1955).

'Tibet and Russian intrigue', *RCAJ* (1958).

'Lord Curzon's Despatch of January 8, 1903: its impact on his Tibetan policy', *Proceedings of the Indian History Congress*, 21st Session (Trivandrum, 1958).

'Kazi U-gyen: "a paid Tibetan spy"?', *RCAJ* (1964).

Mills, J. P., 'Tours in the Balipara Frontier Tract, Assam', *Man in India*, 27 (1947).

'Problems of the Assam–Tibet Frontier', *RCAJ* (1950).

'Mishmis of the Lohit Valley', *Journal of the Royal Anthropological Institute* (1952).

Minto, Mary Countess of, *India, Minto and Morley, 1905–1910* (London, 1934).

Monger, G. *The End of Isolation: British Foreign Policy, 1900–1907* (London, 1963).

Moraes, F., *The Revolt in Tibet* (London, 1960).

Morley, Viscount, *Recollections*, 2 vols. (London, 1917).

Morse, H. B., *The Trade and Administration of China* (London, 1921).

The International Relations of the Chinese Empire, 3 vols (London, 1910–18).

Nanporia, N. J., *The Sino-Indian Dispute* (Bombay, 1963).

Neame, P., 'Tibet and the 1936 Lhasa Mission', *RCAJ*, XXVI (1939).

Needham, J. F., 'Journey along the Lohit Brahmaputra between Sadiya in Assam and Rima in South-Eastern Tibet', *Royal Geographical Society Supplementary Papers*, Vol. II (1889).

Nicolson, H., *Lord Carnock* (London, 1930).

O'Connor, W. F., *On the Frontier and Beyond: a record of thirty years' service* (London, 1931).

Things Mortal (London, 1940).

Oppenheim, L., *International Law: a treatise*, 2 vols. (London, 1948).

Otter-Barry, R. B., 'Mongolia; its economic and political aspects', *RCAJ* (1914).

Patterson, G. N., 'Recent Chinese Policies in Tibet and towards the Himalayan States', *CQ.*, no. 12 (1962).

Peking versus Delhi (London, 1963).

'A Himalayan Confederation', *Far Eastern Economic Review* (6 May 1965).

Pemberton, R. B., *Report on the Eastern Frontier of British India* (Calcutta, 1835).

Report on Bootan (Calcutta, 1839).

Perry-Ayscough, H. G. C., and Otter-Barry, R. B., *With the Russians in Mongolia* (London, 1913).

Phillips, G. D. R., *Russia, Japan and Mongolia* (London, 1942). *Dawn in Siberia: the Mongols of Lake Baikal* (London, 1942).

Prescott, J. R. V., *The Geography of Frontiers and Boundaries* (London, 1965).

Price, E. B., *The Russo–Japanese Treaties of 1907–1916 concerning Manchuria and Mongolia* (Baltimore, 1933).

Pritchard, B. E. A., 'A journey from Myitkyina to Sadiya via the N'maikha and Hkamti Long', *GJ*, 43 (1914).

Pritchard, B. E. A., and Waterfield, F. C., *Report on a journey . . . on the North East Frontier, 1912–13* (Simla, 1913).

Rao, K. K., 'The Sino–Indian Boundary Question and International Law', *International and Comparative Law Quarterly* (1962). 'The Preah Vihear case and the Sino-Indian boundary question', *Indian Journal of International Law* (1962). *International Law Aspects of the Sino-Indian Boundary* (Bombay, 1963). 'The Sino-Indian Boundary Question: a study of some related issues', *Indian Journal of International Law* (1963).

Rawling, C. G., *The Great Plateau* (London, 1905).

Ray, S., *China Strikes* (London, 1964).

Reid, Sir R., *History of the Frontier Areas Bordering on Assam 1883–1941* (Shillong, 1942). 'India's North-East Frontier', *RCAJ* (1944).

Richardson, H. E., *Tibet and its History* (Oxford, 1962). 'Review of *The China–India Border*', *RCAJ* (April 1964).

Roberts, P. E., *History of British India under the Company and the Crown* (London, 1952).

Robinson, J., 'The Chinese point of view', *IA* (1964).

Robinson, W., *A Descriptive Account of Assam* (London, 1841).

Rockhill, W. W., 'The Dalai Lamas of Lhasa and their Relations with the Manchu Emperors of China, 1644–1908', *T'oung Pao*, XI (1910).

Ronaldshay, Earl of, *The Life of Lord Curzon*, 3 vols. (London, 1928).

Rose, A., 'The Chinese Frontiers of India', *GJ*, 39 (1912).

Roy, S., *Aspects of Padam-Minyong Culture* (Shillong, 1960).

Rubin, P., 'The Sino–Indian Border Disputes', *International and Comparative Law Quarterly* (1960).

Sanghvi, R., *India's Northern Frontier and China* (Bombay, 1962).

Sen, C., *Tibet Disappears* (Bombay, 1960).

Seton-Watson, H., *The Decline of Imperial Russia 1855–1914* (London, 1952).

Shabad, T., *China's Changing Map: a political and economic geography of the Chinese People's Republic* (London, 1956).

Shakespear, J., 'Recent events on the Assam Frontier', *Journal of the Royal United Services Institution* (London, 1920).

Shakespear, L. W., *History of Upper Assam, Upper Burmah and North-Eastern Frontier* (London, 1914).

Shao, Hsun-cheng, 'Review of *Tibet in Modern World Politics*, by W. K. Lee', *Chinese Social and Political Science Review*, XVI (1932–3).

Sharma, S. N., 'Assam's relations with NEFA', *United Asia*, Vol. 15, no. 5 (May 1963).

Sharma, S. P., 'The India-China border dispute: an Indian perspective', *American Journal of International Law* (1965).

Shelton, F. B., *Shelton of Tibet* (New York, 1923).

Shelvankar, K. S., 'China's Himalayan Frontiers: India's Attitude', *IA*, 38 (1962).

Shen, T. S., and Liu, S. C., *Tibet and the Tibetans* (Stanford, 1953).

Shukla, B. K., *The Daflas* (Shillong, 1959).

Smith, V., *Oxford History of India from the earliest times to 1921*, revised and continued to 1921 by S. M. Edwardes (Oxford, 1923).
 Oxford History of India, 3rd edition, edited by P. Spear (Oxford 1958).

Spate, O. H. K., *India and Pakistan* (London, 1957).

Sykes, P., *A History of Persia*, 2 vols. (London, 1951).

Tang, P. S. H., *Russian and Soviet Policy in Manchuria and Outer Mongolia, 1911–1931* (Durham, North Carolina, 1959).

Taylor, A. J. P., *The Struggle for Mastery in Europe 1848–1914* (London, 1954).

Teichman, E., *Travels of a Consular Official in Eastern Tibet together with a history of the relations between Tibet and India* (Cambridge, 1922).

Thornton, E., *A Gazetteer of the Territories under the Government of the East India Company and of the Native States on the Continent of India*, 4 vols. (London, 1854).

Tibet Society, *Tibet and Freedom* (London, 1961).

Trenchard, O. H. B., *Report of the Abor Expedition Survey Detachment, 1912–13*, see Burrard, S. G.

Trotter, H., 'Account of the Pundit's journey from Leh in Ladakh to Lhasa, and of his return to India via Assam', *Journal of the Royal Geographical Society*, Vol. 47 (1877).

Tung, L., *China and Some Phases of International Law* (London, 1940).

Waddell, L. A., *Lhasa and its Mysteries* (London, 1905).

Ward, Sir A. W., and Gooch, G. P., *Cambridge History of British Foreign Policy 1783–1919*, Cambridge, Vols. 3 and 4.

Ward, F. Kingdon, *The Riddle of the Tsangpo Gorges* (London, 1926).
'Through the Gorges of the Tsangpo', *RCAJ*, XIII (1926).
'Across Southern Tibet', *HJ*, VIII (1936).
'The Assam Himalaya: travels in Balipara', Pt. 1, *RCAJ*, XXV (1938).
Assam Adventure (London, 1941).
'The Lohit Valley in 1950', *RCAJ* (1951).

Ward, G. L. S., *Military Report on the Mishmi Country* (Simla, 1901).

Weissberg, G., 'Maps as evidence in international boundary disputes: a reappraisal', *American Journal of International Law* (1963).

White, J. C., *Sikhim and Bhutan* (London, 1909).

Whittam, D. E., 'The Sino–Burmese Boundary Treaty', *Pacific Affairs*, 34 (1961).

Williamson, N., 'The Lohit-Brahmaputra between Assam and South-Eastern Tibet', *GJ*, 34, no. 4 (1909).

Willoughby, M. E., 'The Relation of Tibet to China', *RCAJ*, XI (1924).

Willoughby, W. W., *Foreign Rights and Interests in China* (Baltimore, 1920).

Wilson, D., 'Where the World's Roof Ends', *Far Eastern Economic Review* (12 March 1965).
'Who's Right in the Himalayas?', *Far Eastern Economic Review* (18 March 1965).
'Himalayan Honour', *Far Eastern Economic Review* (25 March 1965).

Woodman, D., *The Making of Burma* (London, 1962).

Wright, Q., Lauterpacht, H., Borchard, M., and Morrison, P., *Legal Problems in the Far Eastern Conflict* (New York, 1941).

Yang, R., 'Sinkiang under the administration of Governor Yang Tseng-hsin', *Central Asiatic Journal*, VI, 1961.

Younghusband, Sir F., *India and Tibet* (London, 1910).
'Our position in Tibet', *Proceedings of the Central Asian Society* (November 1910).

Zabriskie, E. H., *American–Russian Rivalry in the Far East: a study of Diplomacy and Power Politics 1895–1914* (Philadelphia, 1946).

INDEX

i